Teacher Evaluation

CORWIN PRESS

The Corwin Press logo—a raven striding across an open book—represents the happy union of courage and learning. We are a professional-level publisher of books and journals for K-12 educators, and we are committed to creating and providing resources that embody these qualities. Corwin's motto is "Success for All Learners."

Second Edition

Teacher Evaluation

A Comprehensive Guide to New Directions and Practices

Kenneth D. Peterson

CORWIN PRESS, INC.
A Sage Publications Company
Thousand Oaks, California

Copyright © 2000 by Corwin Press, Inc.

For information:

Corwin Press, Inc.
A Sage Publications Company
2455 Teller Road
Thousand Oaks, California 91320
E-mail: order@corwinpress.com

Sage Publications Ltd.
6 Bonhill Street
London EC2A 4PU
United Kingdom

Sage Publications India Pvt. Ltd.
M-32 Market
Greater Kailash I
New Delhi 110 048 India

Printed in the United States of America

Library of Congress Cataloging-in-Publication Data

Peterson, Kenneth D.
  Teacher evaluation : A comprehensive guide to new directions and practices / by Kenneth D. Peterson.— 2nd ed.
      p. cm.
Includes bibliographical references (p.   ) and indexes.
  ISBN 0-8039-6882-5 (cloth: alk. paper)
  ISBN 0-8039-6883-3 (pbk.: alk. paper)
  1. Teachers—Rating of—United States. I. Title.
  LB2838 .P48 2000
  371.14'4'0973—dc21   00-008770

This book is printed on acid-free paper.

00 01 02 03 04 05 10 9 8 7 6 5 4 3 2 1

Corwin Editorial Assistant: Kylee Liegl
Production Editor: Denise Santoyo
Editorial Assistant: Cindy Bear
Typesetter/Designer: Marion Warren/Danielle Dillahunt
Copyeditor: Karen Wiley
Cover Designer: Oscar Desierto

Contents

Preface to the Second Edition

This edition adds new chapters on the role of the principal in changed teacher evaluation, how districts can transition from current practice to improved practice, use of national standards, developments in using pupil achievement data, and a new emphasis on developing sociologically sophisticated teacher evaluation systems. The Internet as a resource for local development is encouraged (67 web sites are recommended as starting points). New resources for local development have been added from extensive field testing and analysis: Forms have been improved and district-level principles have been assembled. Substantial material has been added on the topic of responding to deficient teacher practice. Finally, the research literature from the first edition has been added to.

A number of significant developments in education since the first edition have combined to inspire this update. First, the confidence expressed in the performance of teachers and administrators in this country has been bourne out. Academic and scholarly reviews confirm the high-quality work of educators. However, the continued political assault on public schools affirms the need to document the good work and cases of innovative practice already going on. More than ever, schools are in competition with prisons and roads. Good teacher evaluation promises reassurance to audiences and practitioners alike.

Technical progress since the first edition has been reassuring. A national organization, Consortium for Research on Educational Accountability and Teacher Evaluation, has focused attention on diverse work. The Tennessee Value Added Assessment System has illuminated the problems and solutions of documenting pupil achievement, and has confidently pushed their message. Standards of personnel evaluation have been circulated as an additional tool in shaping school district evaluation systems. The Internet has grown into a resource for local development.

Other negative situations also have spurred this work. First, evaluation practice has been slow to develop; most evaluation still relies on the principal as the sole data gatherer and judge. The continued lack of sociological awareness of teacher evaluators has hindered development. Differences in group performances in this country continue to be disturbing—the promise of equal opportunity has still not been achieved.

Many people have inspired and contributed to the new material of this edition. Special appreciation is expressed to Michael Scriven, Tom Chenoweth, Gene Glass, David Berliner, Kathie Bone, Kaye Chatterton, Cathy Cooper, Dave Kassler, Stephanie McBride, Kathy Narramore, Marilyn Oberg, Andy Odoardi, Tom Owen, Verlan Terry, Maureen Unruh, and Chris Wahlquist. The Davis School District (Utah) has been a pioneer in these developments. My own teacher education students at Portland State University have given me the heart to continue work in education; without them I would have sought other endeavors. Finally, thanks to the 90 people who restored our home after the 1996 flood.

This second edition is dedicated to Ben and Jenna.

Preface to the First Edition

A great deal of effort goes into public education in this country. However, this effort continues to meet with much criticism. There is a need to be creative in answering critics and in changing the ways that schools are run. One purpose of this book is to present new directions and practices in teacher evaluation to get the word out to the public about the good and up-to-date work of U.S. teachers. A second purpose is to support innovation in teacher evaluation because it has great potential to affect everything else in education.

Few educational researchers and developers have worked on the evaluation of teachers, who, after all, are the key performers of the curriculum and the classroom. At the same time that its development has been neglected, teacher evaluation is a widespread activity in the schools. In this activity, where good practice should be common, inadequate efforts and materials are the order of the day. Poor practice in teacher evaluation is quietly accepted, according to teachers, administrators, and researchers. Evaluations look about the same in district after district, and for teacher after teacher. When there are problems with bad teachers or bad evaluations, people talk about it like few other educational problems; the rest of the time teacher evaluation is ignored or disparaged.

The purpose of this book is to challenge current evaluation and school practice. Although much recent attention to reform has been focused on education in this country, little substantial change has been made; it is business as usual. This book presents ideas about evaluation that can play a key role in much educational reform. Different data sources, new social power relations, and new ways of thinking about teacher evaluation are needed. The link between these developments in teacher evaluation and school reform is to bring about an increased focus on the most important resource for change: the best practices of current teachers.

The lay public and legislators are not now reassured that good teaching is going on. Teachers themselves are not reassured that their efforts in the face of relatively low income and status make a needed difference for students and the society. Good evaluation should reassure audiences and provide a source of acknowledgment and reward for teachers. It should highlight exemplary practice for emulation and point to good practice to guide teacher education.

Good teacher evaluation requires the participation and control of teachers. Current practice is more something done to workers, rather than something done by professionals. This book presents stages of teacher choice, discusses teacher responsibilities for evaluation, and provides ways for teachers to become more involved and in control of their own evaluation. Administrators must sanction good evaluation, but it requires the active involvement of teachers to make the difference.

Why should teachers want good evaluation? The conventional answer is for improvement; few people think beyond this truism. Yet research that demonstrates improved practice as a result of evaluation is nonexistent. Instead, better reasons for increased teacher evaluation are (in order of importance) practitioner reassurance, teacher security, audience reassurance, development and dissemination of ideas for improved practice for the profession, information for teacher education, and stimulus for research. Feedback for improved practice is a side effect for a minority of teachers.

The practices and insights described in this book come from two primary sources. First, there are three individuals without whom this book would not have been written. The models and conceptualization are greatly influenced by the work of Michael Scriven, an exceptional thinker, evaluator, and (most important to me) teacher. In particular, his "goal-free" evaluation approach was the groundwork for the procedures explained here. Anthony Mitchell clarified many institutional dynamics for me; in our collaboration he was a model school administrator who saw through the appearance of institutions to the underlying human experience, and then had the courage to act. Michael McCoy thought through many applications, especially legal implications, and had good suggestions for description and practice; he encouraged open thinking and doing about the issues.

The second source for this book was the experience of the Utah Teacher Evaluation Project (UTEP) that I codirected with Don Kauchak at the University of Utah from 1981 to 1987. This project was supported by three U.S. Department of Education and one state Office of Education (Utah) grants. This exploration of teacher career ladders provided much firsthand learning concerning teacher evaluation. Two persons in the UTEP who provided creative and critical thinking, professional insight, and hard work were Sarah McCarthey and Dannelle Stevens. The Utah Education Association provided much leadership in explorations of teacher evaluation. The Research Analyst's Office of the Utah State Legislature, League of Women Voters, and Parent-Teacher Association provided additional initiative (no endorsements of the contents of this book by these organizations are implied). Individuals who contributed insights to this book included Jane Abe, Lowell Baum, Tom Chenoweth, Betty Condie, Cathy Cooper, Donna Davies, Connie Della Piana, Gabe Della Piana, Donna Deyhle, Amy Driscoll, Anna Marie Dunlap, Judy Edwards-Allen, Bob Everhart, Judy Haymore-Sandholz, Dave Kassler, Rich Kendell, Dick Krepel, Dave Myton, Dean Osterman, Mike Parsons, Rich Ponzio, Jim Popham, Leslie Rennie-Hill, Carolyn Schubach, Don Thomas, Bill Watkins, Suzanne Weiss, Jean Weston, Henry Whiteside, James Wilson, and Art Wise. Kathy Narramore suggested the organization of the first chapter. Portland State University provided a sabbatical leave to prepare this book.

Finally, personal support for this work was given by Cathy Peterson, Rudi Rudolph, Betty Bennett, and Ben Bennett. My partner in the book was Bonnie Peterson.

About the Author

Kenneth D. Peterson is Professor of Education at Portland State University in Portland, Oregon. He was a classroom teacher, and has over 28 years of experience in teacher education for beginning teachers and veteran inservice education. He has taught at the schools of education of the University of California, Berkeley and University of Utah.

He has conducted research in teacher evaluation for over 18 years. During that time, he was the principal investigator for three U.S. Department of Education research grants to design and study innovative teacher evaluation practices for Utah school district career ladder systems. He has published more than 40 articles concerning teacher evaluation work, and has been a consultant or presenter to more than 60 school districts and state- and national-level organizations on teacher evaluation. He has also been an expert witness on teacher evaluation in teacher dismissal litigation. He is a peer reviewer for the *Journal of Personnel Evaluation in Education, Teacher Education Quartely,* and *Journal of Research and Development in Education.*

PART I

Thinking About Teacher Evaluation

1

New Directions for Teacher Evaluation

Teacher evaluation as practiced in the overwhelming majority of school districts in this country consists of wrong thinking and doing. Administrators occasionally visit classrooms, less often meet with teachers to talk over their work, and fill out annual report forms. Teachers, for their part, put up with the activity and continue to teach as they always have. Educators tell each other, and the public, that the purpose of evaluation is to improve teaching. Few seem to notice that evaluation does not improve practice, and both teachers and administrators continue in their ways in spite of the rhetoric of feedback for change.

Instead of practices that are inaccurate, uninformative, and not useful, teacher evaluation can be made to work. Evaluation can reassure teachers that they are doing good and valued jobs, give security and status to well-functioning teachers, spread innovative education ideas, and reassure the public that teachers are successfully contributing to this society. New directions in teacher evaluation are needed for these payoffs.

HOW SHOULD EVALUATION BE CHANGED?

Twelve new directions for teacher evaluation will bring better results for teachers, administrators, students, and the public.

1. Emphasize the function of teacher evaluation to seek out, document, and acknowledge the good teaching that already exists. *Current practice is to emphasize future improvement, minimal competency, feedback, control, and accountability.*

Evaluation has as much a role of recognizing existing value and quality as it does giving information to improve teachers or keep them in line. Focus data gathering, record keeping, judgment making, and publicity toward the many instances of exemplary practice, effective materials and strategies, strong pupil achievement, good teacher preparation, professional behavior, and routine but valuable teacher accomplishments. Educators who know that much more good teaching is going on in this country than the public hears about need to put their knowledge on the evaluation line. The public needs to get the message and data about the quality of teacher performance. Also, when teachers increase their interest in evaluation because of positive payoffs, other functions of evaluation will be enhanced.

Chapter 2 discusses the multiple functions and purposes of teacher evaluation, including underused ones like teacher reassurance and reward. Chapters 20 and 26 recommend strategies for acknowledging teachers and publicizing their impact on society.

2. Use good reasons to evaluate. *Current reasons for most teacher evaluation systems are to improve teaching and to monitor minimal performance for retention.*

Research presented in Chapter 2 shows little evidence that teacher evaluation actually improves practice, in spite of much rhetoric to that effect. Interview studies indicate that teachers think they already know how to teach better than they do now but lack time to put this knowledge into practice. Teachers ask for more time for uninterrupted work with students, for preparation, and "to be more human." The minority of teachers who rely on feedback data for improvement already have in place idiosyncratic techniques that systemwide approaches merely supplant with little or no net gain in improved practice.

Reasons to evaluate include reassurance of practitioners and audiences (such as taxpayers, legislators) that defensible work is going on. Also, the serious morale problems that sociologists report for classroom teachers who have "endemic uncertainty" are lessened by respected evaluation data. Security is increased for teachers who have worked hard and successfully and can show evidence in data collected in teacher dossiers over many years. Recognition of good teaching practices leads to emulation by others. Finally, better teacher inservice and preservice training can be designed with credible, accurate, informative, and useful evaluation data.

Chapters 18, 23, and 26 present specific new uses for teacher evaluation data and judgments, such as teacher leadership decisions, promotion systems, and public relations information.

3. Place the teacher at the center of evaluation activity. *Current practice is to impose on the teacher a brief visit by a person having little meaningful contact with the classroom or students and summarize the visit on a generalized checklist.*

Make evaluation a task managed by a teacher, and not a thing done to a worker. Have the teacher consider his or her duties, responsibilities, contributions, and outcomes—and direct the evaluation from that point. The teacher should be responsible for data assembly, adequacy of judgments, and the use of evaluation results. In addition, have teachers become involved in the evaluation of their colleagues. The teacher should be a monitor of his or her own evaluation, own practice, and the practice of others. The teacher needs to be engaged in the production of more credible external information about his or her work, and a more public judgment about the quality of that work.

Part I of this book will describe the need for changed teacher evaluation, and subsequent parts will present the tools needed to make the changes.

4. Use more than one person to judge teacher quality and performance. *Current practice is to rely on the annual report of a single administrator.*

Judgments about the quality of teaching should be made by panels that review extensive evidence of teacher performance and background. Panels should be made up of a majority in number of teachers, but include administrators, parents, and at the high school level, students. Although some questions of teaching may be easy for individuals to recognize and report (e.g., Were classes held? Was material presented? Did students pass tests?), others call for judgment from several perspectives (e.g., Did the material interest students? Were the assignments and tests of high quality? Was the amount of learning satisfactory?). The value of much of teaching can easily be agreed on by individuals, but for some questions and situations the perspectives of people in different roles are needed to recognize satisfactory or outstanding work.

Chapter 18 of this book gives guidance and procedures for school district evaluation panels.

5. Limit administrator judgment role in teacher evaluation. *Current practice is to use a building administrator for many tasks: monitor minimal teacher performance, protect young people, induct new teachers, confer with teachers, decide on teacher retention, judge overall teacher quality, lead instruction, remediate poor practice, and praise exceptional teaching.*

Building administrators *can* monitor for minimal performance. They also are on the spot when quick judgments are needed, for example, to stop abusive and acute problem teacher practices. They are in the best position to see the overall teaching picture in relation to parents, school boards, district policy, and large numbers of educators in varied roles. Administrators are more familiar with classrooms on a regular basis than are many other people (e.g., they see more classrooms than most teachers, district-level administrators, parents, university teacher educators, or educational researchers). Administrators significantly affect the morale of a school. Finally, the unique perspective of building administrators is needed in the long run as a piece of evidence about overall teacher quality.

However, there are important limitations and concerns over building administrator roles in teacher evaluation. Chapter 2 will describe over 70 years of research studies that show the inaccuracy of administrator reports of teacher performance. Administrators have a basic role conflict of interest when they are both summative judges and educational leaders with the same population of teachers. Their perceptions and biases are shaped by their role assignment in the school. Sociologists describe a delicate balance of support and control that administrators require from educators in a school; the result is that evaluation activity and decisions become a tool for overall administrator functioning rather than an accurate, informative, and useful report and judgment of teacher quality. Administrator expertise in subject matter content is not as strong as other teachers in the same assignment. Their interpretations of student and parent perspectives are not as accurate as direct information from these audiences. Finally, surveys of administrators show teacher evaluation as the least favored activity and responsibility—they are not motivated to do a thorough job of it.

Chapters 13 and 22 give guidelines and procedures for defensible administrator roles in comprehensive teacher evaluation.

6. Use multiple data sources to inform judgments about teacher quality. *Current practice is to rely on an annual administrator report.*

Good teaching is complex and needs to be documented and recognized in a number of ways. Evaluators need to add such data sources as student and parent surveys, peer review of materials, logs of professional activity, pupil gain data, teacher tests, and other unique evidence. For example, client response is a good indicator of quality. Students are good judges of some parts of teaching (Is new and interesting material available?), but not others (Does this teacher know his subject matter?). Parents can give needed information about how learning is applied outside of school, changes in interests, and positive attitudes about school. Other teachers are in the best position to know both the subject matter content and the reality of presenting it effectively in specific classroom settings. Teacher background and preparation are important to some questions about teacher quality. Although research shows that teachers' knowledge of subject matter is hard to judge by observers, content expertise of a teacher plays a minor role in some classroom situations but is very important in others. Finally, the responsibilities of a teacher extend beyond classrooms to being a member of the school community and a professional who is continually developing. All these factors call for a comprehensive use of separate data sources.

Multiple data sources can replace the current haphazard effect of nonsystematic, hearsay evidence. The occasional overjoyed student, spectacular case, gratifying graduate, irate parent, or intrusive interest group does not have inordinate influence when an evaluation system has representative systematic data from many more dependable sources.

Chapter 4 describes the range of data sources available and recommends procedures for using multiple lines of evidence for teacher evaluation.

7. When possible, include actual pupil achievement data. *Current practice in most districts is to have administrators give crude ratings of pupil achievement (e.g., "satisfactory," "needs improvement," "below standard"). Some states link standardized achievement testing results to all teacher evaluations.*

Several practices are important in the technically difficult task of including pupil achievement data in teacher evaluation. First, the "all teachers or none" approach should be abandoned. Achievement data should be used for only some of the teachers in an evaluation system, where technically defensible and after the teachers call for them. Second, each district system should actively strive to include achievement data with sophisticated measures, consultations, and acknowledgement for teachers who successfully present these data. Defensible data on pupil achievement require teacher choice, agreement on what to measure, good tests (or observations), gain data rather than postinstructional results only, adjustments for prior pupil achievement, stable student populations, sociological stability for teachers in the district, and cost-benefit balance.

Chapter 8 will discuss issues concerning use of pupil achievement data, controversies, and alternative solutions. Several procedures are given and illustrated.

8. Use variable data sources to inform judgments. *Current practice is to use the same standard information on all teachers within a district.*

Good teachers are good for different reasons. Teachers can make learning happen in quite different ways. What makes one teacher good (an effective taskmaster) may not be true of the next one (an inspirer) or still another (a subject matter authority). What allows for this variety is that although much of teaching is simple and straightforward, and done by everyone the same way, other teacher tasks can be quite personal and idiosyncratic, creative, emotionally demanding, and intellectually complex. Teaching at times is replication and at other times innovation, depending on the situation. Thus teachers of different kinds and in different settings need data appropriate to their specific practice. Finally, students have different styles, needs, and preferences in their learning; good teachers match their performance to their students.

What this variation in performance means is that different sources of information and evidence of quality need to be available for each teacher. For some, the best data concern their procedures or process. This calls for systematic observation or a peer review of materials. For others, the results shown in student learning are key. For these teachers, a look at student achievement data is important. In still other situations, the reports of clients (students or parents) give the most direct indicators of quality. In most cases, quality means that each teacher has a constellation of these indicators. But the constellations of quality vary, and thus the data sources reflecting the performance should vary. Finally, data sources for teacher evaluation may have to vary because the best information simply is not available, and evaluation makes do with existing data. A common example of this problem is the difficulty experienced in getting useful student achievement data for teacher evaluation. The result is that good teacher evaluation looks a little to a lot different for each teacher. Some educators object that fairness (and even the law) demands that all teachers be evaluated with the same evidence. However, what fairness actually calls for is the same opportunity to present a case for quality.

Part II of this book presents a variety of data sources and suggests the kinds of evidence that match the variety of practices. Procedures are given so that districts and individual teachers can best select the proper evidence for specific teachers and situations.

9. Spend the time and other resources needed to recognize good teaching. *Current practice is to spend a short amount of time: An administrator visits a classroom for 45 minutes and then fills in an annual form (perhaps in the "best" systems, interview, observe, fill in a form, and finish with an administrator-teacher conference). Time and money spent are minimal and charged to the administrator's usual assignment duties.*

Serious and comprehensive evaluations call for teachers to take individual time to consider their own situations and data. They need to make choices and take initiative in the evaluation process. Time is required for colleague-teacher participation in data gathering and judgment. Evaluation clerks need to administer and score surveys, conduct interviews, and assemble test scores. Money is needed for surveys, postage, test fees, document duplication, transportation and refreshments for focus groups, and record-keeping expenses. Technical consultations are required for teachers to evaluate well. Teacher data need secure storage. Evaluation panels require time and places to deliberate. Although the costs of teacher evaluation are defensible and result in benefits, time and money need to be set aside for teacher evaluation.

The intuitive impression is that one can tell how good a teacher is merely by watching him or her for 15 minutes. However, research shows that good evaluation takes much more time than this. Time is required for some evidence to play out; for example, effects on students make take weeks, months, or even years to see. Good teaching materials take years to develop. Still more profoundly, the practice of teaching is not all instantaneous interactions. Indeed, the greatest effect on most students (our true unit of analysis) is more on the order of what they experience in 2-week periods: Teacher performance, assignments, practice, relationships, materials, and the experience of growth itself are more the stuff of teaching than a brief glimpse into the classroom can show. It takes 2 years to comprehensively evaluate a group of teachers.

Chapter 23 specifies expected costs of comprehensive teacher evaluation, reports experience from field studies, and suggests cost-containment strategies for school districts. Comprehensive teacher evaluation systems easily can be installed and maintained for well under $100.00 per teacher annually.

10. Use research on teacher evaluation correctly. *Current practice is to ignore direct research on teacher evaluation practice itself, but to borrow knowledge bases such as teacher effectiveness for observation form checklists or professional development schemes, such as clinical supervision, as a basis for evaluation.*

Studies of teacher evaluation procedures in the field are a virtually nonexistent basis for policy or practice at the school, district, state, or national levels. Precedent, tradition, and sociological gridlock all are more powerful determinants of teacher evaluation than systematic research on problems, principles, and practices of teacher evaluation. What passes for use of research in teacher evaluation is the borrowed findings from other areas of educational research used to justify practice. One egregious example is to borrow the findings of teacher effectiveness (e.g., wait time, clarity, high classroom structure) and apply these ideas to teacher performance checklists. Another is to borrow the findings of a specialized kind of psychology, such as the isolated learning of nonsense syllables, and apply these to measures of teacher quality in checklists.

Research studies in the literature are ignored. For example, the abundant and noncontradicted research showing the inaccuracy of principal reports has changed virtually no district evaluation systems. New practices, such as including artifacts of teaching, are not used. Sociological accounts using interviews or ethnographic findings that clearly identify teacher needs for reassurance are not a foundation for practice.

It is important to be clear about what good research on teacher evaluation looks like. Research means that evaluation schemes are installed, documented, and examined for their results. Findings are published in peer-refereed scholarly journals. Accurate, informative, and useful research on teacher evaluation reports the reliability and validity of procedures on actual, described populations. Empirical results of recommended strategies, described limitations, and norms with known populations all contribute to the development of defensible teacher evaluation.

Good teacher evaluation research includes a variety of types of inquiry. Empirical reports comparing one data source (e.g., administrator report or pupil survey) with others (e.g., pupil achievement, peer report) in field settings are helpful for designing local district systems. Better understandings of how people make judgments with variable and multiple data are useful. Interviews or ethnographic accounts of how teachers decide quality are necessary to design good practical evaluation systems. Sociological studies that show the extraneous pressure placed on decision makers make for more accurate and satisfactory programs. Studies on how teachers and other audiences use teacher evaluation data are needed to get the most out of evaluation efforts. Cost-benefit analyses are key to evaluation systems that are of value. Finally, studies of evaluation systems are needed—the evaluators themselves must be evaluated.

This book gives accounts of specific useful research in teacher evaluation in every chapter. The methods, techniques, and practices presented are based on field tests and empirical data. The limitations and cautions about techniques, as documented in the literature, are included.

11. Attend to the sociology of teacher evaluation. *Current practice is to ignore the powerful effects of expectations, roles, rewards, sanctions, and relationships in the workplace. Evaluation is done as simple actions of feedback and retention decisions, rather than as a complex, human, organizational interaction and transaction.*

The sociology of the workplace is a great barrier to changed and improved teacher evaluation. The vast majority of school districts do not recognize sociological forces and do little or nothing to prepare the climate for good evaluation. The most technically satisfactory teacher evaluation systems can be brought to the typical school district and should be expected to fail because sociological problems are not addressed.

Many years of research in teacher evaluation have identified significant problems with current practice. Accurate evaluation is sacrificed to social role responsibilities of principals and teachers. Teachers do not trust current methods to correctly characterize what they do in classrooms. Teacher rating systems do not inspire confidence either from teachers or from the lay public.

New directions in evaluation require specific workplace changes. First, school roles need to be addressed. For example, the role of the principal as summative judge needs to be altered to emphasize educational leadership functions. Second, the reward structure of a school should be examined and strengthened. According to sociologists, current school environments are the most reward-scarce settings for any professional work. Teacher isolation and independence should be lessened. Resources (such as consultations) need to be made available to teachers so that they can assume more responsibility and control in their own evaluation. New teachers need radically different and enhanced support. Although these changes take time (on the order of 5 years), they all are required for accurate, informative, and useful teacher evaluation.

Chapters 4, 19, and 23 are specific about sociological barriers to teacher evaluation and give requirements and suggestions for an improved climate for evaluation.

12. Use the results of teacher evaluation to encourage personal professional dossiers, publicize aggregated results, and support teacher promotion systems. *Current practice is to file away annual administrator reports into unused storage. The valuable efforts and results of routine teaching are not made public. Teachers are entirely undifferentiated, and their successful work not acknowledged.*

Veteran teachers with many years of service have files no more than a small fraction of an inch thick that perfunctorily record their performance on checklists, but do not document their results, hard work, efforts outside of the classroom, unique contributions, courses taken, and inservice workshops attended. Veterans do not have the protection and security of serious documentation. The lack of credible information to the public leads to periodic frenzies of criticism of teachers and a chronic pressure for unspecified change. Teachers do not have career ladders, but instead are undifferentiated except for personal power they may accrue unrelated to their performance quality. The purported rewards of "teacher of the year" programs actually result in alienation and other negative sociological payoffs for their recipients.

Teacher personal-professional dossiers tell a teacher's story. They provide security and documentation about value, merit, and worth to a school district. They show that good teaching is a result of much preparation and individual initiative. Dossiers document the unique aspects of good teachers as well as reassure that routine expectations are met. Dossiers give the opportunity to document pupil achievement in narrowly specific, but available, ways. Finally, professional dossiers compress the rich and specific data that might be included in an unwieldy portfolio.

Teacher evaluation findings can reassure audiences that quality education is going on. Aggregated results of teachers within a district should be presented in news conferences, press releases, city and county meetings, parent meetings, legislatures, and to other public bodies. Increasingly, state-level testing of posttest-only school results appear in newspapers. These technically inaccurate, and politically misleading, data need to be countered with reports of specific, concrete teacher achievements.

Teacher promotion and rank systems should be based on those of higher education. Teacher evaluation data, organized in personal-professional dossiers, serve as a basis for a series of titles and pay differentials. Serious hurdle reviews every 5 to 7 years by teacher-dominated promotion panels provide standards for quality performance. Promotion systems reward teachers for effort, results, and time. Success needs to be formally recognized and acknowledged. The sociological need for hurdles and career development should be provided by teacher promotion systems.

Chapters 16 and 18 describe the formation, uses, and judgment of teacher dossiers. Chapter 26 outlines strategies for disseminating and publicizing teacher performances and results. Chapter 18 defines and presents procedures for teacher promotion systems.

CONCLUSIONS

The new directions presented in this chapter represent big changes for educators. If these activities seem too ambitious and even unnecessary, it is only because educators are perceptually, intellectually, and sociologically locked into current systems. The changes in evaluation practice require a gradual introduction and institutional change over perhaps a 5-year period. The procedures presented in this book are not a quick fix or an antidote to immediate attacks on schools. Rather, these new directions are a long-term resource for better relations within schools and with the larger society. Although not overly costly in terms of time and money, they are expensive in terms of changed expectations, relationships, and use of time. Their introduction calls for unusual vision, resolve, and courage.

However, the research literature is clear. Educators should quickly adopt these directions—or continue to have evaluation not taken seriously, miss examining what teachers actually do, fail to address teacher uncertainty and isolation, and suffer a blind spot in educational reform. The present, inadequate practice in teacher evaluation is extremely costly in the long run.

The political situation likewise is clear. This society has become greatly consumer oriented. Citizens no longer take their public institutions at their word, but instead require credible information about how resources are used and what happens as a result. Public schools are in competition with prisons and with roads. Despite much evidence of effective school outcomes, the current climate of public skepticism about teachers and schools will not go away any time soon. Educators need to seriously increase the amount of evaluation data available, make it public, and interact with citizens on questions of teacher impact and value.

Will the results of following these new directions in teacher evaluation justify the efforts? The first purpose of this book is to present field-tested, innovative practices for improved teacher evaluation, along with the benefits to be expected, what needs to be done, how it should be accomplished, and what new players and roles need to be brought into the process. These practices will bring greater satisfaction to teachers, administrators, the public, and ultimately, students.

A second, more important purpose of this book is to stimulate more real-life experience and study in teacher evaluation. Educators need to begin serious research and development in the area of teacher evaluation. More effort in teacher evaluation will produce additional innovations beyond those described in this book. Significant talent and resources should be directed toward the key questions, such as: What is the nature of good teacher evaluation? What techniques are needed? What are the comprehensive costs: direct, indirect, transition, and loss of replaced activities? The intent of this book is to present a state-of-the-art framework for educators to continue this work of questioning and creating high-quality teacher evaluation.

2

The Need for New Directions and Practices

Why the need for new directions in teacher evaluation presented in Chapter 1? Analysts who have taken a close look at current directions and practices have found many problems. Examine these statements of researchers and scholars:

> To this day, almost all educational personnel decisions are based on judgments which, according to the research, are only slightly more accurate than they would be if they were based on pure chance. (Medley & Coker, 1987, p. 243)

> Teacher evaluation is a disaster. The practices are shoddy and the principles are unclear. . . . Using classroom visits . . . to evaluate teaching is not just incorrect, it is a disgrace. (Scriven, 1981, pp. 244, 251)

> The principles and the principals are unclear in [teacher] evaluations. (Epstein, 1985, p. 3)

Evaluators are mistake if they assume they are observing the typical behavior of a . . . teacher with the usual [evaluation] procedure. (Stodolsky, 1984, p. 17)

[Teacher rating scales] generated data that were more a reflection of the rater's point of view than of a teacher's actual classroom behavior. (Cook & Richards, 1972, p. 11)

[Twelve studies from 1921 to 1959] reached the same conclusion: that the correlations between the average principal's ratings of teacher performance and direct measures of teacher effectiveness were near zero. (Medley & Coker, 1987, p. 242)

Means of student ratings of a teacher as instructor are not connected with a single administrator ratings [sic] of the same teacher. Coefficient of correlation is -.078. (Brookover, 1940, p. 286)

Administrator reports, the conventional practice. . ., showed low correlations with other measures [pupil and parent surveys, tests, professional activity] (absolute mean correlation = 0.05). (Peterson, 1987a, p. 316)

Rating differs with individuals . . . and over time and is therefore manifestly unfair. Rating . . . makes unfair discrimination very easy. . . . Rating schemes force the teacher to live up to the scheme and not to teach to good pedagogical principles. Rating forces the teacher to play to the rater and not to the children's interests. (Barr & Burton, 1926, p. 457)

No correlation appreciably different from zero was discovered between the evaluations of the teachers on the different rating scales and the evaluations based on the achievements of their pupils in the subject matter areas. (Anderson, 1954, p. 68)

Almost all respondents [to a survey of 32 district central offices] . . . felt that principals lacked sufficient resolve and competence to evaluate accurately. (Wise, Darling-Hammond, McLaughlin, & Bernstein, 1984, p. 22)

The inconsistency of relations [of teacher behaviors] with . . . outcomes; the frequent violations of expectations . . . ; and the number of competencies that failed to relate [to pupil outcomes] at all

. . . lend little support to our common assumption that beliefs of teachers or experts about the nature of effective teaching are generally correct. (Coker, Medley, & Soar, 1980, p. 149)

Teachers mistrust evaluation. They feel that current . . . techniques fall short of collecting information that accurately characterizes . . . performance. They perceive . . . rating as depending more on the idiosyncrasies of the rater than on their own behavior in the classroom. . . . Teachers see nothing to be gained from evaluation. (Wolf, 1973, p. 160)

Teachers interviewed for this study roundly criticized formal supervision and evaluation practices . . . [saying] that they are . . . not effective for improvement. . . . Administrators are rarely prepared to offer . . . useful advice, . . . virtually never . . . providing an opportunity for learning. . . . Very good teachers . . . regard the practice as an institutional obligation to be endured rather than an opportunity to be seized. (Johnson, 1990, p. 266)

Current teacher evaluation procedures do not distinguish contributions made to minority students, especially by minority teachers. In fact, conventional evaluation underestimates their importance to the educational system. (Peterson, Deyhle, & Watkins, 1988, p. 134)

If a school can justify evaluating all teachers through identical procedures, then the school is probably devoid of innovations. (Travers, 1981, p. 22)

The main direction of recent efforts to upgrade teacher evaluation has been toward so-called research-based approaches. The key process . . . is still classroom observation, . . . but . . . focused on . . . indicators shown to be correlated with teaching success. . . . An approach based on this kind of research . . . cannot be a legitimate method of teacher evaluation. (Scriven, 1987, p. 9)

Superintendents, supervisors, and principals tended to rate good [high student achievement] teachers low and poor teachers high. . . . Ratings by superintendents, supervisors, principals, colleagues or professors in teachers' colleges should not be accepted as the sole or valid criteria until persons in these positions have been re-educated for this responsibility. (McCall & Krause, 1959, pp. 73, 75)

In most school districts, the norms and expectations that sur-
round teacher evaluation preclude a meaningful activity.
(McLaughlin, 1990, p. 404)

Because teacher evaluation is complex, threatening, and not
well-understood, much of current practice involves games
rather than systematic evaluation. (Harris, 1986, p. 12)

Seventy years of empirical research on teacher evaluation shows that
current practices do not improve teachers or accurately tell what happens
in classrooms. Administrator reports do not increase good teachers' confidence or reassure the public about teacher quality. Teacher evaluation as
presently practiced does not identify innovative teaching so that it can be
adopted by other teachers and used in teacher education programs.
Finally, current procedures do not reward exemplary teachers.

Despite these obvious and long-standing problems, school districts
continue to rely on principal reports. This chapter begins with a brief description of current evaluation practice and then follows selected research
and scholarship that shows the shortcomings of current evaluation direction and practice. The chapter concludes with a discussion of why teacher
evaluation has not been improved in spite of the obvious need for new directions.

CURRENT PRACTICE

Most current teacher evaluation consists of a principal's report of teacher
performance, usually recorded on a checklist form, and sometimes accompanied by a brief meeting. These reports are based on informal and formal
classroom visits (Bridges, 1992; Hill, 1921; Johnson, 1990; Lewis, 1982; Peterson & Chenoweth, 1992). More advanced systems add "clinical supervision" components, including preobservation conference, agreement on elements to be observed, postobservation conference, and direct link to
inservice training (McGreal, 1983).

Checklists for teacher evaluation are based on a wide variety of suppositions about what good teaching should look like (e.g., holds students
accountable), includes (e.g., practice time), is characterized by (e.g., brisk
pace), or requires in personal characteristics of the teacher (e.g., enthusiasm) (Boyce, 1915; Good & Mulryan, 1990; Wood & Pohland, 1979). Some
school districts refer vaguely to research bases for item selection. Others favor lists provided by committees or expert consultants. Finally, some dis-

tricts avoid problems of item selection by using open-ended comment topics (e.g., instructional practices).

Although principal reports enjoy wide acceptance, serious flaws with the approach have been identified by researchers and scholars. Chapter 13 suggests a proper role for administrator reports in serious and comprehensive teacher evaluation, but a review of the substantial problems of teacher evaluation with principal reports is appropriate here. The ambitious and practice-altering recommendations of this book rest on the inadequate current practice of teacher evaluation.

RESEARCH ON TEACHER EVALUATION

Research on teacher evaluation shows the problems with current directions and practice. Three kinds of research and scholarship are reported in this section. First, empirical studies present actual observed results with well-described procedures. Second, survey studies report opinions, views, and attitudes of various participants through questionnaires and interviews. Third, conceptual studies analyze the logic, intent, and consequences of practice.

Empirical Studies

Seventy years of research on principal ratings of teachers shows that they do not work well. Well-designed empirical studies depict principals as inaccurate raters both of individual teacher performance behaviors and of overall teacher merit. These problems go beyond simply developing a better rating form, informing teachers of the items on the rating forms, or improving the training of principals as raters, although these strategies are offered by many who are interested in preserving current practice. Instead, research reveals fundamental technical and sociological flaws with present teacher evaluation.

Medley and Coker (1987) obtained ratings of 46 principals on 322 teachers in three roles: (a) facilitating pupil learning of fundamental knowledge; (b) fostering pupil development of citizenship, personal satisfaction, and self-understanding; and (c) being a professional colleague of other educators. The researchers correlated these principal ratings with empirical evidence of teacher performance using achievement tests and colleague reports. The instruments and methods used in the research were specifically described. This study showed great sophistication in statistical controls (regression analysis) for pupil ability, grade level, subject tested, and grade taught. The authors reported low statistical correlation between administrator ratings and teacher roles: 0.20 with Knowledge growth in pupils, 0.19 with Affective growth in pupils, and 0.13 with Professionalism. Medley and Coker (1987) concluded that "the most important finding of this study is the low accuracy of the average principal's judgments of the performance of the teachers he or she supervises" (p. 245).

Stodolsky (1984) studied the stability of observations of 20 fifth-grade teachers teaching social studies and mathematics. Two observers teamed to describe classrooms and report 5-second time samples. The observers spent an average of 8.8 consecutive days in *each* teacher's math class and 8.1 days in social studies. The observers were trained and monitored for their accuracy. The observers had no professional or personal relationships with the teachers they observed. Stodolsky found that teachers taught the two subject areas quite differently, specifically, in variety of formats, pacing, and cognitive level. She also found quite discrepant attention levels in students. For example, the correlation between mean on-task math and mean on-task social studies by teacher was 0.09, "indistinguishable from zero" (Stodolsky, 1984, p.16). Thus teacher evaluation based on observation by classroom visit depends very heavily on what the teacher is observed doing at the time of the visit. Because most administrators have very limited time to evaluate each teacher, the small number of observations results in very unreliable data for evaluation.

Peterson (1987a) reported a study in which 281 teachers were rated for their overall teaching effectiveness on a 4-point scale by their principals. In addition, the teachers submitted other kinds of data to qualify for a promotion in a career ladder system. Other data sources reported in this study were student surveys, parent surveys, involvement in professional activities, scores on standardized teacher knowledge tests (subject matter for secondary, general knowledge for elementary), and years of experience. The data were collected by an external (to the school district) Evaluation Unit, using standardized instruments. The administrator ratings showed low correlations with other measures, as depicted in Table 2.1. Two measures, standardized teacher knowledge test score and involvement in professional activity, were negatively correlated. Peterson (1987a) concluded that these findings "corroborate the criticisms of principal evaluation used without supplementary data from several sources" (p. 316).

Cook and Richards (1972) analyzed the performance ratings of 236 teachers who were observed by their principals and university supervisors of teacher education. Each teacher was rated by both persons at the end of each of his or her first 3 years of teaching on 23 dimensions (e.g., knowledge of subject matter, pupil progress, order, enthusiasm). The ratings were factor analyzed for underlying themes. In an orthogonal varimax factor analysis, the researchers found three factors that accounted for 61% of the observed variance. The first two factors loaded heavily on the role of the rater,

TABLE 2.1 Correlations of Administrator Ratings With Other Measures

Alternative Measure	Correlation (r)
Student survey	0.01
Parent survey	0.09
Teacher knowledge test score	−0.12
Professional activity	−0.11
Years of experience	0.13

SOURCE: Peterson (1987a).

that is, whether the observer was a principal or a supervisor. Observers in this study "generated data that were more a reflection of the rater's point of view than of a teacher's actual classroom behavior" (Cook & Richards, 1972, p. 11). The researchers concluded that

> despite warnings . . . school districts . . . have persisted in using multi-variate teacher rating scales as criteria for teacher competence. It is hoped that [this] . . . study is definitive enough to effect a reexamination of the rationale and use of such scales, especially in instances where they materially effect the teacher being rated. (p. 14)

Coker et al. (1980) reported another key study that challenges current teacher evaluation practices. Although these researchers did not use principals as observer-raters, they demonstrated the problems of using *any* individual observer-raters in a teacher assessment system. Coker et al. followed up previous studies that showed little evidence that any set of observational criteria (e.g., behaviors, competencies, teacher characteristics) can be related empirically to student learning (e.g., American Educational Research Association, 1953). The researchers used a teacher-developed framework of 26 teacher competencies (e.g., gives clear, explicit directions; accepts and incorporates student ideas; respects an individual's right to speak). They made two or more observations in 100 classrooms to record frequencies of performance of the competencies. Students in the classes also completed standardized achievement tests and self-concept measures. Gain scores on these measures were adjusted by pretest score and socioeconomic status (SES). Training of observers and classroom teachers ensured a reliable empirical search for relationships.

Coker et al. (1980) found that the majority of the 52 correlations between frequency of teacher performance of competencies and student gain were statistically nonsignificant. Of those relationships that were significant, only six were positively related to achievement gains, and five were positively related to self-concept gains. However, negative associations were found for five competencies with achievement gains and five competencies for self-concept gains. That is, some competencies identified by teachers as needed by effective teachers were empirically found to show negative effects on achievement and self-concept gains when used with greater frequency. As described by the authors:

> The inconsistency of relations with different outcomes; the frequent violations of expectations, sometimes only at certain grade levels; and the number of competencies that failed to relate at all—these lend little support to our common assumption that beliefs of teachers or experts about the nature of effective teaching are generally correct. (p. 149)

These findings challenge the assumptions that an observer can enter a classroom, use an observational framework of supposedly desirable performances, count or rate the teacher, and draw conclusions about the quality of teaching that can be defended for purposes of teacher evaluation.

Wood and Pohland (1979) studied current teacher evaluation rating forms. They found a problem separate from the issue of accuracy of observation or interpretation. These researchers content analyzed 65 rating scales from actual current use. Wood and Pohland reported that items in the teaching role of teachers (e.g., adequate preparation of lesson plans; techniques in evaluation of student progress; challenges students to think, inquire, and analyze) accounted for only 28% of the total items. The remainder of the items focused on personal characteristics (30%) and lesser percentages in other roles such as administrator/manager and social, professional, and organizational member. Student outcomes constituted only 1% of the total items. The author concluded that

> teacher evaluation serves as organizational maintenance rather than a teaching improvement function. First, rather than focusing primarily on the teachers' classroom instructional behaviors, the items on which teachers are evaluated scan the . . . entire work world. Only a minority of the items are teaching oriented. The items . . . indicate an organizational preference for stability rather than for change. Second, the procedures . . . suggest more concern for assessing minimal competency of neophytes than with . . . instructional improvement. And finally, the formal expectations and conditions which surround the principal/evaluator's role serve to perpetuate the organizational maintenance function of teacher evaluation. (Wood & Pohland, 1979, p. 81)

Workable alternatives to principal-report teacher evaluation are provided in the literature. For example, Peterson, Bennet, and Sherman (1991) reported a study that included evaluation of teachers of at-risk pupils. Their sample included a substantial number of minority teachers. Because current evaluation practices underestimate or miss altogether the contributions of minority teachers (Peterson et al., 1988), the evaluators used a complex, year-long, teacher-controlled data-gathering system in which teachers identified by peers and administrators documented their performance with at-risk pupils. Teachers in this study created varied teacher dossiers. For example, one teacher had pupil surveys, parent surveys, peer review of materials, and documentation of pupil achievement. Another collected test scores (of pupils and teacher), systematic observation report, documentation of professional activity, and administrator report. The collection of multiple and variable sources of data on each teacher enabled the researchers to select a smaller sample of teachers who truly were uncommonly successful with at-risk students. The extensive evaluation went considerably beyond the screening by reputation. This sample then was interviewed for their similar and dissimilar teaching strategies.

Survey Studies

In addition to empirical research studies that show the statistical inaccuracy of principal ratings, interview and questionnaire studies of teachers and administrators indicate extremely low levels of respect for the procedures within the profession.

Wolf (1973) reported an interview study with 293 classroom teachers. In general, he found that teachers mistrust evaluation:

> Teachers . . . believe that the standards for evaluating . . . are too vague and ambiguous to be worth anything. They feel that current appraisal techniques fall short of collecting information that accurately characterizes their performance. They perceive the ultimate rating as depending more on the idiosyncrasies of the rater than on their own behavior in the classroom. As a result, teachers see nothing to be gained from evaluation. One suggested that present teacher evaluation practice does more to interfere with professional quality teaching than to nurture it. (p. 160)

Wolf found that 58% of his sample were not encouraged to evaluate their own programs, and only 8% were. Teachers saw that the institutional climate of the school shaped how they thought about teacher evaluation, for example, that the purpose for evaluation was narrowly for control or broadly to develop teachers, depending on the tradition and culture of the school.

Lortie (1975) found that only 7% of his interviewees saw judgments by their organizational superiors as the most appropriate source of information about how well they were doing. Teachers looked to the students in the classroom for indications of their teaching performance, rather than to outside sources. Teachers reported complex interactions with administrators—depending on them for protection, but simultaneously desiring independence from them in their classroom teaching. Twenty-nine percent of elementary-level teachers and 4% of secondary teachers felt that the principal should "be sure that teachers fulfilled their responsibilities," but other kinds of monitoring or leadership were not valued. In general, Lortie reported that most teachers operated independently of administrator evaluations. They realized that principals had responsibility to evaluate, but teachers placed little direct interest or respect in the process or results of evaluation.

Kauchak, Peterson, and Driscoll (1985), in a survey study of Utah and Florida teachers, found evaluations based on principal visits to be "perfunctory with little or no effect on actual teaching practice" (p. 33). The first problem in current practice identified by these teachers was that evaluation visits were too brief and nonrigorous in their content. Second, teachers complained that the principal was not knowledgeable. Teachers were critical that principals had not taught at their level (elementary) or in their subject area (secondary). Finally, the visits and subsequent reports lacked applicability to the teacher's situation. Principal evaluations said little or nothing about the specific instruction, topics, students, successes, and problems encountered in the actual classrooms observed. Overall, these researchers found that teachers did not see evaluation as instrumental in improving their teaching.

Wise and his colleagues (1984) at the RAND Corporation completed an extensive survey and set of school district case studies on teacher evaluation for the National Institute of Education. The most serious problem they found in current practice was that principals were in a significant role conflict position:

Central office respondents believed that the conflict between the principal as instructional leader and evaluator has not been settled. Noting that collegial relationships lead many principals to want to be "good guys," many respondents felt that principal evaluations were upwardly biased. Principals' disinclinations to be tough makes the early identification of problem teachers difficult and masks important variations in teacher performance. (p. 22)

Also, this study found that principals considered teacher evaluation "a necessary evil or a time-consuming chore" (p. 22).

The RAND study continued with four other major problems of teacher evaluation. Second in frequency of mention was teacher resistance or apathy. Full teacher support was reported in less than half the districts surveyed. The third problem was lack of uniformity and consistency within a school district. Teachers reported that "the present system . . . depends too much on the judgment or predisposition of the principal and leads to different ratings for similar teacher practices in different schools" (Wise et al., 1984, p. 22). The fourth most cited problem was inadequate training for evaluators. Central office respondents reported that evaluators received too little training and guidance for their current responsibilities in evaluation. The final problem area was expertise for evaluation. For some teachers, especially high school and specialists (like P.E., art), subject matter knowledge is essential to good teacher evaluation but is lacking in many administrators.

Johnson (1990) interviewed 115 teachers from the perspective of better understanding of the workplace of teachers. She found that "teachers . . . roundly criticized formal supervision and evaluation practices" (p. 266). As did other researchers, Johnson found teachers well aware of the conflict for administrators to have both the role of making tough summary judgments and responsibility for giving sustained support. When teachers dealt with assessors, they tended to be cautious, but improvement or change call for taking risks. This made satisfactory teacher-principal relationships rare. One way in which both teachers and principals handled this conflict was to minimize the evaluation role altogether. Consequently, most teachers felt that evaluation really exists just for "others," presumably weak teachers.

Teachers in Johnson's (1990) study reported that principals rarely offered ideas for improvement. Instead, orderly performance of the procedures of evaluation was more important than the content of it. Another problem identified by teachers was that the rating forms, with items like "professional demeanor," left teachers puzzled when unaccompanied by descriptions or discussions. Many teachers complained that rating items encouraged principals to be picky in their criticisms—it was easy to find details to criticize just so that administrators will look discriminating. The resulting criticism may have been minor to the administrator but made the teachers feel bad.

The main dissatisfaction of teachers with administrators as evaluators was what the teachers saw as a basic lack of competence on the part of administrators to evaluate: lack of self-confidence, experience, subject matter knowledge, and perspective on what it is really like to be in the classroom. Other teachers faulted the situation and said that observed lessons were pushed by the teacher to be technically better than normal and thus were not accurate views of what teachers actually do—more a "staged production" than a "snapshot."

Systems that rely on teachers to set their own goals received barely more praise from teachers in Johnson's (1990) study. The problem is that "I can't say that anybody's supporting you; you're doing it yourself" (p. 267). When the few teachers who had good reports of administrator reports were identified, it was because of unusual personal qualities of the administrator—good evaluation occurred in spite of present practices. Some teachers did report that they appreciated the praise of administrators.

Overall, teachers in Johnson's (1990) study were quite critical of current evaluation procedures:

> For . . . good teachers, schools offered no systematic way to productively review and improve their practice. The process of . . . evaluation, supposedly meant for all teachers, actually addressed the problems of only the weakest. Evaluators were seldom sufficiently skilled or experienced to offer constructive criticism in subject areas and frequently limited themselves to giving categorical praise. They concentrated on the procedural demands of the process that were subject to legal review in any dismissal case. These consumed enormous amounts of administrative time while diverting administrators' attention from the substance of most teachers' practice. (p. 274)

Three other survey studies found responses corroborating those given above. Trask (1964) found that even elementary school principals were faulted by teachers if they had not taught at the grade level at which they judged teacher performance. Osmond (1978) reported that more than half of his respondents said that not enough time was devoted to evaluation. Rothberg and Buchanan (1981) found that stress was the most negative part of current practice in teacher evaluation. Brevity and infrequency were the second most mentioned negative part of evaluation visits.

Conceptual Analysis Studies

Scriven (1981) provided a thorough analysis of problems with current teacher evaluation practices. His insights have been corroborated by empirical research in the decade since he wrote. Scriven began with institutional prerequisites, things that educational systems need to provide but rarely do in current practice. First, administrators need to be evaluated "to avoid the entirely justifiable resistance of the 'serfs' to being evaluated by those in the castle, who are above such things themselves" (p. 245). Second, the system needs to evaluate carefully other expectations of a teacher's position, for example, faculty committee service, in addition to teaching. Third, the system needs to distinguish between *worth* and *merit* in the evaluation of teachers. Worth is the value of the teacher to the school, not the professional merit (quality) of the teaching. Fourth, the educational system needs to provide an independent support system of some kind, for example, a teaching consultation or Evaluation Unit, that is independent of the administrators and other summative judges. Other institutional requirements include consistent and appropriate evaluation practices (not just rhetoric), some involvement of students (or representatives for their interests), and comprehensive evaluation for all kinds of personnel decisions.

Scriven (1981) was specific about ways *not* to evaluate teaching. He began with classroom visits. First, the visit itself alters the teaching practice. Second, the number of visits is too small to be representative. Third, visitors almost always bring personal prejudices wit them, positive or negative, concerning their interpersonal relations and responsibilities with the individual teacher observed. Fourth, the dominant influence of styles observed in classrooms as a basis for judgment cannot be linked to student learning. Fifth, visitors bring style preferences of their own that cannot be defended by empirical research. Sixth, the visitor has vastly different thought processes than those of the student, due to differences in age, vocabularies, cognitive repertoires, and cultures. Finally, classroom visits are quite costly.

Scriven (1981) identified several further incorrect ways to evaluate teaching. Once such current practice is to evaluate teaching without looking at course content—the quality of what students learn, as well as the quantity of student outcomes. Absence of concern about subject matter content has made educational institutions a laughingstock in the intellectual community and society at large. Another mistake is to focus entirely on teaching processes that merely substitute for style preferences. The literature on structured lesson processes fails to show overall superior results, yet advocates continue to tout certain routines as equivalent to quality teaching. Still another evaluation error is to misuse student questionnaires. For example, it is common to use items that focus on style or teacher popularity. Finally, although appealing, alumni surveys are difficult to do well. Representation numbers are a problem, unless surveys are completed close to the actual exit time. Surveys done later suffer from low return rates and the influence of intervening variables, such as further education and opportunities to put learning into use.

Peterson (1984) identified four areas of need for research and development in teacher evaluation. Without this work, teacher evaluation fails to meet the needs that justify it. First, he maintained that studies should be made on the needs of different audiences for teacher evaluation. Present practice is directed toward a very narrow audience of the administrator-teacher dyad, with the evaluative needs of others (public, teacher educators, legislators, parents) not considered. Consequently, teacher evaluation satisfies very few people who have a direct interest in it. Second, models of evaluation need to be distinguished and tested. Most current evaluation is a kind of discrepant evaluation in which actual teaching is compared to an ideal set of behaviors, characteristics, results, or competencies. Peterson argued that emergent evaluation needs development so that the value of actual teaching performances can be seen more clearly. Third, he called for research and development of additional lines of evidence (e.g., student reports, peer review, student gain, systematic observation) that can be added to, or even supplant, current administrator visits. Finally, Peterson suggested that the metric of teacher evaluation be determined carefully. Current practice of limited categorization (retain, remediate, or dismiss) can be expanded for teacher differentiation in ranks or leadership.

Popham (1987) faulted current teacher evaluation practice for the reluctance of designers and administrators to use professional judgment in their decisions. Instead, most systems divide teaching into a dozen or 20 or even 50 or 100 subtasks that each calls for an isolated judgment. These then are combined to create a final single judgment, apparently independent of the overall opinion of the judge on the key several question of quality. Popham attributed this behavior to a flight from responsibility—it takes little courage to fault a teacher on a minor detail. In addition, because these detailed topics are combined mathematically, there is a false appearance of precision and rigor. Popham (1987) was critical of overquantification in teacher evaluation systems: "Numbers, unfortunately, are no protection against nonsense" (p. 28). He called for educators to abandon pretensions of precision and to instead rely on sound professional judgmental systems—particularly those with multiple judges.

Berk (1988) criticized teacher evaluation based simply on student achievement. He recounted 70 years of research that shows the link between teacher performance and pupil learning to be quite indirect. His "fifty reasons why student achievement gain does not mean teacher effectiveness" (p. 345) were based on a careful analysis of the literature that shows 50 factors beyond the control of teachers that influence pupil learning (e.g., pupil effort, prior achievement, parent support, opportunities for employment and education). He also discussed the technical needs for valid and reliable estimates of pupil learning that are virtually absent in current practice. Berk (1988) concluded that

> between-class, between-grade and between-student variability
> of the 50 sources of invalidity and error render the setting of a
> meaningful criterion for superior teacher productivity nearly

impossible. Although there does not seem to be any single source of invalidity or error (systematic or random) that is large enough to invalidate the pretest-posttest gain score model, the combination of multiple sources analyzed cumulatively does prove fatal to warrant its rejection. (p. 358)

Scriven (1987) criticized the current trend called research-based teacher evaluation (RBTE) in which certain teacher behaviors are used as quality indicators because some teacher effectiveness studies have demonstrated a statistically significant correlation between them and pupil outcomes. He pointed out that there are several kinds of faulty logic (and fairness) in RBTE. First, the difference between correlation and causation is crucial. We would be foolish (and immoral) if we hired all Asian American teacher applicants because as a group they are so successful in schools and universities. Second, there is an important practical distinction between statistical significance and real significance. The large statistical superiority of "Sesame Street" viewers versus a control group was actually a small difference in absolute size of vocabulary learning. (It should be recalled that most teacher effectiveness relationships show correlation sizes in the 0.2 to 0.4 range—statistically significant in large samples, but practically negligible in explaining performance.) He concluded that secondary indicators (attributes that apply to an individual only because of group membership) should be abandoned in favor of the primary indicators, which are samples of criterial performance. Scriven (1987) was critical of RBTE because "it takes inservice attention away from plain duties [e.g., use of tests] and focuses it on stylistic frippery" (p. 21), and he concluded that RBTE "is essentially a contradiction in terms. If an indicator has been 'validated' by empirical research, which can only establish secondary connections to criterial behavior, it is invalid for evaluative purposes" (pp. 22-23).

Peterson and Chenoweth (1992) criticized current evaluation practices because teachers have little control and involvement in their own evaluation. They described three limits to increased teacher participation:

First, recent technical developments . . . , such as peer review . . . , have not been widely adopted. Teachers and administrators alike lack technical expertise or awareness of . . . evaluation options. Second, means to develop teachers to change from passive recipients of evaluation into active participators have not been carefully thought out. Finally, educators who design teacher evaluation systems continue to place teachers into receiver roles, rather than to tap the more powerful functioning of professional evaluation. Researchers and policy makers lack a vision of teacher participation. (p. 177)

The authors described current practice as "faultfinding, discrepancy-reporting, prescriptive, and ritualistic" (p. 181). The advantages of current practice are that it allows teachers to elude responsibility for the quality of their peers, avoids teacher-teacher conflicts, and takes little teacher time. In addition, sociological reactive alliances to evaluation among teachers gives a small measure of a sense of belonging to otherwise isolated teachers.

ADDITIONAL PROBLEMS WITH CURRENT PRACTICE

The research described in this chapter shows teacher evaluation that is inaccurate, not respected, and not well thought out for its needs and consequences. Before turning to reasons as to why evaluation has not been improved, six additional problems need mention.

Teachers Do Not Choose to Support Evaluation Activity

Extensive interview studies of teachers show that they do not want to be evaluated, do not feel they need it to improve, or do not believe that it can be done. As it stands, evaluation is a threat to their livelihood and an intrusion on their time; they do not want or use the results of evaluation. No one wants to be made to look bad at doing something he or she cares about. Classrooms seem to go on well enough without it. There is little or no vision from teacher interview studies about how teacher evaluation could be changed so that it would be believable, credible, useful, and fair.

Difficulties With Teacher Evaluation Are Oversimplified

People who do have a vision of improved teacher evaluation tend to offer simplistic solutions for the rather complicated technical and sociological problems. For example, the suggestion often is made that only the techniques of evaluation need improvement. It is said that the rating form should be improved, perhaps by covering more of what a teacher does, or linking it to some research on what makes a good teacher. Others suggest a change in the circumstances for evaluation, for example, that the principal and teacher should clinically confer over the ideas and topics for evaluation. Still others say that more training is needed—both principals and teachers need to know more about how to recognize good teaching. Some suggest looking more at the results of teaching; there is the perennial siren call for teacher evaluation by student outcomes. Others say that the proper focus is on how one teaches, that process is all important. Another idea, usually of noneducators, is that the content of teaching (e.g., a canon of classical concepts) defines good teacher. Finally, someone generally suggests that the background, education, preparation, and training of a teacher are important. None of these unidimensional suggestions for improving teacher evaluation provides the scope of the new directions of Chapter 1.

Minimal Competency Is Assessed, but Not Appropriate Use of Competency

Current teacher evaluation systems are designed to assess minimal competency. Competency assessments are important. But it is also important that there is no assessment of their appropriate use. For example, if a teacher in the Coker et al. (1980) study were rated high on calling off-task students to attention by inappropriately humiliating students, the academic and self-concept results should have been expected to be negative, contrary to the original hypothesis. If the teacher failed to call off-task students to attention but appropriately allowed self-correcting students to take initiative and responsibility, the outcome results should have been expected to be positive, also contrary to the original hypothesis. The point is that the key element in assessing teacher performance is not mere possession of a competency or demonstration of a behavior, but whether the teacher showed contextually appropriate behavior. What underlies this capacity for appropriate action are understanding, perception, and personal integration—all of which require more complex evaluation schemes than principal reports.

Evaluation Does Not Address Exceptional Teacher Cases

Exceptional cases of teaching that stand out from most common practice suggest that current evaluation is not good enough. First, consider the problem of the bad teacher. Current evaluation practice does not ferret out bad practice. Rather, someone (or many) becomes aware the teacher is not good. Then, the evaluation procedures are used after the fact to "prove" that the teacher was not doing a good job. Second, truly outstanding teaching practice is not identified by teacher evaluation systems. Recognition of exceptional high quality is rare and does not come about as a result of formal evaluation.

Many Systems Feature Overquantification

Many current evaluation systems feature quantitative systems of points, averages, pupil outcome measures, and weightings of data (e.g., Erffmeyer & Martray, 1990; Rakow & McLarty, 1990). This is an attempt to repair the old approaches with more elaborate schemes of "objectivity" and reductionism. A false sense of precision is created by using numbers, categories, and total scores. An additional reason that many choose overquantification is the assumption that the final numerical calculation will make the judgment of quality objectively, independent of the people who assembled the numbers.

Evaluation of quality teaching calls for high levels of professional judgment. Teacher evaluation is not the mere sum of moves or characteristics, but a complex, dynamic, and appropriate set of interactions that differs with every application—in short, a very human kind of performance to demonstrate as a teacher and to recognize as an evaluator.

Laypersons Are Not Reassured by Current Teacher Evaluation

The lay public is not reassured about the quality of teacher performance as a result of current evaluation procedures. Few data are available to make decisions about voting additional money for schools. There are doubts stemming from indirect comparisons with other countries, especially economic competitors like Japan and Germany. The costs of public education have risen, but it is not clear that the quality or effect of teachers has changed.

Laypersons are puzzled by the practice of teacher evaluation. They do not understand a profession that relies so much on testing its clients (students) but does not support testing of its own practitioners. Noneducators are unsure why students are not included more often in judging teachers—they certainly must know who the good teachers are. Also, the public emphasizes the role of student learning in judging teachers much more than educators do. If students are learning, then other issues matter very little. Achievement test scores appear to be an answer to teacher evaluation completely missed by teachers and administrators. Although these issues are complicated, the failure of current practice to address them satisfactorily is a problem for laypersons.

WHY TEACHER EVALUATION PRACTICE HAS NOT CHANGED

If teacher evaluation is so bad, why do practically all those involved continue to do it the way they do? Why has practice not changed? There are several reasons. Good teacher evaluation is difficult to do. It has many short-term costs and only long-term payoffs. Evaluation has few champions and many critics. Very little talent and resources of the profession and the society have gone into development of teacher evaluation. Effective and satisfying alternatives rarely have been demonstrated. Precedent and tradition maintain strong influences on practice.

Two Evaluation Stories

John N. is a third-grade teacher. He has taught for 11 years. Sarah H. is his principal. She is the third principal he has had. She has visited his class for six or seven specific, nonevaluative visits. She has formally observed twice in the 3 years she has been principal. On the last occasion, she included a preobservation conference, using the district procedures. The procedures include a checklist of behaviors linked to a research basis of effective teaching.

John has a good reputation for teaching. Each year, several parents request his class. His "male influence" is valued in a school that is 85% female in its teaching staff. John and Sarah both are comfortable with the evaluation procedures. Overall monitoring is adequate, and the procedures take relatively little time. His item ratings at the last formal visit were all superior, except for lesson planning. John disagrees with this last rating but considers it a small issue.

John has proven himself, and Sarah is respectful of his teaching.

Bill T. is a first-year high school science teacher. Nancy F. is a veteran principal. Nancy was involved in the hiring interviews, although they were teacher dominated, following the initial district screening. Bill is scheduled to have two formal visits during the year.

Bill's teaching is exciting, if a bit unrealistic in time and energy demands. Students take well to his ideas about inquiry. Nancy has given advice on acquiring chemicals from a teacher in another school in the district. Bill's department chair has helped to get articles to supplement the textbook. Although Bill is nervous about the evaluation procedures, he sees himself fairly treated and is pleased with the specific suggestions for resources. Nancy is satisfied that a good selection has been made and that the early rough spots in practice are being made up by enthusiasm and dedication. Bill is making a contribution to the entire faculty with his energetic beginnings.

Both of these examples include just enough appearance of evaluation to cover most external pressures on administrators and teachers. It is difficult to argue that *no* teacher evaluation is going on. In both of these cases, professional life seems to be going on well enough. What more could be desirable?

School districts have operated satisfactorily for a long time without good teacher evaluation. Most teachers give good service, and the evaluation process does not interfere much with their work. Current evaluation practice may take only several uncomfortable hours each year, until the reputation of teacher is established. Then, subsequent evaluations become perfunctory. The exceptions to this innocuous practice are the feelings of terror for some beginning teachers and the irritation to veteran teachers caused by an administrator who recently has attended a workshop and wants to impose a latest fad in evaluation. A major block to reform in evaluation is that current evaluation practice, as inadequate as it is, appears to work in the sense that it is a minimal bother to the majority of teachers who are currently doing a good job and major problems do not exist with the majority of teachers. Thus the general inadequacy of evaluation is hidden, with a few exceptional troublesome cases of bad teachers. In the real life of schools, we are generally unaware of teacher evaluation unless teachers are never visited, unless administrators are overly authoritarian and teachers are excluded from all deliberations and procedures, and where bad teachers are merely transferred from one school to a less suspecting one.

Except for a few troublesome events, current teacher evaluation practice has been reduced to a most innocuous bottom level of activity that bothers participants the least. Because it is difficult to argue that no teacher evaluation should be done, the corrupting contract among educators is to do the least disruptive activity and call it adequate. However, this agreement ignores many important principles of education and evaluation and means that the benefits of good teacher evaluation must go unrealized.

3

Principles of Teacher Evaluation

This chapter presents the major concepts and perspectives that underlie the design and use of teacher evaluation systems. Consideration of these ideas is important because it is not good enough merely to have an evaluation system, it also is necessary to understand it. In addition, the ideas presented in this chapter introduce techniques detailed later in this book.

The evaluation of teachers is a complex activity and not as simple and straightforward as current practice makes it look. Educators need to think through the assumptions, procedures, expectations, and relationships that they use in evaluating teachers. Profound issues such as "What is quality teaching?" and "Who can best recognize teacher quality?" require discussions before action begins. Debate about basic and controversial ideas is the best foundation for effective practice.

This chapter presents a complex collection of basic and controversial ideas. It begins with an examination of the many purposes of teacher evaluation. Next, the central questions of decision making about teacher value are discussed in a lengthy section on how to judge teacher quality. Then follows a working definition of teacher quality, a difficult concept to identify. The next topic is the key idea that teachers should have more extensive control and participation in their own evaluation. The chapter continues with discussion of costs, which too often are ignored in thinking about evaluation design. The next section describes what constitutes good teacher evaluation. Then, the point will be made that although it is not a popular activity, there is a strong case for increased teacher evaluation. The chapter concludes with recommendations for improved practice.

PURPOSES OF TEACHER EVALUATION

The overall purpose of teacher evaluation is to determine the value, worth, or merit of teaching (Scriven, 1973a). More specific purposes are to protect children, reassure teachers that they are doing good jobs, assure audiences interested in teacher performance, make personnel decisions, inform teacher educators, and shape further practice. Most current teacher evaluation systems overemphasize the function of evaluation to improve practice. Actually, there is little evidence that evaluation actually does improve practice, but good teacher evaluation has a number of other important purposes.

There is a heavy responsibility for teachers to be evaluated, relative to other occupations (Scriven, 1973a). The main reason is that their clients are young and nonvoluntary. Thus monitoring teachers for protection of the young is essential. Also, most other professionals have a strong evaluation mechanism in return clientele that teachers do not have. For example, the adequacy or quality of a dentist is affirmed by the number of her return patients. Teachers normally are assigned classes of students regardless of how well the teacher has performed in the past. Therefore, teachers should receive a relatively larger amount of evaluation than is visible in most other occupations.

Another central purpose of teacher evaluation is reassurance of practitioners and their audiences. Lortie (1975) described teaching as a profession remarkably barren of feedback that indicates quality and authoritative reassurance. Much of a teacher's results are barely visible in the short run, or are confounded with other simultaneous experiences of students. Because perhaps 60% of the variance in pupil gain is accounted for by their prior achievement, it is difficult for teachers to be clear about just what effects their efforts have. Other professionals generally can see their results more directly. A legal case may receive a clear judgment, or at least direct comparison with written precedents. An architect is able to see the adequacy of a bridge design as it physically is put into place. Likewise, a dentist is easily able to judge the quality of her bridge design as reported by a patient. Good teacher evaluation has the potential to let the teacher know, in ways that he trusts, that he is doing a valuable, worthwhile, and needed job. This central function of teacher reassurance is rarely designed in, in ways that are most valued by classroom teachers. What teachers want and how they use evaluation has been the subject of little research and development (a notable exception is Lortie, 1975).

Beyond reassurance, credible evaluation data that focus on good teaching (preparation, process, or results) that already exists enhance teacher job satisfaction. As described by Owens (1991),

> A greater motivational need [than for pay, security, and advancement] . . . is for teachers to achieve feelings of professional self-worth, competence, and respect; to be seen . . . as people of achievement, professionals who are influential in their workplaces, growing persons with opportunities ahead to develop even greater competence and a sense of accomplishment. (p. 113)

An important purpose of teacher evaluation is to document and acknowledge teacher achievement, influence, and professional activity.

Reassurance for the audiences of teachers also is important. Teaching is not done just for the practitioners or even the students, but also for parents, elected representatives, society, and the profession. There are many stakeholders in quality teaching. Comprehensive teacher evaluation has the purpose of letting interested groups know how well, and in what ways, teachers contribute to their students and to society.

The most visible purpose of teacher evaluation is for staffing decisions (Bridges, 1992). These decisions are to hire, retain, remediate, or terminate. This activity receives a great deal of attention and forms the single common ground of interest of participants and audiences. In particular, the few cases resulting in dismissal drive much of current teacher evaluation practice (Lawrence, Vachon, Leake, & Leake, 1993). As a result, other kinds of staffing decisions are virtually nonexistent. For example, school districts do not have systematic evaluation that identifies teacher leaders, promotes teachers to advanced ranks (as is done in colleges), or gives recognition and security to long-serving, successful teachers.

The most discussed purpose of teacher evaluation is to improve practice. This function receives much lip service, although there is not much evidence that practice actually is improved. The supposition is that feedback, with specific praise and criticism, helps professionals to self-regulate. Tuckman and Oliver (1968) reported evidence that pupil survey data assisted teachers to make improvements. However, other than a few examples like this one, the research literature is surprisingly empty of specific cases of evaluation resulting in improved practice. There are not empirical research studies that show evaluation practices that pay off in pupil achievement, changes in teaching methods, better attitudes among teachers or students, or even greater teacher satisfaction. There are no published evaluation studies of teacher evaluation programs that show important, durable, cost-effective, educational results in terms of improving teachers or increasing student learning.

A final purpose of teacher evaluation is improvement of the profession. This function goes beyond individual teachers and addresses the larger group of educators. Teacher training programs could benefit from well-documented evaluation reports of successful teachers; such reports are not available from current evaluation systems. Development of a "knowledge base" (Wang, Haertel & Walberg, 1993) for teachers to follow often has been advocated. One source of a knowledge base for teaching and learning is academic, social-scientific research. However, there have been recent criticisms of the value of a knowledge base of education based on scientists distant from the action of classrooms (Kliebard, 1993). Again, well-documented teacher evaluation programs are a promising source of information for general professional practice. Current teacher evaluation programs are not up to this challenge. Chapter 26 of this book shows how data about the value and effect of individual teachers can be aggregated to inform general practice and the design of teacher preservice and inservice education.

HOW TO JUDGE TEACHER QUALITY

Judgments in teacher evaluation concern how decisions about teacher quality are made. Of related concern is the preparation that should be given to those people who make decisions about teacher data. Judgment making is a crucial area of teacher evaluation that rarely is discussed or thought about. It usually is the last step in evaluation (although evaluation of the evaluation should be the last step) and ignored until then. Judgment decisions usually are examined in only the most difficult and unsatisfactory cases—as in controversial teacher dismissals—and then only for the specific case (Bridges, 1992; Lawrence et al., 1993).

This section on judging teacher quality begins with a review of selected research literature. The research literature on decision making in teacher evaluation is relatively sparse. Certainly, more work needs to be done on this topic. This section will review several conceptual and empirical research studies that give good clues for defensible judgment making. This section concludes with a summary discussion of the roles of objectivity and subjectivity in judging teacher quality and the implications of the studies. There is a lack of thinking on these topics, and many assumptions are made before the principles are clear.

The first kind of literature selected for review addresses teacher evaluation judgments themselves. These are studies and analyses of teacher evaluation systems. The literature reviewed here includes conceptual and empirical studies. For additional guidance, two other kinds of literature on human judgments are presented. First, psychological research on human decision making in general helps to understand some pitfalls and limitations of human judgment and to improve the teacher evaluation process. Second, descriptions of decision making in courtroom juries are helpful to understand human judgment making in another setting with parallels for teacher evaluation.

Selected Literature: Conceptual Studies

Educational Evaluation

Scriven (1973a) created a number of key ideas for teacher evaluation as he refined his model training program for qualitative education evaluation. Although these ideas were targeted more generally at problems of program evaluation, their importance for personnel evaluation is clear. Scriven (1973a) defined educational evaluation as

> the process whereby judgments of worth or merit . . . are given objective substantiation. It involves many of the skills of experimental design and data analysis, including statistics, but it also involves a major qualitative component. Somehow one must develop a framework of value criteria in which to insert the observational data, and . . . [to] substantiate that framework. (Module 1, p. 1)

Scriven (1972, 1973b, 1973c, 1976, 1977) raised the important issue of where the value framework for judgment should originate. On what basis can we know whether the data submitted by teachers for their evaluation are good? This is an especially intriguing question because many people suppose that evaluators should be value free, in the sense that evaluators should not subjectively interpose their preferences and beliefs, but let the evaluation evidence speak for itself.

One common source for values used in educational evaluation is the *goal statement* of the enterprise (e.g., program, curriculum, personnel). Many evaluators use lists of program or personal goals or ideals to compare to the data gathered about actual implementation. Scriven pointed out that this discrepancy strategy is used a great deal in formative evaluation. However, for summative judgment making, there is even a larger scope of value than whether the person (or project) is meeting his or her (or its) planned goals. Even if the teaching is right on target of the plans of the teacher or institution, it may not be all that is needed by the clients. Thus the evaluator is responsible for going beyond the intentions and goals of the educator and bringing in the larger picture of value for clients, audiences, and theoretical understanding of the profession.

Table 3.1 presents 10 pathway tasks or analyses (not necessarily in sequence) recommended by Scriven (1973a) in preparing for an evaluative judgment. (Scriven's original list of steps for general educational evaluation have been modified in this table to correspond to specific requirements for teacher evaluation.) These considerations are important because they suggest the depth and nature of thought that goes into the assembly and judgment of teacher evaluation data. Scriven's analysis of evaluation tasks is a sound guide for understanding the preparation and thinking required for judging teachers. Chapter 18 presents recommended practices and forms for carrying out these tasks.

Peterson (1984) described teacher evaluation as a highly judgmental process. He identified the current common practice of "discrepancy" judgments (Provus, 1971) in which teacher quality is recognized by differences between an a priori ideal—a list of some behaviors, characteristics, duties, attitudes, outcomes, preparation, and/or experiences—and evidence about the actual teacher under review. Thus a standard of good teaching is defined, and all teachers are compared to it. Those teachers most closely corresponding to the ideal are considered to be of the highest quality.

For example, in applying discrepancy teacher evaluation it may be decided that a certain set of instructional behaviors (e.g., clarity or giving guided practice) are keys to good teaching. Then, observation or anecdotal reports are used as evidence that the individual teacher can perform ("competency based") or characteristically performs ("performance based") the desired process; hence quality has been demonstrated. Conversely, teachers not showing these behaviors are said to be of low quality. A second example is for the discrepancy evaluation design to center on the ideal payoff of pupil achievement. With this ideal, evidence is gathered on student outcomes, for example, biology test gain scores or self-concept measure increases. Data showing such growth are indicators of teacher quality. Absence of student learning indicates lack of teacher quality.

In discrepancy evaluation, an a priori ideal is selected as a standard for comparison, or determination of difference from the ideal. Some themes that are used for discrepancy systems include behaviors identified in teacher effectiveness research ("research based"; e.g., McGreal, 1983), competencies exhibited by ideal teachers (competency based; e.g., Houston & Howsam, 1972), performance or systems analysis (performance based; e.g., Heath & Nelson, 1974), teacher task analysis ("duty based"; e.g., Scriven, 1987), student achievement (e.g., Berk, 1988), managerial-

TABLE 3.1 Evaluation Pathway Model

1. *Characterization.* What grade and subjects are taught? What methods does the teacher use (e.g., hands-on, direct instruction, project-based)? Describe the nature of the teaching that is being documented and evaluated.
2. *Clarifications with audiences.* What do people want to know about the teacher (e.g., results, processes, comparisons, background)? Discuss the needs, purpose, and nature of the evaluation with school boards, teachers, parents, students, and legislators.
3. *Client characteristics.* What are the needs and priorities of the students? of the parents? of the school board? of the community? What are the students like? What are their futures? Perform client needs analyses; describe clients.
4. *Causation.* What exactly does the teacher make happen—distinct from pupil background, school, and community resources? Describe nature of teacher's impact, activity, and preparation.
5. *Consequences.* What are the results of this teacher's work, including unintended side effects (positive and negative)? Gather data on teacher impact, activity, and preparation.
6. *Conceptualization and compression of data.* What are the best objective data available (quantitative and qualitative; documented, organized, analyzed, summarized, archived)? Present data.
7. *Costs.* Does this teacher cause (or save) any extraordinary costs? What are the costs of the evaluation of this teacher? Perform cost analysis.
8. *Critical competitors/comparisons.* What are the results of similar teachers in similar settings? What consequences are other teachers responsible for? What data are presented by other teachers like this one? How does this teacher compare to an ideal? Present parallel data from others, and population norms.
9. *Credentialing.* What credible, authoritative reassurances are there about the data? How important are goals and methods? the conceptualization and compression? the characterization and needs analyses? Who says that these are important? Obtain experts' reactions to goals, methods, and results.
10. *Conclusions and communications.* What is the judgment of the value of the teacher's work? Who should be informed? What consequences are there? Judge the teacher. Present decisions and documents. Disseminate results.

SOURCE: Adapted from Scriven (1973a, 1973c). Used with permission.

administrative (e.g., McGreal, 1983), or humanistic (e.g., personal qualities; Combs, 1965). A more recent theme is content-based knowledge of teachers (Shulman, 1987). Research and development in teacher evaluation that emphasizes discrepancy evaluation is a continuous search for more appropriate a priori understandings of quality teaching.

One purported advantage of discrepancy judgments is that they are objective and allegedly more accurate and fair than are subjective judgments. Some claims are made that discrepancy decisions are free from the prejudices, biases, arbitrariness, and less than perfect knowledge of human judges, who must operate subjectively. However, as discussed in the following section on objectivity and subjectivity in teacher judgments, the superiority is not clear on closer analysis.

However appealing the logic of discrepancy evaluation and an a priori understanding of teacher quality, there are significant faults with using them in teacher evaluation (Peterson, 1984). First, no comprehensive list of what a teacher does exists. A teacher's tasks vary from mundane, repetitive, and pedantic acts to more spectacular perceptive reactions and creative innovations. Each job description so far available has captured only a part of the total job universe. A teacher's job is open ended, not solely controlled by the teacher or the school district, and complex. Current job descriptions or duty-based evaluations may capture much or what a teacher is supposed to do, but all leave a significant "negligible" remainder.

A second fault with the discrepancy approach to teacher evaluation is that any comprehensive job description would not be agreed on. Even if an encyclopedic description of teacher tasks could be produced, differing views of education, such as behavioral, cognitive, pragmatic, or classical, render such task lists unusable. The assumption in the early stages of assembly of comprehensive teacher job description is that an agreement among evaluators is in the offing. In fact, it is not.

Third, the context of teaching calls for different performances or solutions, as appropriate. The ideal description of teacher behavior, competence, or approach assumes a specific context. A change in context actually may call for the opposite performance. For example, the structured lesson called for by beginning students on foundation material gives way to less teacher structuring for advanced pupils on elaborated applications. Good teaching means that teachers perceptively take on different duties as called for in specific instructional settings.

Fourth, teachers are effective for different reasons and with varied styles. Although all teachers need to be successful at engaging their pupils in learning, this can be done by giving specific details or letting students invent; uniformly directing or allowing students to be independent; having students react to negative teaching or emulating positive teacher examples; students' responding to a teacher's attractive personality or their avoidance of a negative one; providing structure or opportunity, inspiration or boredom, creative planning or spontaneity; opportunities to satisfy oneself or others; or flexibility or rigidly adhered-to plans. The combinations of teaching simply are too varied to be narrowed to a specific a priori concept that can be used to evaluate teachers by searching for discrepancies.

Fifth, a theoretical problem with discrepancy teacher evaluation is evident when current systems uncover situations where a recognizably good teacher does not fit the a priori criteria. No matter how quality teaching is defined, one can point to cases of excellent practice that contradict the specific definition. For example,

> Analysis of a group of highly effective teachers suggests that they have a characteristic interpersonal perspective that places

student problems ahead of teacher problems, expects problem solving, and values time spent with students. This perspective, because of a demonstrated relationship (correlation) with student learning, is considered to have inherent value.

This *a priori* value is applied to teacher Betty Jones who considers the classroom to be the province of the teacher, and not a place for resolving individual problems, has routines for every foreseeable problem, and will not schedule individual student conferences. Yet she has excellent pupil test scores, is highly rated by students, and enjoys the admiration of fellow teachers. Additionally, evidence is that her students become unusually self-reliant and able to include many other school activities.

Betty Jones is judged to be inadequate. (Peterson, 1984, p. 65)

Even a single disconfirming case undermines the theoretical backing of the evaluation system and destroys its credibility among practitioners.

The final problem with discrepancy teacher evaluation systems, according to Peterson, is that they inevitably involve criteria and applications that are clearly unfair for some individuals or groups. Seeing this unfairness, other teachers prevent the system from operating. Any particular definition of quality teaching faces crushing pressures in practice when used as a sole and universal description. Even combinations of a priori descriptions (often assembled by committees) face the same problems.

Peterson (1984) suggested as an alternative to current discrepancy decision making the use of emergent judgments in which the

actual demonstrated impact and merit of teachers are used as a basis for value judgments and decisions. Essentially, a distinct analysis is made for each teacher in terms of what that particular teacher has done within a specific setting. The focus is on the crucial, salient elements of the particular performance, whether the elements be intended goals, side effects, or unique outcomes or processes. The emphasis is on . . . the actual teaching performance or results. . . . The basis for value judgments is how events and outcomes emerged in an actual case of teaching. (pp. 64-65)

Using this view, the judgment for teaching merit has four premises:

1. teaching is a complex phenomenon with multiple desirable solutions or expressions of value,
2. value in teaching is in relation to a specific audience,
3. value in teaching is context dependent, and

4. value may take into account a precursor, process, or potential, as
   well as payoff. (p. 66)

The proper question for deciding about quality, then, is "What case can be
made that: an expression or solution occurred, the expression is of defensible value, the value is to a specific audience, and the expression occurs in a
context that suggests merit?" (Peterson, 1984, p. 66). Using an emergent
point of view, teacher evaluation is a process of making a case for quality,
using supporting lines of evidence or data sources, and then judging the individual case for adequacy or comparative merit.

Popham (1987) discussed the need for "good professional judgment"
in teacher evaluation. He criticized what he called the "champagne bub-
ble" evaluation approach of using many detailed items on a checklist in
which "the judgmental process is either circumvented altogether or, more
commonly, subdivided into a series of such minuscule judgments that no
single judgment, by itself, is terribly important" (p. 25). Popham called for
educators to show courage and to use "the only instrument capable of dealing with the enormous complexity of a teacher's instructional efforts . . .
professional judgment" (p. 28).

Alternately, Mehrens (1990) well represented the evaluation tradition
of reducing complex phenomena to numbers. He discussed the benefits of
using data from multiple sources for summative scores or decision making. He distinguished between clinical and statistical methods of combining data. Clinical methods are defined as "eyeballing the various pieces of
data to arrive at a final score [or] decision" (Mehrens, 1990, p. 324), whereas
"statistical weighting is the use of fixed weights for the data in a mathematical equation" (p. 324). Mehrens cited researchers who maintain that statistical prediction is better than clinical prediction when a criterion measure
(a number, in this situation, that rates teacher quality) is available. Nisbett
and Ross (1980) maintained that statistical predictions are preferable even
when the outcomes are "logically derived algorithms" (Mehrens, 1990),
such as would be used in teacher evaluation decisions.

Psychology of Decision Making

Nisbett and Ross (1980) provided an extensive view of the psychology
of decision making, especially focusing on the strategies and shortcomings
of human inference. Their thesis was that the intuitive inference of the
layperson is much less reliable than the statistical inference of the formal
scientist. The advantage of the formal scientist as a decision maker about
quality is that he or she uses normative principles (agreed-on procedures
for evidence and standards of quality, e.g., Occam's razor) and three inferential tools. These tools are (a) knowledge structures, that is, broad and

specific information; (b) judgmental heuristics, that is, active search for data for expected categories; and (c) weighting of data for salience and vividness, that is, information ranked for importance and appropriateness. Scientists also consistently gather data well (sample reliably), recognize covariation, seek causal inferences, predict, and test theories.

The authors contrast this decision making with that of laypersons who may use "simplistic inferential strategies beyond their appropriate limits" (Nisbett & Ross, 1980, p. 3). As a result, "in ordinary social experience, people often look for the wrong data, often see the wrong data, often fail to ask the correct questions of the data, often weight the data improperly, often fail to ask the correct questions of the data, and often make the wrong inferences on the basis of their understanding of the data" (p. 12). These cautions have important implications for how we decide to judge teachers. Good teacher evaluation must guard against these demonstrable problems of decision making by attention to bias and training of judges.

The remedies recommended by Nisbett and Ross (1980) are the methods of the professional scientist, or the trained social scientist. First, decision makers should adopt procedures that are normative: "a consensus among formal scientists that the rule is appropriate for the particular problem" (p. 13). Second, decision makers should learn statistical thinking and methods (e.g., concepts of covariation, regression, probability). Third, the authors recognized "the very impressive results [decision making] of organized intellectual endeavor" (p. 250). That is, inferential decision making can be improved by conducting it in a social context. This occurs for three reasons: Group decision making permits a cultural transmission of knowledge, a group imposes effective quality controls, and the resulting consensus often works very well, even if it is not entirely accurate.

Although much of the writing of Nisbett and Ross (1980) focused on the psychological problems of human decision making, they were optimistic that defensible inferences can be made using less than the strictest strategies of the professional scientist. The norms of the applied scientist, less concerned with the underlying nature of reality and more with the pliability of the real world, are adequate. Also, decision makers are asked merely to use theory, rather than test it. And the requirement of decision makers is to action, rather than understanding. Finally, the costs of benefits of formal decision making are not always justified versus those of intuitive strategies.

Nisbett and Ross (1980) gave advice about training for high-quality decision making. First, judges should be trained in the preconditions of good judgment: sensitivity to the possibility of errors and visible demonstrations of errors and bias. Second, the judges should be trained in statistics, including inference, sampling, probability, regression, and covariance. Third, decision makers should encounter concrete illustrations and vivid anecdotes. Fourth, trainers should use maxims and slogans, such as "It's an empirical question" and "Which hat did you draw that sample out of?" to press the key ideas of formal scientific inference. This advice has great value for developing good teacher evaluation programs, especially for preparing Teacher Review Panels.

Psychologists, such as Nisbett and Ross (1980) and Meehl (1954) have distinguished between clinical judgments and statistical judgments. The latter are advocated as preferable because they are based on a more reliable process. Statistical decisions, the argument goes, are more consistent and supportable. Gathercole (1968) described the ideal statistical decision-making routine for psychotherapy:

> The aim is to produce a test with standardization such that when administered to a patient, his score can be checked against the tabulated scores of standardization groups and he can be classified accordingly. When research has produced the kind of data for this method to be adequate there is no subjective interpretation of results and no use of clinical acumen in the classification of an individual patient's score. Once the patient has produced a score the classification of that score can be done by anyone trained to read the tables—a person Meehl calls a statistical clerk. (p. 44)

This statistical decision-making ideal has a parallel in teacher evaluation where many evaluators have sought numerical score systems that enable mere clerks to read off the final judgment of quality (Erffmeyer & Martray, 1990; Rakow & McLarty, 1990). In such a teacher evaluation system, there is no need for fallible, subjective, clinical judgments.

However, advocacy for the superiority of objective, statistical decision making in teacher evaluation should be challenged. First, clinical decisions are highly defensible when based on experience, training, and public performance. As described by Rodger and Mowbray (1961):

> The clinician behaves like the craftsman in that he attends quickly to what he knows to be significant, his skill develops with experience, and his work involves economy of effort. Like other crafts, it is dependent upon the assimilation of a body of knowledge which is shared by others; but expertness increases with practice until the practitioner is capable of recognizing clinically significant features with such rapidity that his steps of reasoning are not discernible to the uninitiated. (p. 167)

Also, clinical decisions can be guided by appropriate statistical inferences, when they are available. Finally, teacher quality is not a simple enough construct to be reduced to a single, statistical decision.

Continuing the challenge about the superiority of statistical judgments was the analysis of Scriven (1976). Recall that Nisbett and Ross (1980) used the ideal of the scientist as decision maker. Scriven (1976) maintained that science means value judgments (as done in clinical decision making):

> There can be no such thing as science . . . if it were not for the fact that science was an evaluative activity. For science can only be distinguished from pseudo-science in one way; namely, by distinguishing between good and bad evidence, between good and bad explanations, between good experimental designs and bad ones, between good instruments and bad ones, and between good arguments or inferences and bad ones. These are the value judgments on which the very possibility of science rests. The very words "science" and "scientific" are thus evaluative, meaning part of the body of *well*-supported claims, as opposed to *badly* supported ones. (p. 364)

The decisions to use certain measures, to select one tool but not another, to analyze a certain way but not another, and to interpret one way but not another are all clinical judgments. Thus "statistical" decisions themselves rely on "clinical" judgments. Indeed, one way to think about statistical judgments is that they are merely the last stage of an extended line of clinical judgments.

These issues about clinical and statistical decision making are important to teacher evaluation system design. Many current systems seek to present themselves as statistical arguments: Tally so many points, achieve certain levels on scales, and match specific descriptions and the statistical, reliable decision is made (e.g., Erffmeyer & Martray, 1990). Popham (1987) called this a flight from responsibility and challenged teacher evaluators to return to their clinical responsibilities.

Jurisprudence

A third kind of literature that is helpful to understand the process of judging evidence about teacher performance is that related to decision making of juries in the legal system. Here, groups of people hear evidence, discuss their reactions, vote, and deliver a decision.

One particular area of research gives valuable guidance on procedures to be used in judging teacher evaluation data. O'Barr (1982) summarized the research literature on the persuasiveness of language in the courtroom. He reported that certain styles were significantly effective in conveying the message that the speaker was competent, trustworthy, dynamic, attractive, and convincing. These patterns included powerful speech (lack of hedges, super politeness, and tag questions and presence of humor and paraphrase); smooth narration (vs. fragmentary); normal grammar and usage (vs. hypercorrect); and balanced interchange (vs. conflict, overlap, and domination). O'Barr also found significant differences favoring male witnesses. Other influences on the effectiveness of testimony included structure, organization, interaction, storytelling, explicit conclusions, use of emotion, and order of presentation. These findings show the unfairness and irrelevant bias introduced by having teachers make in-person presentations of their evidence for quality performance.

Lloyd-Bostock (1989) described a series of psychological studies on courtroom juries that have importance for designing defensible teacher evaluation decision-making panels. First, she outlined the importance of clear instructions to juries. In particular, it is important to use simple and direct language. This includes short sentences, removal of unusual words and phrases ("two sigmas of pupil gain"), avoidance of negatives, and use of easily grouped, logical steps. Instructions to jurors should be given before as well as after evidence is heard. Instructions should be given in writing as well as verbally. Note taking should be encouraged. Finally, it is extremely difficult for juries to follow the instruction "disregard this information."

Lloyd-Bostock (1989) provided useful information on jury deliberation that is informative for setting effective teacher evaluation review panels. Although Kalven and Zeisel (1966) found that jury deliberations changed little of the outcomes, there are important other functions for the social discussions before rendering verdicts. First, greater accuracy (recollection) of evidence is achieved by pooled viewpoints. Second, preexisting biases are neutralized in that negative moods are dissipated by deliberation. Lloyd-Bostock also provided evidence that group deliberation facilitates leniency.

Lloyd-Bostock (1989) reported additional studies about jury functioning. First, social status outside of the group influences the status created within the group. Second, the size of the jury is important to deliberations: "Experiments with six-person juries have shown that usually everyone speaks, whereas in a 12-person jury, sometimes individual jurors make no contribution to discussions at all" (p. 58).

Hastie, Penrod, and Pennington (1983) determined important patterns of jury deliberation. Early preliminary votes move deliberations from preliminary discussions to conflict resolution. Secret ballots encourage split decisions. These authors distinguished between verdict-driven and evidence-driven deliberations; that is, early voting in the deliberation process encourages verdict-driven decisions because positions are taken and defended.

Selected Literature: Empirical Studies

McCarthey and Peterson (1987) reported a study that compared multiple peer teacher judgments with individual principal judgments of teachers. The subjects in this study used teacher-selected and teacher-presented materials as a basis for recommendation for rewards in a career ladder incentive program. The authors found that teacher judgments were more critical and selective than principal judgments. In 50 reviews, principals recommended 45 (90%) for career ladder reward, whereas teacher panelists (three per reviewee) recommended only 36 (72%). Teacher reviewers reported high levels of confidence and satisfaction in their ability to make judgments of teacher quality. The authors concluded that teacher teams were able to make highly defensible decisions regarding the quality of teacher materials.

Peterson (1988) did a study of panel judgment reliability in a career ladder system in which 26 members of promotion decision panels reviewed 12 teacher dossiers. The panelists in the study had experience on school district promotion panels. The dossiers contained data from a minimum of four sources such as student surveys, administrator report, teacher tests, parent survey, peer review of materials, and pupil gain data. Overall, 73.1% of the 312 decisions were for promotion. Panelists agreed on 90.4% of the decisions (Cohen's kappa = 0.81). For study purposes, the judges were then asked to rank the dossiers in order of quality (a procedure not recommended for teacher evaluation programs). The mean rank order correlation (Spearman's rho) between individual judges and a single composite-judge ranking was 0.84. Peterson (1988) concluded that groups of teachers can make highly defensible decisions regarding the quality of teacher data: "These findings suggest defensible consistency and promise for an alternative teacher evaluation practice" (p. 95).

Meehl and Dahlstrom (1960) reported studies in which they compared statistical decision making to clinical methods. They used 16 rules to classify 988 test results of the Minnesota Multiphasic Personality Inventory (MMPI) as indicating either neurotic or psychotic conditions and reached correct (according to case study classification) categorization on 76%. Then, the authors compared clinical judgments of 29 Minnesota psychologists as they reviewed responses on the MMPI for the same distinction. None of the clinicians correctly identified as many patients as did the objective rules. This study favored statistical decision making, but on a relatively narrow and simple set of criteria. That is, the clinical judges had very little data (only MMPI responses) to base their choices on.

Peterson (1990b) did a computer simulation of professional judgments on teacher promotion using an expert system computer program. The expert system DOSSIER consisted of 111 questions organized into 117 rules (Peterson, 1987b). Questions and rules were derived from interviews of career ladder promotion panel members in Utah. The human judges used a clinical decision-making system. DOSSIER represented a statistical method of combining multiple data, specifically, a compensatory system (Mehrens, 1990).

Peterson (1990b) found that DOSSIER recommended a promotion rate of 75% compared with that of 73.1% by the 26 human judges. The computer expert system agreed with 90.7% of the judges' 312 decisions, who had a 90.4% within-judge agreement rate. DOSSIER had 100% agreement with the 12 majority promotion decisions, as did 10 of the 26 human judges. The mean rank order correlation coefficient (Spearman's rho) of the expert system with the human judges was 0.77, compared with the corresponding value among 325 judge-pairs of 0.73. The DOSSIER rank order of the 12 teachers correlated at 0.92 with the composite rank order generated by averaging the 26 human judges. Six of the 26 judges had higher rank order correlations with this consensus than did the expert system.

These findings demonstrate the statistical support for using human clinical judgment. However, mere statistical agreement does not mean that the best quality judgments have been made. That one agrees with the consensus of others is not the only argument for making the best judgment, although that certainly is an important consideration. Minority opinions may carry valuable perspectives. The statistical argument is that lower variance is the best indicator of quality. However, quality may lie outside of the decision that showed less variance. The human judgment may call for recognition of appropriateness, special cases, and justifiable bias. In short, teacher quality may be more complex than a numerical summary of relationships. Certainly, the judgment of quality teaching is just such a phenomenon.

One example from DOSSIER is telling. The study promotion system had a clear rule that four lines of evidence were required. However, one art teacher submitted three lines—two very strong and one outstanding. The outstanding line was organization of a community art festival in which students not only displayed their own work but organized businesses, schedules, and city government to put on an outstanding community and educational program. DOSSIER decided not to promote, whereas a majority of the human judges did. Although DOSSIER performed well, it should not substitute for the human clinical decision-making process. Quality teaching is an emergent phenomenon that requires recognition of context, need, and comparison in order to recognize quality.

Research on the sociological conditions of teachers suggests that major, conscious, and deliberate changes are required for teachers to begin judging the quality of each other. Yet these same studies show the needs and benefits of such change. In current teacher culture, it is not considered desirable to judge one another. Also, it is not good form to go public with exemplary practice. Thus districts should expect reluctance, awkwardness, and even resistance to increased teacher involvement. Once these inhibitions to teacher participation are broken through, teachers become quite good and enthusiastic judges (McCarthey & Peterson, 1987).

Sociologists report that at present teachers are quite distant from personnel evaluation judgments (Johnson, 1990; Lortie, 1975). These threaten the delicate relationships needed for day-to-day functioning. Currently, teachers are not in a role position to acknowledge or praise good practice. Aside from the reluctance to judge at all, teachers see praise of some teachers to be a threat to the scarce rewards that are available to all teachers. Finally, teachers lack confidence in their own ability to participate in evaluations (Kauchak et al., 1985).

Change requires recognition of the emotional and political dynamics of evaluation, trial programs to gain experience, and a commitment on the part of teachers to make this professional innovation (Peterson & Chenoweth, 1992). Judgments of teaching by teachers will not ultimately be imposed from administrators, politicians, or the lay public—teachers are in a strong position to subvert any such fiat. Greater teacher involvement can be initiated and made available by administrators but then requires the action and backing of teachers. Improved teacher evaluation primarily is a choice of teachers themselves.

Objectivity Versus Subjectivity: A Summary

Much conventional thinking on teacher evaluation has it that good judgments about teacher quality should be objective. Objective evaluation should be easily agreed on by all who see it. Good decisions should require little thought or discussion. If, the reasoning goes, decisions are done well or set up well, there should be little room or need for discretionary judgment or relativity—both attributes of subjectivity, which should be avoided at all costs. Discrepancy evaluation is held out as a good model because it offers the hope of high levels of public agreement on ideals, methods to document actual practice, and easily agreed-on demonstrations of discrepancies (McGreal, 1983; Provus, 1971; Stronge & Helm, 1991).

This conventional wisdom needs to be challenged. Teacher evaluation decisions are made in relation to needs of clients and audiences. These needs may be ambiguous and subject to the perspective of participant, observer, or patron. Decisions about need and quality are value judgments made by human beings. Thus teacher evaluation decisions have an inherent subjectivity. However, as Scriven (1973a, 1976) said, there is good subjectivity and bad subjectivity.

Good subjectivity requires four conditions: (1) the logic of the action is made explicit, (2) decisions are made on the best objective evidence available, (3) inherent biases are balanced, and (4) the interests of all parties are involved. For example, judgments about the adequacy of a teacher's relations with parents are better when the logic of teacher interaction with parents is described and justified before action is taken. Judgments are better when based on the results of systematic surveys over a period of 3 years rather than on the impressions of a principal. The judgments are better when teachers, parents, and administrators were involved in setting up the procedures used to obtain and use parent survey data. Finally, the judgments are better when decisions are made by a panel consisting of teachers, administrators, and parents who counter each other's bias and contribute their respective values.

Many current teacher evaluation systems attempt to avoid subjectivity by overquantification (e.g., Erffmeyer & Martray, 1990; Popham, 1987; Rakow & McLarty, 1990). That is, they seek evaluation systems that reduce teacher performance to scales and categories that receive numerical or categorical ratings. Then, the components are somehow aggregated, and a final number results. The numerical solution judges the teacher, rather than judgment by a person. This may comfort some that they have not subjectively judged others, but in fact they have been subjective when they set the so-called objective system in place.

This procedure, of course, merely removes the subjectivity from the final judgment and places it in a series of preliminary subjective decisions. Why were *certain* categories of behavior chosen to rate and not others? Who decided to *weight* indicators more heavily than others? Who gave one rating, whereas another person provided the second rating? Who decided to gather some evidence (e.g., pupil options) but ignore other evidence (e.g., pupil achievement)? All of these questions are subjective and aggregate to make complex evaluation systems as subjective as the professional judgment system recommended in this book.

Implication of Studies

The methods for judging teacher quality through dossiers recommended later in this chapter rely on clinical judgments of district-level evaluation review panels. Review panels are recommended to have a membership of four teachers, two administrators, and two parents. The validity of this decision making is based on using the best objective evidence available, using multiple judges to balance bias, having social decision making, and relying on clinical judgments. Teachers are not allowed to present or discuss their materials in person. Although review panel deliberation may not change many teacher evaluation decisions, it has additional functions in the education setting (namely, development and dissemination of educational ideas and enhanced expertise of the panel members). A number of empirical studies support the wisdom of this recommended strategy for determining teacher quality.

A DEFINITION OF QUALITY TEACHING

A concept of quality teaching is important in order for educators to talk about values and to design effective evaluation procedures. Each approach to evaluation implies a concept of quality. Later discussions in this book of how to document good teaching are based on understanding what constitutes good teaching.

An Alternative to Discrepancy Evaluation: Quality Teaching as an Emergent Phenomenon

This book uses quite a different view of teaching quality than reliance on some a priori ideal. Rather than to generalize ahead of time what quality teaching consists of, we set up ways to recognize quality as it emerges from a specific case of teaching (Peterson, 1984). For purposes of teacher evaluation, it is possible to recognize (and agree on) the value of a specific act or case of teaching for a given setting and specific clients. What we look for is a professional (or clinical) judgment, rather than a highly defined and explicit discrepancy from a clearly described ideal. Instead of adherence to some ideal, the methods in this book are based on the following definition of *quality teaching* as

> a specific educational act or solution that meets the demonstrated educational needs (and demonstrated priorities) of the clients. Quality is best recognized by the participants themselves or their representatives. Quality may be in the payoff, process, or teacher potential for education. The act or solution of teaching is of value in a specific context and to the interested clients, audiences, and other participants. The teaching meets ethical and fairness requirements. Quality is best understood in comparison with competitors in terms of effectiveness, costs, durability, and side effects. (This definition draws heavily on the qualitative ed-

ucational evaluation ideas of Scriven, 1972, 1973a, 1973c, 1987, and professional judgment ideas of Popham, 1987.)

This concept of quality teaching is significantly different from the discrepancy evaluation (McGreal, 1983; Provus, 1971; Stronge & Helm, 1991) so widely used in current teacher evaluation practice. In the view used in this book, it is possible to recognize good teaching after it has occurred and to conduct meaningful and useful teacher evaluation based on it.

What's the Difference?

The difference between discrepancy and emergent evaluation is fundamental in how teachers are judged. In discrepancy evaluation, the design is to have one means by which all teaching is evaluated, or, if multiple measures are used, to specify a weighting among measures to prespecify quality. In the emergent view, the evaluation effort is to document the practice or performance after it has happened and then to recognize it and describe its value through human judgments.

TEACHERS' INVOLVEMENT AND CONTROL IN THEIR OWN EVALUATION

Teachers need to take an active, decision-making role in their own evaluation (Peterson & Chenoweth, 1992). The main technical reason for this involvement is that teachers are in the best position to know the key indicators of impact for their own case. Thus they are able to select the best combination of data sources for their own evaluation. Their participation enhances accuracy and appropriateness of evidence used to judge them. Because data self-selection may raise doubts in the minds of consumers, credibility can be increased by using independent evaluation personnel to gather and summarize the data, increasing the involvement of peers, students, and additional administrators.

The second argument for extensive teacher participation and control in selecting the data sources is a sociological one. Teacher evaluation systems require the supportive backing of teachers. The current passive teacher involvement is not sufficient to support more comprehensive evaluation. New payoffs, such as teacher and lay public reassurance, and new, more extensive data gathering, such as surveys and activity log books, call for high levels of teacher participation and control.

Careful structuring of a school district's teacher evaluation resources is required for optimal teacher involvement. The following three provisions are needed for increased teacher participation and control:

Technical Information and Consultations

Teachers require information and advice about how best to participate in an extensive teacher evaluation system. This preparation requires some systematic training (as in inservice courses) and opportunities for consultations on individual situations.

Teachers need information on how data sources work, their limitations, and payoffs. Teachers need training in data use and storage. Other information includes political and sociological understandings of teacher evaluation data, for example, that state legislatures find pupil achievement data in relation to expenditures most useful, and peer assessment increases some kinds of teacher security while threatening other kinds.

Independent Evaluation Unit

Teachers need assistance in collecting and interpreting data. However, this help should not be from the people who do the summative evaluation in the district (Popham, 1988). Teachers, understandably, are reticent to explore and use data that might be held against them. Indeed, the current reluctance of teachers to support serious and comprehensive teacher evaluation shows the need for separation of formative and summative functions.

It is recommended that districts form an independent Evaluation Unit consisting of administrators, elected teacher leaders, and clerical help. The unit gives information, provides surveys and other materials, and assists with data interpretation and presentation. Chapter 18 further describes organization of this unit.

Data Sources Are Selected at Two Levels by Teachers

Teachers should have two levels of control in teacher evaluation data collection and presentation. First, teachers decide from among the possibilities the data sources that best tell their stories. These decisions are based on what is available, appropriate, and (in most cases) data that look best. Teachers may make first choices of sources they are most confident of but also try out others that they are not sure of.

The second level of control for teachers comes after data have been collected and reviewed by the teacher. At this point, teachers may take the option of having summaries of the data kept in professional dossiers and used for subsequent evaluation decision making and dissemination. Or, teachers may choose to have the summaries returned to them with the original documents (e.g., survey forms, peer review notes) and no record of the evaluation activity or results to be kept by the Evaluation Unit or district. This option permits a best case data-gathering and review system. The logic of best case evaluation systems is discussed in the next chapter. For most teachers, four to six different kinds of data make the strongest case for quality.

COSTS OF TEACHER EVALUATION

No discussion of teacher evaluation is adequate without a consideration of costs (Peterson, 1989c; Scriven, 1973a; Thompson, 1980). Most often school districts act as if teacher evaluation has zero expense; it is a normal and included part of administrator responsibility. However, two truths of life are that love hurts and evaluation costs. The expenses of teacher evaluation include data gathering, decision making, personnel usage, and emotions of participants. There are evaluation costs in terms of money, time, materials, and morale. Also, there are expenses of installing evaluation systems (training and disruption) and costs of *not* doing other activities that are precluded by evaluation (e.g., additional inservice time and activity on other topics).

The value of teacher evaluation must be understood in relation to the costs. Discussions and decisions about new directions, policy adoption, and specific techniques all need to be done in light of specific and explicit cost-benefit analyses. Some group within each school district needs to make a comprehensive determination of costs and then encourage debate about the values of current and possible teacher evaluation program design. A one-shot, ad hoc committee decision or single administrator fiat decision is not adequate to the needs of teacher evaluation ongoing and complex cost-benefits decisions for a school district. Chapter 18 recommends a district-level Teacher Evaluation Board that includes this function, among others.

Chapter 22 also addresses specific costs and options that districts have to manage the levels of teacher evaluation expenses. Districts can gauge the amount of evaluation activity and allocate resources of money, time, and personnel initiative to get teacher evaluation activity to desirable levels.

WHAT IS GOOD TEACHER EVALUATION?

Not only can teaching practice be examined for quality, the performance of teacher evaluation systems likewise should be continuously looked at (Scriven, 1973a, 1981). Good teacher evaluation systems are fair and just, meet demonstrated needs of clients, answer the questions of interested audiences, are cost-effective, and are free from unjustifiable side effects. Formative and summative functions should be separated in purpose, time, method, and personnel. Good teacher evaluation systems should be technically sophisticated enough to encompass the full range of teacher types and duties. They should be sociologically and politically complex. Defensible systems should be research based and involved themselves in ongoing studies of validity and reliability. Good teacher evaluation systems are themselves evaluated. Empirical data should be gathered on levels of participant satisfaction, teacher performance norms, and system performance in terms of its claims. Systems should be compared with other competitors for outcomes, long-term effects, expenses, and problems. Finally, good teacher evaluation systems are credentialed by outside experts and knowledgeable educators.

THE CASE FOR INCREASED AMOUNTS OF TEACHER EVALUATION

As Scriven (1973a) stated, the question is not whether to evaluate but whether to evaluate well or poorly. Unsystematic teacher evaluation happens all the time: Students comment about how well a teacher works, a few parents rave about specific events or complain about problems, the media focus on declining test scores, personal qualities stratify teacher ranks, and innovative teachers are harassed. These examples produce little useful information, certainly less than the better results than can be obtained from the new directions presented in this book. The challenge for improved teacher evaluation is to upgrade practice to the point where it pays off for teachers, administrators, parents, legislators, and students. This is the case to increase what to this point has not been a popular activity: teacher evaluation.

Good teacher evaluation means that teachers and others working at schools will have to do more tasks and spend more time than with present systems. The costs of good teacher evaluation are real. Time is the most valuable and scarce commodity for educators. However, there are many reasons to increase the amount of activity and do good teacher evaluation. The professional burdens of teachers for evaluation should be met. Increased documentation of good work increases teacher job satisfaction. The changing political climate of consumer orientation demands recognition of good teachers and defensible results. Instructional practices can be altered and improved, and then documented, judged, and disseminated. The knowledge base of the profession should be added to, not only by research and conventional professional wisdom but by useful evaluation data. All these are reasons to increase the amount of teacher evaluation activity. If we believe teachers are doing good and needed work, we have to put these beliefs on the evaluation line.

RECOMMENDATIONS FOR IMPROVED PRACTICE

Many scholars and researchers on teacher evaluation have given directions for improved practice. The following examples clearly show that there are many positive ideas for changes in current practice. Scriven (1981) recommended independent support systems for teachers, evaluation of administrators as well as teachers, judicious use of student questionnaires, consideration of quality and professionality of teaching content and process, use of actual learning gains, inclusion of a professional development dossier, and use of exit interviews. Travers (1981) encouraged appropriate nonuniformity in teacher evaluation methods within a district. McGreal (1983) recommended using six data sources in addition to the mainstay of principal observation: parents, peers, student performance, self-evaluation, students, and artifact collection. Peterson (1984) pointed out the need for multiple data sources, variable data sources, research and development lines of evidence, and use of decision-making panels. Epstein (1985) called for use of multiple judges in teacher evaluation, specifically, the use of parent survey data in addition to principal viewpoints. Popham (1985, 1987) called for research and development in the measures of teachers and emphasized the central role of professional judgment in good decision making. Brauchle, McLarty, and Parker (1989) advocated a portfolio approach to using student performance data to measure teacher effectiveness. Good and Mulryan (1990) called for student and parent ratings to be used in teacher evaluation. Bird (1990) outlined a portfolio as a central part of teacher evaluation.

The teacher evaluation practice recommended in this book is to downplay the principal-based observation and checklist routines in favor of multiple and variable data sources, increased teacher control and participation, and panel decision-making bodies. It also is critical to attend to the sociological and political realities of teacher evaluation; the current professional climate is not conducive to good teacher evaluation nor to making the recommended changes. These changes can be installed gradually, say, over a 5-year period. This recommended approach to teacher evaluation has additional, but defensible, costs. The result is evaluation that reassures teachers for doing a good and valued job, gives security and status to well-functioning teachers, spreads innovative educational ideas, and reassures the public that teachers are successfully contributing to this society.

4

Problems of Teacher Evaluation

Teacher evaluation often is discussed as if it were merely a technical problem: "What instrument [observational checklist] should we use?" House (1973) called this the good instrument assumption. With a bit more sophistication, the question is, "How can we get valid and reliable information about teacher performance?" Technical questions, such as how to get and use good data, are important. However, the problems of teacher evaluation go beyond technical questions to sociological and political dimensions. The major problems of teacher evaluation are not only technical in nature but also include the human social and political context of evaluation activity.

Sociological problems concern the group dynamics of evaluation activity. These include expectations, roles, relationships, rewards, recognition, and sanctions in the social group in which teachers work. Evaluation profoundly affects how people work together, think of their work, solve problems, and take initiative. Sociological forces are subtle but crucial determinants in educational programs, including evaluation of teacher quality.

The politics of teacher evaluation concern who controls evaluation, who decides on data gathering, and to what uses data and decisions are put (Bridges & Groves, 2000). Politics decides the aims of evaluation—for the greatest good or for a narrow purpose. Politics involves decisions about scarce resources, or the economics of evaluation. Still other issues are power and status within the society. For example, questions of the professional status of teachers involve who is in charge of evaluation (Etzioni, 1969).

The three sections of this chapter examine technical, sociological, and political problems of teacher evaluation as if they were independent. Substantial thinking and work are required on each of these problem areas. However, subsequent chapters of this book will present new directions for teacher evaluation practice that integrate these three problem areas.

TECHNICAL PROBLEMS OF TEACHER EVALUATION

This section discusses nine problems or complications of teacher evaluation. These topics need to be discussed and planned for at a school district level in evaluation systems that deliver satisfactory results.

Multiple Audiences

Teacher evaluation has a number of audiences with an interest in the resulting information and judgments: school administrators, teachers themselves, parents, voters, legislators, business and industry, and teacher education universities (Peterson, 1984; Scriven, 1973a). These audiences differ in the kinds of questions they ask, types of evidence they want, and even the language they use in talking about evaluation. With some groups, such as school administrators, the needs and procedures are well known. For other audiences, such as voters, only scant information about specific questions and uses has been developed. For example, parents have shown interest in newspaper publication of local school standardized test results (a technically mistaken and politically misleading practice). For these traditionally neglected groups, development of effective teacher evaluation practice requires a more complete understanding of their needs for data and subsequent interpretation.

Audiences differ in evaluation needs because they have different roles and uses for teacher evaluation data. For example, state legislators have as a primary function the judicious use of taxpayers' money. In this respect, the teacher evaluation data of most interest help to answer questions such as "Is the taxpayer getting a good return for the tax dollar?" and "Are there more cost-effective ways of allocating education funds?" School administrators, by contrast, are more concerned with teacher evaluation data that provide information about the quality of their programs and teachers. In this sense, they are interested in both formative and summative teacher evaluation data to be used to shape future decisions and make personnel decisions. Teachers constitute a third audience for evaluation data. As professionals, teachers need to know when their actions are effective and ways in which their teaching can be better. In addition, there is increasing evidence that teacher satisfaction with the profession can be strengthened by reassuring and respected feedback about effectiveness.

Another way of understanding the evaluation needs of different audiences is in terms of scope. State legislators typically are not interested in teacher evaluation data dealing with individuals; instead, they find broad, descriptive data comparing programs, districts, or states to be most helpful. By contrast, the most valuable data for teachers interested in improving their own practice must be quite specific and individualized.

Most current teacher evaluation is designed for one very narrow audience: principals and individual teachers. Development of a teacher evaluation system for a school district should consider the different views of all of its audiences. Meetings, discussions about the results of trial runs, and public presentations all help educators and their audiences to design more effective evaluation systems.

Formative and Summative Evaluation

Teacher evaluation has two major uses with teachers themselves (Scriven, 1967, 1981). First, assessment data may be used as feedback to shape performances, build new practice, or alter existing practice. For example, information from a student survey that not enough practice time was provided in class calls for a change in instructional timing. This use of evaluation is called *formative*. A second use for evaluation is to make decisions or judgments, for example, to retain teachers. This use is called *summative*.

The distinction between formative and summative evaluation is important because very often different techniques, and even personnel, must be used according to the intended purpose (Popham, 1988). In practice, it may be difficult or impossible to accomplish both types of evaluation at the same time. For example, a teacher may want student survey feedback if it is merely to be used privately by himself but will be quite cautious about putting his reputation on the line for the opinions of a ninth-grade general science class if the results are to be made public. For example, the stated goal of evaluation to improve practice (formative) is seriously weakened by the overriding goal of summative judgments to control teachers.

The audiences for teacher evaluation may have either formative or summative uses in mind but should be clear about what their intentions are. Summative evaluation techniques, because of their consequences, usually are more narrow in scope and thus require more rigor and systematic application in practice. Most current teacher evaluation mistakenly attempts to use principals to mix formative and summative purposes.

Nature of Teacher Evaluation Data

When teacher evaluation moves from current practice (principal reports) to more comprehensive designs, it gets more complicated. One technical complication is that data on teacher performance become more varied. Information used for evaluative judgments may be in the form of numbers, such as test scores and ratings; in the form of verbal descriptions, such as reports and comparisons; or in lists, such as log books that document professional activity. The event that is assessed determines the form of the data. Most teacher evaluations should involve both quantitative and qualitative data. For example, observers can rate some aspects of a teacher's performance on a numerical scale that can be compared with similar performances of other teachers. Other kinds of performance, for example, the strategy of beginning a class, cannot easily be reduced to numbers. For these aspects we must rely on verbal descriptions. Most important, the kind of data gathered in evaluation must be appropriate and the best available for that situation.

Problems arise with evaluation systems that are overquantified—when decisions or judgments predominantly rely on satisfying numerical requirements. It is rare, in something as complicated as teaching, that a numerical decision by itself is adequate. Most often, this approach is an illusory attempt to strengthen the objectivity of a teacher evaluation system.

Multiple Data Sources

It is important to use as many different sources of data as possible when making the value judgments required in teacher evaluation (McGreal, 1983; Peterson, Stevens, & Ponzio, 1998). To take an example from another topic altogether, the value of a new commercial product such as laundry detergent is not judged by washing one sample load of laundry, but by sales records, market studies, manufacturing cost-effectiveness, consistent performance adequacy, competitor comparisons, and absence of undesirable side effects. The process of evaluating teachers is an even more complicated task that requires correspondingly more data sources and indicators of quality.

Multiple data sources in evaluation require that information be gathered from a number of locations in addition to traditional administrator reports. Use of a variety of data sources is important because no one source tells all about what a teacher does. For example, one perspective of teacher quality concerns the benefits, outcomes, or gains for students. From another viewpoint, we care about how much subject matter a teacher knows herself—we value knowledgeable teachers over those who lack knowledge. At times we should be concerned about how the classroom looks and works. Another consideration is that a teacher is a member of a school community—a good school requires more than a collection of independent teachers. Because of various views of what we expect of teachers, multiple data sources are required in a comprehensive teacher evaluation system. There is no single person, checklist, test, set of characteristics, body of knowledge, training, or kind of outcome that, by itself, defines or indicates good school teaching.

Another reason that good teacher evaluation requires multiple data sources is that no single data source works for all teachers. As important as student achievement data are in teacher evaluation, Chapter 8 shows the great difficulties of getting dependable information on student learning outcomes that can be used defensibly in teacher evaluation. Although it is true that in many cases students can tell us where good teaching is going on, Chapter 6 outlines specific situations in which student reports are inaccurate, misleading, or not needed for good evaluation. There are some very good teachers whose materials are scant, or whose instructional strategies contradict the statistical norms of teacher effectiveness research, or whose background does not fit the usual sequence of college training experiences. Thus teacher evaluation systems require multiple data sources to document the range of quality performances.

It is not necessary for each teacher to use all available data sources. A good case for teacher quality can be made using only the data sources that are most important and available for that teacher. As will be seen in the next section, sometimes valuable information (e.g., student gain) simply is not available. When this happens, a good evaluation almost always can be made using the data sources that are available. Finally, using all available data sources is not necessary to make a satisfactory judgment; evaluation can be overdone and cause unneeded and indefensible costs.

Glass (1974) proposed an "observational-judgmental" teacher evaluation system that contained multiple data sources. He recommended use of (a) systematic observation data from trained observers, (b) pupil evaluations of teachers, and (c) collateral data that include professional training and examinations of teacher knowledge. His evaluation system differs from the one presented in this book in three respects. The first difference is a smaller number of data sources. The second difference is mandatory and uniform use of the data sources rather than a teacher-controlled and variable use as described in the next section. The final difference of the Glass proposal is his lack of specification of the person(s) performing the judgment on the data.

Variable Data Sources

One requirement of good teacher evaluation is that multiple data sources are used for each teacher. Another requirement is that the combination of data sources used for different teachers can and should vary

(Peterson, Stevens, & Ponzio, 1998). The sources are somewhat customized for teachers' contexts and styles. For example, one teacher may present data on student gain, parent surveys, pupil reports, and teacher tests, whereas a second teacher may use peer review, administrator report, systematic observation, student focus groups, and documentation of professional activities. This strategy addresses a number of problems found in conventional teacher evaluation. No single data source is sufficiently reliable, works for all practitioners, addresses all that a teacher does, or is agreed to by all educators. In addition, excellence in teaching comes in a variety of configurations and areas of performance. As Travers (1981) said, "If a school can justify evaluating all teachers through identical procedures, then the school is probably devoid of innovations" (p. 22).

One reason for variable data sources is that not all data are available in every setting. For example, parent surveys are difficult to obtain and interpret for older high school students because of relatively low levels of communication between students and parents. Teacher knowledge is difficult to test at the primary grade level because we have few up-to-date, appropriate tests. Thus we should expect the specific evidence for each teacher to vary.

Another reason that data sources should vary is that teachers differ in the ways in which they work. Good teaching comes in a variety of forms and styles. Some teachers are good because of their materials. Others are especially strong because of their insights into learners and subject matter. Still others use engaging personalities, whereas some rely on experience. Some teachers are effective because they are innovative, others because they apply tried-and-true traditions of teaching so well. Thus the kinds of information that that are most helpful in understanding quality vary from one teacher to another. A good teacher evaluation system recognizes these differences and provides for variation in data sources.

Finally, the contexts of teaching vary considerably. Teaching young children is different from teaching older adolescents. Beginners and novices require different resources from a teacher than do students with developed knowledge and skills. Some teaching situations are difficult—with high student turnover, many distractions, low skill levels, poor motivation, and few parent and community resources. This means that a teacher evaluation system must be prepared to use a variety of data sources as appropriate to specific settings and contexts in which the teachers perform.

Mandatory Data Gathering Versus Best Case Evaluation

Most school districts currently have a mandatory data-gathering system in which all teachers must have the same information gathered on their practice for teacher evaluation purposes. This book presents a clear alternative in which teachers choose among available data sources to best represent their activities and contributions as teachers. This "best case" system of teacher control is a permissive one. However, the approach is easily defended. There are good best cases and bad ones. There are superior, adequate, and inadequate best cases. Truly bad teachers are hard pressed to show *any* positive results. Thus the procedures and judgments made with best cases are technically the same as those of mandatory data-gathering systems.

The advantages of a best case system are considerable. Teachers are more likely to participate when they feel that an accurate and appropriate picture, or case, is being constructed about their teaching. Exploration by teachers of unfamiliar or even uncomfortable data sources is encouraged. Incorrect evidence is easily managed by being excluded. Even when data are not included by the teacher for evaluation purposes, the opportunity remains for them to use the data for formative purposes. Districts that have installed such systems report an outstanding level of evaluation activity and discussion (Peterson & Mitchell, 1985).

Best case, teacher-controlled systems have important sociological advantages. Too often, the present teacher culture operates against evaluation activity. When data are gathered on all teachers, a few instances of unfairness are bound to happen. For example, a teacher who takes on high-transition students with low initial achievement has unfair comparisons made on achievement tests. Or an effective teacher with a businesslike style challenges students and receives lower pupil ratings. These few inaccurate evaluation situations are talked about by groups of teachers who begin to discount the evaluation procedures for everybody else. Teachers then rally around their colleagues and subvert the entire system.

Best case systems are less subject to this subversion. The question and challenge for teachers is not to defend a specific data source (e.g., student reports or achievement data), but how will *you* document *your* impact, merit, and value? No single data source needs to be defended for all teachers. If a single teacher complains about parent surveys in her situation, no administrator or teacher leader has the burden to demonstrate that they should be used. Instead, the burden remains with the complaining teacher to demonstrate her merit while *not* using parent surveys.

Evaluation of Other Educational Components

It can be easy to make the logical mistake of assigning all responsibility for the outcomes of education to the teachers. Of course, there are other contributors to student learning: pupil effort, parent support, community resources, future employment or educational opportunities, school board quality, buildings and materials, administrators, and other factors. In the long term, all of these need to be taken into account to get a useful perspective on what difference teachers make. Teacher evaluation systems need some means of using this broader perspective. However, the problem is that it is virtually impossible to get reliable, useful data on all factors of student learning.

The contributions of these other educational components are not trivial. For example, research suggests that on the order of 60% of the variance in pupil gain is accounted for by where students began in their learning. High prior achievement usually means having strong basic skills and good attitudes toward additional learning. Thus, accurate teacher evaluation needs to take into consideration student prior achievement. However, although teachers may account for a small part of the total variance in pupil learning, the difference between good and bad teaching is very significant. Good teaching has a large effect on learning. There is a great deal at stake with the quality of teachers, and with their accurate evaluation.

Often overlooked too is the effect of successive years of good teaching, which is the largest teacher effect on students. This increased time frame not only permits the results of one good teacher to take full effect but increases the impact when students receive assistance in different settings with different styles of instruction. Also, the roles of practice, application, and repetition in learning are reinforced with more time than that of a single school year.

The problem in teacher evaluation is to use some level of estimates of the effects of other contributors in the teacher evaluation system. We seek an accurate representation of teacher work, in light of the specific context for success in which they work. Otherwise, the work of the teacher gets lost in the environment of pupil motivation, district wealth, parent income and education, and economic and educational opportunities for students. For example, is the teacher in question in a district with a 97% college entrance rate, or a 62% high school graduation rate? At present, principals are expected to factor in these various influences, in some informed subjective way, as a part of their annual teacher evaluation reports. However, compensation due to contributing factors of learning is not done explicitly. Instead, in their evaluations teachers are left to assume full responsibility for student learning—whether inaccurately good or inaccurately bad. In either situation, we simply do not get a good report of how well teachers are doing.

Good teacher evaluation means that knowledge of local district conditions for teachers, as imprecisely as they may be assessed, are taken into account. Somewhere in school districts, people occasionally should talk about the dynamics that contribute toward (or detract from) learning in the school and district. Absent such discussions in current teacher evaluation practice, this book recommends Teacher Review Panels, described in

Chapter 18, as the place to include this imperfect knowledge and perspective in judgments about teachers. This group of teachers, administrators, parents, and students needs to describe the quality of the individual teacher in light of the context for success in which the teacher works.

Although not all of the co-contributors to student learning in a district can be precisely assessed, a good place to start is to evaluate other educators: administrators, support personnel, and specialists. The resulting information is helpful to better understand the impact of individual teachers. Chapter 20 outlines methods for the evaluation of these educator groups.

Timing of Evaluation Activities

Effective and thoughtful timing is key to good teacher evaluation. To say that teacher evaluation is an ongoing process is an oversimplification. Rather, timing of various evaluation activities should depend on the purpose for the activity. The frequency, depth, procedures, personnel, and purpose of teacher evaluation all vary according to complex considerations. This section will discuss four issues of timing.

Evaluation for beginners should look quite different than that done for veterans. It should be more frequent, and with an eye to the important retention decisions to be made after the first 3 years. It should be attuned to the problems of the beginner, for example, taking into account gaps from the preservice training (Peterson, 1990a). Beginning teacher evaluation should at the same time be supportive (new teachers are insecure in their positions) but allow less teacher choice (a broad spectrum of data from students, parents, and colleagues is desirable).

Another issue of timing is how much time it takes to do good teacher evaluation. Complete teacher evaluation cannot be done in a simple visit-and-report procedure. In some respects, the most comprehensive teacher evaluation takes on the order of 2 years to complete. (This, of course, does not mean that egregious practice cannot quickly be recognized and dealt with.) Time is required to see the effects of pupil outcome. Patterns of professional activity and growth must be played out over a period of years. The collection and development of instructional materials takes years to accomplish. The stability of data, for example, pupil reports, requires a series of years to demonstrate.

Determination of leadership and exemplary practice differ from routine monitoring. Once a teacher has been established in a career, and questions of retention have been addressed, evaluation can be used to determine how superior performances can be used to better the district beyond the individual classroom. Teacher evaluation can document successful teaching that should be emulated throughout the district. For example, most changes advocated for the schools (such as an increased focus on job preparation) already are implemented in some isolated classrooms within a school district. Teacher evaluation can be used to identify such practices and bring them to the attention of others in the district.

Finally, it is possible to spend too much time and resources and overevaluate. For example, pupil surveys work well for many teachers. However, once a pattern is established for a teacher over a period of several years, annual surveys may not be necessary. There are teachers and situations where a thoughtless, continuous monitoring is wasteful and even harmful to professional morale. Evaluation activities should be timed carefully throughout a career in a staged fashion.

Validity and Reliability

Educators in local school districts have the responsibility to evaluate what they should assess and what they say they assess. This task is done in a number of ways. It begins with reflection and discussion about purposes and needs. It continues with external checks on what audiences need, what pupils and parents need, and what professionals claim is important. It is strengthened by comparisons, of methods and results, to see that state-of-the-art evaluation practices are used. It requires follow-up studies of the actual use of evaluation data, and educational consequences in graduates. All of these activities are done to support the validity of the teacher evaluation system.

Validity is an abstract idea. A valid evaluation system may be described as "sound; well grounded on principles or evidence; able to withstand criticism or objection, as an argument" (Friend & Guralnik, 1960, p. 1608). This means that it is necessary to do what we have done in this chapter and the previous chapter: Think about principles, examine evidence, criticize, and answer objections. Teacher evaluators have the responsibility to continuously validate their work.

Educators also have the responsibility to see that their evaluation tools (e.g., surveys, lists, reports) and the resulting judgments are accurate, consistent, and dependable. This task also is done in a number of ways. Surveys should be tested to see that they show the same results independent of the time of day, day of the week, or time of the year. When samples are used (e.g., 8 parent interviews rather than all 28 from a classroom), care must be taken that the number is truly representative. Some data, for example, student ratings, should be checked over a period of years to see that results are consistent. Lists assembled by teachers, for example, of inservice courses completed, should be verified on occasion. Classroom observers should be monitored for report correctness. All of these activities for accuracy are done to support the reliability of the teacher evaluation system.

Construction of a teacher evaluation system requires attention to both validity and reliability. Once evaluation procedures are in place, efforts need to continue to ensure their well functioning. Chapter 25 presents specific ideas to accomplish these tasks and more technically detailed descriptions of these characteristics of quality evaluation.

SOCIOLOGICAL PROBLEMS OF TEACHER EVALUATION

Although technical questions of teacher evaluation are the most frequently addressed by researchers, other concerns need to be examined. The most technically excellent teacher evaluation system can be installed in a school district but be doomed to failure if the sociological dynamics are not addressed. A selected number of sociological constructs having implications for teacher evaluation are presented in Table 4.1. Sociological problems concern the effects of the larger social structure (e.g., expectations, norms, power) on the behavior of individuals and subgroups within that structure (Goodman, 1992; Homans, 1950, 1961; Larsen & Catton, 1962; Parsons, 1937, 1964). Sociological dynamics often describe the real-world fate of teacher evaluation programs better than a systems analysis flow chart, theoretical formulations about effective teaching behavior or duties, or exhortations to increased professional behavior. Educational sociologists, such as Cusick (1973), Jackson (1968), Lortie (1975), and Johnson (1990), have shown how workplace culture powerfully shapes educational and evaluation practice.

Sociological interventions in teacher evaluation largely determine whether the organizational structure elicits compliance and support for the technical procedures, or actions contrary to the goals of the organization and participant efforts to defeat the evaluation program itself.

This discussion calls attention to the need to include sociological analysis and provisions in the practical application of teacher evaluation systems. The need is great because sociological perspectives are underrepresented in most research and development in teacher evaluation. This discussion will not present a complete sociological analysis of teacher evaluation systems, nor point to all issues concerning this topic, but will illustrate the nature of needed sociological perspectives.

Roles

In current practice, accountability for educational results is the central responsibility and role of the principal. Numbers of persons and perspectives in this role can be expanded by having teachers responsible for mak-

TABLE 4.1 Selected Sociological Constructs Having Implications and Applications for School Teacher
Evaluation

Alienation	Endemic uncertainty	Justice
Anomie	Energy	Leadership
Approval	Entrepreneur	Norm
Author/pawn	Equilibrium	Power
Authoritative reassurance	Exchange	Relationship
Authority	Expectation	Reward
Charisma	Function	Role
Coercion	Gemeinschaft/Gesellschaft	Sanction
Contract	Information	Sentiment
Control	Influence	Status
Culture	Innovation	Symbol
Emergent phenomenon	Investment	Value

ing their own case for quality—by thinking through what is of importance and value in their work, and then gathering evidence that they address it. Teachers can become more responsible for evaluating their own professional practice. Teachers also can assume the role of aides in evaluation with their colleagues. They can be called on to serve as peer judges, panel reviews, and informal consultants to other teachers.

The conflict in roles of the principal can be lessened by focusing on the role of educational leader and by being a cheerleader for colleague success. These functions currently are repressed by having the principal as sole formative and summative judge. Principals can retain the essential monitoring role to prevent short-term detrimental teacher practices.

Other participants in schools can benefit from having more of a role in teacher evaluation. Students and parents can be called on to contribute their views. Specialists, like librarians, can become more involved. These role changes increase the amount and diversity of accountability in the entire system and the number of people working on it.

Relationships

The roles people play in social organizations like schools affect relationships and ways of working with others (Cusick, 1973; Johnson, 1990; Lortie, 1975). The relationships educators have with each other affect the ways they solve problems, create, cooperate, and feel about each other. The role alterations suggested by the new directions in teacher evaluation in this book lead to changes in relationships. Some of these changes lead to clearer identities and better functioning for educators; other changes cause more stress. Relationships between teachers and the others they interact with in schools (administrators, fellow teachers, students, and parents) are complex, dynamic, and even involve contradictions.

Teachers' relationships with others are affected by their role and power in governance issues inherent in evaluation (Peterson & Chenoweth, 1992). DeCharms (1968) and other psychologists have demonstrated the benefits of changing a worker from a "pawn" (one to whom evaluation is done) to an "author" (one who assumes responsibility in evaluation). Teacher relationships are enhanced by increased role responsibility in evaluation. Specific, concrete data from colleagues (in review of materials), students, and parents do much to allay the endemic uncertainty and the feeling of "is anything happening?" that are so much a negative part of current teacher culture (Lortie, 1975). It is helpful to examine specific relationships as they interact with teacher evaluation activity.

Teachers and Principals

The current relationship of teachers with their principals certainly is complex (Cusick, 1973, Johnson, 1990; Lortie, 1975). On one hand, teachers depend on their administrators. They need support and protection from the principal. Teachers appreciate kind words and reassurance from administrators. They need a shield against disgruntled parents. They need backup in difficult discipline situations. On the other hand, teachers want to be independent of the principal. They feel solely responsible for their classrooms and for their successes with students. At times, they resent the greater social status given to principals, who, after all, do not have to do the frontline educating work of the schools. Teachers have some resentment about their dependency on the principal. When the principal is the sole summative judge, as in current teacher evaluation systems, teachers are more guarded, conservative, and reserved around the principal.

Increased teacher responsibility for evaluation can lessen the feelings of conflict in teacher-principal relationships. Teachers can, to some degree, become more independent of the opinion of the principal. They can be less guarded, more innovative, and more expressive as a result of their independence. This allows for a more satisfying and productive professional relationship. Principals, for their part, can lessen their judgment roles and spend more time supporting, encouraging, and leading their teachers. This alleviates the role conflict inherent in current practice (Lortie, 1975; Wise et al., 1984).

Teachers and Colleagues

Teachers need to work with each other (Cusick, 1973; Johnson, 1990; Lortie, 1975). They need to cooperate on details. Teachers need to keep confidences. They need each others' approval and inclusion. They can survive being on the outs with the principal but rarely thrive unless accepted by each other. They need to not be bothered or distracted by each other. Significantly, teachers need to not be shown up by one another, as happens when one or more teachers are singled out for recognition. When teachers have no part in the evaluation of each other, they are less guarded, conservative, and reserved with each other. However, they also are less concerned with quality, results, innovation, and their own reputation.

Increased teacher involvement and control in evaluation of colleagues changes relationships (Peterson & Chenoweth, 1992). Some of this is negative. Competition can be increased at the expense of collaboration. Isolation can increase because of fear of judgment. However, more changes are positive. Involvement in evaluation means greater attention to each others' work. Greater awareness of good teaching spreads desirable practices. Although there is more of an opportunity for conflict in increased teacher involvement in evaluation, there also is more of an opportunity for admiration and pride.

The greatest change in relationships is a positive one regarding teacher isolation. Lortie (1975) described much of schooling as happening in "cells of instruction"—individual classrooms with one adult teacher and a group of young students. Contacts among adults during the school day are outside of the reward system and thus are downplayed by teachers. Negative mechanisms, such as petty, complaining teacher lounge talk, develop to trivialize encounters. Meetings with administrators and parents likewise are not intellectually and professionally satisfying. The result is extreme feelings of isolation for most teachers. Increased teacher evaluation activity, such as in peer reviews, review panels, and informal consultations on data gathering and dossier formation, all can break down the isolation felt by teachers. Conversations over data have the potential to be nontrivial and close to the intellectual and personal concerns of teachers in their classroom work.

Teachers and Parents

Teacher relationships with parents also have mixed dynamics (Lortie, 1975). Teachers want some distance from parents; after all, the primary work and responsibility of teachers are with students and not their parents. From the teacher's point of view, most meetings with parents are over problems and do not result in much progress. Teachers resent intrusions on their work when parents, especially when unscheduled, break into the day. For their part, there is the danger that parents may harbor bad feelings from their own school backgrounds and resent teachers' success with their own children. Parents may fear confidences the children may have shared with the teacher. Involvement of parents in teacher evaluation, through parent reports (surveys, systematic interviews, focus groups) changes these relationships.

A greater involvement of parents in teacher evaluation helps make teacher-parent relationships more positive. Although there is some chance for hurtful opinions, there is a far greater likelihood of an expression of appreciation (Peterson, 1989b). There is a chance for greater security because a pattern of appreciated work has been documented. A small group of parents suddenly presenting grievances should be considered in light of the pattern of parent responses over the career of the teacher. Finally, positive parent reactions do much to allay the uncertainty of teachers.

Teachers and Students

Students and teachers often have distant relationships, especially as students grow older (Cusick, 1973). Teachers are responsible for making students work and behave in a group setting. Teachers evaluate students in a one-way power relationship. Students are not voluntary participants in schooling. Teachers must work in a large group gathering. On the other hand, teachers are vulnerable to students. For example, students have an indirect power in terms of gossip and isolated complaints.

Involvement of students in teacher evaluation, through student reports (surveys, systematic interviews, focus groups), makes positive changes in these relationships. Although there is some chance for hurtful opinions, there is a greater likelihood of an expression of appreciation (Peterson & Stevens, 1988; Peterson, Stevens, & Driscoll, 1990). There is a chance for greater security for teachers because a pattern of appreciated work has been documented and confirmed by review.

Rewards

Teaching is an exceptionally reward-scarce occupation (Cusick, 1973; Johnson, 1990; Lortie, 1975). Acknowledgment is limited to those teachers whose classes appear to be under control, with work getting done, and students showing respect to the teacher. Extremely few teachers are rewarded for exceptional results, hard work, creativity, brilliance, subject matter knowledge, instructional excellence, human competence, care, love, commitment, dependability, maturity, sacrifice, concern, unique contributions, and humor. In current school culture, it is not considered good form for teachers to go public with exemplary practice and be recognized for excellence. For example, Peterson's (1987b) study of high teacher test scorers (99th percentile of national norms) showed that *none* wanted public acknowledgment. Such behavior is seen by fellow teachers as making an end run around the conventional reward system.

Current teacher evaluation systems limited to minimal expectations and competencies do not highlight the specific contributions of individuals. The new directions presented in this book enable teachers to extensively document their work and to show their unique combinations of value. More comprehensive evaluation, with multiple lines of evidence, can more accurately point out effective teaching so that it can be rewarded with recognition and acknowledgment.

Beyond mere recognition, credible teacher evaluation systems can support additional reward structures. One such structure is to form teacher leadership positions based on a series of successful panel reviews. This merit-based appointment increases the amount of leadership within a district and rewards those who seek and earn such a position. A second new reward structure is a promotion system similar to the successful one used in postsecondary education. Ranks based on successful panel reviews are an effective reward technique. Chapter 18 gives specific guidelines for creating these new reward structures in a school district.

(One additional reward structure advocated by many—merit pay—has been a disaster because it generally sets unrealistic quotas, is based on far too short a time period, uses narrow and unreliable evidence, and creates a premium on isolated and competitive rather than collaborative teacher work.)

Endemic Uncertainty

Lortie (1975) described the work of even competent veteran teachers as having endemic uncertainty about value, meaning, results, and importance. Teachers in his studies reported wondering at times if anything is happening in spite of lack of visible problems and apparently routine activity.

Increased teacher evaluation activity can answer some teachers' uncertainty about the progress and effects of their work. Concrete data from students, parents, peers, materials, and results can do much to allay doubts about one's work. Truly respected teacher evaluation systems can bring to teachers some measure of the authoritative reassurance about their efforts and results that they now lack in current practice.

Sanctions

Current sanctions that teachers have for each other are almost exclusively confined to a subtle, but effective, exclusion of the targeted teacher from the local teacher society (Lortie, 1975). Teachers who have been offensive or threatening are sanctioned by perhaps a barely perceptible social isolation. The worst punishment for most teachers is to be excluded by fellow teachers. However, once a teacher has renounced her transgressions, subtle inclusion begins.

Increased teacher evaluation activity for the most part has the potential to make teacher relationships better. However, just as teacher evaluation expands the rewards that teachers can create for each other, it also increases the number of sanctions available to teachers in the school workplace. A new kind of sanction available to teachers is that of reaction to inadequate or bad practice, as evidenced in teacher evaluation results, that threatens the welfare of students or teachers as a group.

POLITICAL PROBLEMS OF TEACHER EVALUATION

"Evaluation is political. It is used to allocate resources, cover up mistakes, build reputations and make money. It is also used to correct mistakes, improve programs, reward merit, and tell parents what is happening to their children" (House, 1973, cover overleaf).

Political problems of teacher evaluation pertain to how policy is determined, particularly to decisions about what data to gather, from whom, and for what use (Bridges & Groves, 2000). One example is access to information. Restrictions on who can see and use peer review of materials reports are political decisions. For another example, it is politically important to teachers if a policy is made to use peer review of materials in teacher evaluation. If teachers make the decision, their professional standing is enhanced in the eyes of the public. If administrators cause the change, teacher-teacher conflict is exacerbated. This section discusses how political policy changes affect educators in the schools, administrator control, teacher job security, and decisions about schools in the larger society.

Local District Internal Politics

Local district politics can support or thwart the most technically excellent teacher evaluation systems. Power relationships, governance, and policy-making patterns must be attuned to good teacher evaluation. If they are not, symptoms show up in problems that can look like interpersonal conflict, but actually are technical and sociological problems that doom the evaluation effort. Two clusters of political factors are essential for well-functioning teacher evaluation systems.

The first cluster of political factors are general principles of political functioning. To begin with, a district must practice rational decision making, a tradition in which choices are made on the basis of deliberation, backed by evidence, with goals of the greatest good for the most participants, using priorities of clients as a value base, and inclusion of minority views. Second, this process necessarily must be carried out with open deliberation and public debate. Third, a good, local political climate for teacher evaluation requires some intentional manipulation of power relationships, that is, some measure of authority must be specifically altered to carry out new roles and relationships inherent in judging teacher value. Collaterally, a corresponding degree of shared governance should be evidence of a political framework that supports expanded teacher evaluation. Finally, good politics for teacher evaluation means that teacher participation in policy setting and decision making has increased beyond current levels in most school districts.

Lortie (1967) discussed attributes of rationality in evaluation policy making. For example, active debate and decisiveness on value conflicts, rather than burying them, facilitates rationality. Delineation and certainty about responsibilities, especially for superintendents, principals, and teachers, is important. Lortie recommended specific terminology for actions, rather than use of general and hazy language. An emphasis on agreement on goals suppresses nonrationality. Decision, rather than compromise, is characteristic of rational systems. Finally, more use of clarity and definition, and restraint in use of vague pressure tactics are important.

Lortie (1967) described two kinds of rational decision making in schools. The first is a tight managerial model in which authority is used openly to enforce decisions about goals, procedures, and educator behavior derived from knowledge about teaching and learning. An alternative is a separation of powers among board, superintendent, principals, and faculty, where spheres of decision making coexist and overlaps are adjudicated with the goal of best outcomes. Both of these rational plans are distinct from murky organizations functioning to avoid trouble and upset. Nonrational approaches focus not on substantive, large-view decisions, but on specific procedures that offend the fewest. The sum of many specific decisions is not rational, but protective and defensive. The legal and organizational realities of public schools "makes it difficult for decisions to be made within an entirely rational framework. It is more difficult . . . publicly to announce . . . specific objectives . . . with clear output than it is to organize to avoid trouble" (Lortie, 1967, p. 6). Lortie recognized that the second kind of rational decision-making plan is professional in form, and expensive. It calls for "years of preparation, a light teaching load, allowance for privacy, [and] opportunity for professional recognition" (p. 8).

Corwin and Edelfelt (1976) showed the contrast between rational and organic organizations. Rational organizations are characterized by clear-cut goals, well-planned and coordinated activities, easily available information, informed decisions, sufficiently centralized control to get things done, compliance with long-term goals, and formal authority based on expertise. On the other hand, organic organizations are characterized by an accretion of policies adopted without a long-term plan. In addition, organic organizations have independent units with interests more important than those of the total organization, status as an end in itself, status determined independent from contribution, survival as a main goal, decision made by bargaining and compromise, no group with sufficient power to get things done, and authority based on seniority or persuasiveness.

Erlandson (1973) stated that strong, centralized, and aggressive evaluation by an administrator works against nonrationality in a school. He saw such action as protecting the educational program from political pressures, special interest groups, fads, and haphazard events.

Peterson and Chenoweth (1992) argued that teacher participation is a political factor that is at the same time a cause, mechanism, and result of good teacher evaluation. Its importance reaches beyond establishing technically and sociologically good evaluation. Having teachers take greater initiative on their own evaluation is related to their taking greater initiative on other education problems. Currently, we depend on a few unusual administrator leaders to create novel changes in schools. The media feature stories that show individual schools led by dynamic principals who install drastic changes in response to problems. The authors argue that what is needed is the opportunity for *teachers* to take more of this leadership. The current evaluation systems that have teachers at the mercy of administrators and mundane checklists do not encourage the kind of teacher initiative needed in an era of high, visible demand for change in public education.

The second cluster of political conditions was identified by Wise et al. (1984) in the RAND Corporation's case studies of effective practices in teacher evaluation. These authors attributed much of the success of four school districts with technically sophisticated teacher evaluation practices to four similarities. First, organizational commitment means that the entire district from top to bottom is directed toward quality evaluation. Specifically, this means that efforts are focused, time provided, concrete mechanisms invented, and resources provided to evaluation as a central mission. Second, competence must be demonstrated by players in the district, whether they are decision makers, evaluators, teachers, or recipients of evaluation data. Political functioning at some point depends on people doing their job well. Third, collaboration of people in various roles—teachers organizations and administrators in particular—is essential. Finally, strategic compatibility means that other district policies and procedures, such as inservice and personnel, are tuned to work with teacher evaluation structures.

In sum, the internal politics of a school district must function well to support new directions and practices in teacher evaluation. This can be accomplished with attention to the processes of decision making, inclusion of participants, and coordination of efforts of a complex organization.

Administrator Control

The increased involvement and control of teachers in their own evaluation means significant power relationship changes for administrators. These new directions may be seen as a source of problems from overall diminished administrator authority. For example, administrators are concerned with how hard it is to dismiss a bad teacher in present practice (Bridges, 1992). They are concerned about how difficult it will be to get rid of a bad teacher who has been evaluated by peers and parents as good. Because of this new hurdle, it will be more difficult to control those teachers who act in detriment to the district, for which the administrators are ultimately accountable. Increased participation might work well for the majority who are teaching quite well, but the few bad teacher problems are made significantly (even irrevocably) worse in the eyes of some administrators.

Erlandson (1973) argued for keeping teacher evaluation as a strong central tool for administrators. He described the governance of the school as dependent on the authority to evaluate. The administrator "must retain real control of the process. Complete delegation means either that the subordinate has been given the power to run the school or, if the administrator chooses to disavow a distasteful report, that the evaluation has been emasculated" (p. 22).

However, the new directions of teacher involvement and control in their own evaluation can be seen as merely a shift of responsibility. The new emphasis of responsibility of administrators is threefold. First, more time can be given to educational and organizational leadership. This will call for a change in expectations and relationships, and teachers and central office administrators must adjust to this new role emphasis. The second responsibility shift is for administrators to heighten their monitoring function. It must be clearer to all participants that administrators are responsible for alerting others to the beginning of problems, or acute difficulties. Although this is a current function, it is not as apparent as it could be. The third shift keeps administrators involved in the problem of the bad teacher. The heightened responsibility will be to focus on the specific problem of poor practice. That is, although much of the teacher's practice may be supportable, or even praiseworthy, the specific problems need to be concretely and narrowly addressed. This causes problems for administrators who lose the tools of reporting general insubordination, general poor performance, and general problems. Replacing these must be specific problems, with specific evidence and specific consequences.

The result of this change means more precise personnel actions on the part of administrators. In some cases, this merely means doing their job better. In other cases, it will require additional work and initiative on their parts. Others in the district will need to alter their relationships with administrators. Certainly, teachers will have to change their expectations of administrators' roles. Especially, they will have to increase vigilance and support for administrators to go after bad cases, as well as to participate in this action themselves.

A final problem in changed administrator control is that they will have to undergo much of the same evaluation as teachers. Although they remain accountable to superintendents, similar expectations for a range of data will exist. Principals should create their own dossiers of performance data. Increased participation of teachers, office staff, parents, and even students will have a great effect on administrator power. Indeed, the basis of power will change.

Tenure

Teacher tenure is defined differently in various states, but essentially is long-term security of employment and seniority privileges that follow a 1- to 3-year probationary period (Strike & Bull, 1981). Tenure represents a long-term commitment on the part of a district to its teachers. The rigor of current tenure decisions varies a great deal by district. Most often, it involves a presumption of competence conferred by the state teaching license and a lack of performance problems for 3 years.

Scriven (1981) challenged the existence of tenure for compelling reasons. He argued that tenure should be phased out:

> Previous fears about violations of academic freedom, which were the most important basis for tenure . . . certainly can be taken care of through protective contracts, whether formal or informal. The residual infamy of tenure, due to the number of people who are burned out (or wrongly tenured) but kept on by it, stands as a proclamation of lack of responsibility that is becoming increasingly prominent as the hard times for education develop. We cannot afford to continue that way, and we cannot move any other way without a rock-solid process for evaluating teaching and for improving it. (pp. 266-267)

The political decision to retain or strengthen tenure should be based on strong sociological arguments for enhanced teacher performance and a technically strengthened teacher evaluation system. Tenure decisions can be justified through both administrative approval and serious review by a district evaluation panel. Chapter 18 presents recommendations for the organization and function of this panel. This represents a serious and rigorous hurdle for professional development. Lortie (1975) found a detrimental lack of such devices in teacher culture that define, acknowledge, and reward growing competence.

A counterargument to this recommendation for a more complex award of tenure is to add this serious hurdle to the already precarious and, in many ways, unattractive lot of the beginning teacher (Peterson, 1990a; Wise & Gendler, 1990). Beginning salaries of teachers are marginal for many talented people in the society who have other opportunities. A bright person considering teaching will have to put up with at least 1 additional year of schooling, low initial salary, and the added uncertainty of tenure based on rigorous evaluative review.

Educational Political Issues in the Society

External politics reflect how others in the society use and influence teacher evaluation. For example, the recent increase in newspapers' publication of standardized test scores by school has implications. The national push for standardized testing will affect how teacher quality is measured and thought of. The national program of Education 2000 includes common educational goals. This outcome-based emphasis will inevitably lead to technically ill-advised comparisons of states, districts, schools, and eventually, teachers. Accuracy and appropriateness of these comparisons may not be challenged. Districts that have extensive, defensible data will be in a better position for political debate.

Another example of political considerations is how noneducators view different kinds of teacher quality data. Teacher evaluation systems that somehow do not include pupil achievement data have virtually no chance for credibility with the public. Also, few, if any, noneducators understand how teachers justify using testing as a cornerstone of their teaching, but resist using tests to assess teacher quality. Lay persons remember the intense and often negative experience they had with tests when they were in school and are resentful when teachers excuse themselves from the same experience.

Schools are not unlike other public institutions—the era of intense scrutiny will not pass soon. Questions involve not only the outcomes of student learning but how teachers conduct themselves as a group: Do they take initiative? Do they self-regulate? Do they raise their own questions of quality? All of these issues begin as questions directed to teacher evaluation but end with immediate consequences for the overall well-being of teachers and other educators.

Part of the challenge of greater political awareness and interaction with the public concerns the presentation of teacher evaluation data. MacDonald (1973) presented useful advice for using evaluation data to inform decision makers and audiences of evaluation data. Although his recommendations were in the context of program evaluation, his ideas also are sound for teacher evaluation. He recommended being careful of specific technical language and translating where necessary. Basic premises of the activity need to be clear and articulated to all concerned. He outlined the need to be explicit about problems in design and interpretation. MacDonald pointed out the need to state circumstances, situations, and operations. Finally, he reminded educators to be careful of the timing of the presentations.

Although there are reasons to increase the amount of evaluation and research activity surrounding teachers, it is important to be aware of the intense political nature of such activity. There are positive benefits, but there also are increased controversy and uses of data in nonrational power moves (Cohen, 1973; House, 1973; Read, 1973). Evaluative data can and will be used to change power relationships. Even the *existence* of data-gathering procedures and data itself will be subject to power relationships. Care must be taken by educators in thinking through the control and ownership of teacher evaluation data.

Control and Disclosure of Teacher Evaluation Data

Although this book has taken the position for rationality, openness, and more public disclosure for teacher evaluation data, this change should reflect the important political realities of data reporting. Installation of dossier, panel-review teacher evaluation systems should follow guidelines from Chapter 16. Once teacher evaluation systems and data are created, their control and usage will be subject to power maneuverings. Issues such as truth, accuracy, appropriateness, accountability, privacy, fairness, and conscience will be subject to power manipulations (Cohen, 1973). Clearly those involved with teacher evaluation have an important responsibility for caution and clear thinking.

House (1973) described how once evaluation data are in the public domain, they are subject to widespread and, in the views of many educators (e.g., Read, 1973), inappropriate comparison and use. House (1973) gave the example of program evaluation in Michigan:

The Michigan Department of Education was forced to reveal test scores for individual districts. At first local districts were promised that local scores would not be made public. Generally state officials were for such reporting and school people were opposed. However, once scores showing relative standing of districts were made available to local school people, a storm of demand came from legislators for the same data. At first, the state department resisted. . . . [But then] like all bureaucracies under political pressure, the department finally crumbled. Local test scores were made public. Local superintendents were incensed; one charges that, "the [program] is really politics, masquerading as research." . . . [As Kearney and Huyser, 1973, stated,] . . . assessment programs are political. As such they must serve the interests of competing groups. All in all, the Michigan assessment has been the center of more controversy than any other education program in the state. (p. 44)

Chapter 16 will fully present the following safeguards to protect the political sensitivity of teacher evaluation data gathered in teacher dossiers for district panel review:

1. A phased introduction of practices begins to gain local knowledge of issues, procedures, problems, and safeguards.
2. Dossiers and panel reviews should begin as advisory to current administrator evaluation procedures.
3. Dossiers and panel deliberations should be treated initially as private teacher property or privileged personnel information.
4. Dossier assembly and panel review are teacher options.
5. Dossier contents are teacher options.
6. Dossier contents are variable by teacher, and not directly comparable out of context.

Following the introductory 5-year period, districts can decide evaluation policy that is politically more aggressive.

Although teacher evaluation activity does stir up political problems, it also can lead to greater public satisfaction with schools and teachers and to new levels of public support. It is tempting for educators to take the least troublesome strategies of noncontroversial, vague, authoritarian, difficulty-avoiding, and minimally required evaluation activity. However, this policy leads to less long-term satisfaction, perennial political weakness in social decision making, and ultimately, is not trouble free in itself. Clearly, political courage and effectiveness are a part of the new directions of teacher evaluation.

POLITICS OF SCHOOL QUALITY: A NATIONAL CONTROVERSY

The politics of teacher evaluation is largely a matter of local controversy (Kimbrough, 1964). However, one national-level political debate concerning education does have implications for teacher evaluation practice. The charge that schools are declining in quality makes a difference in how teachers should be evaluated. For example, a true crisis in quality would call for more use of mandatory techniques, and fewer options for teachers as recommended in this book.

A Nation At Risk (National Commission on Excellence in Education, 1983) began a series of national policy documents that claimed the performance of U.S. schools was in great decline. The complaints of these influential reports included falling achievement as evidenced by lower standardized test scores, unfavorable international comparisons, and inadequate performance of U.S. public school graduates in the workplace. The role of teachers in these critiques varied, but in no case was the teacher seen as a well-functioning, valuable contributor. This negative view of U.S. schools and teachers became generally accepted in the lay public, media, and government (Lind, 1997; Schrag, 1997).

The *Sandia Report* (Carson, Huelskamp, & Woodall, 1993) was the first academic analysis of the question of school and graduate quality. The findings of the report were quite unequivocal: The evidence for decline in quality simply does not exist. Rather, the data point to either constant levels or even a slight increase in some subgroups. Other studies began to confirm this more optimistic view (Berliner & Biddle, 1995). Finally, popular journalists began to take up the corrections (Applebome, 1995; Schrag, 1997).

If the critiques of school and teacher quality were not based upon a preponderance of the data, what reasons can be advanced for their sudden and widespread appearance? Lind (1997), a political journalist, called these controversies "an intersection of scholarship and politics" (p. 158), rather than rational analysis. Further, he presented evidence that the "sacrifice of objectivity to political expediency has gone beyond the normal tendency of partisans of all persuasions to stack evidence in favor of policies they prefer" (p. 157). Lind suggested that partisan politics were behind the critiques, rather than scholarly, rational, or objective decision-making politics. For example, the interests of organizations or office-seeking candidates can be advanced by diatribes against public schools. Spring (1997), a political scientist, added that a sense of crisis serves the interests of many points of view in the process of educational policy making. For example, liberals interested in securing more money for schools can use the sense of crisis as justification. Others interested in private schools or vouchers use the claim of crisis as backing for their preferred changes. Table 4.2 summarizes reasons for partisan critiques of education, rather than objective, scholarly, or rational debate.

Political debate and decisionmaking concerning the quality of U.S. schools directly affects teacher evaluation thinking and practice. If schools, and by association their teachers, are declining in quality, then emphasis

TABLE 4.2 Reasons for "Partisan" Rather Than "Objective," "Scholarly," or "Rational" Debate on School Quality

Justify government financial support for private schools where religious and political expressions can be made (e.g., creationism, prayer)

Acquire votes for candidates of certain political groups, parties

Acquire financial contributions for certain political groups, parties, organizations

Advocate school control centralization versus local control

Advocate large-scale standardized testing

Emphasize school curriculum for work preparation, international competition, economic development

Advocate standards-based education

Sense of crisis important to stimulate educational reform

Sense of crisis important to increase school resources

TABLE 4.3 Differences in Teacher Evaluation if Quality Is Declining or Stable

If Teacher Quality Is Declining	If Teacher Quality Is Stable or Improving
Improve teachers	Document current effectiveness
Identify incompetence as a main goal	Identify incompetence as only a component
Discriminate among teachers	Highlight effective practices
Reward best teachers	Acknowledge best practices
Mandate evaluation practices	Give teachers choices

should be given to goals and procedures that halt the erosion. Table 4.3 shows issues at stake in the debate.

The new directions and practices presented in this book assume that teacher quality is either stable or increasing, and that international comparisons generally are equivalent or favorable to the U.S.

INTERNET RESOURCES

American Reform Party

> http://www.americanreform.org

Christian Coalition

> http://www.cc.org/

Educational Excellence Network

> http://www.edexcellence.net/

Feminist Majority

> http://www.feminist.org

House Democrat Research

> http://www.house.gov/democrats/research/

House Republican Research

> http://www.house.gov/republicans/research/

Hudson Institute

> http://www.al.com/hudson/

Libertarian Party

> http://www.ag.uius.edu:8001/liberty/libweb.html

National Organization for Women

> http://www.now.org

People for the American Way

> http://pfaw.org/

Rainbow Coalition

> http://www.cais.net/rainbow/

Rethinking Schools

> http://www.rethinkingschools.org/

PART II

Multiple Data Sources for
Teacher Evaluation

5

Introduction to Multiple and Variable Data Sources

This chapter begins presentation of sources of data for teacher evaluation. The following chapters in Part II of the book discuss nine data sources in detail. Each chapter presents descriptions, advantages and disadvantages, selected research literature, materials (e.g., forms), procedures, and guidelines for use. The last chapter in this part concludes with a discussion of eight data sources, such as self-report, that are *not* recommended.

The data sources presented in this book assess all or most of what teachers do. The information includes preparation for good teaching such as participation in inservice education, effective practice documentation such as systematic observation of classroom performance, and evidence about the quality of outcomes such as student achievement data. Each data source contributes evidence to making a larger case for teacher quality. Each data source has advantages and limitations. Not all enjoy the same levels of credibility and importance. No data source works for all teachers in all settings, but all recommended in this book were effective in field tests.

Following the recommendations of this book, teachers decide which data sources should be used in their situation. After the evidence is gathered and summarized by an independent district Evaluation Unit, it is reviewed by the teacher. If she judges the data to be relevant and supportive to her case for quality, she has the summary reports placed into a professional dossier. Chapter 16 describes assembly of teacher dossiers. Dossiers are judged for quality by a school district Teacher Review Panel, as described in Chapter 18. Aggregated data from the teachers in a district are used to communicate teacher quality and accomplishments to the public; these activities are described in Chapter 26.

SOME DATA SOURCES ARE PROMISING, OTHERS ARE NOT

Although many information sources are useful in adding to the picture of quality performance of individual teachers, some other initially attractive data sources, such as self-reports and graduate follow-ups, have problems that preclude their use. For data sources to be acceptable in teacher evaluation systems, they must meet tests of logic, empirical trial, fairness, legality, and cost.

Logical tests establish the validity of a data source by positive answers to questions like those presented in Table 5.1. Examples of data that pass the test of validity are documented pupil learning gains and descriptions of teacher materials made by knowledgeable peers. Examples that do not pass are teacher appearance, use of specific instructional techniques, and personality type. Chapter 25 addresses more issues of validity in teacher evaluation.

Empirical trials of possible data sources test reliability (accuracy, dependability, consistency) in actual use, logistics, and the presence of practical flaws not apparent in logical analysis. For example, student reports on some topics (e.g., presence of disruptive rowdiness in class) have been shown to be quite accurate in trial tests (Peterson & Stevens, 1988). But other data sources, such as unsolicited student testimonials, are not nearly as dependable as well-designed pupil surveys.

Fairness tests concern such questions as equal opportunity for teachers in different settings and with different assignments, timely notice of expectations, logistical support, data storage security, absence of conflict of interest in judges, and opportunities for appeal. Legal tests of possible data sources are relatively straightforward and often coincide with fairness issues (Strike & Bull, 1981); for example, teachers must not be judged on the basis of membership in organizations. Other legal issues are addressed in Chapter 25.

Finally, possible data sources for teachers should be defensible in terms of costs. One-to-one clinical interviews of students may give rich information but should not be done because of time demands on students and expenses of interviewers. Chapter 22 reviews the costs of teacher data.

TABLE 5.1 Tests of Acceptability of Data Sources

Are the data caused by (or the responsibility of) the teacher?

Are the data included in the job description of the teacher?

Are the data linked to student learning, welfare, or other needs?

Are the data of *primary* importance in consideration of teacher quality (e.g., student gain)?

(If no to last question) Do data predict or consistently associate with questions of primary importance (e.g., student report)?

Are better data available on the same issues?

Some data sources should be dismissed for more than one reason. For example, testimonials of colleagues miss on three tests. First, teachers rarely are in a knowledgeable position to judge each other's classroom work (validity). Second, testimonial statements are seriously inaccurate in representing the views of colleagues (reliability). Third, colleagues in the same school have serious conflict-of-interest problems in rating each other (fairness). A listing of poor data sources is in the last section of this chapter; they are discussed in detail in Chapter 15.

RECOMMENDED DATA SOURCES

The following data sources have successfully passed the tests for recommendation. Each of these data sources works when it has been selected by the teachers under review and is used systematically. Systematic use of these data sources means that care is taken for representativeness, sampling, accuracy of recording and reporting, use of state-of-the-art procedures, attention to bias control, and descriptions of procedures.

Student Reports

Student reports are evidence taken from students about their views of a teacher's performance, usually gathered on surveys with multiple items and scaled responses. Other information-gathering techniques are interviews with representative numbers of students—in individual or group settings—and focus groups that discuss topics in an open-ended fashion. Students' views may be reported with an average of the ratings on a single global item (overall quality of teaching), or by responses to specific parts of the teacher's performance (e.g., opportunity to learn, perceived fairness of grading). Student reports are reliable, cost efficient, and key for understanding the pupils' point of view of teacher quality. Studies have shown good results at the earliest grades through high school.

Peer Reviews of Materials

Peer reviews of materials are restricted judgments in which teachers (usually a team of three) examine and report on instructional materials, classroom artifacts, and student work assembled by a teacher. Most often, the materials occupy no more space than a single box. The actual review period requires from 30 minutes to several hours. The peers are from the same grade level or subject area assignment as the teacher under review. Reviewing teachers do not know the teacher they review and are not connected to him or her by program or school assignment. Peer review does not include visits to the classroom, or opinion surveys of fellow teachers. Peers are a unique and valuable source of information about subject matter, instructional quality, and the realities of classroom work.

Student Achievement Data

Student achievement data focus on pupil gain information, taking into account prior achievement (usually difference between preinstruction test and postinstruction tests). The sole use of postinstruction test scores is not helpful because of the tremendous influence of previous achievement on learning, independent of the teacher. Standardized tests are easiest to interpret; however, teacher-made tests can be used. Peer teachers are helpful in interpreting teacher-made tests (peer reviews often include such data). Student achievement data often include group averages and distribution information (e.g., ranges, standard deviations). Data comparing the teacher under review to similar teachers and settings are useful, but rare. Pupil achievement data can be difficult to obtain, but they are the single most compelling line of evidence about teacher quality. In addition, noneducators are not likely to respect any teacher evaluation system that does not include student achievement data in some form.

Teacher Tests

Teacher tests are standardized measures that include subject matter knowledge, professional knowledge, and academic aptitude. Subject matter knowledge may be quite broad for elementary school teachers and includes science, language arts, social studies, mathematics, fine arts, foreign languages, and physical education. For high school teachers, tests may be more narrow and designed for specific subject areas. Professional knowledge tests assess information about classroom strategies, human development, social needs of children and youth, educational laws, and relations between schools and communities. Other kinds of teacher tests examine leadership knowledge and group process skills. Teacher tests do not include performance tests, which will be described in Chapter 15 as ineffective for teacher evaluation.

Parent Reports

Parent reports are systematic evidence of parent or guardian views of teacher performance. Most often, parent reports are prepared from surveys of parent opinion. For some special settings, parent interviews or focus groups may provide useful information. One good topic for parent reports is the level of communication offered by the teacher, specifically expressed in overviews of the class, descriptions of pupil progress, and ideas for home support of learning. Other valuable parent views are whether the child knows teacher expectations, level of challenge to students, and overall parent satisfaction with teacher. Parents should not be asked about classroom events (such as time allocation) or materials for which they have no direct knowledge.

There is a great range of knowledge of parents about teacher activity according to the age of the student. Parents of kindergartners tend to be highly involved and knowledgeable about school events. Upper grades begin to show diminishing involvement and interest. Parents of middle school- and high school-age students are knowledgeable about some teachers, but not others.

Documentation of Professional Activity

Documentation of professional activity concerns teachers' work outside of the classroom as they complete professional obligations and expectations. Categories of professional work include updating competence (e.g., inservice training, advanced degrees, workshops), serving the profession (e.g., helping colleagues and beginners), being involved in the school community (school committees, teacher leadership), and serving the larger community (e.g., advisory work at city library). Evidence includes log books, lists, and supporting documents (e.g., transcripts, letters, grade sheets, descriptions of meetings). Although professional activity is removed from the primary work with students, data from this source help to round out a view of quality for many teachers.

Systematic Observation

Systematic observation documents classroom activity and the process of instruction as performed by teachers. Analysis of transcripts of classroom interaction and class descriptions helps in understanding the meaning of classroom results. Good observation data are difficult to obtain, and not the kind collected in current teacher evaluation practice. Observers in good systems are independent of the school district administration and decision-making procedures. They are trained and monitored for accuracy. *Systematic* means that time is accurately controlled—representative observations are made over perhaps 5 to 10 selected (but unannounced) hours of classroom time. Classroom audiotapes are used to prepare verbatim transcripts for analysis and teacher feedback. Experts in classroom interaction analysis categorize teacher and student behavior. Common categories for observation and analysis include use of time, level of pupil cognitive engagement (e.g., as in Bloom's Taxonomy; Bloom, Engelhart, Furst, Hill, & Krathwohl, 1956), opportunity to learn (new material, practice time, performance time), and equal opportunity to learn (boys and girls, high and low achievers, differently abled, ethnically different). Specific instructional systems (e.g., structured lessons) should not be the subject of observation for teacher evaluation purposes. Systematic observation is useful for teachers who use technical skills to create good opportunities to learn for students.

Data for systematic observation include numerical summaries of distributions, graphical displays, and prose descriptions. As with other data sources, comparisons with teachers in similar settings are very helpful to evaluators. Systematic observation is one of the most costly of data sources.

Administrator Report

The administrator report recommended in this book is a highly restricted version of current practice. First, like other data sources, its use is optional. Second, it is limited to topics for which the principal has expertise and direct knowledge.

The recommended administrator report is a one-page form. It begins with notation of sources of information: discussions with teacher (how many?), classroom visits (how many?), talks with other persons (chairpersons, team leaders, students, parents), student achievement data, and other district-level information. Next follow items for which the principal has direct knowledge: overall rating, classroom order, classroom progress, teacher as member of school community, health and safety, compliance with state and district guidelines, and ethics. The teacher and principal may negotiate on other report items, if documentation is provided that the principal has direct knowledge of these topics.

Other and Unique Sources

Teachers should have the option to assemble other kinds of data than those listed and described above. This provides teachers the opportunity to document and have taken into account unique contributions and creative endeavors, or to adjust to unusual teaching assignments or circumstances.

The burden in evaluation is on the teacher to present information that shows that a unique data source is pertinent to his or her situation, to make claims for educational need and quality, and then to document the accomplishments. One example of data in this category is a complex community project in which a teacher had students study spring vacation disruptions on a small beach city. The findings of the study changed school schedules, city traffic patterns, curfew practices, and small business planning cooperation. A second example is an art teacher whose students plan the local art festival by working with city government, businesses, artists, and the tourist bureau. A third example is a teacher who is effective with a highly transient, migrant-worker-family, student population. These three teachers should customize their data collections to document these outstanding contributions.

USE OF MULTIPLE DATA SOURCES

Two reasons to use multiple data sources are the limited nature of the sources themselves and the need to address the multiple responsibilities of classroom teachers. Table 5.2 summarizes characteristics of data sources for teacher evaluation. The multiple responsibilities of teachers, and corresponding data sources that best document performance of these responsibilities, are presented in Figure 5.1.

DATA SOURCES THAT ARE NOT RECOMMENDED

A number of additional data sources frequently are advocated for teacher evaluation. However, at present their problems make them unworkable, and the alternatives from the previous section make them unneeded. Table 5.3 names these sources. Chapter 15 discusses these techniques and their fatal flaws.

TABLE 5.2 Characteristics of Teacher Evaluation Data Sources

Positive Characteristics	*Negative Characteristics*
Work well for many teachers	Do not work for *all* teachers
Can add to total picture of quality	Do not, by themselves, disclose total picture of quality
Should be selected by teacher	Mandated use is not appropriate
Work well with technical assistance	Can badly misfunction for specific teachers and situations

Figure 5.1 Teacher Performance Areas and Corresponding Data Sources

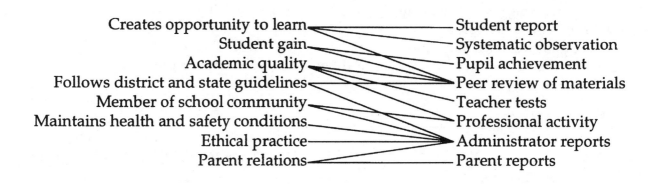

VARIABLE DATA SOURCES

This book advocates the use of different configurations of data sources for each teacher. This key innovation in teacher evaluation is important because the issues of quality vary for each teacher (Peterson, Stevens, & Ponzio, 1998). Variable data sources are important for the acceptance by teachers of the new directions described in the first chapter. One controversy of current teacher evaluation is that each of the data sources does not work for every teacher. Thus the focus of much current discussion is on statements like "Well, student reports don't work for me because . . ." and "Teacher tests are not good at our school because . . ." or "I know a teacher who tried parent surveys once and the problem is . . ." The burden in current practice is on advocates of the data source to show that it works in all possible situations, which is an impossible task.

TABLE 5.3 Teacher Data Sources That Are Not Recommended

Testimonials
Peers visits to classrooms
Peer consensus
Graduate follow-up
Teacher competencies
Microteaching performance
Self-evaluation
Classroom environment

In the new directions and practices, interest changes from how data sources do not work in certain cases to a focus on how each teacher does his or her work well. The burden shifts to the teacher: "How will *you* demonstrate *your* merit?" The task is for teachers to establish their own case for quality performance and credibility in documenting it.

DISADVANTAGES OF MULTIPLE AND VARIABLE DATA SOURCES

Although there are many advantages of the innovations of multiple and variable data sources for teacher evaluation, some significant drawbacks need to be faced openly. Four disadvantages are particularly notable.

Multiple data sources require more time and initiative from teachers than currently is expected of teachers in the evaluation process. Time is perhaps the most valuable and scarce commodity of teachers. Estimates of these new demands are provided throughout this book.

Although multiple data sources give a more complete picture of teacher practice than do current administrator reports, they do not provide an entirely complete picture of the work and impact of any one teacher. Some roles are always left out because they are impossible to document, or simply are not worth documenting for that teacher. Although this need not affect the overall satisfaction with evaluation, it can conflict with unrealistic expectations of teachers to present a total representation of their work. The temptation for some teachers is to add more to their dossiers, when additional data are not justifiable.

Teachers will get less than perfect results with their data sources. For example, student ratings for teachers in a school district are very good (4.91 average on a 5-point scale; Peterson & Stevens, 1988). However, in current reward-scarce practice, teachers with less than perfect results (i.e., 5.0 averages on 5-point rating scales) are disappointed. This dissatisfaction comes from the unrealistic expectations of current practice. Experience with actual data eventually shows teachers what is reasonable and realistic. But in the meantime, initial reactions may include disappointments.

Finally, although use of multiple data sources emphasizes the individuality of teachers, it is inevitable that objective data will lead to comparisons. A value for cooperative, noncompetitive interactions may conflict with this reality. This disruption lessens with time and experience, but it requires districts to aggressively install new rewards for teachers, as outlined in Chapter 18.

USING THE FORMS PROVIDED IN THIS BOOK

The forms included in the following chapters on data sources are intended to be guides for local school districts to begin development of their own forms and procedures. Although these forms have been field-tested, with results published in refereed journals, each contains details that should be adjusted to local conditions and preferences. The best advice is to begin with the forms provided in Part II of this book in pilot test applications with volunteers, and then use these results to revise and adapt the items and strategies.

TWO TEACHER EVALUATION SCENARIOS

As we saw in Chapter 2, scenarios of teacher evaluation are helpful for understanding the ideas behind the practice. This time, notice the effect of using multiple and variable data sources.

Richard is a fourth-grade teacher with 8 years of experience. His evaluation dossier contains information from peer review of materials, student and parent reports, teacher tests, professional activity, and administrator reports.

His peer review of materials had an overall rating of "contributing, well-functioning teacher; with outstanding activity plans and evidence of pupil achievement." The review was done 2 years ago, by two teachers from other district schools and one from his own. The review notes focused on his projects with canoes. In these, he integrated science, math, social studies, and art. The teachers noted "impressive and exciting math analysis (using computers) and clearly, competently written student essays reporting their inventions and applications with canoe building." Another comment noted "his outstanding logistics for including individual student and group goals" in his planning materials. He has begun a student portfolio evaluation system. Richard meets with four other teachers in the district on portfolio development.

Student reports were just above district averages (4.7 on 5-point scale) on the global item ("this is a good teacher"). They have been stable for the past 6 years, with much lower standard deviations than the district levels. Parent averages were just below the district means. They have varied somewhat. Parent comments included several of the nature: "My daughter showed more interest in school, because of the canoe project, than ever before." More than a dozen commented on the hard work shown by Richard. One parent said that his son had trouble explaining his grade card to him.

Richard's teacher tests include the 87th percentile in a professional knowledge test and a 91st percentile in a nationally normed test for academic graduate studies in the social sciences. The former test was taken before or during his licensure program; the latter test was taken 2 years ago.

Richard has completed a master's degree in social studies education. His thesis was a project on cooperative learning of historical concepts. A letter from his university adviser praises his insights and initiative in research; he contacted four principal investigators of research studies on cooperative learning and visited two of these university sites. His study used a pre-, postinstruction holistic scoring device that Richard created and student peer writing judgments. Richard has served on 13 district and school committees, including chairing the thematic integration committee. He has completed 23 subject matter or instructional technique workshops or inservice presentations.

Eight administrator reports give Richard the highest rating ("Professional") at each report.

Angela is a high school math and social studies teacher. She has 18 years of experience. Her dossier contains information for pupil achievement, professional activity, administrator reports, student surveys, and parent surveys.

Pupil achievement data include 3 years of results on the district social studies essays. These holistically graded student products were characterized as "meeting all district expectations." The department mathematics tests show an expected number of students passing minimum competencies and qualifying for subsequent classes in the math sequence. Her gain score analysis (posttest minus pretest) is accompanied by student work samples that interpret the numbers into applications.

Her professional activity includes community involvement. She is in a church choir that teams with a youth choir. Her previous work experience includes 5 years as a day care employee. She has been a volunteer organizer in four political campaign organizations. Angela has been appointed to both the city Youth Gang Task Force and the Mayor's Council on the Homeless. She has continued course work at the local community college in mathematics in occupations courses, and at the state university in advanced mathematics topics. She has completed six courses at the mathematics education center.

Student reports are consistently above school averages. Focus groups held 2 years ago produced a report from the Evaluation Unit that students see her as demanding, challenging, tough, happy, and with a message that "you can do it!" She sees students as not only capable of passing the district graduation test but exceeding it by at least 10%. Students reported a record-keeping system that helps them keep track of progress and keep up with the great deal of class work. They also mentioned a math invention fair.

Parent comments include her influence on students through choir: "My son brings up her name all of this last year." She has a very high return rate (69%) on parent surveys for the high schools (48%) in the district. Her global item average score is 4.94 for the 5 years that she has used parent surveys.

Administrator reports for 8 of her 18 years give her the highest rating ("Exemplary"). Previous district forms gave her a "Satisfactory" rating. The principals reported that they knew her work well and talked to parents and students about their views of the teacher.

6

Student Reports

One bit of folk wisdom about teacher evaluation is to "ask the kids, they know who the good teachers are." Indeed, a very good source of information about teacher quality is that group of people with whom teachers work most directly and spend the most time. Student reports are systematic collections of information about pupil perspectives on teachers. Tools to collect student views include survey forms, interviews, and focus groups. Defensible use of student reports avoids using them on *all* teachers, haphazard statements of individuals, certain topics (e.g., "teacher knows subject matter"), and judgments unbalanced by other information (e.g., peer review of achievement data). Although student reports are common at the college level, they rarely are used for schoolteachers. This chapter discusses why there no longer are excuses for not having student reports as an important part of teacher evaluation.

Advantages

Important, useful, and reliable data can be obtained through student reports about teacher performance. Student ratings produce a main source of information regarding the development of motivation in the classroom, opportunity for learning, degree of rapport and communication developed between teacher and student, and classroom equity. In addition, student ratings provide unobtrusive information on course elements such as textbooks, tests, and homework. Students are good sources of information about their instructors because they know their own situation well, have closely and recently observed a number of teachers, uniquely know how students think and feel, and directly benefit from good teaching.

Student reports are defensible sources of information about teacher performance for additional reasons. The availability of a large number of students for use as reporters provides high reliability for many kinds of teacher performances. Class data reliability in the 0.80 to 0.90 and above range is reported in the literature (Peterson & Stevens, 1988). Student report data, most often obtained through questionnaires, are relatively inexpensive in terms of time and personnel; data summarization is the major cost (Peterson, 1989c). Finally, student reports can be justified in terms of students as consumers and stakeholders of good teaching (Mark & Shotland, 1985; McKeachie, 1979).

Disadvantages

Although students are in a good position to report much useful information, they also have definite limitations as judges of teacher quality. Students at this level are not mature adults; thus their judgment may differ from that of adults who have ultimate responsibility for schools. Students are not subject matter experts (all the way through postsecondary education). They are limited in their ability to take an overall perspective of a classroom in favor of their own particular case. Younger students can have difficulty understanding some concepts of teacher performance, or even reading survey forms. Teacher styles vary and equally effective teachers may differ in popularity with students. As with any reporters of human behavior, students may be dishonest for trivial or self-interest reasons.

Necessary relationships between teachers and students may cause problems in assessment. For example, an occasional student may, in the judgment of the teacher, call for correction, a stern demeanor, or insistence on doing things the student does not want to do. The reports of these students may not be an accurate picture of teacher performance.

Another problem with pupil surveys is that they may encourage teachers to pander to students to get high ratings. Teachers may change their practice while focusing on student ratings rather than the best, long-term interests of their students. A few teachers oppose using student views in systematic evaluation on defensible philosophical grounds (Kauchak et al., 1985).

Some teachers are in a disadvantaged situation relative to other teachers, for example, those assigned to students who do not like school, transient pupils, students with low prior achievement, or unusually large classes. There is evidence from higher education research that teachers of elective courses rate higher than those having required courses (Landis & Pirro, 1977). Some studies (e.g., Goebel & Cashen, 1979; Peterson & Stevens, 1988) suggest that females are rated higher than male instructors.

Survey studies of teachers show that, in general, student reports are not trusted by teachers when required (Kauchak et al., 1985). They question limited student perceptions, worry about bad rating forms, and readily report anecdotes about problems with student opinions. One common fear is that students are too easily influenced by extraneous factors. Although much research and development has been done with student ratings in higher education, the corresponding literature for schoolteachers is much less available.

SELECTED LITERATURE

Recognizing a lack of quantity at the K-12 level, student rating of instructors still is one of the most heavily researched topics in teacher evaluation. Aleamoni (1981, 1987) provided extensive reviews of the literature on student ratings of instruction at the college level; they should be read by persons developing pupil reports for any age group. The results of this research are positive for teacher evaluation practice (Braunstein, Klein, & Pachio, 1973; Centra, 1980; Haak, Kleiber, & Peck, 1972; Marsh, 1980; McGreal, 1983; McNeil & Popham, 1973; Morine-Dershimer, 1976; Peterson & Stevens, 1988; Scriven, 1994; Wright & Sherman, 1965). Researchers have found that student ratings of teachers are consistent among students and reliable from one year to the next. Studies also show that students differentiate between teaching effectiveness and other affective dimensions such as attitude, interest, and friendliness of the teacher. Student ratings are neither capricious nor whimsical; students can consistently differentiate among instructors, and ratings are not based solely on popularity factors, a fear expressed by teachers. One compelling argument for student ratings is that they do relate to the amount learned in a course. In a comprehensive analysis of 41 studies reporting on 68 courses having multiple sections, Cohen (1981) found the mean correlation between the overall instructor rating and student achievement to be 0.43; the mean correlation between overall course ratings and student achievement was 0.47. Significantly, Cohen found that these results were not affected by the type of institution or class; these results were consistent in hard and soft disciplines, in pure and applied areas, and in life studies as well as other content areas. In addition, Aleamoni (1981, 1987) found that student ratings were positively related to colleague ratings, expert external judge ratings, and graduating senior and alumni ratings.

In addition to summative purposes, student reports have been shown to be useful for formative evaluation. Tuckman and Oliver (1968) found instances in which supervisor ratings produced negative reactions in teachers, whereas student reports of the sample topics were well received by teachers. Thus student ratings may be more influential for teacher improvement than feedback from other sources.

Studies of student reports at the school-age level suggest that children and youths can evaluate teachers in a reliable and consistent manner (Amatora, 1954; Christensen, 1960; Driscoll, Peterson, Crow, & Larson, 1985; Driscoll et al., 1990; Peterson & Stevens, 1988). The validity of student reports is supported by a study that found the ratings of 11th and 12th graders to be quite similar to those of experts (Bryan, 1966). Haak, Kleiber, and Peck (1972) reported that ratings of older students are remarkably reliable. These authors also summarized studies that indicated teacher ratings by younger students (down to second grade) are valid; in addition, they cited six studies that indicated that elementary student reports of peers are quite reliable.

Haak et al. (1972) analyzed an instrument designed for young nonreaders used to assess pupil views of teachers. The instrument was presented by an external assessor and requested students to deposit picture symbols in one of two receptacles: a mailbox for positive responses and a trash can for negative responses. The researchers reported a defensible factor-analytic structure for responses, reliable internal consistency, and logistical success. The authors argued for "the reasonableness of assessing teacher behavior by at least obtaining young children's perception of it" (p. 13).

Peterson and Stevens (1988) reported on the use of student survey reports as optional evidence for 373 K-12 teachers in a career ladder promotion program. Student surveys were well accepted by teachers; more than 80% chose to collect student reports. In turn, the pupils rated their teachers highly. The teacher averages on the global item ("my teacher is a good teacher") ranged on a 5-point scale from a low of 1.50 to a high of 5.00, with a mean of 4.57 ($SD = 0.42$). The authors found that elementary grade students rated their teachers higher than did their junior and senior high school counterparts (statistical significance); this suggests that results should be examined by grade level. Women teachers were rated higher on 4 of the 12 items and the total of all items.

Peterson and Stevens (1988) presented statistical analyses (descriptive, variance, factor, regression) of more than 21,000 individual surveys that showed that the global item ("my teacher is a good teacher") well represented all other items, and total and factor ratings. Table 6.1 presents an item analysis for grades 7 through 12 student reports. The internal reliability (alpha) of the 12-item instrument was 0.85. Correlation of ratings between two years on a subsample was 0.67. The authors concluded that "both the levels of usage and discrimination suggest that student reports present an important additional data source for school teacher evaluation" (p. 29).

Peterson, Driscoll, and Stevens (1990) analyzed student reports from 1,023 K-2 students in 43 classrooms in five schools. The survey form was a 3-point scale, 11-item, individual colored-page book with face symbols and text administered verbally by a researcher unfamiliar to the students. Factor analysis revealed three factors: "learning new things," "time and support," and "ability to work in class." The global item well represented other items, factor score, and total score ($r = 0.73$). Internal reliability (alpha) of the form was 0.64. The researchers concluded that "student rating forms used in this study presented sufficient variance in results to suggest that primary students do discriminate among teachers' performances" (p. 171) and "pupil reports may help to provide teachers with credible information about their impact in the classroom, an important resource not presently available" (p. 172).

Driscoll, Peterson, Browning, and Stevens (1990) reported an analysis of 318 student reports of preschool, kindergarten, and first-grade pupils. Internal reliabilities for the form were 0.70 for preschoolers and 0.62 for K-1. The researchers found that the preschool students were significantly more negative in their teacher ratings than were the older children. The authors explained this finding in terms of the psychological development of the younger students. The researchers concluded that "this study . . . demonstrates that 4-years-olds can follow directions and respond with reliability to an instrument in a group setting" (p. 77).

Ostrander (1995) concluded that "the fairest and most comprehensive performance appraisals may involve multiple judges, each offering a unique perspective on teacher effectiveness" (p. ii). In her studies, she found that students were somewhat more critical in their reports of teacher performance than were either administrators or parents. Stronge and Ostrander (1997) argued for including student reports as an optional data source because of the inadequacies of administrator reports. They recommended use of pupil report data for formative purposes and presented two model surveys (K-3 and 9-12) for practitioners and researchers.

Global items are single-rating items that best represent other items, and can be used as a summary of survey results (Peterson, Gunne, Miller & Rivera, 1984). Global items might be the following:

	Agree (High)				*Disagree (Low)*
This is a good teacher	5	4	3	2	1
Rate the quality of the teacher					
Overall teacher performance					

The global item strategy is to rely on these items as overall summaries of student reaction to teacher. In other words, the most important score on a

TABLE 6.1 Item Analysis for Grades 7 Through 12 Student Surveys

Item	Load Factor 1	Load Factor 2	Corr.[a] With Total	Corr. With Item 7	Corr. With Item 5	Alpha if Deleted
1. I know what I'm supposed to do in class	.80	.07	.69	.60	.55	.830
2. Teacher shows us how to do new things	.79	.10	.67	.65	.64	.825
3. There is enough time to finish class work	.63	.24	.58	.48	.54	.828
4. This class is not too noisy or rowdy for learning	.01	.87	.20	.18	.24	.885
5. I learn new things I can tell you about	.76	.28	.74	.61	—	.819
6. I know how well I'm doing in this class	.67	.15	.59	.56	.48	.829
7. This is a good teacher	.81	.18	.72	—	.61	.823
8. We have enough materials and supplies to learn	.77	.10	.66	.65	.60	.832
9. At the end of class, I understand well enough to finish the assignment	.69	.15	.61	.50	.51	.828
10. I know why we learn what we learn in class	.80	.09	.69	.59	.64	.825
11. This class is not too slow or fast to learn well	.23	.56	.32	.27	.26	.857
12. The rules in class help us to learn	.73	.14	.63	.59	.55	.825

SOURCE: Peterson and Stevens (1988). Used with permission.
a. Correlation.

pupil survey is the global rating. This is the result reported to the teacher and used by summative judges. Alternatives to the global item are (a) total scale score or (b) some weighting in significance of items giving some more importance than others (e.g., "I learn new things in this class" is given twice the weight of "I enjoy coming to class"). The total scale score equates all topics and themes. On the other hand, a weighting system is very hard to agree on, or to defend in all cases. The global item is conceptually most central to the question of teacher quality. However, it is important to check to see that it empirically well represents what is expressed in all other items.

The question about how good the global item is can be answered empirically by seeing how well it correlates with other scores. First, the global item should correlate well (and highest) with the total scale score. Second, the global item should correlate well with other items. Third, the global item should correlate well with factors that underlie the items. Fourth, the global item should correlate well with various combinations of items. If the global item does these things well, it is defensible to use the global item as the summative report from the survey. Table 6.2 shows the empirical results of comparisons derived from three studies.

RECOMMENDED PRACTICES FOR STUDENT REPORTS

As with other data sources, each teacher should control the use of student surveys with the safeguards presented in Chapter 4.

Survey Form Guidelines

Research and field-testing of student survey forms provide useful suggestions for design (Aleamoni, 1981, 1987; Good & Mulryan, 1990; Peterson & Stevens, 1988). First, individual teachers should not construct and administer their own survey forms; too many design and credibility hazards exist. Committee production of forms should carefully use the findings of the literature. Standardization of procedures within a district can aid fairness and useful interpretation. However, some level of individual teacher choice and customization is possible.

The general format of surveys is to have a number of items—statements about the teacher, class, or pupil—presented with a scale to indicate the student view. Some surveys have a space for open-ended comments. Information about the class should be included, so that surveys can be identified if misplaced. Most often, surveys are filled out and collected anonymously.

A section on the survey form for comments is appealing to many; but open-ended statements are very difficult to interpret. The main problem is that individual comments are given inordinate importance by teachers relative to their representational importance. People tend to be more concerned about individual statements, rather than the more representative and reliable central tendencies of group average perceptions. For example, in one field test for a single teacher, only two surveys out of an entire class had complaints about unfairness. In a discussion of the survey results, the teacher was so distracted by this criticism that she missed the fact that her "opportunity to learn" item and global item averages were impressively above district means. Thus the recommendation is to avoid comments altogether, or to downplay their importance with small spaces and not reporting them in summaries. Good surveys should be representative, and comments are weak in this area.

TABLE 6.2 Global Item Correlates From Three Studies

	Correlation of Global Item With		
Study (level)	Survey Total	Other Items	Factor 1
Peterson, Gunne, et al., 1984 (university)	0.86	0.64	0.75
Peterson and Stevens, 1988 (high school)	0.72	0.52	0.81
Peterson et al., 1990 (K-2)	0.75	0.61	0.45

Surveys with a few items are better than long surveys that try to do too much. Educators may be tempted to ask a great deal—they are curious about many things that students may think. A variety of topics are possible: materials, classroom structure, learning, teacher behavior, how learning gets used outside of school, and comparisons with other classes. However, every data source tells something, but not everything, about a teacher. For the students, too many items are tedious to respond to and cause lower reliability because of diminished student attention. Having many items results in greater response interaction; inaccurate halo effects are strongest on long rating forms. For most purposes, between eight and a dozen items is sufficient. The entire form should fit on one page.

Items That Work Well

Some types of items work well for many teachers and settings. One such type is "opportunity to learn," examples of which appear in Table 6.3. These items center on the students' perception of how well the teacher makes learning available. Opportunity-to-learn type items are *teacher-style independent*, which makes them suitable for a wide range of teachers, settings, and subject areas. These items pay less attention to the frameworks (e.g., behavioral structure, discovery) of teaching and more to the results. Opportunity-to-learn items avoid involving teacher teaching styles and personalities.

Another good type of item addresses classroom management and discipline. This is a complex topic because there is no evidence that certain types of classroom environments consistently result in greater learning for students. For example, extremely orderly rooms may or may not produce student learning. Extremely supportive and emotionally warm classrooms may or may not foster student achievement. It is good for students to experience the full range of class structures in their educational careers so that they at times have the advantages of a preferred environment, and at other

TABLE 6.3 Sample Opportunity-to-Learn Pupil Survey Items

	Agree				*Disagree*
I learn new things in this class	5[a]	4	3	2	1
Learning is not too hard or too easy					
I know what I am supposed to do					
I can hear the teacher					
The pace in class is *not* too fast or slow					
I get to practice what I learn					
I will use what I learn in the future					
I can use what I learn outside of school					
Schedules and assignments help me to learn					

a. In actual forms, this scale would appear with each item.

times learn to cope with a nonpreferred environment. However, there is a level of disorder at which learning ceases for most or all students. This point may be addressed with an item like "class is *not* too disorderly or rowdy for learning." This item is negatively stated and presents some problems for young readers. If so, another kind of discipline item may be needed: "The rules in this class help me to learn."

Although student surveys should be neutral in terms of teacher style, there is a concern with inordinately tough or harsh treatment that interferes with learning with a substantial number of students. Students do recognize the value and effectiveness of discipline, order, and challenge presented by some teachers. But the concern is for the extreme situations where teacher demeanor substantially interferes with learning. This type of item is called unreasonable negativity: "Teacher is *not* too unkind or unfriendly." This item also is negatively presented and may require special explanation to make sure that students understand its meaning and intent.

Older students, that is, those above sixth grade, can answer a few more difficult items that call for a larger perspective, or metaknowledge, such as "I know *why* we learn what we learn in class," "At the end of class, I understand well enough to finish the assignment alone," and "I know how well I am doing in class."

Items That Do Not Work Well

Some potential items do not work well. These items are included in student surveys because the forms are constructed by people who have lit-

TABLE 6.4 Examples of Poor Pupil Survey Items

Teacher is fair
Teacher makes me want to do my best
Teacher makes the school work interesting
I like my teacher
This teacher and her assignments help me to learn
Everyone gets called on alike in this class
Teacher treats everyone alike in class
Teacher knows her subject matter
My teacher is better than most other teachers

tle experience or expertise with teacher evaluation. Some examples of poor items are presented in Table 6.4.

One example of a poor item is "fairness." Although we do value fairness in teachers and recognize how a teacher perceived as unfair may have difficulty, having students report unfairness is not a good strategy. A sense of fairness depends on one's own private and idiosyncratic experience and is difficult to generalize to others. Another test of item quality is an empirical one, that is, does it work well in practice? A clue to items that do not work well is large variance (standard deviation) in distributions. This generally means that individual students interpret the item with such disagreement that the resulting averages make little sense. Another way to identify poor items is to interview students about why they responded the way they did. Topics like "fairness," "subject matter knowledge," and "participation of other students" all show that students quite disagree on what is being called for. Their answers are idiosyncratic and contradict one another.

"Knowledge of subject matter" is a student report topic that does not work well. Research indicates that students are not good judges of teacher knowledge all the way through advanced graduate school. The "educational seduction" studies (Perry, Abrami, & Leventhal, 1979) demonstrated that even college students can be overly impressed by language, appearance, clothing, and performance personality (Christensen, 1960). Content knowledge items also show the large variance (standard deviations) characteristic of misunderstood or idiosyncratically interpreted items.

"Whole class perspectives," such as judgments about what other students experience, or generalizations to others (e.g., "everyone gets called on in class"), are not reported accurately by students. Although students know their own situation well, they are not good judges and reporters of how others in the room experience their education and teachers. Being a student in most classes is rather an independent experience.

"Individual treatment" is not a good item in most situations; it especially is unfair to teachers who have large classes. Although individualized instruction has been held as an ideal in American education, its actual application has been virtually nonexistent. Except for laboratory settings, individualized instruction simply is not done—especially with groups larger than a dozen. Some studies suggest that individualized instruction can damage students for conventional classroom group learning. Thus individualization and related items ("teacher is available") are not good items.

"Responsibility for learning" and "teacher causes me to do my best" are not good items because they blur the responsibility for learning; it can be argued that students should develop the will to do well on their own. Also, such items are easily misused by students; for example, students may punish teachers for their own purposes. Finally, empirical tests of such items show a large variance and are described idiosyncratically in student interviews.

Survey Form Format

Survey forms should be as simple as possible, with few distractions. The form should have a statement of anonymity. Some class identification information helps to keep forms from being misidentified during scoring. Large print makes reading and responding easier. One option is a small area provided for comments. A standard introduction on the form, such as the following, is helpful:

> The purpose of this survey is to give your teacher your opinion about this class so that he or she can make it a better place to learn. Do not write your name on this sheet or make marks so that someone can identify you. Write your own opinion, not what other people think.

Nonreader students can participate in surveys, but need special forms and procedures. The form is more complex and requires multiple pages. As shown in Figure 6.1, a booklet (4 in. × 8½ in.) is made with each item printed on a separate colored page. Responses are made on one of three faces with labels: "Yes, Sometimes, No" to indicate scale preference.

The nonreader form should be administered as described in the following section, Administration of Forms. For nonreaders, it is helpful to give directions using a large chart that looks like a response booklet page. A sample item (e.g., "chocolate is my favorite ice cream") helps students to see how to mark their options. The data gatherer then reads each page

Figure 6.1 Pupil Survey Booklet for Young Nonreaders

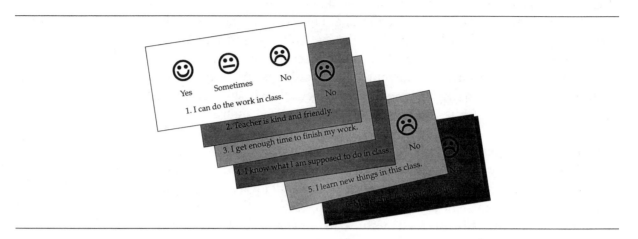

while the students follow along and mark their preferences. The data gatherer can scan the room to see that students are on the same colored page as the item he or she is reading. A gentle correction will keep most self-pacers on the same page as the group (of course, a few self-pacers are entirely on their own!).

Survey items for elementary nonreaders are presented in Table 6.5. Forms for elementary readers and middle and high school students are presented as Forms 6.1 and 6.2.

Administration of Forms

Survey forms should be administered by a neutral person, separate from the administration and other teachers in the school. Ideally, a trained clerk from an independent Evaluation Unit should be used. The teacher should give a brief, *standard* introduction of the data-gathering person such as "The purpose of this survey is for me to get ideas about how I can make this a better class for learning. Please follow the directions of Mr. (Ms.) . . ." The attitude of the teacher as she sets up the class is crucial. A teacher can make the task pleasant, important, honest, positive, and productive—or the opposite. The teacher then leaves the room as the clerk gives directions, distributes, and monitors completion of the forms. The clerk takes the forms, thanks the students, asks for general questions, gives reassuring answers, and asks the teacher to return. It is important to communicate to students that their responses will be taken seriously.

Teachers with multiple classes, that is, high school and some junior high school teachers, should sample classes (e.g., three taken at random from a six-period schedule).

TABLE 6.5 Nonreader Student Survey Items

	Yes	Sometimes	No
I am able to do the work in class			
Teacher is kind and friendly			
I know what I am supposed to do in class			
I learn new things in this class			
Class is *too* noisy and rowdy to learn			
We have plenty of paper, pencils, things to learn with			
Teacher shows us how to do new things			
My teacher is a good teacher			
The rules in class help us to learn			
Teacher lets me do what I want			

NOTE: In actual forms, the face symbols would appear with each item.

Analysis and Presentations of Forms

The clerk hand scores the forms as soon as possible. Two copies of a summary sheet are made: one to return to the teacher for inspection and one to be included in the teacher's dossier if she chooses. If the teacher decides to include the summary sheet in her dossier, the original survey forms and summary sheet should be archived for 5 years. If the teacher decides not to use the summary sheet, all original forms, summary sheets, and other materials should be given to the teacher and no records kept by the Evaluation Unit. Administrators and other teachers should not be told who is, and who is not, collecting student report data.

The most important analysis is of the global item. It is helpful for the clerk to compute means (arithmetic averages) and standard deviations. An up-to-date calculator can perform these computations. As described in Chapter 17, computers can analyze these numbers, make graphic displays, and keep records of these and similar data. Histograms (bar graphs) are helpful for complex, mixed, or bimodal distributions. A similar analysis of other items completes the scoring. District data—averages and distributions—can be kept for examination by individual teachers or used in public relations.

Interpretation of Results

Field studies of the student surveys presented in this book (Driscoll et al., 1990; Peterson et al., 1990; Peterson & Stevens, 1988) showed positive

FORM 6.1 Elementary Reader Student Survey Form

	Agree	Not Sure	Disagree
I know what I'm supposed to do in class	3	2	1
Teacher shows us how to do new things	3	2	1
There is enough time to finish class work	3	2	1
This class is not too noisy or rowdy for learning	3	2	1
I learn new things I can tell you about	3	2	1
I know how well I'm doing in class	3	2	1
This is a good teacher	3	2	1
We have enough materials and supplies to learn	3	2	1
This class is not too slow or fast to learn well	3	2	1
The rules in class help us to learn	3	2	1

FORM 6.2 Middle School and High School Student Survey Form

	Agree		Not Sure		Disagree
I know what I'm supposed to do in class	5	4	3	2	1
Teacher shows us how to do new things	5	4	3	2	1
There is enough time to finish class work	5	4	3	2	1
This class is not too noisy or rowdy for learning	5	4	3	2	1
I learn new things I can tell you about	5	4	3	2	1
I know how well I'm doing in class	5	4	3	2	1
This is a good teacher	5	4	3	2	1
We have enough materials and supplies to learn	5	4	3	2	1
At the end of class, I understand well enough to finish the assignment	5	4	3	2	1
I know why we learn what we learn in class	5	4	3	2	1
This class is not too slow or fast to learn well	5	4	3	2	1
The rules in class help us to learn	5	4	3	2	1

reactions of students to their teachers. Students like and appreciate their teachers. This supportive feedback is good for teachers and reassures the vast majority of teachers who are doing a good and needed job.

However, experience also shows that many teachers have unrealistic and vulnerable expectations for student report data. Few teachers will get perfect 5.0 ratings. This can disappoint teachers new to student report data. It should be pointed out to these teachers that perfect scores are rarely desirable. Most classrooms have some students who need stern attention from teachers at times. Some students require pressure from teachers to do things they do not choose to do, or do not choose to do well. This interaction may result in a lower (but desirable) student rating. A realistic pupil rating is slightly bimodal: Many students rate the teacher highly, but a few react negatively to positive teacher pressure for performance. Review panels use their expertise to take this into account in their judgments of teachers (Peterson, 1987c, 1988).

Finally, results of student reports should be interpreted differently by grade level. Studies consistently show higher ratings by elementary grade pupils relative to middle school and high school. The greater complexity of reaction of older pupils shows up in fewer of the highest responses by individuals.

Costs

Costs for students surveys include duplication of forms and clerk time for administration and scoring. Teacher time is minimal: making the decision to gather data, time waiting for students to fill out forms, and inspection time of results. Student time is 6 to 10 minutes per class. The Peterson (1989c) study of middle school and high school student surveys found a cost of $8.50 per teacher. Because not all teachers elect to gather student surveys (15% of the sample did not), and those who do will not use them every year (three times every 5 years is recommended), the final estimated cost per teacher per year was $4.34.

Districts may want to experiment with electronically scored forms. Field experience is that the final costs and time required are surprisingly often in favor of hand scoring and distribution. Spot checks on accuracy are important regardless of the scoring method selected. Mistakes in computing or reporting seriously damage credibility.

Suggestions for Use of Pupil Survey Forms

Student report data have a number of possible uses. Teachers may want to use them for purely formative data several times during the year, then talk them over in class meetings. Some inservice training may be organized around ways for teachers to get more positive results; this relatively trivial beginning turns into a profound opportunity to work on larger issues of teacher quality. Beginning teachers can be encouraged to talk over district norms, while not disclosing their own results.

GROUP INTERVIEWS

Group interviews are semistructured question-and-answer sessions with students conducted by a person who is not the teacher, administrator, or fellow teacher at the school. Student responses are recorded by the interviewer, and a summary report is prepared. The teacher reviews the summary and decides whether to include it in his professional dossier.

As an alternative to survey forms, group interviews give more perspective, detail, and spontaneity. They are less representative and more expensive. Their interpretation and comparison with other teachers are more complex. Group interviews are a stronger formative evaluation because of the useful information they give, and a weaker summative evaluation because they are less useful for comparison. They are as valid and reliable as surveys but serve a different purpose. They are less standard in content, but equally standard in procedure.

Interviews should involve a large sample of a class (e.g., 15 students), rather than the entire group. For high school, students from several classes may be gathered for a group interview. The following questions are helpful for a group interview setting: "What is one thing that could be done to improve the class?" "What is one thing that should be done more often in class?" and "What is one way in which tests or grading could be improved?" Group interviews may be used in years when surveys are not gathered. Another use is an unusually intensive year when both surveys are used and interviews are held. In the majority of cases, these data are needed only every 3 to 5 years. Group interviews are cost-effective.

Individual interviews are rarely needed. They do permit discussion of more sensitive issues that students in groups might be reluctant to discuss. Care must be taken for representative numbers. Individual interviews are expensive in interviewer time, analysis, and presentation of results.

FOCUS GROUPS

Focus groups are sessions of six to eight students discussing their views and ideas about a teacher for an extended period (45 minutes) with a lightly structured set of questions, but an expert leader (Krueger, 1988; Morgan, 1988). Group leaders should be experienced and familiar with the literature of focus group technique. Focus groups are more expensive than surveys or interviews. They require greater expertise in leadership and reporting. They are more open to the direction of the students. Although the procedures are standard, the contents most often are quite unique. They are more likely than surveys or interviews to conform to unique strengths or problems of teachers. Focus groups elicit valuable formative information.

Focus groups will collect additional information, allow teachers to try out ideas, and increase the amount of two-way communication. Focus groups are not as representative of overall student reaction to teachers (small samples are usually involved), but they do have the potential to create more ideas and topics for understanding the work of teachers. Focus groups should be arranged by persons other than the teacher.

Focus groups are helpful for some teachers, especially after surveys have been made. Focus groups help to fill in specific details about performance, for example, exactly which teacher strategies were best for helping students to learn. They also may be of assistance for evaluation of special teacher populations, such as teachers having difficulty, teacher leader selection, or teachers at a promotion time in their careers.

Focus group meetings should be designed as a positive, productive, and satisfying experience for the student participants. A comfortable environment, such as a lounge or neutral setting in a school library, is important for good discussion and idea development. The goal of a focus group meeting is not agreement and consensus but production of new ideas and perspective for the teacher. Focus groups are different from other data-gathering strategies in that a central goal is to have participants influence each other *during* the session with social interaction and interplay of ideas. Preexisting social status among students can be a barrier to a productive group.

School districts may assign members of the Evaluation Unit to lead focus groups. Another staffing possibility is to solicit volunteer teachers to conduct sessions for other teachers (with whom they have no social or professional contacts). Coleaders can ensure reliable note recording and productivity of sessions. The task of the focus group leader is to moderate, listen, observe, and record. The session should be based on a small number of predetermined but open-ended questions and follow-ups. Resulting notes and audiotapes are content analyzed for central ideas. Rather than an encyclopedic report of the session, good focus group reports highlight a workable number of ideas for use by the teacher and evaluators.

CUMULATIVE BENEFITS OF PUPIL REPORTS

Systematic use of pupil reports means that students will get more and more familiar with the procedures as years pass. Although nonreader responses are somewhat less reliable than upper grade responses, the *experience* of younger students participating in pupil reports means that their reliability and validity will increase as students become more accustomed to the expectations and ideas. This has a short-term payoff in that second graders who have 2 years of experience with surveys are more reliable than second graders with no experience. In the longer term, high school students who have done pupil surveys throughout their elementary school years are more reliable than students for whom this is a novel activity. This longer term perspective should be kept in mind by educators who are considering adopting these practices: Years of experience for both students and teachers are required for teacher evaluation systems to acquire their full functioning and utility. This includes sociological and political experience with teacher evaluation as well as with the technical changes outlined in this chapter.

INTERNET RESOURCES

Davis School District, Utah

http://www.davis.edu/stafdev/eas/index.htm

Williamsburg-James City County Public Schools, Virginia

http://admin.sbo.wjcc.k12.va.us/public/teacheval.html

7

Peer Review of Materials

Peer review is a process in which teachers use their own direct knowledge and experience to examine and judge the merit and value of another teacher's practice. The term *peer* means that the teachers in both roles are equivalent in assignment, training, experience, perspective, and information about the setting for the practice under review. Teachers who review peers should not teach at the same school and should not be connected with each other socially or through professional politics. Peer review means, for example, that a third-grade teacher is reviewed by another third-grade teacher of similar experience and training, who knows the students and school conditions of the teacher under review. It does not mean using any teacher of any grade level, having vastly different experience and training, having special preparation in teacher evaluation, or currently teaching in a socioeconomically different school.

Teacher peer review brings the expertise and experience of the profession into evaluation as does no other assessment technique (French-Lazovik, 1981). Teacher colleagues are familiar with school goals, priorities, values, and problems. They know subject matter, curriculum, instruction, and materials. At the same time, they are aware of the actual demands, limitations, and opportunities that classroom practitioners face. They are in a position to address both the quality of teaching and the real limitations of actual teaching situations. Peer evaluation is a sine qua non of professionalism (Etzioni, 1969), yet it is an underdeveloped and underresearched data source for teacher evaluation (Batista, 1976; McCarthey & Peterson, 1987).

Advantages of Peer Review

Arguments for the development and use of peer review are compelling. Experience with how classes work and how children learn permits judgments that are realistic and knowledgeable. The peer teacher balances the knowledge of a curriculum expert or the university education specialist with the experience of teaching immature, nonvoluntary persons in a group setting. This is a unique and valuable perspective to determine quality in teachers.

Teachers in the same subject area can give highly specific feedback. At the high school level, for example, a science teacher is able to recognize different strategies for balancing student learning of facts, concepts, and scientific processes. One science teacher is in a good position to judge the resourcefulness displayed in setting up hands-on experiences for students by another. It requires a practicing science teacher to discern the dangers to be avoided and exciting moments for learning created by another teacher. The value of home support of learning for a particular group of students in the form of parental education, home computers, stimulating conversation, hopes for future occupations and education, and travel and recreation in natural settings all are recognized by science teachers as significant to classroom quality, but more often overlooked by people who are not currently teaching science. These examples are similar to other subtleties experienced by teachers in other subject areas or at different age levels.

Peer review gives one of the few good estimates of teacher knowledge for purposes of evaluation. Although students, classroom observers, and administrators are poor judges of teacher knowledge (Peterson, 1987a), peers can give some good estimates of subject matter expertise. Other teachers are in a position to recognize how knowledge is organized and made available for students. The experience of peers enables them to deal with subject matter knowledge at developmentally appropriate levels. Without this perspective, it is easy to miss the realities of how an eight-year-old does mathematics, or how an adolescent views the history of her country.

Because of how close they are to the teaching situation, peer reviewers also provide a way to include student achievement data in teacher evaluation. The technically difficult task of holding non-teacher-explained variance constant in judging a teacher's results (e.g., generally, approximately 60% of the variance in pupil gain is explained by previous achievement) can be approximated by a fellow teacher.

Peer review provides a sociologically powerful role for teachers. The very fact that teachers are involved in evaluation changes relationships among teachers, and with administrators. Peer review can be healthy for the professional life of teachers; it encourages professional behavior and helps lessen teacher isolation (Etzioni, 1969; Lortie, 1975). A sense of professionalism is strengthened with the idea of shared craft knowledge. Peer review makes it possible to exchange information and techniques. It makes exemplary practice available for others to follow. Finally, the professional and political standing of teachers in the society is enhanced with the self-regulation of peer review.

Disadvantages of Peer Review

The present difficulties with peer review in teacher evaluation are considerable. Chiefly, they stem from lack of reliable procedures, credibility to outside audiences, precedent, teacher preparation, and a negative teacher culture for peer evaluation. Problems also arise because peer review is not an established and administrator-sanctioned part of educational systems. Often, teachers' organizations take a stand against peer evaluation of any kind.

The bulk of research on peer review has focused on one topic, the effectiveness of peer classroom visits. Teacher visits are as unreliable as those of administrators and other supervisors. Studies suggest that the unreliability is due to the few number of observations, judgments based on political consideration or friendships, and overreliance on style preferences that have little to do with the objectives of teaching (Cohen & McKeachie, 1980; Scriven, 1981). As Centra (1977) stated, "Colleague ratings of teaching effectiveness based *primarily* on classroom observation would in most instances not be reliable enough to use in making decisions on retention and promotion" (p. 105).

The present culture of teachers is not to participate in peer review (Lieberman, 1972; Lortie, 1975). Teachers avoid the responsibility and prefer to leave the task to others. Teachers feel that the delicate balance of cooperation needed in a school for day-to-day functioning is upset by peer evaluation relationships (Alfonso, 1977). Teachers have doubts about their own training and abilities for peer evaluation (Kauchak et al., 1985; Lortie, 1975).

Advantages of a Materials Review

Review of instructional materials has distinct advantages over other forms of peer review, most notably peer visits to classroom or peer surveys of overall impressions. For one thing, reviews of materials are reliable. Levels of agreement among practicing teachers about the quality of materials are high (McCarthey & Peterson, 1987). Use of three or more reviewers adequately controls for bias. Competitor techniques like peer classroom visits or surveys are very difficult and expensive to make as reliable. The logistics of reviews of materials are practical. Teachers can participate without having to leave their own classrooms during instructional time. This saves valuable contact with students, saves money for substitutes or administrators, and makes classroom disturbances of the teacher under review unnecessary. Materials review means that peer reviewers do not have to be removed from classrooms for short- or long-term assignments. Some evaluation systems have designated peer teachers for year-long appointments (French, 1984). Such strategies are expensive, mean the loss of good teaching, and place people in a role where they are not true peers in attitude, value, or perspective.

Review of a teacher's materials helps to avoid the irrelevant focus on classroom style. Although all teachers have preferences for classroom climate, no one style (e.g., task oriented) has been demonstrated to be superior to another style (e.g., participant oriented). A restriction to materials evidence keeps the focus on tools, results, and solutions to common teaching problems.

Materials reviews examine discrete elements of teaching that are important indicators of quality (Sergiovanni, 1977). For example, the structure and sequence of a classroom program usually are apparent in the materials. Student achievement often is evident. Elements of an opportunity to learn—such as new material, practice and performance time—should be apparent. Quality of the teacher's feedback to students can be discerned. Fairness and equity may be evidenced, for example, for different levels of achievement, boys and girls, and different background. Finally, much of the complex, subtle, and idiosyncratic elements of teaching can be examined in a peer review of materials. Other methods miss these considerations.

Disadvantages of a Materials Review

Of course, using materials is only a part of what a teacher does. The overall picture of teacher quality does not come through in a materials review. Not all teacher are effective through the use of their materials; some very good teachers work with spartan materials. Other teachers who might be misevaluated by peer review include teachers who have little access to resources or time to create or accumulate materials.

Professional or social connections can dominate peer judgments (French-Lazovik, 1981; Scriven, 1981). If teachers are friends of one another, or linked by school ties, a disruptive bias is almost sure to result. Beyond these personal connections, peer reviewers are biased by style considerations. For example, a teacher who herself uses a hands-on approach will value this in others, even though such a technique is not always or necessarily superior. Lewis (1975) showed how college-level peer judgments can be weakened by considerations irrelevant to teaching.

SELECTED LITERATURE

French-Lazovik (1981) reviewed the advantages, materials, procedures, data, and outcomes of peer review of materials for teacher evaluation at the college level. She noted the central role of this data source.

> So deeply rooted as to be almost universal in American colleges and universities, peer review is the procedure by which a faculty member's work is judged by peers in all matters of academic and disciplinary decision—appointment, promotion, . . . tenure, the selection of manuscripts for publication, the approval of research grants. Its essential function is to guarantee that members of an academic community have control over their own standards, their own membership, and the future course of their disciplines. (p. 73)

French-Lazovik recommended that peer review materials include detailed descriptions of courses and procedures for assignments and grading. She specified for exclusion lecture notes, descriptions of teaching style, and self-evaluations. She listed five questions for reviewers on (a) quality of materials, (b) kinds of intellectual tasks called for, (c) knowledge of subject matter, (d) duties related to mission of department, and (e) evidence of striving for quality.

French-Lazovik (1981) stressed the need to control bias in peer reviews by attending to friendships, anonymity, competition, expertise, and sufficient numbers. She recommended peer review committees of three to six members. Peer reviews should be held once every other year for untenured faculty, and every fifth year for tenured members.

Kauchak et al. (1985) interviewed 60 teachers from a variety of schools and levels in Utah and Florida. In general, the teachers were open to the benefits of peer evaluations as a formative activity in which information was shared. As one teacher said, "More than anyone else, another teacher can appreciate the problems you're dealing with, more than a parent, more than an administrator, more than kids . . . they have more of a feel for what you're trying to do and what you're working with" (p. 36). Teachers in this study felt that the evaluators should come from the same subject matter area or grade level. Interestingly, although teachers saw peer evaluation as positive, they were reluctant to serve as evaluators themselves. Reservations focused around disturbances of the professional relationships and dependencies in a school setting. Fears were expressed that peer reviews might lead to isolation, bad feelings, and detrimental competition. Teachers expressed a lack of confidence in their own abilities and worries about taking on a function that was not appropriate. As one put it, "You're treading on very delicate ground . . . because we all teach differently and I might get results out of a kid that another teacher may not and another teacher might do things that I would never dream of" (p. 36).

McCarthey and Peterson (1987) studied peer review of materials in a career ladder reward system in a large urban school district. Fifty teachers (36 elementary, 7 intermediate, and 7 high school) selected the optional data source as part of their case for performance bonus or to quality for additional duties for additional pay. Teachers collected materials that demonstrated their individual, unique teaching practice as well as to represent "expected and routine" teaching. Materials were collected in one box per teacher over 5 months. Teachers included such items as curriculum outlines, instructional materials, grade records, student work samples, tests, photographs, activity descriptions, letters to parents, and schedules. Teachers reported a median of 10 hours of assembly time. Each box of materials was reviewed by three peers (same grade level or subject area) for approximately 1 hour. Peers were district teachers but were not personally acquainted with teachers they reviewed. Reviewers conferred and they filled out a report form with a recommendation: "Pass" or "Insufficient information to pass." Review costs were $29.00 per teacher. For the purposes of this study, the principals of the teachers under review judged the materials using the same procedures.

McCarthey and Peterson (1987) concluded that

> the findings do suggest considerable promise for improved teacher evaluation. Peer involvement in judging teachers may serve to heighten a sense of professionalism. . . . [R]eview of teacher artifacts, rather than direct observation will lessen negative teacher attitudes toward their evaluation. (p. 267)

These authors found that the teacher reviewers were more stringent in their judgments than were the principals (72% pass rate vs. 90% pass rate). Surveys showed that participants were positive about their experiences. On a 5-point rating scale, reviewees reported a mean rating of 4.05 and reviewers a mean of 4.47 on the item "peer review should be kept as an optional line of evidence." Other survey data showed a similar vote of confidence, with the reviewers more positive about the experience.

McGreal (1983) recommended including teacher artifacts in teacher evaluation. He pointed out that teaching means student interaction with teacher-made and teacher-selected materials, as much as it means interaction with the teachers themselves. He reported studies (e.g., Rosenshine, 1980) that showed that students spend 40%-70% of instructional time learning from teacher-made and teacher-selected materials. McGreal offered a framework for analyzing the artifacts of teaching. The evaluative framework included content (e.g., validity, clarity, relevance), design (e.g., sequencing, engagement, meaningfulness), and presentation (e.g., time, pace, quality). He included recommendations for differences in artifact collection between beginning teachers and veterans.

McGreal (1983) reviewed the literature explaining the considerable teacher resistance to peer evaluation (e.g., Lieberman, 1972) and technical accuracy problems (Bergman, 1980; Cohen & McKeachie, 1980). However, he based a recommendation for the use of peers in teacher evaluation on limiting their role to one of peer consultants. This voluntary relationship involves mutual teacher agreement, joint goal setting, and reliance on already existing team-teaching arrangements. McGreal recommended a slow development of peer evaluation with increasing emphasis on professional discussions of topics of mutual interest.

Bird (1990) provided an extensive discussion of teacher portfolios as a data source for teacher evaluation. He suggested nine modes of thinking about portfolio contents. These included teacher entries (elective, guided, or required), jointly produced entries (collegial, negotiated, or proctored), and entries produced by others (commentary, attestations, or official records). Bird distinguished portfolio contents between teacher tasks (teaching a class, planning, student evaluation, professional exchanges, and community exchanges) and teacher concerns (responsibilities, subject matter, individual students, and class organization). Bird (1990) concluded that "the schoolteacher's portfolio belongs to an occupation of schoolteaching that we don't have now, but should be organizing for the future" (p. 255).

Portfolios and dossiers are distinctly different collections of materials (Peterson, 1984; Scriven, 1973a, 1973c). Dossiers are more compressed and interpreted and contain multiple data source summaries, including, perhaps, a portfolio (materials) review report. Chapters 16, 18, and 26 present principles and practices for teacher dossier construction, judgment, and use.

RECOMMENDED PROCEDURES

Peer review of materials is an option for teachers to collect documents and artifacts from their teaching, store these in boxes or portfolios, have them reviewed by knowledgeable peers (same grade level or subject area, but not socially or professionally connected), and receive a summary report for teacher choice for inclusion in the professional evaluation dossier.

Timing

It is best if teacher materials are collected along the way rather than as a result of a separate housecleaning or "cram session" effort. Teachers need to both plan for collection and more spontaneously recognize the value of artifacts for review as they use the materials in class. Materials may take 1 to 2 years to collect and organize; 6 months is a reasonable minimum.

A review of materials is not an annual event, but appropriate every 5 years or so. Peers are able to recognize the quality of materials from a sample and do not need to see every piece that a teacher has selected or developed. The limited opportunity to create and collect materials should be recognized for first- and second-year teachers who might choose a review of materials. The teacher under review is the best judge of how often reviews are needed to make his or her case for quality.

Materials

Teachers should be guided in their selection of materials by the question, "What materials would be helpful or necessary for you if you were reviewing the teaching practice of a peer?" Table 7.1 suggests materials for peer review. These are offered as possibilities for teachers and not requirements or even expectations.

Examples of written feedback have shown great value for reviewers (Scriven, 1972). Although this is not an expected practice of routine teacher performance, analysis of feedback discloses a great deal to peer reviewers. The process begins with the teacher selecting an important teaching episode, like a unit goal, written paper, student project, or similar major objective. At the end of the activity, the teacher writes extensive comments (one half to three fourths of a page) to 10 students selected at random or by explicit criteria. The resulting pages are included in the materials review. What is disclosed to the reviewers by this feedback are such things as

- Topics chosen to comment on
- Language, vocabulary, and technical detail
- Depth and subtlety of assessment
- Variation in feedback by individual student
- Use of knowledge about the student other than immediate classroom experience
- Subject matter tutelage included in feedback

TABLE 7.1 Suggestions for Peer Review Materials

Curriculum outline
Schedules and timelines
Sample instructional materials
Reading lists
Video- and audiotapes
Activity descriptions
Tests
Student achievement data
Comparisons with other similar classes
Examples of student work
Results of quizzes and tests
Grade records
Audiovisual and computer instruction descriptions
Lesson plans
Examples of written feedback
Classroom rules and discipline procedures
Handouts and worksheets
Diagrams and photographs of room
Messages sent to parents

This optional artifact of feedback statements is a rich source of information. Other materials likewise can be expanded creatively or prepared by the teacher to demonstrate his or her teaching merit.

Review Procedure

Teacher Control

As with other data sources, each teacher should control the evaluation process with the safeguards presented in Chapter 4: initial selection of the procedure and inspection of results before deciding to keep them for review in the professional dossier.

Reviewers

Peer review teachers should volunteer for the service. One compensation for their time and effort is professional status derived from their selection. Another compensation is the chance to learn from the materials of a colleague who sees this to be a strength of his practice. An agreement should be made ahead of time that reviewers can borrow ideas from the reviewee owner. This is a considerable benefit for the reviewers and can disseminate good practice. Still another compensation is money, for example, at wages paid to substitutes. Strategies for compensation should be made in market terms, that is, what is the lowest cost payment needed to get high-quality reviewers in the given setting?

Appointments should be made by a knowledgeable, neutral agency—such as a district Teacher Evaluation Board (see Chapter 18 for district-level committees). The Teacher Review Panels should identify a pool of reviewers for consideration by the board. Thus peer review participation is based on successful dossier review. Reviewers should have knowledge of the school conditions and students under consideration. However, care must be taken so that social and professional connections are avoided. At times, reviewers will have to be shared with other districts, for example, in small school districts. In some cases of very limited opportunity, it may be necessary for perhaps one of the reviewers to be connected to the reviewee.

Review Procedures

Teacher materials are stored and submitted for review in boxes. Most often, one box (12 in. × 28 in. × 8 in.) is enough. For all but a few extraordinary situations (e.g., oversized portfolios), two boxes is a reasonable limit. Boxes should be stored and delivered for review by the district Evaluation Unit, after submission by the teacher.

Boxes of materials are presented to the reviewers in an area where reviewers can spread out material and talk over their findings. The workroom should be comfortable and contain supplies such as paper pads, video- and audiotape equipment, slide projectors, and computers. The review area should have privacy and not be disturbed by outside distractions. The respect given to the work area should be commensurate with that deserved by the process of peer judgment of colleagues.

Time control is important for reviewers to have. Reviewers should decide the optimum arrangements for their work. It may be scheduled on Saturdays or evenings for some reviews but include mid-weekday sessions for others. Teachers have important differences of opinion, responsibility, and styles that should be accommodated in teacher evaluation activities. Significant teacher resistance to increased evaluation stems from lack of respect for teacher needs and preferences.

Individual reviews should be scheduled flexibly. Most reviews take less than 1 hour per set of materials. Reviewers should be free to look at the materials together or work alone. They can make notes for discussion, later use in completing the report form, or for their own personal use.

FORM 7.1 Sample Peer Review of Materials Summary Form

REVIEWERS:

After examination, review, and deliberation concerning the instructional materials submitted by

_____ *of* _____, *we conclude that this teacher is:*

        ___ Well functioning, contributing

        ___ Well functioning, contributing, AND shows exemplary practice in these areas:

        ___ Not well functioning in these respects:

        Signed _____

                    _____

                    _____

        Review supervised by _____

One review team may complete as many as three to four reviews in a half-day session.

Report Forms

Two feedback forms are used in peer review of materials. The first form is for the professional evaluation dossier. A recommended format for

Figure 7.1 Completed Peer Review of Materials Summary Form

Peer Review of Materials Summary Form

REVIEWERS:

Betsey Jenkins, 1st-grade teacher, Sattursby School, King City School District
Kent Hyret, 1st-grade teacher, Glen Eden Elementary School, King City School District
Esther Morane, 1st-grade teacher, Fredericks Elementary School, King City School District

After examination, review, and deliberation concerning the instructional materials
submitted by **ANNE MARLOWE** *of* **Woodside Elementary School**, *we conclude*
that this teacher is:

                    ___ Well functioning, contributing.

                    <u>xxx</u> Well functioning, contributing, AND shows exemplary
                          practice in these areas:

1. Excellent communication with parents—consistent, positive, readable ideas
2. High degree of organization in instructional materials, sequences, timetables
3. Many creative activities; a variety of activities to teach skills
4. Excellent at-home reading program
5. Nice incorporation of reading throughout your program
6. Excellent use of *webbing* in which concepts in various curricular areas are related to each other in students' learning
7. Art activities supplement rather than supplant the core curriculum
8. Remarkable fit with District core curriculum goals
9. Student work samples show student individuality and choice
10. Record keeping (to be passed on to 2nd-grade teachers) is outstanding
11. Your children must love school!!!!!

                    ___ Not well functioning in these respects:

                    Signed_____

                            _____

                            _____

                  Review supervised by _____

this form appears as Form 7.1. Following the review, this form is examined by the teacher, who then decides on what is to be done with it. If the teacher chooses it for her professional dossier, two copies are made by the Evaluation Unit: one for the dossier and one for the teacher. If the teacher decides that the summary form will not be used in the dossier, both copies are given to the teacher and no further records are kept. Figure 7.1 is an example of a completed peer review report form.

The second form recommended for peer review is a formative report that includes informal feedback given only to the teacher under review. This personal communication between reviewers and teacher does much to reassure the person under review. It contains brief notes about what was noticed and reactions to the materials. It often contains praise, questions, or criticisms. It may give ideas for changes in format of the materials presentation. It may become more complex and suggest areas for consideration for change of practice. It might include suggestions for inservice education. It will most often not be extensive nor diagnostic but will reflect some sense of the direction and focus of the review.

8

Student Achievement

Student achievement, how much and what pupils learn, is the single most important concern about educational programs. To many, it is the most compelling evidence about teacher quality. In particular, the interest is in what students gain while working with the teacher—the difference between where pupils start and end in their achievement. Essentially, this data source requires a determination of the contributions of the teacher, or *teacher effects*, on student learning. Advocates for using pupil achievement in teacher evaluation argue that if students are learning important things well, other issues like teacher preparation and teaching methods are not of much concern.

As desirable as student achievement data are for teacher evaluation, good pupil gain information is technically difficult to get for many teachers (Stake, 1973). Advocates of teacher evaluation by pupil outcome need to understand that useful, extensive pupil achievement data may be available for fewer than half of the teachers in a typical school district. First, dependable achievement tests do not exist for all parts of the curriculum. Another problem is that achievement *prior* to the time with the teacher under review generally accounts for on the order of 60% of the variance in student learning as measured by paper-and-pencil tests; it is difficult to isolate and document teacher effects on pupil learning. Finally, student motivation, parent support, school facilities, and opportunities for future education and employment all play large, but indeterminate, roles in student learning in addition to the teacher effects.

Advantages

The argument for using student gain data in teacher evaluation is relatively simple. Pupil achievement appears to be the most direct measure of teacher quality. The logical connection is that good learning equals good teaching, and vice versa. Inevitably following this line of thinking is the comparison: Better teachers get better learning results.

The overwhelming commonsensical appeal of measuring student learning to evaluate teachers gives a definite advantage of popularity to this data source. Using pupil achievement as evidence of teacher quality makes a great deal of sense to many people, especially noneducators. Alternatively, an evaluation system that does not include pupil achievement in some way is not credible to many audiences.

Another apparent advantage of pupil achievement is economy of evaluation. If the kinds and amounts of student learning are assessed, then the teacher evaluation problem is simplified from the task described thus far in this book. If teacher contributions to learning (the primary task of the teacher) can be accurately assessed, then evaluators need only check for a few crucial ancillary concerns: outside-of-class responsibilities, ethics, welfare of children, lack of abuse, legality, and long-term effects (e.g., durability, effects on other learning). They need not be much concerned with teacher preparation, methodology, classroom strategies, use of materials, opinions of peers, or inservice education.

Disadvantages

A close examination of the use of pupil achievement in teacher evaluation discloses a surprising number of limitations (Stake, 1973). It turns out that this prime contender for assessing teacher quality is much like the other data sources described in this book: It will work for some teachers but not for others. It must be used carefully and in conjunction with at least several other data sources. In spite of these limitations, pupil achievement remains a most compelling data source for teacher evaluation, if only evaluators can defensibly get it for the teacher under review!

There are three major obstacles to using student achievement in teacher evaluation. First, the logical connections between teacher performance and student learning are indirect and have mixed causality. Second, there are many technical problems in getting defensible data about teacher effects on student learning. Third, the distorting effects of pupil-gain-based teacher evaluation on the educational system are significant.

Teacher quality and effort are not always directly tied to student learning. For example, lack of student effort can thwart the effects of the most brilliant teachers. In addition, research shows that such factors as parental expectations, prior achievement, socioeconomic status, and the general educational quality of the home (values, reading, conversation, travel) add up to a greater influence on pupil learning than does the teacher (Borich, 1977). Many other school factors that are beyond the control of teachers affect pupil growth. These include classroom resources, number of students, and learning environments such as the size of the room. Finally, teacher effects vary in their potency according to the age of students and the nature of the material that is to be learned; teachers with different teaching assignments cannot easily be compared.

The technical problems of accurately measuring student learning for the purposes of evaluating most teachers seem insurmountable at present. Five major problems are the following:

1. What should be measured is not clear.
2. Good (valid, reliable, usable) tests for summative evaluation purposes are not widely available.
3. Administration of student tests, for summative teacher evaluation purposes, is difficult and expensive.
4. Pupil gain data are needed, not merely end-of-instruction achievement.
5. Stability of teacher influence (over populations, materials, and time) is low.

There is general agreement on what teachers should be doing, namely, enabling students to learn important subject matter that consists of information, skills, and attitudes. However, there is less agreement about how teachers should perform other important teacher tasks. Teachers at times are expected to help students recognize their increasing competence, feel better about themselves, become good citizens, develop more responsibility, increase in problem-solving ability, prepare for a world of work, exhibit moral values, think critically, collaborate in groups, lead healthy lives, and develop independence. When these additional important goals of education are considered, it becomes difficult to narrowly specify and measure the job of a teacher. Fairness demands that a teacher be evaluated on the basis of the total job expectations rather than just a narrow segment of the task. Because the overall task of teaching is complicated and context dependent, it is very hard to measure teacher success in terms of student outcomes.

Even if the purposes of teaching were relatively narrow and agreed on, there remains the problem of a lack of good, standardized achievement measures for all levels and topics of learning. Existing tests often are very useful for curriculum decisions, choices of learning materials, pupil diagnosis, feedback for learning, promotion decisions, and assessment of qualification for further learning—they rarely are good for the purpose of determining teacher effects. One reason is the discrepancy between the content of standardized tests constructed at the national level and the goals and programs of individual classrooms, schools, or districts. Typically, standardized achievement tests measure outcomes that are different from the goals of the teachers and do not measure what teachers are assigned or choose to teach. Locally constructed achievement tests offer one solution to this problem but are difficult and expensive to construct, require validity and reliability studies, are not generalizable to other settings, and are not justifiable in terms of increased student learning.

Even when and where valid achievement tests are available, they need to be well administered if summative decisions about teachers are to be made. In practice, large-scale testing requires expert test administrators and well-controlled testing conditions. This is not true of current standardized testing in most districts, where classroom teachers administer the tests to their own students, a practice not to be permitted for reliable teacher evaluation uses. Defensible testing is expensive and difficult to ensure.

An additional problem in using achievement test scores to evaluate teachers is the selection of test scores for analysis. The worst practice with achievement tests is to use only posttest scores. Rather, the appropriate measurement is of the amount students learn from a given class (difference between posttest and preinstruction test). However, the gain score itself is influenced by prior achievement levels of the students, their individual abilities, and the resources available to the teacher during the class. It is patently unfair to judge or compare teachers without estimating the percentage of final achievement resulting from factors outside the control of the teacher.

Even if gain data are sought rather than posttest-only scores, they are difficult to determine with reliability. As Borich (1977) pointed out, if both the pretest and posttest have reliabilities of 0.80[1], and the correlation between the pretest and gain scores for large populations is 0.70 (both of these coefficients are common and expected values in educational settings), then the resulting reliability of the gain score is 0.33. This low reliability is unacceptable for judging teacher performance with any significant consequences (including feedback to teacher). Even more elaborate statistical techniques (residualized gain scores) rarely approach necessary lower limits of reliability. Whereas the practice of computing student achievement gain scores is defensible for research studies, it rarely is done for general teacher evaluation. (The exception is for individual teachers who make the case for pertinence and data availability and quality for their unique setting.)

The best statistical technique for using pupil achievement data is to compute residualized gains. This is often done in research, but rarely in teacher evaluation programs. Residualized gains are based on the outcomes expected of a given class because of (a) its pretest score mean on a standardized test and (b) the correlation between the pretest score and gain (posttest minus pretest) found in (large) standardization samples. Knowing (a) and (b), a prediction is made from a regression analysis formula of where the class mean on the posttest "should" be, if it is an average class relative to the standardization samples. The evaluation logic is that an actual class average gain above the expected gain can largely be attributed to the class experience that is the teacher's responsibility. In other words, prior achievement has been taken into account. A teacher with relatively low posttest scores and low gain scores may have high residualized gain scores. These results have been known to surprise many educators, where (as in an actual example) "everyone knows that the high test scores and large amounts of gain are to be found on the [affluent] East Bench schools." Residualized gain data often show that the good classroom influences are more evenly distributed in a large district than are the posttest scores or even the gain scores. A very good example of a system that meets these stringent requirements is the Tennessee Value Added Assessment System (Sanders & Horn, 1995a, 1995b, 1998), which is discussed later in this chapter.

The final measurement problem of pupil achievement data is the stability of teacher effects. What effects a teacher has in one instance is not necessarily what he or she will have in another situation. Estimates of reliability for teacher effects on student learning range from 0.08 to 0.30 across two educational settings (Medley, Coker, & Soar, 1984; Rosenshine, 1970). To generalize about a teacher's performance, data need to be gathered in at least five situations with more than 15 students in each situation. This is impossible to accomplish within a year for elementary teachers who have only one class.

Even if the above measurement problems are dealt with, there is a third major obstacle to using achievement test scores as sole or central data for teacher evaluation. Teacher evaluation based on pupil achievement has a strong potential to distort teacher practice in favor of better score results at the expense of pupil interests. For example, teachers will tend to narrow their focus in classrooms to those issues on the test, rather than to allow current student interests and needs to alter the planned curriculum. Teachers may begin to teach to the test and to emphasize narrowed goals of learning to the detriment of the broad scope and goals of most school subjects. For example, basic principles of chemistry that are to be tested may preclude spontaneous exploration of serendipitous topics (e.g., ecological implications or industrial applications) if teacher test results are at stake. Or, teachers may focus more on certain students who can show the biggest gains in testing, to the detriment of students who will not. Also, often ignored are difficult-to-measure educational goals such as personal initiative, aesthetic growth, problem-solving abilities, critical thinking, and cooperative group applications. Reliance on achievement test data for teacher evaluation tends to make teaching and learning more trivial and rigid.

Although this narrowed focus is precisely what goal- and measurement-driven educators value (Cizek, 1993; Knezevich, 1977; Popham, Cruse, Rankin, Sandifer, & Williams, 1985), their position begs the question of why teachers do not teach the "desired" curriculum. Critics of teacher latitude cite teacher error, incompetence, lack of focus, misunderstanding, or (most often) that the reason for deviation is irrelevant—the standardized results have been agreed to and are needed for quality education. However, this position places the teacher in the role of technician, who can be corrected or controlled by external forces. Madaus (1988) called this a kind of "psychometric imperialism." This is contrary to the position of this book, which is that teachers need to be placed in a central location of decision making for their own classes. Teachers are capable of this responsibility and even if they were not, external controls simply do not work. Applying external controls, such as measurement-driven education, rarely returns the errant teacher to the agreed-on fold of educational objectives and, more important, meanwhile does damage by lowering the morale of the majority of teachers who are capable of balancing their curriculum to the needs of the immediate students, society, and integrity of the subject matter.

Taking all the problems of achievement test results into account, they present both much promise and much effort to be used as a major criterion in teacher evaluation. Although most teachers' organizations publicly disavow any evaluation system that employs them, many other consumers of teacher evaluation, such as legislators, are not likely to find an evaluation system that ignores pupil achievement satisfactory. These positions illustrate the polarity of views on this controversial subject.

Specialized Methods: Simulation Teaching
Achievement and Outcome-Based Teacher Evaluation

Two specialized variations of teacher evaluation based on pupil achievement deserve attention: simulation teaching/standardized student achievement and outcome-based teacher evaluation. These specialized methods attempt to address some of the problems inherent in using student gain information. In addition, they gain support from educators who favor the educational structures or procedures associated with each of these methods. However, both of these strategies fail to address the general problems of using student gain data in teacher evaluation and add problems of their own.

Simulation Teaching Achievement Data

Glass (1974) described what he called the Popham-McNeil-Millman (PMM) method (Popham, 1971) in which teachers are

> given advance notice of a few hours or a day or more that they are to teach a particular topic to an unfamiliar group of pupils. The teachers . . . study reference materials, instructional objectives, and even test items comparable to those which will be used as posttests. Frequently, the topic to be taught is one with which the teachers have had little prior experience [e.g., auto carburetion, electronic power supplies] . . . groups of six to thirty or more pupils are randomly formed . . . for the [instruction and] assessment. The pupil group is taught for a period of thirty minutes to an hour. (Glass, 1974, p. 12)

Glass described how this approach strives for objectivity in teacher evaluation to avoid the hobgoblin of subjectivity. However, he pointed out that every case of scientific inquiry involves human judgment (including aesthetic and value judgments). Another problem with this view of teacher evaluation is that it simplifies the activity to one of the teacher's role in changing student behavior. Another important consideration, according to Glass, is to enable students to "grow in a supportive and interesting environment," which, of course, is not considered in the PMM evaluation simulation. Finally, the focus on unfamiliar content removes the additional dimension of subject matter mastery and wisdom as an element of quality in teaching.

The empirical evidence for simulation/controlled student teaching methods is not supportive. Rosenshine (1970) stated that "when teachers taught different topics to different students, the directions of the correlations were . . . erratic, and few correlations were significant" (p. 660). Popham (1971) found nonsignificant differences in pupil achievement among experienced teachers, college students, garage mechanics, and electronics workers. He reported that "experienced teachers are not particularly skilled at bringing about specified behavior changes in learners" (p. 601). Glass (1974) concluded his review of the empirical research literature by examining the 21 correlation coefficients produced to that time. He calculated that only four of their confidence intervals did not include zero and that the reliability of the PMM technique was in the range of 0.20 to 0.30.

Outcome-Based Teacher Evaluation

A more recent strategy for including pupil achievement in consideration of educational quality is an emphasis on "pupil outcomes" (Rosenshine & McGaw, 1972). Outcome-based education (OBE) is a movement in which general agreement is sought on what students ought to be able to perform as a result of their education. For example, Brandt (1993) quoted Spady defining an education outcome as "a culminating demonstration of learning . . . what the kids will actually do" (p. 66). There is an increased emphasis on performance capacity, as opposed to static knowledge of information. Evaluation of pupil achievement calls for demonstrations of ability, rather than test scores of completion of courses of study. Another feature of OBE is reliance on expert judgment for evaluation; systems of judgmental rubrics can be used to reliably define the expected performances. Standardized testing is to be avoided in favor of performance sessions. Authentic learning and evaluation are hallmarks of the movement.

The application of OBE to teacher evaluation consists of holding teachers accountable for the agreed-on outcomes of schooling. However, the mere replacement of standardized testing with performance assessment does not mean that advocates of OBE have solved the problems of using student learning in teacher evaluation. This use of pupil achievement has virtually all of the drawbacks of using standardized test results, with less of the measurable reliability of paper-and-pencil test data and having group norms for comparisons.

SELECTED LITERATURE

Kerlinger (1971) argued that student achievement should be a prime determinant of teacher quality. Although he focused on college-level teaching, Kerlinger made the case that the primary teacher responsibility was for pupil learning. Peterson and Kauchak (1982) reported the popularity of student achievement assessment for teacher evaluation purposes. In particular, they found that legislators seek objective data about student learning as a way of determining teacher quality.

Glass (1974) described the problems concerning pupil gain data in teacher evaluation, and the "danger that some school district might use pupil gains on standardized achievement tests to evaluate teachers" (p. 11). He called the use of commercial standardized achievement tests as "patently invalid and unfair" (p. 11). Such tests are useful to show problems with basic educational skills and content, but they are not designed to "reveal the variety of ways in which teaching and learning can be creative, favorably opportunistic, and uniquely meaningful to students" (p. 11). He cited several studies that back his contention about the limitations of standardized tests for teacher evaluation. In addition, Glass pointed out that attribution of pupil gains to teachers (even in the form of residualized gains) requires random assignment of students, a practice clearly impossible in actual school settings. Next, he reviewed the problems of determining stability of results over a period of years, even if good measurements and attributions were possible for a single year. Finally, Glass pointed out the policy problems of such teacher evaluation: Teachers would teach to safe objectives, could not administer their own tests, would require expensive test administrators, and still potentially lose the trust of the audiences for their evaluation.

Medley et al. (1984) and Soar, Medley, and Coker (1983) provided a useful technical review of problems associated with using pupil achievement data in teacher evaluation. They concluded that the validity and reliability of achievement measurements are "far too low to be useful" (Medley et al., 1984, p. 40). They gave evidence that stability of gains within a classroom is about 0.30; at this rate "it would take 20 years to find out by [achievement tests] whether an elementary teacher is competent or not" (Soar et al., 1983, p. 242). The researchers identified a multiplicity of factors (e.g., pupil IQ) not under teachers' control that affect pupil achievement. In addition, they recognized that "available achievement tests do not measure some of the most important outcomes of teaching" (Medley et al., 1984, p. 40). Finally, Medley et al. worried that students, aware of the use of achievement tests for teacher evaluation, might "do poorly on a year-end exam, merely to punish a teacher" (p. 40).

Berk (1988) reported a review of the research literature on the limitations of pupil achievement data in teacher evaluation in his article "Fifty Reasons Why Student Achievement Gain Does Not Mean Teacher Effectiveness." This analysis of 83 published studies identified 50 factors of pupil achievement scores that are not under the control of teachers. Thus to use pupil achievement data to assess teacher performance or quality is virtually nondefensible.

Berk (1988) first identified 17 variables associated with student characteristics: pupil intelligence, attitude, socioeconomic status, race/ethnicity, sex, age, and attendance. Next, he specified 21 variables associated with school characteristics: school conditions (e.g., class size, enrollment, library) and instructional personnel. For example, he cited a study (Glasman & Biniaminov, 1981) that found a significant positive correlation between reading achievement and school library size. Next, Berk reviewed factors influencing student achievement data that arise from the testing or measurement process itself: type of achievement test, curricular and instructional validity, and test score metric. Finally, he specified 11 problems with pretest-posttest measurement designs (that are needed to establish pupil gain): history, maturation, statistical regression, small class size ($N < 30$), overall school effects, test-wiseness, score conversion errors, minor variations in test administration, teaching to the test, coaching on test-taking skills, and random error. Bert (1988) concluded that

> between-class, between-grade, and between-student variability of the 50 sources of invalidity and error render the setting of a meaningful criterion of superior teacher productivity nearly impossible. Although there does not seem to be any single source of invalidity or error (systematic or random) that is large enough to invalidate the pretest-posttest gain score model, the combination of multiple sources analyzed cumulatively does prove fatal to warrant its rejection. (p. 358)

Stiggins (1989) reviewed the potentials and problems of student achievement data in the evaluation of teachers and recommended resolutions to the debate. First, he recognized the problem:

> On one hand, we believe that one legitimate source of evidence of the effectiveness of teacher performance should be whether students are learning. We feel certain that if teachers are held accountable for student achievement, then teacher and student performance will improve. Yet, on the other hand, the one index of achievement that we always thought we could count on—standardized achievement test scores—cannot and will not do the job. (p. 7)

Then, Stiggins recommended two resolutions to the dilemma. First, he advocated formative uses for pupil achievement measures, rather than summative. He recognized that summative evaluation identifies very few inadequate teachers in practice. Formative evaluation has the potential to help a great many more teachers improve by themselves as part of their expected professional activity. Thus the beneficial effects of student achievement data on teachers are indirect.

The second Stiggins (1989) emphasis was on classroom assessment, as opposed to putting most resources into large-scale standardized testing. Rather, he focused on the considerable evaluation activity that already is part of individual classrooms, and the goal to improve it with further training. Teachers should be encouraged to use a full range of the possibilities (e.g., paper-and-pencil tests, textbook, observation/judgment, assignment, pupil self-assessment, group measurement) and to get as much as possible out of each one. Stiggins advocated the support and improvement of classroom-based teacher assessments of pupil achievement. He stressed that training programs for better teacher evaluation of student learning should fit the classroom realities.

TENNESSEE VALUE ADDED ASSESSMENT SYSTEM (TVAAS)

The Tennessee Value Added Assessment System (Sanders et al., 1994; Sanders & Horn, 1995a; 1995b) is a technically sophisticated achievement test and linear regression analysis procedure for estimating annual academic gains by individual students, adjusted for each student's multiyear performance history. The system uses each child's previous scores as a blocking factor to control for concomitant variables (e.g., family income). The resulting score is a standardized measure in relation to the *expected gain* for that student, given the relationship (correlation) empirically determined in an analysis between score(s) of a large sample population and annual gain. TVAAS can be used with any scalable, norm-referenced, linear-metric achievement test (e.g., California Achievement Test, Iowa Test of Basic Skills, or state-level testing program).

TVAAS shows a number of innovative features. The use of previous test history solves many problems of pretesting: cost, time, appropriate timing, equivalent forms, student time and attitude, and missing data. This blocking factor approach adjusts the gain in light of previous achievement of the student herself. This effectively solves the problem of controlling variables in pupil achievement concomitant to teacher effects (e.g., SES, ethnicity, local resources, individual student effort and attitude). The regression model mixes fixed effects (not having their own distribution—e.g., school, class size, teacher) and random effects (having own distribution—e.g., certain interactions and error term); this "mixed methodology" approach solves problems of missing data, regression to the mean, and variation in modes of classroom instruction (e.g., self-contained or departmentalized school organization). These innovations make TVAAS a powerful tool for documenting teacher effects on pupil achievement.

Research on the TVAAS database has produced a number of significant conclusions about measurement of pupil achievement (Sanders & Horn, 1998). For example, researchers have found the most underserved group in schools assessed with TVAAS was that of previous high achievers; their posttest scores were high, but the gains were routinely less than expected. Other findings include wide variation in school sites, and that cumulative effects of good teaching are large. Certainly this line of research deserves much attention.

The Tennessee Value Added Assessment System has been advocated as an important tool for teacher evaluation. In some settings, it has been presented as a centerpiece of teacher evaluation; it may be advocated as the best way to evaluate teachers. While TVAAS procedures are to be highly recommended as a technical advance for pupil achievement data, there remain significant limits to this line of evidence for complete teacher evaluation. For example, not all teachers in a school district can participate in TVAAS. Another example is found in the logic of the procedure. National norms stand in as an indicator of quality, which means that a relative value can be misrepresented as an absolute value. In plain English: What if considerably below-norm results are all that are possible in a given setting, and thus are very good? These gaps mean that this very compelling data source is not the ultimate in objective data for teacher evaluation, or a reason to abandon the multiple- and variable-data-source approach. A more comprehensive list of concerns not addressed by TVAAS is presented in Table 8.1.

Perhaps the greatest limitation of TVAAS is that it is available to a limited number of teachers in a school system. For example, the requirement for 3 previous years of data means that primary grade teachers are excluded. Also, because serious testing of students may not begin until the third grade, the middle grades may be excluded. Table 8.2 lists other categories of teachers who are not able to participate. Thus, a situation is presented much like other kinds of evidence about teacher quality: Single data sources are not available that are appropriate for all teachers in a system. Therefore, a complex array of data sources is required, and no single data source should be promised as the end all indicator of teacher quality, even one so compelling as pupil achievement (Bingham, Heywood, & White, 1991)—documented so well by the TVAAS approach.

RECOMMENDED PROCEDURES

Four strategies for using pupil achievement data in teacher evaluation work well. The first strategy is for individual teachers to develop a local scheme for collecting and analyzing data on representative classroom goals. This procedure will be presented at the end of this chapter. The second approach is for the small number of teachers who can prepare a traditional, but technically rigorous, presentation of student-gain data on nationally normed standardized tests. These data must include residualized gains based on legitimate pretest data. The third strategy is to have the TVAAS procedure available for teachers to elect as their data for student

TABLE 8.1 Contributions and Gaps Afforded by Tennessee Value Added Assessment System

Problems Solved, Controlled, or Trivialized	*Problems Remaining*
Pupil gain adjusted for prior achievement	Not all teachers can use system
Family income, socioeconomic status	Previous year content may vary
Missing data (especially pretests)	Test content = universal desirable outcomes?
Pretest problems: cost, time, forms	Test content may not represent class content
Many concomitant variables can easily be added to analysis, such as class size	Testing may not include affective domain: content interests and attitudes, citizenship, civility, occupational development, psychosocial development
Wide variety of tests and domains can be included in assessment	Shorter term teacher effects (< 150 days) not included
	Side effects (e.g., attendance, vandalism) not addressed
	Delayed effects of individual teachers
	Activities of teachers that might be expected to greater future effectiveness not used
	"Teacher" = program, materials, relationship
	Norms are relative; value may be absolute

TABLE 8.2 Teachers for Whom TVAAS Is Not Available

Primary grade (K-2) teachers: Inappropriate testing, no 3-year longitudinal data
Grades 3-4: No 3-year longitudinal data
Teachers in subject areas without good tests
Teachers in subject areas that vary by year (e.g., adequacy of "biology," "chemistry," for "physics")
Teachers transferred from systems without comprehensive testing programs

achievement. These three approaches result in pupil achievement data as a separate data source. The fourth strategy is to include some student achievement data in another data source (e.g., peer review of materials or teacher as curriculum designer).

Basic Ideas in Using Pupil Achievement Data

The procedures for using pupil achievement data begin with the same safeguards as for any other data source. The individual teacher should elect to gather the information and inspect results before choosing to include them in his professional dossier for evaluation review. Student achievement data do not work well for all teachers in a school district, although they are a most compelling line of evidence for teacher quality. Once a teacher has decided to use achievement data, the collection, analysis, and presentation are the teacher's responsibilities.

Our advice differs from Stiggins's (1989) or Schalock, Schalock, Cowart, and Myton's (1993) in that we recommend that *some* teachers submit pupil achievement data for summative evaluation purposes. Other recommended practices for using pupil achievement data do follow Stiggins: A wide range of classroom assessment techniques should be considered and used by the teacher. Likewise, the literature for validity and reliability should be used by the teacher. The teacher should provide for as much pertinence and accuracy (validity concerns), dependability (reliability), and good sampling of time and numbers of students (validity and reliability) as he or she can. Such techniques are recommended in the next section of this chapter.

The procedures recommended here are for sampling of the teacher's ability to foster learning in students, and not an encyclopedic record of all of the achievement that can be attributed to the teacher. We are more interested in the potential of teachers than in recording all of the teacher's professional achievement. This is an important distinction for all participants to keep in mind. A final consideration is that most teachers will require substantial advice from consultants in the preparation of pupil achievement data.

Classroom-Based Achievement Data

Table 8.3 presents the recommended procedures for using pupil achievement data from the local development strategy. The teacher selects several year-long goals and several short-term (3- to 6-week duration) goals. He designs the evaluation procedure to include preinstruction assessment (tests, inventories, observations, work samples), goal or objective statements, postinstruction assessments, and explicit descriptions of the educational significance and benefits of the learning that has been measured. If possible, he collects comparison and control data to help Teacher Review Panels to understand the achievement information.

The first step of this strategy is for the teacher to identify several major goals for data gathering, analysis, and presentation. The major goals should be significant ones, such as the following:

The student reads a paragraph of grade-level-appropriate vocabulary and writes a similar length paragraph that incorporates a personal experience of the same topic.

TABLE 8.3 Steps for Classroom-Based Pupil Achievement Data Collection and Presentation

Step 1: Teacher selects and describes several measurable goals: three major class goals for the year and three major goals from a single teaching unit (3-6 weeks).

Step 2: Goals are validated as "major" and important by principal, department chair, *or* three peer teachers (choice of teacher under review, same grade-level or subject area assignment, *not* professional or social colleagues of teacher under review).

Step 3: Measures (assessments) are assembled. They may be teacher-made, departmental, or standardized. May be paper-and-pencil tests, inventories, performances, products, and objective item *or* subjective item, and norm or criterion referenced.

Step 4: The report should be limited to two pages of data, descriptions, comparisons, graphic representations, and validation statements.

Step 5: Include a brief statement from three peer teachers (other than in Step 2), describing the educational and professional significance and value of the data.

> Given a novel discrepant event, the student designs an experiment, including hypothesis testing, measurement, controls, and comparison.
>
> Given three word problems involving geometric relationships, the student (a) recalls the appropriate proof, (b) applies the proof to get a correct numerical solution, and (c) writes a word problem that calls for the same geometric principles.

The teacher should then write a measurement protocol, which clearly describes how pupil achievement is measured. The protocol should include instructions to students, timing schedule, sample scoring, and other criteria.

The goals and measurement protocol then are given to educators of the teacher's choice. These persons may be an instructional leader (such as principal, curriculum director, or department/grade-level chairperson) or three peer teachers. They write brief statements of the importance and value they see in the teacher's plans for student learning and assessment of gains. Time should be allowed by the teacher for revisions, and rereview if necessary. These educators serve a credibility function. The Review Panel needs authoritative reassurance that the goals and assessments are legitimate, important, and credible.

The teacher collects pre- and postinstruction scores or performance samples. Observer assistants can add credibility to this stage. Archiving individual student tests or production materials further documents the assessment. Next, the teacher prepares a data analysis and presentation document, which includes group average changes and visual data displays.

FORM 8.1 Classroom-Based Pupil Achievement Data

I.   Goals—sample goal statements
    A.   Long-term goals: (September data, May data)
        1.   Student performance goal:
        2.   Student achievement goal 1:
        3.   Student achievement goal 2:
    A.   Short-term goals: (October-November unit; pre-, postinstruction data)
        1.   Student performance goal:
        2.   Student achievement goal 1:
        3.   Student achievement goal 2:
II. Measures and Other Assessments—performance protocol and rubrics, test descriptions
    (teacher made or standardized)
    A.   Long-term performance:
    B.   Long-term achievement 1:
    C.   Long-term achievement 2:
    D.   Short-term performance:
    E.   Short-term achievement 1:
    F.   Short-term achievement 2:
III. Goal and Measurement Credentialing—statements about importance and value of
    (a) goals and (b) measures
    Signatures, titles, locations of (teacher chooses one): district curriculum director, principal,
    department chair, grade-level chair, or three peer teachers (3 needed)
IV. Data Analysis and Presentation—analysis by individual student, group averages,
    analysis by class subgroups (e.g., high and low achievers); data tabled, graphed,
    artifact archive
V.   Peer Statement About Results—three independent peer reviews of results
    (peers *not* included in III; peers selected by Evaluation Unit)

The final preparation step for teachers is to have three peers comment on the results. They should write brief statements to the merit and value of the results they have seen. This professional perspective is quite helpful for outside reviewers; no other persons are in as good a position for review as front-line teachers. Form 8.1 presents expectations for teacher data concerning pupil achievement.

Judgment of the teacher's pupil achievement data consists of a Review Panel determination that the teacher has been responsible for *some* important degree of valuable pupil achievement. Only a few cases will present enough data to show quantity and extent of pupil gain attributable to the teacher.

INTERNET RESOURCES

Consortium for Equity in Standards and Testing

http://www.csteep.bc.edu/ctest

Resources related to Classroom Testing

http://odl.fsu.edu/edf5443/resource.htm

Classroom Assessment Checklist

http://www.delta.edu/~library/html/a_checklist_for_avoiding_p
robl.html

Tennessee Value Added Assessment System (TVAAS)

http://www.shearonforschools.com/TVAAS_index.html

NOTE

1. Rules of thumb for levels of reliability coefficients are the following: above 0.92 if individual educational decisions are to be made about students; above 0.80 if group decisions are to be made (e.g., curriculum selection); down to 0.70 for research purposes, unless no alternatives are available; and below 0.50 is territory of little or no use except for population association trends.

9

Teacher Tests

T eacher tests are assessments of teacher knowledge. One type of teacher knowledge is the subject matter content (information, skills, attitudes) they teach to their students. Another type is what teachers know about teaching in schools; this includes knowledge about professional education issues (pedagogy), human development, communication, school organization and law, and the role of schools in society. Both types of knowledge play important roles in understanding overall teacher quality. Any one or combination of kinds of knowledge may be used by teachers to be good performers and to assist students to be good learners. Shulman (1987) included all these types of knowledge in a dynamic and complex model of "pedagogical reasoning and action."

Tests of teacher knowledge most often are standardized, paper-and-pencil assessment based on multiple-choice items (Harris, 1981; Madaus & Mehrens, 1990). More recent developments are performance or simulation tests that disclose applications of teacher knowledge (Delandshere & Petrosky, 1994; Glass, 1974; Haertel, 1990). Peterson (1987b) distinguished between two uses of testing for teachers. The first measures minimal qualification levels for admission to training programs or state licensure (Gunne & Peterson, 1990). Testing to ensure minimal competency in prospective professionals for the protection of clients is a common provision of state licensing (Fortune, 1985). The second use is comparative performance in which individuals are compared with population norms. This use of teacher tests is widely advocated but virtually nonexistent in teacher evaluation practice.

Teacher knowledge is not the same thing as teacher quality. However, that oversimplification is offered in debates over teacher testing. Teacher knowledge is most directly related to teacher quality as it affects pupil learning. As depicted in Figure 9.1, teacher knowledge has an important, but indirect, effect on student learning. Many factors in addition to teacher knowledge also play important roles in student learning.

If teacher knowledge is considered as a part of evaluation, care must be taken that the kind of content assessed is of high quality itself. It is not particularly useful to assess static information with little direct utility to the complex act of teaching. Table 9.1 presents desirable attributes of teacher knowledge.

Veteran teachers generally have little value for teacher tests as a part of teacher evaluation (Harris, 1981; Kauchak et al., 1985). They resist programs of teacher testing and do not show respect for colleagues who test well. On the other hand, many audiences for teacher evaluation, such as legislators and the lay public, do value tests. It is difficult for these audiences to understand teacher resistance when public schools use tests on an almost daily basis and other occupations so routinely use them for professional licensing (Peterson, 1985).

Advantages of Teacher Tests

Subject matter mastery, intellectual capacity for academic work, professional information, professional insight, basic academic skills, awareness of human development and cognition, and performance-knowledge potentials all are valuable resources for being an effective classroom teacher. Teacher knowledge plays a role in student learning that varies by student and situation from negligible to crucial. The role of teacher knowledge may be circuitous, context dependent, concomitant, and difficult to isolate and measure—but it nevertheless is an important part of quality teaching.

Paper-and-pencil tests are commonly used and accepted in this society (Harris, 1981). Tests for determination of professional quality are well known. For example, licensure tests for lawyers, physicians, dentists, accountants, and architects are commonly accepted assurances of competence and good practice (Fortune, 1985). Standardized tests are created by educators for schools and classrooms. Teachers are known to support and refer to tests for decision making with their pupils. Virtually everyone remembers testing as a part of his or her own school attendance. The question of whether we want to employ teachers who themselves test low is an-

Figure 9.1 Role of Teacher Knowledge in Pupil Learning

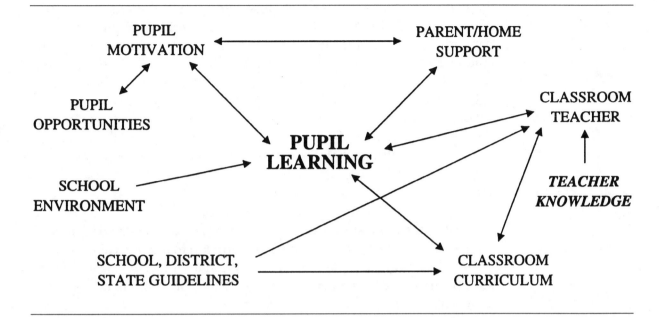

TABLE 9.1 Desirable Attributes of Teacher Knowledge

Up-to-date
Extensive
Available
Related to student knowledge
Applicable
Organized
Conceptualized
Rehearsed
Theoretical
Part of processes
Can be renewed

swered quite differently by different audiences such as lay public, legislators, teachers, parents, and principals (Peterson, 1985). Teacher resistance to testing creates the impression among many laypersons that teachers do not know their subject matter, are afraid of tests, and do not much care about quality ("Help! Teacher Can't Teach!" 1980; Lyons, 1979).

Standardized test scores have meaning in assessing the qualities of *some* veteran teachers (Harris, 1981; Peterson, 1987b) for several reasons. Some good teachers are good because they have a high level of verbal knowledge and are able to use it well in their teaching. High test scores, particularly on multiple choice or comprehension items, indicate strong reading ability. Knowledge of a significant amount of verbal subject matter can be assumed for those who score highly. In addition, good tests estimate abilities for application, analysis, and judgment. Strong test scores indicate *academic environmental wisdom*—a capacity to understand and follow directions and discern intent. This ability may serve teachers and their students well in school settings that are themselves primarily academic.

Disadvantages of Teacher Tests

Although there are several distinct values in teachers who score high on standardized tests, low test scores are difficult to interpret as clearly because there are other explanations in addition to deficient teacher knowledge (Hyman, 1984; Peterson, 1987b). There may be a poor match between knowledge used in classrooms and the content of the teacher test. Veteran teachers specialize in their content, and may forget other information that is in tests but inconsequential in their classroom. Also, test-taking ability is measured by tests, but is hardly worth rewarding by associating it with quality teaching. Another important reservation about using test scores in teacher evaluation is that although cultural bias has been addressed by test producers, criticisms of unfairness remain (Smith, 1984). The minor role of subject matter knowledge for some teachers (e.g., those who teach basic reading, basic science, basic mathematics) should be kept in mind. Finally, high test scores are not necessarily important for *all* teachers, because in many settings effective teaching comes from other characteristics such as interpersonal relations, motivation, hard work, creativity, and caring.

Many educators criticize standardized teacher tests, pointing to the narrow content and scope of current teacher tests, questionable validity, and the problem of some teachers who know their subject matter, but perform poorly on standardized paper-and-pencil tests (Glass, 1990; Hyman, 1984; Stedman, 1984). Critics say that tests are not fair for all teachers, for example, minorities, veteran teachers who have lost test-taking abilities through years of not taking tests, and good teachers who do not function well in a performance limited to 2 hours. They add that testing is associated with faulty generalizations such as "low test scores mean poor teachers, and high scores mean good teachers" or "test scores tell us *nothing* about teacher quality."

Disadvantages of Testing All Teachers or None

Current teacher evaluation practice is to test all teachers in a given category (e.g., applicants to teacher training, state licensing), or to test none (e.g., teachers in a school district, candidates for tenure). Current practice is not to test teachers for hiring, retention, leadership, promotion, or other rewards. This practice means that good teachers who do not test well are protected. However, if no tests are used, many audiences (e.g., legislators) are disappointed, and some veteran teachers lose the chance to document what for them is a valuable asset.

The current practice of either minimal competency tests for all or the use of no tests at all does not satisfy needs for information about teacher quality. For example, erratic and haphazard testing of teachers does not answer the question as to whether the profession has a share of the academically talented persons in the society (Schlechty & Vance, 1981). Although it is the case that good teaching comes from a variety of talents (care, hard work, resourcefulness, perseverance, creativity, intelligence), educators need to encourage the academically talented. Sociological research suggests that academic talent of the kind assessed by standardized tests is ignored, downplayed, or even negatively sanctioned by teacher culture (Lortie, 1975; Peterson, 1985, 1987b). Teacher tests can be used to acknowledge and reward a kind of teacher quality (academic competence) where currently only a disincentive exists.

Advantages of Testing at the Teacher's Option

Separate from the issue of minimal competency testing, standardized tests for teacher can be used to identify and acknowledge teachers who score highly (Peterson, 1987b). Teachers can self-select and choose among academic achievement, pedagogical knowledge, and other tests to present evidence that strengthens their case for quality. This use does not create a need to test all teachers, but only those who desire (or need) such recognition. It is unfair to deny test data to teachers whose excellence *can* be documented on tests. On the other hand, fairness does not necessarily mean that everyone gathers the same evidence but that all have an equal opportunity to demonstrate merit and worth (Strike, 1990).

The first advantage of optional testing is that teachers who use high levels of verbal knowledge as part of their quality work are able to get acknowledged for it. The second advantage is that the profession then has a mechanism to account for teacher knowledge, and to use it in the evaluation and reward systems (without disadvantaging some other teachers who do not use test scores); the teaching profession expresses its value and place for teacher knowledge. The third advantage for the society is that teacher knowledge is given a place in the view of the community: Teacher knowledge is valued and worthwhile.

Peterson (1984, 1987b; Peterson & Mitchell, 1985) called for optional use of teacher tests. Teacher evaluation systems that use multiple and variable data sources, such as presented in this book, create an opportunity for teacher-chosen use of teacher tests. This innovation enables school districts to use teacher tests and other controversial data sources. In optional use systems, teacher tests are not used for minimal protection, but for acknowledgment of a certain kind of quality (knowledge) in certain teachers. Such elective use results in greater participation, less teacher resistance and subversion, and increased risk taking (Peterson, 1987b).

SELECTED LITERATURE

Conceptual Studies

As described earlier, the testing of teachers may be done at screening periods (when candidates are admitted to teacher preparation programs, licensed prior to practice, or hired in school districts) or routinely during practice (to maintain the assurance that teachers know what they ought to know). This section will discuss the issues that arise for these distinctly different uses of teacher tests.

Issues Concerning Testing of Veteran Teachers

Glass (1974) recommended testing of high school teachers for subject matter knowledge as part of a multiple data source evaluation system. He argued that "there are minimum levels of subject matter knowledge below which teachers are incompetent to teach . . . it's hard to justify paying high wages to ignorant teachers" (p. 31). He suggested that such testing be repeated throughout a teacher's career. This practice should have the purpose of controlling for teacher misassignment; it should not be used to grade or rank teachers. His judgmental evaluation system included the collateral data of test scores along with expert observation of classroom behavior and pupil reports of the teacher.

Scriven (1981) critiqued a number of current practices in teacher evaluation. One particular problem is that of evaluating solely what is presented to students, and not what is learned by them. Another problem is that the content of the classroom (or the teacher) is not evaluated. He said that the emphasis on methods in schools of education, rather than including a strong assessment of the quality of content, has made schools of education "a laughingstock in the educational community, and increasingly in the total community" (p. 252). Correspondingly, the quality of a teacher's knowledge of content should be important in teacher evaluation.

Murray (1986) provided an extensive discussion of policy options for testing teachers. He listed four reasons to test teachers: limit number of incompetents, encourage professionalism, promote public confidence, and promote excellence. He identified five uses of teacher tests: admission to teacher training; licensing; job selection; recertification; and granting promotion, rewards, or special status. Another valuable analysis by Murray was identification of nine major pitfalls (and corresponding guidelines) of teacher testing programs. For example, districts may fail to establish clear purposes for the testing. The remedy guideline is to fully debate these policy issues among the interested audiences. A summarized listing of Murray's pitfalls of teacher testing programs and guidelines for effective practice is presented in Table 9.2.

Shulman's (1987) description of teacher knowledge is the most complex. First, he acknowledged that simple views of teacher knowledge miss the point about how teachers use their organized insight:

> Assessments of teachers in most states consist of some combination of basic-skills tests, an examination of competence in subject matter, and observations in the classroom to ensure that certain kinds of general teaching behavior are present. In this manner, . . . teaching is trivialized, its complexities ignored, and its demands diminished. Teachers themselves have difficulty in articulating what they know and how they know it. (p. 6)

Rather than a single domain of information for recall and direct application, Shulman described a much more complex and dynamic organization of teacher professional insight. His model of "pedagogical reasoning and action" included comprehension, transformation, instruction, evaluation, reflection, and new comprehension. He described a teacher's application of knowledge as starting with a text (syllabus, textbook, material), followed by an intellectual cycle through a unique kind of thinking to prepare, recall, sense, adjust, monitor, and integrate material for and with the student. Shulman's professional teaching knowledge or capacity comes from scholarship in the disciplines, materials and settings of the school in-

TABLE 9.2 Pitfalls and Guidelines of Teacher Testing

Pitfall	Guideline
1. Unclear purpose(s)	Debate policy goals; decide purposes(s)
2. Unrealistic expectations	Establish, test, get advice, plan for expectations; clearly state expectations
3. Inadequate funding	Plan, budget, fund realistically
4. Unrealistic timelines	Plan, schedule, document
5. Unresolved stakeholder differences	Identify, involve, use stakeholders
6. Unmet legal requirements	Know requirements, cases; follow and document procedures
7. Inadequate test security	Use standardized procedures
8. Low-incidence content areas	Cost-benefits analysis
9. Changing job requirements	Review recommendations annually

SOURCE: Summarized from Murray (1986). Used with permission.

stitution, research on teaching and learning, and the wisdom of practice itself.

According to Shulman (1987), the proper focus for assessment of teaching is on the "intellectual basis for teaching performance rather than on behavior alone" (p. 20). His recommendation for teacher evaluators is to get behind the manifest behavior to the regularized and internalized structures of thinking that underlie teacher decisions and actions. Shulman's acknowledged frame of reference from the psychologist Piaget translates the cognition of general thought to the specialized thought of the teacher. Thus evaluation of teacher knowledge calls for examination (by professionals) of teacher processing in an educational setting that *uses* subject matter knowledge, pedagogical planning, monitoring of learning, and teacher-learning from the situation itself.

Harris (1981) and Peterson (1985) analyzed the various political positions of agencies interested in teacher testing and found quite different points of view among audiences in the teacher testing debate. Tests for veteran teachers are desired by the lay public, legislators, and sociologists (e.g., Etzioni, 1969; Lortie, 1975). They are opposed by teachers' organizations such as the National Education Association and American Federation of Teachers (Harris, 1981). Teacher tests are not used by school districts for personnel evaluation. Tests for beginning teachers are favored by the lay public, legislatures, teachers' organizations, sociologists, and "middle persons" such as state offices of education and district persons who hire teachers. Mandated teacher tests for beginners are questioned by teacher training institutions, who desire autonomy and judgment in their preparation of teachers.

Issues Concerning Minimal Scores for Screening Teachers

Occupational licensing routinely includes standardized testing as a way to protect society from unknowledgeable practitioners (Shimberg, 1985). Late in the 19th century, the American Medical Association began to lobby legislators to require medical practitioners to be licensed by the states and to meet requirements of medical boards. Licensing is distinct from certification, which is a voluntary activity of professional or occupational agencies. Teacher testing as a part of state licensing is a relatively late addition, which may be surprising in light of the extensive use of standardized testing by teachers, and its rarity in the practice of other occupations.

Popham (1984) identified what he called the "Devil's Dilemma" of teacher testing in which "educators must set the passing standards on . . . competency tests high enough to satisfy the public's demand for quality, yet low enough so that certain constituencies are not systematically barred from the teaching profession " (p. 5). Popham recognized that one central reason for testing teachers is to assure the lay public that teachers know what they are supposed to know (mastery of basic skills). However, the public nonprofessional expectations often confuse the technical use of "cut" scores, which have the function of cutting off persons who are too low to function as teachers, with optimal scores, which describe high average levels of knowledge. If passing scores are set high enough to satisfy outside audiences, they almost assuredly are higher than needed to screen out actual poor performance due to low knowledge. High passing scores systematically will exclude some teachers who are good because of other factors, and not bad because they test relatively low. The performance of minorities on standardized testing is one example of this dilemma (Peterson et al., 1988). Well-functioning cut scores are quite low, and politically difficult to defend. Testing all teachers exacerbates this problem.

Empirical Studies

Veteran Teacher Knowledge Tests

Peterson (1987b) reported a study in which 297 veteran teachers selected teacher tests as one of several data sources in career ladder promotion and reward systems of three Utah school districts. This number was 29.7% of those participating in optional career ladder reward systems. Of those taking tests, 215 (72.4%) reported results to decision-making panels. The highest rate of test taking (39%) was in the district that paid for the tests. Test score rankings ranged from the 17th percentile to the 99th percentile (national norms). The median score for the total of 297 teachers was the 84th percentile for the appropriate test. The median score for the 274 successful (promotion or merit pay award) teachers was at the 86th percentile. The median score for the 23 (7.7%) unsuccessful teachers who took tests was at the 66th percentile; their individual rankings ranged from the 24th to the 98th percentile.

Although the trend in the Peterson (1987b) study was toward reward of those teachers who had high test scores, the result in individual cases was more complicated and interesting. Outlying examples included a teacher with a score at the 98th percentile who was denied reward and a teacher with a score at the 17th percentile who was given reward, both based on other data in their promotion dossiers:

> These outcomes may be discouraging to those seeking a simple answer to the problem of quality recognition and reward, but supportive of those who recognize the complexity of documentation of the qualities of teachers. High test scores should not be rewarded without corroborating evidence. Also, teachers who do not present high test scores should not be excluded from a consideration of quality. This logic is closer to what is known about good teaching than oversimplifications that tests tell all or nothing about teacher quality. (Peterson, 1987b, p. 22)

Because teacher evaluation is an important political event, there were several political outcomes to the Peterson study. First, a newspaper article stated, "297 Utah Teachers Strut Their Stuff, Score in Top 18% on National Test" (1986). Second, state legislators requested discussion of the results in an interim study session. Testimony included the observation that Utah teachers tested ahead of the students, so that resources should be used to reduce class size, improve programs for the most able students, and increase teacher morale.

> The use of teacher tests as demonstrated in this study may have positive professional and political implications. The focus on top performances provided by this study can be a good feature for the profession. A clear premium was created for high academic

achievement as evidenced by test scores. Public arguments about teacher testing can change from "We can't test teachers," which is not well understood by legislators and the lay public, to "We can't test *all* teachers, for several reasons." This latter argument is an easier one politically. (p. 22)

We can, and should, test to show and encourage high levels of teacher knowledge.

Administrator Assessment Center Performance Simulation Tests

Haertel (1990) described developments of teacher performance simulation tests. These "performance exercises" are "designed to elicit specific, expert teaching knowledge and skill" (p. 282). Haertel used examples from instructional vignettes (how to teach fractions with calculators to each of four average fifth-grade students), topic sequencing (17 mathematical topics such as ratios, common denominators, cross multiplying), documentary history (content, use in the classroom, instructional goal development), and other exercises (analysis of teacher lesson presented to six students, analysis of videotape of lesson in progress, textbook analysis, discussion of pedagogical strengths of three computational algorithms, evaluation of student papers).

These performance exercises have at least two advantages over more traditional multiple-choice tests for teachers. One strength is to include the element of *teacher application* along with the concern for *teacher knowledge of subject matter*. Another advantage is a more ecologically valid setting for assessment; the focus is on a classroom/pupil setting for demonstration of knowledge.

However, performance exercises have important limitations to keep in mind. Like all other standardized assessments, their goodness of fit for particular teachers and situations is not perfect; they are, after all, samples of general capacity rather than cross-sections of actual teacher work. Also, the application lacks the information and context of real students; teachers in actual classrooms use the knowledge they have about Chandra Billings and Jimmy Fredricks and recent classroom history to shape their applications of teacher and subject matter knowledge. The current interest in professional performance assessment tests for teachers, particularly as a part of national-level certification, has little empirical evidence at this point to suggest its effectiveness (Haertel, 1990). Although more time and effort are needed to permit such inquiry, preliminary evidence from a similar setting provides cautionary findings.

Educator assessment center performance simulation tests for prospective and practicing administrators have been studied empirically. Bryant (1990) reported that "the results of the . . . analysis . . . suggest the . . . Assessment Center does not capture the assumed expertise (experience) possessed by participants on many dimensions" (p. 359). The vast majority of correlations between center assessments and those in the field were below 0.15. Schmitt and Cohen (1990) reported relatively low criterion-related validity (0.20-0.40) both in their review of the literature and in their own empirical studies.

RECOMMENDED PROCEDURES

Teacher test scores should be an optional data source for documentation of teacher quality. School districts should take Murray's (1986) advice, presented in Table 9.2, about policy and planning for use of teacher tests. Debates and decisions about purpose, attention to details, and security of records are important. Additionally, teacher control over test score usage is essential. As described in Chapter 4, teachers should first choose to take tests for school district evaluation purposes (or to use prior test scores) without administrative knowledge. Then, teachers should inspect test results before deciding to include them in their professional dossiers.

A sample report for teacher test data is presented as Form 9.1. One document, with several supporting pages, is adequate to report all test information on the teacher. In this document (to be placed in a teacher's professional dossier) is information about the test(s), test company, population-norming information, and location of further information on the test(s). Also of interest are statements about how the test results are related to the teacher in question. Information about why the test scores are important is best provided by the teacher him- or herself. Finally, several supporting pages may include photocopies of test results.

Appropriate Tests

Several types of teacher tests are appropriate for classroom teachers. The most common are subject matter knowledge or professional knowledge examinations. Other kinds of tests that may have additional bearing on overall teacher quality include academic ability, basic academic skills performance, specialty area advanced tests (e.g., Graduate Record Examination), interest inventories, organizational theory tests, and the newer

---

FORM 9.1 Teacher Tests

Teacher name:
School address:

Test 1:
Test:
Test information:
Test description:
Date of test:
Scores:
    Raw:
    Normed:
Statement of pertinence:

Test 2:
Test:
Test information:
Test description:
Date of test:
Scores
    Raw:
    Normed:
Statement of pertinence:

---

performance exercises. In every case, it is the responsibility of the individual teacher not only to arrange for the test scores but to justify explicitly the meaning of the scores for her case. This means that the teacher is responsible to select tests, describe their role in the quality picture, and show links to her practice.

District Logistics

Teachers can arrange on their own to take many kinds of teacher tests at regional testing centers, most often local universities. This location has the advantage of teacher anonymity. In addition, district Evaluation Units can schedule and arrange supervision for many kinds of teacher tests to be given in the district itself. This has the advantages of showing district values for testing, being more convenient in location for many teachers, and simplifying the logistics of test administration for many participants. Most often, local administration costs will be slightly higher than for regional testing centers.

The district has responsibilities to have an Evaluation Unit that is knowledgeable and capable for supporting teacher activity. It also is responsible for having Teacher Review Panels that are able to interpret and use teacher test scores. Review panels need to know the advantages and limitations of teacher tests.

Costs

Teacher test costs include testing fees, facilities for district-based testing, and some personnel costs for monitoring tests. Tests themselves may cost in the $25.00 to $45.00 range. However, these costs are not annual but may require updating every 5 to 7 years for the greatest credibility. Also, not all teachers in a school district will use tests. In field tests, Peterson (1989c) found that 29.2% of teachers elected to take teacher tests as an optional data source for career ladder reward. Thus the cost estimate for teacher tests was $2.35 per teacher per year in a school district.

Districts can control test usage costs by paying for test costs if usage is low, and sharing test costs if usage is high. The cost percentage thus ranges between 100% teacher responsibility to 100% district subsidy. This is a policy decision best made by each local district, depending on its needs to initiate or maintain teacher testing levels.

INTERNET RESOURCES

Educational Testing Service, PRAXIS series for teachers, Graduate Record Exam

http://www.ets.org

Massachusetts teacher tests

http://www.doe.mass.edu/teachertest/info_booklet/
TSTINFO_toc.html

http://www.doe.mass.edu/teachertest/info_booklet/
TSTINFO_subj.html

Controversies on testing teachers

http://www.csmonitor.com/durable/1998/07/03/p1s2.htm
http://www.familyeducation.com/article/0,1120,5-7156,00.html

Educational Policy Analysis Annals

> http://epaa.asu.edu/epaa/v7n4/

FairTest

> http://www.fairtest.org/empl/ttcomp.htm

The Massachusetts News

> http://www.massnews.com/mtafear.htm

Study for Wyoming Legislature

> http://legisweb.state.wy.us/school97/post/reports/taer.htm

10

Parent Reports

Parents and guardians play an important role in student learning, and they are a significant audience for teacher performance (Epstein, 1985; Peterson, 1984). Parent reports of teachers are systematic collections of information about parent or guardian perspectives on teacher quality. Tools to collect parent views include survey forms, interviews, and focus groups. Defensible use of parent reports avoids using them on *all* teachers, haphazard statements of individuals, certain topics (e.g., classroom events), and judgments not balanced with other information (e.g., peer review of achievement data, teacher test scores, or student surveys).

Advantages

Parents are in a good position to assess their own interactions with the teacher and to know about the student's reaction to the teacher's performance. Although parent reports give an indirect view of the classroom, they provide a direct view of the set of teacher duties dealing with parents (Gestwicki, 1987; Murphy, 1987; Scriven, 1988) and of student reactions to the teacher expressed outside of the classroom. Systematic (valid and reliable) inclusion of parental views in teacher evaluation recognizes the partnership of parents in education. Parents are clients and taxpayers; the rights of consumers have been established in evaluation practice (Mark & Shotland, 1985).

Parents are involved in current teacher evaluation practice; however, parent input in most school districts consists of haphazard, unreliable single-case reports, hearsay, and single-issue- or single-event-driven involvement (Lortie, 1975; Peterson, 1989b). Teachers are at risk of inaccurate and unfair evaluation when information is unsystematically gathered and reported. To develop valid and reliable parent participation, as described in this chapter, is to strengthen and make more useful an already present data source for teacher evaluation. Systematic parent report data are economical, usually well respected by teachers, and most often very positive and supportive of teachers (Epstein, 1985; Peterson, 1989b, 1989c).

Disadvantages

There are substantial arguments against parent participation in teacher evaluation for all teachers. Most teachers are familiar with instances of negative parent influence based on hearsay complaints and unrepresentative episodes, and the disruption and threat they bring to teachers' livelihood (Lortie, 1975). Popularity with parents is positive but not compelling in determining teacher excellence. Although in many cases parents are expert in raising their own children, they are not expert at classroom teaching. There are significant problems with comparing parent views of teachers of different age students because of the large variation in parent interests according to pupil age (Peterson, 1989b).

Although parent relations and some parent involvement are a part of the duties of any classroom teacher, it should be recognized that some excellent teachers go little beyond a minimum of activity in this area. Good teaching does not directly equal exceptional reactions from parents. Unless teachers are recruited to work with adults, hired to work with adults, given specific preservice and inservice training in working with adults, and are rewarded for working with adults, we should not expect all teachers to emphasize parent relations and reactions in their evaluation.

SELECTED LITERATURE

Conceptual Studies

Some arguments for parent participation are formalized in the evaluation concepts of *stakeholder evaluation*. Mark and Shotland (1985) described two dimensions of stakeholders in evaluation: power and legitimacy. Stakeholders are involved in evaluation in the sense of power because of their capacity to affect the enterprise. In the case of teacher evaluation, parents clearly influence pupil achievement, and they can support (or disrupt) teacher performance. Groups may be included in the second sense of legitimacy because they have substantive contributions to add to the process or outcome. Parents can present *some* important information about teacher quality. For either dimension, the decision to include stakeholder groups in evaluation is a value judgment. Problems may arise if the only purposes are peremptory involvement of parents (e.g., to avoid criticism) or pseudo-empowerment to achieve a diversionary façade of participation. Mark and Shotland provided guidelines for appropriate and effective stakeholder participation in evaluation. They emphasized the necessity to (a) set aside sufficient time, (b) provide training, (c) acknowledge contributions, and (d) set clear limits to the involvement.

Lortie (1975) described sociological concerns about parent-teacher relations that complicate the evaluation process. Essentially, parents and teachers have different points of view that cloud the relationship. For example, parents see the child as a prized individual, whereas the teacher must see the child as a member of a class group. Parents may fear that the child has told the teacher embarrassing family secrets; the teacher resents the intrusion of parents on valuable teaching time. Both experience the fact that most parent-teacher meetings are nonproductive. Teachers are not awarded for good work with adults, only when they appear to control students and get work out of them. Other examples of difficulties in parent-teacher relationships are that teachers resent the power to disrupt possessed by parents, whereas parents envy the authority and influence possessed by teachers. Relationships between teachers and parents are not the simple, positive, cooperative, and unambiguous interactions pictured in some idealistic stereotypes.

Empirical Studies

Epstein (1985) reported a landmark study of parent views in teacher evaluation. She correlated principal ratings of 77 teachers with those of 1,051 parents of their students. She found that higher parent ratings are associated with teachers who (a) involve parents with learning activities at home, (b) provide ideas for them, (c) send them communications, (d) improve parents' understanding of the school program, and (e) send the message that parents should help learning at home.

Epstein (1985) found a correlation of 0.27 between parent and principal ratings of teachers. She concluded that parents and principals base their judgments on different dimensions of teacher performance. Principal ratings are influenced by situational factors (conditions of difficulty or support) and the extra work that establishes some teachers' leadership within the school. Parent ratings are influenced by connections teachers make with families, the quality of classroom life their children experience, and by resources and ideas offered to parents by the teachers. Among other findings was that the variation among ratings increased with the grade level. Epstein (1985) concluded that "parents can make valuable contributions in the evaluation of teachers" (p. 3) because they have an important perspective on performance and provide another view of excellence. She called for the use of multiple judges in teacher evaluation.

Peterson (1987a) studied the correlations between parent survey ratings of 252 teachers and other data sources. He found the parent ratings to correlate at 0.09 with principal ratings and at 0.58 with pupil ratings of the same teachers. He concluded that parent and principal ratings "showed independence from one another" and that these data sources "may have assessed different constructs of quality" (p. 316).

Peterson (1989b) analyzed the parent surveys used by 337 K-12 teachers in two school districts having career ladder systems. More than 12,000 individual parent rating forms were used in this study. He found that 48.1% of the teachers (of the 701 teachers in the career ladder program) used the surveys as an elective data source. The average rating and return rate by grade level are presented in Table 10.1. The correlation between the global rating of teachers by individual over 2 years was 0.41 (the same teacher population student report stability was 0.67). Parent surveys were spontaneously reported as valuable feedback by 76.6% of the teachers. Parent comments were seen by a substantial number as "helpful or more helpful than the global item ratings for understanding parent reactions to their classes" (p. 246).

Ostrander (1995) found that parent ratings of teachers differed from teacher self-ratings and administrator ratings. She reported that parents viewed teachers in a positive light but were more critical than administrators. She found a significant degree of agreement between students' and parents' rank ordering of teachers. Ostrander concluded that "the fairest and most comprehensive performance appraisals may involve multiple judges, each offering a unique perspective on teacher effectiveness" (p. ii). Stronge and Ostrander (1997) recommended client surveys, including parents, as a state-of-the-art remedy for deficiencies in most current teacher evaluation practice. The authors argue for collaboration, legitimacy of judgment, and practicality of data gathering; they presented several prototypical forms.

RECOMMENDED PROCEDURES

Survey Form

A survey rating form is an effective means for determining parent opinions about teacher performance. Form 10.1 was used in field tests of

TABLE 10.1 Parent Ratings and Return Rates by Grade Level

Grade Level	Mean Rating[a] (SD)	% Return Rate (SD)
K-3	4.72 (.18)	86.2 (.10)
4-6	4.63 (.23)	85.3 (.12)
7-9	4.35 (.37)	60.8 (.15)
10-12	4.48 (.26)	46.0 (.20)

SOURCE: Peterson (1988).
a. Global item, 5-point scale (highest ratings is 5).

teacher evaluation for career ladder promotion (Peterson, 1989b). The survey form and a cover letter by principal or district Evaluation Unit are mailed to parents, with a school-addressed, stamped envelope. An alternative distribution method is to have parents fill out forms as a part of their regular parent-teacher meetings. This procedure saves mailing costs but produces some alteration in results because of the influence of the meeting itself.

For elementary school teachers, all parents should have an opportunity to complete forms. For multiple-class teachers (middle and high school), a representative sample of three classes is sufficient.

Teacher Control of Survey Use and Review

As with other data sources described in this book, it is important that the safeguards of Chapter 4 be used with parent surveys. First, the individual teacher should decide if parent surveys are to be made. Second, the survey should be conducted, scored, and reported by a third party (preferably an Evaluation Unit) other than the teacher him- or herself or the principal supervisor. Third, the teacher should inspect the results summary and decide whether to include it in his or her dossier for Teacher Review Panel inspection. If the teacher decides not to use the survey results, all original forms, scoring sheets, and summary reports should be given to the teacher—and no records kept of their use.

Interpreting Survey Results

The report form presents numbers of responses, class averages on each of the nine items, and verbatim copies of comments. The global item (Item 9, "Were you satisfied with your daughter's or son's overall classroom experience as provided by this teacher?") is used as the central datum for evaluation decisions. Comments may be included with the item results

FORM 10.1 Parent Survey

Teacher's name _____

Your child's teacher has asked for a survey of parents so that he or she can see your opinions. Please check the following items that describe your experience with the teacher. No individual parents will be identified with these survey forms. Thank you for helping.

Have you asked the teacher for: Yes   No

      1. An overview of class content and goals?   ___   ___

      2. Description of student's progress?   ___   ___

      3. Ideas for home support of learning?   ___   ___

Has the teacher provided you with:

      4. An overview of class content and goals?   ___   ___

      5. A description of your child's progress?   ___   ___

      6. Ideas for home support of learning?   ___   ___

For each of the following, circle the number that best describes your opinion:

	Yes				No	Don't know
7. Did your child seem to know what was expected of him or her in this class?	5	4	3	2	1	0
8. Did the classroom work seem to be the right challenge, not too hard or too easy?	5	4	3	2	1	0
9. Were you satisfied with your daughter's or son's overall classroom experience as provided by this teacher?	5	4	3	2	1	0

Comments for teacher (and his or her professional file if he or she chooses):

for the dossier, or they may be excluded. A good ground rule for use of comments is to include them all, or exclude them all, but not to select among them for reporting in the professional dossier.

Another ground rule for deliberation about the survey results is to include levels of parent interest (reflected in Items 1-3) in judgments about teacher performance (Items 4-9). Classes in which parent interest and involvement are high should be expected to be matched by high teacher activity and communication with parents. Correspondingly, classrooms with little parent interest might be well matched by teacher activity higher than the parents, but lower than other classrooms with more parent interest.

Minimal return rate expectations should be established and publicized. Some teachers, particularly at the high school level, may have difficulty in getting representative numbers of returned surveys. This may happen outside of their control and regardless of the quality of teacher performance. Too few parent survey results can make interpretation difficult or inaccurate. A specific percentage, for example, 60% or two thirds, should be established as district policy for expected return reliability.

Perspectives about specific item results should take into account a number of factors. Results will vary significantly by age of pupil. District and school averages will vary according to parent populations. Some teachers show great stability in results year after year, whereas others vary yearly, according to external circumstances. Teacher Review Panels have demonstrated their capacity to take these mitigating factors into account when judging teacher quality (Peterson, 1988, 1990b).

As with other data source results, it takes time and experience for teachers to interpret parent survey data. Field tests have shown that teachers unfamiliar with objective teacher performance data are unrealistic in their own expectations for results. Several years of experience are required for teachers to understand that less than perfect (5.0) ratings are usual and positive. In fact, reports below the district averages still encompass good practice. Field studies have indicated that more than 70% of field test teachers were well appreciated by parents. This means that a number of "below average" teachers are providing quality performance; the term *average* must acquire new meaning in the context of teacher evaluation and thinking about teacher performance.

Frequency

As with any other data source, most teachers do not have to gather information about parents every year. Beginning teachers may want formative information for several years in succession, after their first year of teaching. Once a veteran teacher has established a pattern of parental responses, occasional monitoring every 3 years is adequate, This is particularly true for teachers who have consistency in their parent surveys.

An exception to maintenance monitoring is the opportunity for teachers to establish baseline parent response data, then to enrich their parent involvement practice and gather subsequent data to look for changes. This practice can encourage teachers and support improved parent relations.

Costs

In the field studies (Peterson, 1989b, 1989c), parent surveys cost 44 cents per student for mailing and $2.50 per class for aide time, for an approximate cost of $15.00 per class. Time requires was approximately 5 minutes for teachers and 20 minutes for the aide per class.

Focus Groups

An option to surveys for data collection about parent views are focus groups (Krueger, 1988; Morgan, 1988). This strategy will collect additional information, allow teachers to try out ideas, and increase the amount of two-way communication. Focus groups will not be as representative of overall parent reaction to teachers (small samples are usually involved), but they do have the potential to create more ideas and topics for understanding the work of teachers. Focus groups should be arranged, conducted, and interpreted by persons other than the teacher.

Focus groups are helpful for some teachers, especially after surveys have been made. Focus groups help to fill in specific details about performance, for example, exactly which teacher strategies were best for helping parents to support home learning. These findings have great value for formative teacher evaluation. They also may be of assistance for evaluation of special teacher populations, such as teachers having difficulty, teacher leader selection, or teachers at a promotion time in their careers.

Focus group meetings should be designed as a positive, productive, and satisfying experience for the parent participants. A natural environment, such as a home or neutral setting in a school library, is important for good discussion and idea development. Focus group membership should be from 6 to 10 persons. The goal of a focus group meeting is not agreement and consensus but production of new ideas and perspectives for the teacher. Focus groups are different from other data-gathering strategies in that a central goal is to have participants influence each other *during* the session with social interaction and interplay of ideas. It is best if the parents or guardians do not know each other previously—preexisting social status can be a barrier to a productive group.

School districts may assign members of the Evaluation Unit to lead focus groups. Another staffing possibility is to solicit volunteer teachers to conduct sessions for other teachers (with whom they have no social or professional contacts). Coleaders can ensure reliable note recording and productivity of sessions. The task of the focus group leader is to moderate, listen, observe, and record. The session should be based on a small number of predetermined, but open-ended questions and follow-ups. Some examples are the following: "In what ways does this teacher effectively communicate with you?" "What are some practices that should continue or increase?" and "What is one change this teacher could make for the better?" Resulting notes and audiotapes are content analyzed for central ideas. Rather than an encyclopedic report of the session, good focus group reports highlight a workable number of ideas for use of the teacher and evaluators. The report should be limited to a single page.

INTERNET RESOURCES

Davis School District, Utah

   http://www.davis.edu/stafdev/eas/index.htm

Williamsburg-James City County Public Schools, Virginia

   http://admin.sbo.wjcc.k12.va.us/public/teacheval.html

11

Documentation of Professional Activity

Documentation of professional activity summarizes important preparation and credentials for teaching, current inservice efforts to maintain and update professional skills and knowledge, and performance of ancillary duties expected of the teacher. Professional activity describes the background of the teacher, things done to prepare for classroom teaching, and nonclassroom responsibilities, such as participation in school governance and professional organizations. Documentation of strong professional activity is a good indicator that a teacher is prepared to teach well, works to keep quality performance, and is up to date in his or her practice. In addition, it shows that the teacher supports good practice of colleagues, participates in the larger school program, and contributes toward educational concerns outside of the classroom.

Documentation of professional activity addresses one important part of teacher quality. Teachers are good professionals when they do activities like those listed in Table 11.1. A teacher does not have to do all of these to be considered a good professional, but certainly should exhibit substantial and significant activity in this direction.

TABLE 11.1 Activities of Teachers With Good Professional Performance

Take initiative to get best quality curriculum and instruction

Evaluate their teaching systematically and objectively

Systematically improve and update their practice

Give and get advice from colleagues

Show concern about the quality of their work

Think about the implications of their teaching

Are self-critical about their practice

Support colleagues in good work

Support the larger school program

Take responsibility for education concerns outside of their classroom

Advantages

Advantages of documenting professional activity are that it is an expected part of the teacher's role, good professional preparation is at least an indirect indicator of teacher performance, professional activity affects the performance and morale of colleagues, teachers care about a record of their efforts, and documentation is inexpensive.

A comprehensive view of quality for teacher evaluation encompasses as many expected duties as possible (Murphy, 1987; Scriven, 1988). Included in teacher duties are service on committees, collaborative program planning, student supervision out of the classroom, and relations with the community. More generally, teachers are expected to participate in organizations that further subject matter knowledge or general professional welfare. Good evaluation specifically includes information on these topics and does not rely on a secondary person's recollection, such as in administrator report evaluations.

One view of teacher quality concerns the preparation of a teacher. This dimension includes such things as "Has the teacher studied the *subject matter content* she is to teach?" Evidence for quality may consist of a list of university courses in subject areas, backed by official transcripts. Another example of professional preparation is inservice courses on methods of teaching. The assumption is that a teacher who has specific training in classroom organization, discipline, or instructional procedures is at least somewhat more likely to perform well than a person who has not. Of course, the ultimate proof is in the classroom performance and student learning. However, the concern in teacher evaluation is to get as much good evidence as possible; at times, data concerning preparation for teaching are the best evidence available. Research shows that the people who judge the data, such as review panelists, are able to distinguish between primary indicators of quality (e.g., pupil gain or parent satisfaction) and secondary indicators (e.g., *preparation* for pupil gain or parent satisfaction; Peterson, 1988, 1990b).

Still another advantage of including professional activity in teacher evaluation is that it recognizes and encourages positive efforts that assist other teachers and the larger school organization. A teacher who shares her knowledge can help the performance and morale of other teachers. A teacher who studies school organization issues is in a position to give ideas to school reform committees. A teacher who participates in a community activity extends the influence and recognition of herself and other teachers.

Documentation of professional activity is desirable because it costs relatively little to do. Once teachers have prepared extensive resumes, annual updates require little time, virtually no materials, and no need for others to be involved.

Finally, attention to professional activity in teacher evaluation is an advantage because teachers care deeply about recognition for these efforts. One need only talk to teachers to understand the importance of activity recognition. Most teachers spend considerable time and effort to attend inservice training, are involved with colleagues, and represent their schools and professions at various meetings. In current practice, no one is responsible for documenting and recognizing this activity. Teachers may assume that their districts keep track of courses taken and institutes attended, but they do not.

It is important to specifically document professional activity apart from mere mention in administrator reports. Peterson (1987a), in a study of 214 classroom teachers, found that teacher-made records of professional activity frequency correlated at $r = -0.11$ with the overall rating of teacher equality made by their principals. This small but statistically significant negative relationship indicates problems with current levels of recognition for important teacher professional activity.

Disadvantages

Care must be taken to give the proper perspective to the role of professional activity in overall teacher quality. The main teacher responsibilities, activities, duties, and payoffs are in the classroom. Mere totals of outside experience and contributions do not necessarily contribute to classroom teaching effectiveness.

Credentials do not assist in evaluating the immediate, manifest performance quality of teachers. For example, associations between credentials and student learning have been found to be weak (Guthrie, 1970) or nonexistent (Rosenbloom, 1966) for several reasons. First, training programs and courses may be directed toward specific abilities that are not assessed by the measures of teaching effectiveness. Second, credentialed backgrounds do not affect in a systematic way any specific categories of behavior across populations of teachers. A third reason for the lack of a direct connection between credentials and teacher quality is the individual nature of the teaching act. Each teacher operates in the classroom based on unique and perhaps idiosyncratic structures of teaching knowledge, skill, and attitude. It is difficult to parcel out individual, specific contributors to these underlying structures and then to demonstrate a relationship with concrete, manifest teaching performances. Experience, by itself, or a particular academic background, by itself, has not been found to be a detectable contributor to teaching ability. This conclusion, in terms of teacher evaluation, is not surprising; parallels exist in other professions. Although degrees in law, medicine, architecture, or business assure minimal levels of competence, the level of performance quality within these licensed populations varies considerably.

As with other data sources, it should be recalled that not all possible dimensions of teaching define all instances of good practice. Excellent teaching can exist with undocumented or relatively little professional activity. There are instances of teachers responsible for high levels of student learning and positive responses from students, parents, and administrators who perform only the minimally expected duties outside of their classroom. Valuable teaching can come from teachers who engage in relatively little professional activity. Also, a detailed accounting of trivial and barely relevant activity is not, by itself, a major part of teaching quality. However, field studies (Peterson, 1988) suggest that Teacher Review Panels have little difficulty distinguishing between pertinent professional activity and its role in teacher quality, and lists of irrelevant busywork.

RECOMMENDED PRACTICES

As with other data sources, each teacher should decide whether documentation of professional activity helps to make his case for quality performance. If he does, he should assemble and maintain two documentation tools. First, a professional activity records file may contain documents, lists, letters, program descriptions, resumes, job descriptions, transcripts, test score reports, and clippings. It should range in size from an accordion folder to a storage box. Second, a dossier entry on professional activity should reduce this information collection to no more than two pages.

Specific entries for documenting professional activity many include

- A list of classes taken, with dates and description (transcripts can be included in records file)
- A list of professional organization memberships and offices held
- A list of education-related community activities and role descriptions
- Descriptions of particular ways that colleagues have been assisted, including names, topics, locations, dates, and phone numbers
- Descriptions of special services performed for school or district
- A list of visits and consultations, with names and dates
- A list of special training activities
- Evidence of successful completion of advanced degrees

Sample presentation for an individual teacher appears as Form 11.1.

Teachers can begin their documentation by a thorough review of their own records; it is not likely that others, such as school districts, have much comprehensive information. Then, the teacher can write the first extensive resume, including the suggested information above. It is best to use a computer word processing format for future updating and revision. Next, a two-page summary is prepared for the dossier. Finally, a selection of primary materials is made for storage in the backup folder or box.

An annual update and revision of the documents keeps them current and avoids losing track of activities and accomplishments. For most teachers, this activity is a concrete, satisfying affirmation of their time and energy expenditures. For other teachers, it is a time of consideration and reflection for increased professional involvement.

Costs and Teacher Usage

Field test teachers estimated the first-time preparation of professional activity lists and folders to take several hours, best spread over several work sessions (Peterson, 1989c). They estimated a time cost of 1 hour per year to maintain and update their professional activity records. This included duplication of documents, list typing, phone calls for confirmation, and organization of materials into statements and folders. The estimated cost per teacher was $2.00 per year. Professional activity documentation was a very popular optional data source, with over 90% of the teachers electing to collect and use these data.

FORM 11.1 Sample Documentation of Professional Activity (excerpts)

Teacher: Mary Samuels

School: Richardson Elementary, Riverside School District

Assignment: 3rd grade

Former school: King City, 1988-90

Education preparation:

        B.A., history, Northern Oregon State College, 1988

        Teacher Licensure, Graduate Teacher Education Program, Central Oregon State College, 1989

        M.Ed., Central Oregon State College, 1989; Project: "Professional networks"

Inservice education:

Math in the Mind's Eye	Portfolios of student writing
Cooperative learning	Caring communities
Storyline	Discipline With Love and Logic
Oregon Writing Project	Judicious Discipline

School committee service:

Playground redesign	Parent-Teacher Discipline
Curriculum articulation committee	Public relations presentations
PTA	

District committee service:

Curriculum articulation	Parent-Teacher Discipline
Transitions to Site Councils	Public relations
KCEA Building representatives	

Professional colleague contact (excerpts):

Teacher Jim Whittaker	Lincoln	Team teaching	1/14/90
Teacher Sandy Janes	King City	Team teaching	2/2/90
Counselor Ben Taggert	King City	Schoolwide discipline	3/24/91
Teacher Seth Everts	Lincoln	Schoolwide discipline	3/26/91
Teacher Betty Thomas	Lincoln	Community contracts	4/18/91
Principal Judy Haymore	King City	Schoolwide discipline	

Community activities (related to teaching):

Public relations:

King City Kiwanis Club	1992
King City Rotary	1992
City Council, King City	1992

12

Systematic Observation

Systematic observation is a process in which a classroom observer records the visible performance of a teacher and an expert analyzes the record using some conceptual framework. This technique, usually performed by the principal, is the most common form of teacher evaluation (Lewis, 1982; McGreal, 1983; Stodolsky, 1984). Evertson and Burry (1989) said that "the classroom observation is probably the single most important element in systems that assess the competence of classroom teachers" (p. 297). The intuitive appeal of classroom observation is great: A direct look at the teacher in action with students seems to afford good information for judging teacher quality. However, research has consistently revealed problems with assessing teachers by direct observation. Careful conceptual analysis led Scriven (1981) to say that "using classroom visits . . . to evaluate teaching is not just incorrect, it is a disgrace" (p. 251).

Advantages

Some good teachers are good because their manifest behaviors (classroom moves) help students learn and can be documented by systematic observation. For example, some teachers are effective because they model new learning for their pupils in a way in which it is easy for students to acquire. Evertson and Holley (1981) claimed that views of classroom climate, rapport, interaction, and functioning are provided by systematic observation better than by any other data source.

Transcripts of actual classroom sessions are compelling evidence for outsiders to consider in their deliberations of quality. One can look at transcripts for use of time, wide involvement of students, and appropriate responses of teachers to student statements (Borich, 1990). Good systematic observation data are useful for many teachers as formative information. Patterns of using time, interaction with students, and communication are made available for teachers to analyze and consider for improvements.

Disadvantages

Watching a classroom teacher in action is not the best way to determine teacher quality. Visits are disruptive to normal class operation, student participation, and teacher behavior. What you see in classroom visits is not what you get in routine teacher performance (McLaughlin, 1990). Good, reliable observation data are difficult to get, and they are an expensive line of evidence about teacher quality (Peterson, 1989c). There is not even good agreement about what to look for when in the classroom. Also, classroom observation reports most often are inaccurate because of observer style preferences, sociological role conflicts, social biases, and political axes to grind.

Classroom observations for teacher evaluation show still other problems. For example, although observation data may capture the immediate events of the classroom, they do not present the nonobservable forces that shape the manifest behavior. As stated by the advocates of classroom observation Evertson and Burry (1989):

> Observations do not take place in a vacuum; they are a function of environments—social, psychological, political, organizational, and physical. All of these environment co-occur and impact what happens in the classroom. Observational methods that are sensitive to these contexts and are still efficient enough to be used in large numbers of classrooms are extremely rare. (pp. 297-298)

Finally, it is important to understand that not all good teachers are good because their immediate, manifest classroom behavior fits a given conceptual framework for most desired practice. Some very good teachers (i.e., having good levels of student learning, positive colleague reviews of materials, great respect of students and parents, and extensive professional activity) are quite technically awkward. For example, they may not model new learning for their pupils, but otherwise allow student initiation, discovery, and interaction for acquisition of the subject matter. For these teachers, observation gives a misleadingly low measure of overall quality.

What Makes Observation Systematic?

Before reviewing selected literature concerning the data source of systematic observation, it is important to limit the activity to a technically defensible format. Not all classroom visits can be called systematic observation. In fact, little or none of what passes for observation data gathering for teacher evaluation qualifies under the technical standards for observational data. The following criteria are minimal requirements for systematic observation data to be used in teacher evaluation (Peterson & Kauchak, 1982):

1. The observer is a neutral outsider to the school system, trained in observation techniques, having established reliability, and monitored for ongoing reliability.
2. Observations are taken from a reliable number and timing of visits. Number of visits is based on stability (regularity) of teacher performance. Often this means six to eight or more unannounced visits.
3. Focus of observation is limited to a few categories of events, and not a wide-ranging collection of attractive but elusive, high-inferential themes.
4. Recording systems (checklists, narratives) are systematic, verifiable, permanent, and have reliability in practice established.
5. Data are analyzed with a single, coherent, limited, public, validated, and agreed-on conceptual framework, linked to student learning.

Absence of any of these requirements, for example, by using a building administrator to cut costs, fatally threatens the fairness, accuracy, and credibility of systematic observation. Good systems of systematic observation can be devised to contribute data for teacher evaluation, but they are expensive and technically difficult to construct. As with other data sources presented in this book, individual teachers should decide to have systematic observation data collected, and then inspect the results before including them in professional dossiers.

SELECTED LITERATURE

Limitations of Teacher Evaluation by Looking

The first problem with judging teachers by observation is that there is no single set of practices, behaviors, strategies, or events by which we can judge the value of teacher performances (Centra, 1977; Peterson, 1984; Rebell, 1990). Braskamp (1980), in a review of the research literature on the components of teaching, concluded that because "there is no one standard in which effective teaching can be evaluated, diversity in teaching styles is to be advocated" (p. 63). He also concluded that "the definition of teaching effectiveness is contingent upon the expectations and instructional goals of the institution, the type of students enrolled, course goals, and the instructor's teaching style" (p. 64). He recommended, as an alternative to evaluation by observation, use of a variety of perspectives derived from multiple data sources. Thus it is clear that great caution must be taken in selecting, analyzing, and making claims for classroom observation systems and data. There is general agreement that classroom observation provides quite limited data on questions about teacher quality, in spite of (a) the great intuitive appeal of "evaluating by looking" and (b) the vast preponderance of observation-based systems in current teacher evaluation practice (Lewis, 1982; Manatt & Daniels, 1990; Manatt & Manatt, 1984; McGreal, 1983; Stodolsky, 1984).

Scriven (1981) was clear about why classroom visits should not be used for the evaluation of teaching. First, visits change the teaching performance itself. Announcing the visit ahead of time makes the alteration worse. Second, a visit (or even several) is just too small a sample of the teaching behavior to make any judgment. Third, the personal and social relations between observer and teacher (positive or negative) threaten the accuracy of reports. Fourth, research has produced no systematic links between what is observed in a classroom and student learning. Fifth, observers believe that their biases for certain teaching styles actually do represent a standard for good teaching; in reality, biases destroy a common ground for judging teacher quality. Finally, classroom visitors simply do not think the way that students do. In the long run, student perception of the classroom affects their learning, not the view of short-term adult guests in the classroom.

Good (1980), a teacher effectiveness researcher who used classroom observation for a great deal of productive research, noted a great number of problems of using the technique to evaluate teachers. First, he reported that school districts casually adopt observation systems without understanding their purpose or limitations just because they are used in other locations, or they are readily available. Second, most observation systems in use are far too simple to capture the complexity of real classrooms. Third, there is a tendency to overinterpret the findings and make them mean more than their actual limited scope. Fourth, it is rare that enough observations are made to generalize about the classroom. Fifth, many teacher proactive behaviors are ignored or not visible during the observation period. Sixth, Good (1980) recognized that "there are some [teacher] behaviors that simply cannot be explained in terms of the present, ongoing situation by an outsider who has missed most of the interactions that have occurred in a classroom earlier in the year" (p. 33). Next, student perceptions of classroom events are crucial and may not match what an observer reports. Finally, every evaluation system has an inherent value system that produces the judgment to use it. The choice of a particular set of topics to observe is a subjective act, not the purported objective, hard data gathering so often claimed by classroom observation advocates.

Stodolsky (1984) studied the research observations of 19 fifth-grade mathematics and social studies lessons. Approximately 260 hours of observations were analyzed. (Compare this amount of time with that used in teacher evaluation observations by principals.) Stodolsky reported that "the same teachers teaching the same children in the same physical setting used very different instructional arrangements as they switched from math to social studies lessons. Full day observations showed variation in other subjects as well" (p. 14). The instructional arrangements included format (e.g., seat work vs. group work), pacing, and cognitive level (as in Bloom's Taxonomy; Bloom et al., 1956). In addition, she reported that "teachers often produce discrepant attention levels in students when teaching two different subjects" (p. 16). Stodolsky concluded that "assumptions of internal consistency made in connection with teacher evaluation procedures [using classroom observation] must be seriously questioned" (p. 16).

Coker et al. (1980) studied research observations of a total of 100 classrooms that were observed twice on four "valid and reliable low-inference observation instrument[s]" (p. 133). Frequency counts of target behaviors ("absence of teacher scolding, humiliating student," "motivates with privileges, prizes, grades") were correlated with pupil achievement and pupil self-esteem measures. The authors reported that "the results are startling in the mixed and negative support they offer for our best ideas about how an effective teacher of cognitive skills and content behaves. They call into question some of our strongest convictions about teaching" (p. 149). These findings show how difficult it is to select a conceptual framework with which judgments about teacher performance can be made.

One particular dilemma of classroom observation systems is to choose between observation topics or variables that do not call for judgment on the spot (e.g., "teacher responds to student questions") and those that make use of the expert judgment of the observer (e.g., "communicates and fosters a respect for learning"). The former variables are called *low-inference* observations because the observer merely records an observable event without much analysis of the behavior in front of her. In *high-inference* observations, the observer must subjectively judge the presence, adequacy, and probable consequences (given the context) of the behavior in front of her. Of course, these terms are relative—there are no absolutely behavior-free or judgment-free observational recordings. Low-inference observations may be described as more objective than high-inference notations. At times, advocates of classroom observation claim that this results in less subjective evaluation. However, as many researchers have noted, the *choice* to observe some factors in a classroom but not others is, of course, subjective in itself.

What Can Be Observed?

Once it is recognized that classroom observation data have significant limitations in classroom teacher evaluation, a number of research studies have suggested some possible kinds of data to attend to within these limits. For example, Evertson and Burry (1989) reported a study using an observation system termed the Classroom Activity Record. It called for an observer to complete coding sheets that record use of time in six categories (content development, directions, seat work, administrative, transitions, academic), teacher-initiated contacts (number, questions, behavior, individual), student-initiated contacts (number, questions, comments, academic), contact content (praise, criticism, academic, behavioral), and student engagement (on task: definitely, probably, off). Training for use of this system consisted of a 2-day session that included manual study, practice by recording scripted dialogues, making their own dialogues, and coding videotapes. At the end of training, group criterion-referenced agreement with the rating of a coded master tape was described as "high—85% or above" (p. 300). Use of this system was illustrated in a study of class size effects for elementary reading and mathematics instruction. Use of the observation system was sociologically and politically neutral in that the observed teachers were either (a) on videotape or (b) interns rather than veteran teachers participating in a summative evaluation program.

McGreal (1983) exemplified a research-based approach to determining topics for classroom observation. He recognized the need to focus observations. He concluded that the focus should come from a "combination of current teacher effectiveness research and portions of Madeline Hunter's [1976] work" (p. 71). In particular, he included the four components of climate (contact, extended questions, success, handling incorrect responses), planning for effective time management, Hunter lesson design (anticipatory set, objectives, input, modeling, check for understanding, guided practice and independent practice), and management (rules, consequences, eliminate interruptions, academic goals, whole-group work, clarity, practice, feedback, review, monitoring, transitions, accountability, climate).

Scriven (1987) reacted to a research basis for teacher evaluation (RBTE). He concluded that *"research-based teacher evaluation is a contradiction in terms;* i.e., an approach based on . . . [observation focused on a number of indicators shown to be correlated with teaching success] cannot be a legitimate method of teacher evaluation" (p. 9). One problem with RBTE is that the individual links between teacher behavior and student outcome are not necessarily additive, as is implied in complex teacher effectiveness systems. Second, the weighting of various links is impossible to defend. Third, correlation is not explanation. Fourth, statistical significance is not the same as educational significance; statistical values may merely describe very small differences that did not occur due to chance. Finally, it is indefensible to use secondary evaluation criteria (behaviors *related* to primary job criteria) instead of the primary criteria themselves.

Direct Instruction as a Basis for Classroom Observation

Zahorik (1980) offered direct instruction research findings as a focus for systematic observation of teachers. He emphasized this use more for teacher study, formative information, and program implementation than for summative teacher evaluation. Much of what teachers are expected to do falls in the category of direct instruction of academic material for achievement learning (Good, 1980; Good & Brophy, 1980; Peterson, Kauchak, Mitchell, McCarthey, & Stevens, 1986; Zahorik, 1980). This includes, for example, much of the content of chemistry, reading for comprehension, and computational skills. (It does not include, for example, effective participation in group teamwork, perseverance in making a difficult measurement, or taking initiative in a comprehensive report.) Some research suggests that teachers produce greater academic learning in students when the teachers (a) effectively use time, (b) provide an opportunity to learn, and (c) deal equitably with students—high and low achievers, both sexes, of different socioeconomic and ethnic groups.

Effective use of time has been found to affect student learning (Fisher et al., 1978; Rosenshine, 1980). Fisher and his colleagues called this instructional factor academic learning time (ALT) and described three distinct components. The first part is time allocated to academic learning. Simply put, student learning is increased if more time is actually spent on the subject matter, rather than on organizing, ordering, generally discussing, or making decisions. Dishaw (1977) reported that *allocated time* in second-grade classrooms that she observed varied from 62 to 123 minutes per day, and for fifth-grade classrooms, from 17 to 134 minutes per day. Clearly, some teachers are more adept than others at providing the time necessary for essential learning time. The second component of ALT is *engaged time,* that is, time in which students are actively involved in learning the material during the allocated time. Dishaw reported engaged times that ranged from 38 to 98 minutes per day for the second-grade classrooms, and from 49 to 105 minutes per day for fifth-grade classrooms. Again, she found distinct and important differences in the amount of time teachers provide for students to actually be at the work of learning academic material. The final part of ALT that has been shown to influence student learning is the amount of *successful time* that students have with the subject matter. Teachers have been found to vary considerably in the amount of time their students practice new learnings with accuracy, correctness, and the good feelings of newly found competence (Rosenshine & Stevens, 1984).

It needs to be clear that these authors specifically cautioned against the use of principles of direct instruction for widespread summative teacher evaluation. Far too many teacher evaluation systems in current practice have borrowed the limited findings of direct instruction research and mistakenly applied them to teacher evaluation. These good moves define a very narrow sense of teacher quality and do not take into account the context of teaching and learning, other important goals and kinds of learning (e.g., indirect instruction), and the very appropriateness of using direct instruction at any given time in a classroom. Various textbooks on the techniques of classroom observation (e.g., Borich, 1990; Ober, Bentley, & Miller, 1971) give information and methods for formative uses. They refer to research studies, but not to summative teacher evaluation.

Domains and Levels of Teaching and Learning

Bloom et al. (1956) edited a taxonomic collection of educational behaviors to provide a common vocabulary for educators.

> It was pointed out that we were attempting to classify phenomena which could not be observed or manipulated in the same concrete form as the phenomena of such fields as the . . . sciences, where taxonomies of a very high order have already been developed. . . . It was the view of the group that educational objectives stated in behavioral form have their counterparts in the behavior of individuals. Such behavior can be observed and described, and . . . classified. (p. 5)

These authors distinguished among cognitive, affective, and psychomotor domains of teaching and learning that described (respectively) intellectual, attitudinal, and motor skill performances. They began a fuller description of these domains with their identification of levels of educational behavior within the cognitive domain. Six cognitive domain levels are knowledge, comprehension, application, analysis, synthesis, and evaluation.

Krathwohl, Bloom, and Masia (1964) edited a companion description of the affective domain, which included levels of receiving, responding, valuing, organization, and characterization. These taxonomies have enjoyed widespread dissemination and acceptance by educators (Woolfolk, 1993).

Equity in the Classroom

There is general agreement that good teaching means equity in the classroom (Grayson & Martin, 1990). One kind of equity involves equal treatment and opportunities for students who look different because of their ethnicity. For example, Jackson and Cosca (1974) reported a study in which Chicano students were found to be systematically treated differently than Anglo students by teachers in classrooms. This study found statistically significant positive differences toward Anglos in the amount of teacher praising or encouraging, acceptance or use of student ideas, questioning patterns, positive feedback, noncriticizing talk, and student speaking time. Instructional theory suggests that equal treatment of students is required for equal learning results (Woolfolk, 1993). Basic values for fairness demanded equal classroom treatment (Scriven, 1981).

Good and Brophy (1987) described differences in treatment between high and low achievers shown in more than 50 empirical studies. These differences include such teacher behaviors as waiting less time for low achievers to answer, seating low achievers farther from the teacher, praising low achievers less, giving high achievers the benefit of the doubt, more smiling and friendliness toward high achievers, and more acceptance of high achievers' ideas. The authors stated that "ultimately this [differential treatment] will affect student achievement and other outcome[s]. . . . High-expectation students will be led to achieve at or near their potential, but low-expectation students will not gain as much" (p. 121).

Increasingly, consciousness has grown about differential treatment in teacher behavior between boys and girls (Grayson & Martin, 1990). Some specific topics demonstrated in research studies are instructional contact, grouping and organization, classroom management, enhancing self-esteem, and evaluation of student performance. Good, Sikes, and Brophy (1973) reported that males have more contacts with teachers, but a higher proportion of the females' contacts is positive. These and other teacher performance differences lead to lower female achievement and attitudinal growth than is possible with equitable treatment. Again, fairness requires equal treatment and opportunity for pupils.

Summary

It is clear from a review of these and other authors that topics for systematic observation need to be limited, clear, and agreed on. Systematic observation is a much more restricted data source than commonly understood.

How Should Observations Be Conducted?

Flanders (1970) made significant refinements and conceptual advancements to earlier practices of systematic classroom observation. He identified three purposes for studying classroom interactions: (a) to keep track of selected events while ignoring others, (b) to "help an individual develop and control his teaching behavior" (p. 3), and (c) to "discover through research how to explain the variations which occur in the chain of classroom events" (p. 3). He did not include teacher evaluation in his listing; formative evaluation was included along with research functions.

Flanders (1970) recommended that "the *fewest* number of ideas necessary to help a person develop and control his teaching behavior" (p. 3) be used in systematic observation systems. He reasoned that parsimonious thinking is important because the teacher faces more variables at any given time than can be directly dealt with, and only a few of the most key ideas are manageable.

Also, Flanders (1970) recommended that an observer sit in a classroom (or view a videotape) and keep a record on an observation form. Depending on the recording system, an observer can be expected to be able to record some "10 to 30 symbols per minute" (p. 6). He stated that verbal communication is an important topic for recording and analysis. Flanders (1970) maintained that "it is relatively easy to learn the skills of interaction analysis. Like any other assessment technique it only requires some practice, a little guidance, and some time to think about what you are doing. The more difficult problem is how to use these skills wisely" (p. 8).

Evertson and Holley (1981) described classroom observation as "valuable for personnel evaluation" (p. 90). Although they did not prescribe a specific instrument or system, they suggested how such systems could be developed. They began by describing how to establish a climate for observation in terms of human relationships and communication. Next, they discussed the importance of selecting a good instrument and recommended several resource books (e.g., Borich & Madden, 1977). They described conditions for effective use, including understanding of purpose, selection of observation times and duration, integration of observation into other data sources, work with faculty for understanding and support, and provision of follow-up procedures when necessary.

Evertson and Holley (1981) recognized seven constraints on the use of observation systems for teacher evaluation. These were time, focus and selection of behaviors, integration and coordination of data with other sources, aggregation of data, communication of data, the law, and training of observers. All of these topics or activities require the judicious use of supervision and decision making to set up an observation system that works well.

Also, Evertson and Holley (1981) specified four features that ought to be expected in observation systems. First, the requirements and purposes are limited and specified to all participants. Second, observation forms are made mandatory; all observers should use the same form. Third, the role of observers in the system should be clear to all and specified. Fourth, observer training needs to be ample and cyclical.

Finally, Evertson and Holley (1981) addressed the technical questions associated with classroom observation. Essential for successful observation are (a) a systematic approach and (b) reliable and valid instruments. Systematic means that there is a careful focus by the observation instrument on the topics of interest and that classrooms events are attended to in a methodical way. Systematic recording may be done by frequency counts, ratings, or narratives. Valid instruments do what they are supposed to do and meet the objectives of their use. Reliable instruments have a known error of measurement. Such errors may come from (a) event instability, (b) observer disagreement, or (c) inconsistency in the instrument itself.

McGreal (1983) described four tenets of classroom observation that should be included in training to perform systematic observation. The first emphasized the importance of information *before* the observation is performed. Much of this advice is similar to that of clinical supervision (Acheson & Gall, 1980). First, the observer should know the teacher's goals and concerns. The second tenet is that a narrow focus of observation is highly preferably to a wide-ranging report. Training is required to stick to an agreed-on format and instrument. The third tenet is that the way in which data are record is crucial to success. Options here include rating scales, category systems, and narrative. The fourth tenet is that the way in which data are presented to teachers affects subsequent relationships and willingness to improve. This means that data should focus on such things as performance rather than personality, observations rather than inferences, descriptions rather than evaluation, specific rather than general, the present rather than the past, information rather than advice, and requests rather than impositions.

Peterson and Kauchak (1983) and Peterson et al. (1986) reported use of systematic observation in teacher evaluation for a career ladder system. This analysis used four criteria: use of time, opportunity to learn, equal opportunity to learn, and taxonomic level of instruction. These authors used trained observers (university graduate students) and transcripts typed from classroom observation notes and audiotapes. Use of systematic observation was optional to teachers, but a popular data source.

RECOMMENDATIONS FOR PRACTICE

As with other data sources, teachers should decide to have systematic observation data gathered about them. Then, a neutral Evaluation Unit arranges for the observation and analysis. Finally, the teacher inspects the summary data before deciding to include it in his or her professional dossier.

Observations are made by a person independent of the district teachers and administrators. The classroom visits are unannounced, but at representative times. The observer takes notes of events, materials, time, and "public discourse," which is teacher talk and student talk directed to the teacher, or heard by a group or more than half the class. An audiotape recorder helps the observer to capture the exact speech of the classroom. The teacher receives a written transcript of classroom public discourse and observer descriptions, audiotapes of the observation sessions, and a summary analysis done by an expert. The dossier entry should be limited to a one-page description of the process and a summary of the analysis limited to three pages.

Observations

Observers

It is crucial that the observer be socially and professionally neutral; thus a person external to the district is needed for systematic observation. Two sources of classroom observers have been identified in field trials (Peterson & Kauchak, 1983; Peterson et al., 1986). One source is graduate-level education students from local colleges and universities. Collaboration between school districts and higher education can result in a helpful exchange of training opportunities, data gathering, and reasonably priced observers (in the minimum wage–$10.00/hour range). A second source of observers is networks of local districts to share staff to gather data in other districts. These persons may be administrators, teachers, or even (in some situations) parent volunteers. These exchanges result in neutral, but expert observers. Local districts are encouraged to be inventive in securing good classroom observers.

Training Observers

Training should begin with discussion of philosophy and approach. It is important for observers to be clear that their purpose is to capture accurately the events and materials of the classroom; complex inferences by observers are not required. Categorization of classroom events (e.g., taxonomic level of instruction) will be done by an analyst, and judgments of value will be made by Teacher Review Panels. This discussion should include alternatives not to be used, for example, principal evaluation observation schemes.

The second stage of training is to have observers prepare narratives based on videotape selections. The observers should watch (and audio tape) videotaped segments of classrooms. During the viewing, observers continuously write verbatim instructional talk, describe events and materials, and note time landmarks. Following the observation period, they extend their real-time notes from audiotapes. The extended notes (containing descriptions and verbatim public discourse) should be read into a second tape recording for typing by a transcript clerk. Problems with note taking, reporting of time, and description of classroom materials can be discussed by trainers after the observers have prepared their reports. Reliability checks at this point should be the verbatim accuracy of observer records and time keeping.

A third stage of training is to provide live practice in classrooms of volunteer teachers. This training is done in groups of three to four observers. After notes are made and transcripts prepared, the observers share impressions, problems, and critiques of their own work. The important issues here are accuracy, unobtrusive behavior (of observers) in classroom, and ground rules for contacts with students. Once again, reliability checks should be made for accuracy.

A final stage of training follows the first several sessions of actual observation. At this point, the trainers and analysts should give the observers critiques of their solo efforts. This should focus on inclusiveness of descriptions, useful formats for reporting, and specific problems reported by the observers.

Once in place, observers should be checked in two ways. The first is occasional monitoring in which a trainer arranges with the observer to visit the classroom to do parallel recording and to discuss the common experience. The second kind of monitoring is to collect teacher reports of observer activity: Is the observer unobtrusive? Does the observation cause problems for the students or teacher? How representative are the sessions? These reports can be solicited on a brief questionnaire.

Observations

The classroom observations should be from 30 to 50 minutes in length, with an emphasis on capturing some episode of instruction—a coherent unit or collection of classroom activity. For most classrooms, four to six observations will provide sufficient coverage of variety in instruction. A few classes having great variety may require an additional one to two visits. The observation should be scattered over a 30- to 60-day period.

Class observation visits should be unannounced. Special lessons or changes in teacher routine are not desirable for the teacher, analysts, or teacher panels. Teachers should operate with as little disruption to their original routines and plans as possible—some disruption is inevitable. Observations should be scheduled on typical days, that is, not just before a holiday. Other days to avoid are Mondays or Fridays (in general). The schedule should aim to encompass a variety of classroom instruction. This means that the observer should confer with the teacher about his or her general plans for the several months of observations.

The observer should be friendly to classroom participants, but as unobtrusive as possible. The observer should be introduced by the teacher as someone who has been invited in to help her do a better job and to show others how the teacher does her work. The audiotape recording should be described to students as a way for the observer to complete her notes; audiotapes should be erased after transcripts are produced. Contacts with students should be limited to brief, general statements like "I am watching the class and writing notes to help the teacher to know more about her classroom. The tape recording is given to the teacher after I use it to complete my notes to her."

Transcript Preparation

The central activity of the classroom observation recommended in this chapter is to prepare printed transcripts of samples of classroom descriptions. The descriptions contain brief observer notes about the classroom, such as objects, furniture arrangement, equipment, and people paths. Much of the transcript consists of public talk. Names of students should be recorded (they will be changed later) for interpretation, for example, of high achievers and ethnically different students. Major events, such as beginning of instruction, people coming and going to the room, location shifts, and distribution of materials, should be noted. Time landmarks should consist of regular intervals (usually every 5 minutes) and at the beginning and end of major class episodes or events. The observer makes notes of public talk and classroom events. An audiotape recorder is aimed toward the teacher and left running during the observation period. Often, the notes of talking consist of the first parts of sentences or the incomplete phrases. These are completed after the observation session by the observer as she listens to the audiotapes.

After leaving the room, the observer reviews and completes notes by listening to the audiotape. Descriptions of the room, materials, and major events are extended. At this time, the observer may recall additional details and give additional perspective. Verbatim quotations are completed. Student names should be changed at this point, with notation of indicator students for ethnic and cultural differences and high and low achievers.

Finally, the observer reads her extended notes into a second tape recorder. These notes include classroom descriptions, time indicators, verbatim talk, identification of students (with altered names), and punctuation. The typist listens to this tape and prepares a transcript for analysis. Figure 12.1 is a sample page of classroom transcription.

Transcript Analysis and Reporting

The narrative transcript is given to a designated expert for analysis. The analyst should be socially and professionally neutral. Often, the analysis can be done without knowing the name or location of the teacher. The analyst's task is to make the components of the framework for interpretation visible. (Value judgments for the levels of these components are made by the subsequent Teacher Review Panel.) Four themes for analysis are recommended, and discussed next.

The first theme is an estimate of the *use of time*. Percentages of class time in several categories are useful information for outsiders considering the quality of the classroom instruction. Sample categories of time usage are whole class, individual seat work, small group, activity center, directions, transitions, and nonacademic. Graphic presentations of data are often helpful for teacher and reviewers. Figure 12.2 is a sample comparison of two kindergarten teachers' use of time.

The second theme for analysis is *opportunity to learn*. This includes provisions such as those presented in Table 12.1. By using a framework of opportunity to learn, the analyst can pick out specific moves and activities that contribute to learning. Other possible categories have been suggested by authors such as Borich (1990). Specific categories should be agreed on by teacher and Evaluation Unit.

Equal opportunity to learn is the third theme of systematic observation. This category focuses on opportunities to learn being equitably applied by the teacher. This means that the teacher does not distinguish between high and low achievers, girls and boys, and ethnically different students. The analysis is begun by having the teacher identify by name a small group of the high achievers in the class and an approximately equal-sized group of low achievers. Student ethnicity is included by having the teacher supply names of ethnic minority students. The analyst notes frequency and nature of interactions with teacher.

The final recommended theme of analysis is the *level of teaching and learning* (Bloom et al., 1956). The most useful analysis consists of selecting

Figure 12.1 Sample Classroom Transcript

TEACHER C SESSION 4 PAGE 5

1 "Who's absent today? TJ's not here, and Whitney's on a trip. So I'll put
2 two. Cam, fix that for me would you? OK, it's your teacher's turn. Thirteen
3 girls are here today, 12 boys are here today, 25 children are here today, two
4 children are absent today. Everyone, read for me." The students repeat the
5 numbers. It's now 13 minutes into the class and the teachers says, "Tony,
6 take care of that for me (referring to the pointer). It's our second day so we'll
7 have only one listening time. Mrs. Strom's turn." She begins to read a poem
8 off the chart; it is Z sounds of initial consonants. She asks the students to
9 read it after she reads and they do. Teacher says, "Lee, Astro chose a poem
10 about a zipper because zipper begins with what letter? (Lee says Z.) OK.
11 Zachary, Astro chose a poem about a zipper because Z begins with what
12 sound? (Zachary says the Z sound). Perfect. Ask me at snack time (to Bill).
13 It's our second day for this one too, so we'll just have one listening time."
14 The teacher recites a poem on tails. It's a repeat from a previous session.
15 The students are attentive and participating. Hadley gets up quietly, goes to
16 the bathroom (ground rule is 1 at a time, no permission needed). Teacher
17 says, "Read with me (students read tail poem loudly). Good. Sunshine lead
18 gentlemen come. OK, read to class." Marshall leads in an initial consonant
19 song. Teacher says, "Read for the class now, all sing." Students sing and
20 teacher joins them at the letter *I*. Teacher says, "OK, leave that for the lady.
21 Molly, do you want to do the sound chart or the toy chart? Which one do
22 you like best?" Molly selects the sound chart that the students have just
23 used. Teacher says, "Whenever you're ready?" (she prompts the beginning of
24 the song). Molly begins to lead and the students follow enthusiastically.
25 Molly smiles broadly at conclusion. It is now 17 minutes into the class. The
26 teacher reads a poem about a rabbit and asks, "Matthew, what could you be
27 seeing?" (There is no clue from poem.) Matthew says, "A boy coming." Teacher
28 now asks every student who raises hand what the rabbit could possibly be
29 seeing. Students raise hands and answer: fox, another rabbit, carrot, tree,
30 hunter, lion, snowman. After each response teacher gives a neutral acknowl-
31 edgment. (Cassie, Damien, Hadley, Steven, Jason, Katie, Brecken, Molly,
32 Darcey) After 30 min. teacher continues divergent questions: "Think up some-
33 thing brand new, that he could see, that a rabbit has never seen before!"

examples from each level, and some estimate of time percentage spent at
each level. The analyst should note balance of emphasis. Another consideration is the teacher's competence to work at each level. As with the other
three categories, the ultimate value questions ("Is this a good use of time to

TABLE 12.1 Teacher Provisions for Student Opportunity to Learn (theme for interpretation of systematic observation data)

New information and skills (content) are available to learn

Information and skills are modeled, examples are given

Information and skills are of appropriate challenge for this group

Materials to learn the content are available

Time is allocated for learning the content

Practice time is provided

Students know what is expected of them, why they are doing what they do, and how well they are doing

Feedback from teacher is frequent and focused ("This is right because . . .")

Praise is limited to direct feedback

Student rehearsal, successful performance, and review are apparent

Rules and logistics are tied to work and learning

Absent: Class is not *too* rowdy, noisy for learning

Teacher is not *too* harsh, intimidating for learning

have 13% at the *synthesis* level?") must be answered in the Review Panel deliberations where the teacher context is taken into account.

Reliability of analyst reports should be established by triangulation of several experts at the initiation of the process. Confidence needs to be established that one analyst will produce reports quite similar to others.

Usage and Costs

Systematic observation is popular with teachers (Kauchak et al., 1985; Peterson, 1989c). Field studies showed 80% of teachers selected this data source. Teachers are attracted by the attention to the classroom, feedback and reassurance of a classroom visitor, opportunity to review their own work, and safety of control of data.

Systematic observation is an expensive data source. Peterson (1989c) estimated a per teacher cost of $85.00, two hours of teacher time, and 16 hours of Evaluation Unit staff time (including expert analysis). His recommendation for frequency of systematic evaluation was for the second or (preferably) third year of teaching, and then once each 7 years throughout a career. As expensive as systematic observation is for each teacher application, systemwide costs are defensible. If the $85.00 cost is understood as applicable to only 80% of the teachers in the district, and the usage is one seventh per year, then the final cost per teacher in the district per year is $9.72. This makes systematic observation competitive in costs with parent surveys and pupil gain data.

Figure 12.2 Time Usage of Kindergarten Teachers

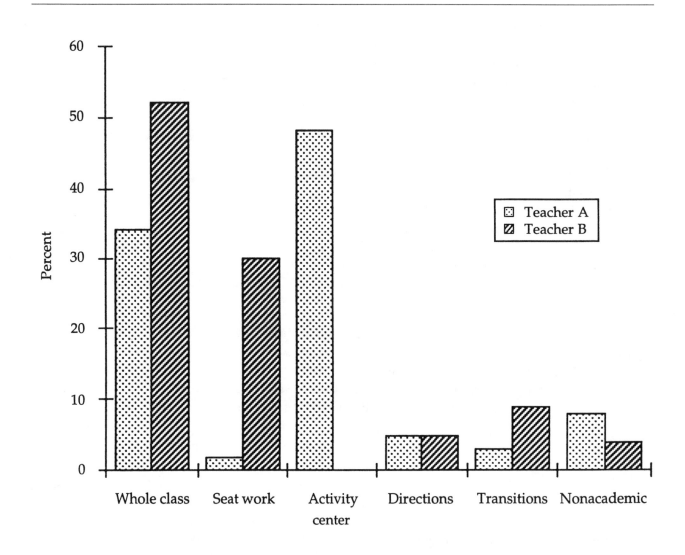

13

Administrator Reports

In current teacher evaluation practice, principals or vice principals have a long history of being the sole (or primary) data sources and summative judges of teacher quality. This book has taken the position that school administrators presently are too involved in teacher evaluation. More precisely, they are too involved in the wrong ways. This chapter describes new roles for administrators that balance their expert views with the best objective evidence available, involve them at points in teacher evaluation where they best perform, and recognize the essential monitoring function of school administrators.

The most defensible administrator involvement in teacher evaluation is of two kinds. First, they are effective monitors of minimal teacher performance and acute teacher problems. This watchdog function involves interventions with few teachers, but is absolutely necessary to the well-being of the entire school system. Second, at the request of individual teachers, administrators can provide specific information about the merit and worth of teacher performance. This corroborative evidence function applies to the majority of teachers.

Some teachers may fall in between the watchdog and corroborative evaluation functions of administrators and thus not require administrator reports at all. These teachers consist of two kinds. One is the occasional teacher who is good to excellent in her performance, but does not see eye-to-eye with her current administrators. The other kind is the teacher who meets minimal expectations and is not bad enough to merit immediate intervention but who is not strong enough to gain enthusiastic administrator support. However, reviewers of overall teacher quality, such as district Teacher Review Panels, need to reserve judgment about these specific teachers in the absence of administrator reports. More data sources (than the recommended four) may be needed to judge quality in the absence of administrator reports.

Advantages

Building administrators are in a good position to see different parts of a teacher's work, are familiar with the performances of many teachers, and are aware of the needs of virtually all of the audiences for teacher evaluation. Administrators most often have been trained and hired for their ability to work with teachers. Administrators do have the duty to monitor for minimal performance and to guard against bad and abusive teacher practice.

Administrator evaluation of teachers enjoys strong acceptance by precedent; after all, this is the way that teachers have been evaluated in this country for well over 100 years (Darling-Hammond, Wise, & Pease, 1983; Medley & Coker, 1987). Legal judgments often reflect this respect for tradition and administrator authority (e.g., Rebell, 1990: *Shelton v. Tucker,* 1960). Parents and others in the community respect the views of the administrator (Epstein, 1985; Lortie, 1975).

Relative to other groups, administrators are good judges of teacher performance. The practical limitations of using them in teacher evaluation stem from administrators' precarious sociopolitical role in the school (Cusick, 1973; Johnson, 1990; Lortie, 1975) and limited opportunities to collect reliable and valid data about teacher performance (Kauchak et al., 1985). Although research studies have found the administrator's report to be unreliable (Barr & Burton, 1926; Cook & Richards, 1972; Medley & Coker, 1987; Peterson, 1987a; Stodolsky, 1984), any other group of persons (teachers, students, parents, researchers) is no better in a sociopolitically neutral judgment (Centra, 1975). The difficulty is not with the administrator as a person as much as the role and that one single observer is not as reliable a reporter of events as the average of multiple judges in that same situation. That is, systematic pupil surveys are preferable to the opinion of the principal concerning certain classroom events (e.g., "gives sufficient guided practice"). If it were possible to have 15 principals in a teacher's class for 20 hours, their average report would be quite accurate and dependable. However, obviously this would be both too disruptive and expensive to justify.

Another advantage to administrator reports is that they are relatively inexpensive to obtain (Peterson, 1989c). A simple form can be filled out quickly by a principal, using information already present as a result of normal supervisory activity and interactions with the teacher.

A final advantage to administrator reports is the wide range of topics on which they can provide information. As depicted in Figure 5.1, administrators can usefully report on teachers' performance as members of the school community, maintenance of health and safety conditions, teacher compliance with district and state guidelines, and overall ethical behavior.

Disadvantages

There are many disadvantages to administrator roles in teacher evaluation. Reliance on administrators as the central evaluator leads to sociological domination, which in turn detracts from teacher functioning and morale. Principals face serious role conflicts when they have the tasks both of educational leaders of professionals and summative judges of teachers (Cusick, 1973; Lortie, 1975). Administrator reports are not always the best objective evidence available; systematic parent surveys, pupil reports, peer reviews, pupil achievement data, standardized achievement tests, and documentation of professional activity all routinely are more reliable than principal reports (Peterson, 1987a, 1990b). Finally, administrators may not have been selected for their role because they were themselves the best classroom teachers.

RECOMMENDED PRACTICES

Recommended practices for administrators in teacher evaluation are two roles as (a) a monitor of minimal practice and acute teacher problems and (b) an optional data source for teachers. These two functions are quite distinct, but both are important to the well-being of the educational system and teacher evaluation program.

The Monitor Role

The principal has the role in the school system to monitor teacher performance, and if necessary to step in to halt incompetent and abusive performances (Bridges, 1992; Lawrence et al., 1993). She also has the duty to suggest or require specific steps of remediation of these problems. Interventions may be infrequent, but this supervisory role is an important one for the protection of students and, ultimately, others having a stake in schools. District employment handbooks having well-defined areas of expected performance and of prohibited practices and limits help to make this judgment role clearer. Administrators who are themselves evaluated for their monitoring role (see Chapter 20) perform a needed and respected service for their districts.

One key intervention of administrators who spot trouble is to require that data be gathered from sources that indicate trouble. The optional use of data sources expected for most teachers can be made mandatory for teachers who have been identified as having problems. This district-level policy decision to have required data for certain teachers should be made by the district Teacher Evaluation Board.

The Data Source Role

Administrators can serve as a valuable optional data source for teacher evaluation. As with other data sources, the teacher should first decide to have the administrator complete a report. Then, the teacher should inspect the form before deciding to include it in his or her dossier for Teacher Review Panel consideration.

The administrator report appears as Form 13.1. The first section indicates the sources of information used by the reporting principal. One important distinction between this form and current practice is that this form does not purport to represent *systematic* observation data, as defined in Chapter 12. It does include *informal* observations that are a part of normal supervision and administrator monitoring. This monitoring is described in Chapter 23.

The second section of the report form has nine rating items for which the principal has firsthand knowledge. The first rating ("well functioning")

FORM 13.1 Administrator Report

Check sources of information used for report:
___ discussions with teacher
___ discussions with other teachers
___ discussions with chairperson or teacher leader
___ discussions with students
___ discussions with parents
___ classroom visits (number: ___)
___ evidence presented by teacher
___ student achievement data
___ district level information
___ other (specify: _____)

FORM 13.1 Continued

	Well-Functioning	Needs Attention	Unsatisfactory
Overall rating	W	N	U
Effective instruction, strategies	W	N	U
Classroom order, discipline	W	N	U
Student progress, achievement	W	N	U
Supports schoolwide goals, procedures	W	N	U
Maintains health & safety conditions	W	N	U
Follows District Course of Study	W	N	U
Follows State Core Curriculum	W	N	U
Ethical practice	W		U
Areas for which teacher may provide additional data to administrator:			
Professional development & activity	W	N	U
Student relations	W	N	U
Colleague, staff relations	W	N	U
Parent relations	W	N	U
Knowledge of subject matter	W	N	U

Additional comments:

For items circled as N or U describe

1. Specific problem
2. Evidence/indicators
3. Concrete effects on student learning
4. Actions recommended for teacher
5. Time frame for remediation, second data gathering, and employment status

[SPACE PROVIDED]

Action Summary:

___ Proficient, well functioning
___ Move to remediation (overall judgment or required for any individual item *U* rating)

_____   _____
(Administrator's signature, date)   (Educator's signature, date)

includes what is expected from the majority of teachers. The second rating ("needs attention") indicates an administrative concern that, at this point, does not require the interest of outsiders. The third category ("unsatisfactory") should lead directly to remediation, remedy, and change of performance on the part of the teacher. Failure to correct these problems in a timely manner should result in employment sanctions (suspension or termination). The item "ethical practice" has fewer than three possible ratings. Ethics simply *must* be present; there are no real degrees of performance here.

Usage and Costs

In our field studies (Peterson, 1989c), administrator reports were the most popular optional data source. They were elected by 95% of the sample of volunteer teachers. Even if the general teacher population used administrator reports at a lower level (our self-selected sample was a group of well-performing teachers), districts can expect that the majority of teachers will select this data source. This is an encouraging indication of positive and supportive relationships between the majority of teachers and their administrators.

Cost data showed 10 minutes each per year for teacher and administrator. (Administrator time is for form completion only, the monitoring time—approximately 2 hours per teacher per year minimum—is figured as normal function with no additional evaluation expense.) Generally, it is recommended that beginning teachers collect 3 to 4 years of administrator reports to establish a pattern, then alternate years thereafter.

14

Teacher as Curriculum Designer, Unique Data Sources, and National Board of Professional Teaching Standards Licensing

In some cases, teacher quality may be evidenced by unusually extensive work on complex contributions that directly or indirectly support enhanced student learning. These teacher efforts may include design and testing of curriculum, student materials for learning, instructional techniques, assessment procedures, and school schedule or other kinds of logistical changes. Three variations of the curriculum design data source are curriculum and instruction design, action research, and participation in school improvement projects. A fourth, related kind of data source is documentation of practices or results unique to an individual teacher. Finally, the documentation of National Board of Professional Teaching Standards licensing may serve as a data source for teacher evaluation.

Curriculum and instruction design involves innovative teacher construction of subject matter content, materials, learning activities, and assessments provided in the classroom (Hass, 1978). Action research is systematic inquiry into a problem or opportunity that involves recommendations for action based upon data (Perry-Sheldon & Allain, 1987). School improvement projects involve faculty groups who decide upon common goals, then align materials, activities, instruction, and assessments to achieve these goals (Holly & Southworth, 1989; Webster & Mendro, 1995). In addition to these extensive kinds of activity in curriculum design, some teacher evaluations may best be served by custom construction of a data source unique to that teacher and her setting. In general, an individual teacher can select one of these four versions as a single data source to be added to others for his evaluation dossier.

Advantages

Thorough documentation of extensive teacher involvement and pay-offs in curriculum design, customized for an individual teacher, may be what is needed to complete the picture of value for the teacher. Although the extensive curriculum work of this data source is beyond the normal duties of most classroom teachers, some teachers feature this contribution. Thus, a comprehensive teacher evaluation system requires an opportunity to document extraordinary efforts and results. This more customized data gathering and documentation opens up important areas of teacher performance, such as the creation of innovative learning materials or testing, which educators otherwise might miss while evaluating teacher quality.

There are a number of other advantages to documenting activity in teacher curriculum design. First, vigorous and successful curriculum work is often linked to other things that educators value: pupil achievement, teacher professionalism, school system improvement, and client or stakeholder satisfaction. Second, opportunities to document curriculum work present an important way to highlight and reward professional innovation for emulation and broader adoption. This feature is important as a parallel to the development of surgical techniques in military field hospitals: Frontline practices may intensely spur important new developments. Third, teacher evaluation that uses and values teacher curriculum work makes a sociological contribution by honoring and fostering teacher authority, leadership, and professional collaboration. Fourth, evaluation of curriculum work may focus professional expectations for out-of-classroom duties and influence in a way that other data sources do not. Finally, the evaluation system provision for "unique" or "other" data sources provides the flexibility to incorporate truly novel performances or contributions.

Disadvantages

There are disadvantages to using curriculum design or unique data sources for teacher evaluation. First, documentation of extensive curriculum development or other performances unique to individual teachers requires additional assessment work on the part of the teacher, relative to other, more standard data sources. This increased demand is also true for the persons performing the evaluation analysis or decision making. Second, this data source has the hazard of reflecting much time, activity, and effort that has little substance or ultimate meaning. Summative judges must be diligent and discriminating in their decisions about quality and value. Third, group, team, or schoolwide efforts are common in advanced curriculum work, but they make the specific role and contribution of the individual teacher unclear. Finally, teachers should rarely, if ever, claim more than one variation of this category of data sources; the proper use is to choose one approach from the four described in this chapter. (One exception is the use of National Board [NBPTS] licensing as a separate data source in addition to one other from this chapter.)

LITERATURE

Curriculum and Instruction Design

Curriculum and instruction (C & I) design may include development of units (e.g., integrated thematic units), learning activities, organization of subject matter content, planned experiences of the learners under the guidance of the teacher, instructional technique, assessment procedures, classroom routines, or a philosophy of learning or life (Hass, 1978; Schubert, 1986; Tanner & Tanner, 1980). The level of impact may be the teacher's classroom, school, district, or even the nation.

Curriculum and instruction design refers to teacher work above and beyond the expectations for curriculum selection, integration, coordination, and implementation tasks of the classroom teacher (Danielson, 1996; Murphy, 1987; Scriven, 1994). The additional performance of this data source requires the teacher to make a claim that her efforts are valuable because she does things such as meet otherwise neglected important needs, innovate curriculum and instruction, or substantially enhance student learning above levels given by current C & I. It is essential that the teacher selecting this data source for evaluation make a specific claim, such as those listed above, and then proceed to document its occurrence.

One example of documenting a C & I design is a teacher who constructs, implements, and evaluates a unit on local problem solving (Nagel, 1995). She may, for example, have her students find a "real-world" problem of a stand of neighborhood fir trees that are dying. The integrated classroom unit has students investigate the causes, gather data, create solutions, and implement the solutions (which may include rechanneling storm water). To use this real-world problem solving as evidence in her evaluation, the teacher should document the need, demonstrate the gains in knowledge and attitude, look for comparisons of similar units and results by other teachers, analyze what was given up by adopting this unit (e.g., systematic instruction in math computation skills), and present statements of credible educators as to the choices, contents, and results of this activity. The evaluation components of documented payoffs to students and the credentialed educational value of the goals, in addition to the unit itself as experienced by the students, are essential to the use of this data source.

Action Research

Action research is systematic inquiry into some specific part of school curriculum with the purpose of acting on current local practice to improve, change, or initiate better ways of doing things in schools. It rarely has only the purpose of a better theoretical understanding of educational practice or widespread dissemination. Action research is performed by practitioners, uses local resources (wisdom, materials, data analysis, practices, and dissemination), and employs a variety of data-gathering techniques. Its procedures, processes, and standards are shaped by the nature of the problem studied, local resources, and the applications in which it ends. Action research shares a number of features in common with "academic research" such as importance, techniques of data gathering (e.g., surveys, focus groups, and interviews), and reliance on empirical data. However, action research is distinct from academic research in a number of respects. These commonalties and differences are presented in Table 14.1.

Action research may be described as having sequential steps. For example, Perry-Sheldon and Allain (1987) listed stages of reconnaissance, planning, action, and reflection. Sagor (1992) presented a sequential process much like academic research that includes problem formulation, data collection, data analysis, reporting of results, and action planning. However, action research also may be described as an interactive, nonlinear process. Mills (2000) advocated a *Dialectic Action Research Spiral* that acknowledges the realistic mutual development of components. He suggested that the determination of an area of focus, data collection, data analysis and interpretation, and action plan all act upon one another as an actual study progresses.

School Improvement

The North Central Regional Educational Laboratory (2000) described school improvement as a local activity in which a team of educators and

TABLE 14.1 Differences Between Action Research and Academic Research

Action Research	*Academic Research*
Seeks to suggest action	Seeks to disprove theory
Determines a decision	Determines truth
Researcher often a participant	Researcher often not a participant
Aims at specific audience	Aims at multiple, unknow audiences
Focuses on specific problem	Focuses on generalizable problem
Meets demonstrated need	Meets need of a theoretical framework
Local standards of validity, reliability, control, prediction and explanation	General standards of validity, reliability, control, prediction, and explanation

community members participate in cycles of school betterment. Each cycle consists of four phases:

1. Schools and communities define their problems using their goals
2. They draw on an understanding of learning to select improvement strategies
3. They initiate changes in accordance with local conditions
4. They evaluate and decide what more needs to be done to meet their goals

The process is enhanced by the team incorporating the following resources:

- Research-based knowledge
- Expert advice
- Demonstrations of successful practice
- Resources in key educational areas
- Critical issues to stimulate and inform the improvement process
- Indicators of engaged learning
- Self-study tools

Thus, school improvement is an ongoing, continuous group process of systematic review, redesign, assessment, and reflection. Individual participants may move in and out of the projects, but the group itself stays intact as a regular function of the school or district. Specific topics for improvement (e.g., "aligned curriculum and assessment," "standards-based learning," or "community service education") are adopted as appropriate to the setting.

Webster and Mendro (1995) described a specialized kind of school improvement mandated at a district level. Although individual schools were given a great deal of latitude in specific applications, this form of nonelective study and improvement is not the most common form of school improvement effort. However, the methods described by the authors did emphasize site-based decision making and a cycle of study and change.

Unique Data Sources

There are two central reasons for allowing teachers to create data sources for themselves other than those described thus far in Part II of this book. First, the particular *teacher practice* may be so unique that it cannot be captured by the usual and expected data sources. For example, a teacher who is responsible for a community-based art project involving city government and business requires a complex and unique evaluation design. For this teacher, the data sources of professional activity, student report, and peer review do not depict the value and merit of the teacher performance. The second reason is that the *teacher circumstances* may be exceptional enough to warrant unique evaluation treatment. For example, a teacher who is assigned to a migrant student population where turnover is very high requires data on short-term accommodation successes, establishing continuity with diverse former achievement, and teaching coping skills to mobile students. As with many other decisions, the judgment to move outside of the normal data sources can be left to the teacher. She needs only to document the reasons for her additions and begin to make them.

Quality teaching comes in a variety of forms. Some performances that are recognized as excellent are quite situation specific or unique to individual teachers. Teachers are expected to innovate and to contribute individual features or provisions as part of their professional work. Some teachers are good because they routinely step outside of usual practice; some good teachers do not. Also, the data sources described so far do not include every possible indicator of teacher quality. Thus teachers should be encouraged to consider designing and completing an additional line of evidence that deals with a unique contribution, student outcome, or district service that extends beyond the usual professional expectation.

One example of a unique data source is a teacher whose business classes get recognition every year at statewide Future Business Leaders of America competitions. She shows her preparation, specific social-learning and school-to-work transition benefits for students, and includes parent and pupil surveys of the value of the teaching. She documents and discusses the downsides of this activity, for example, what happens to students who do not participate ("In what ways are they deprived?"). This documentation is a unique combination of materials review, parent and student reports, and professional activity

Contributions of Minority Teachers

Another example of use of a unique data source is documentation of a contribution made to students because of the teacher's unusual experience, knowledge, activity, insight, contacts, or access to materials. One specific case of this is the minority teacher's potential to further student learning (minority or majority student) because of the teacher's cultural or economic experience (Peterson, Deyhle, & Watkins, 1988). Teacher minority status does not necessarily confer value (rolemodeling may be an exception [Castaneda & Gray, 1974]); not all minority teachers should be assumed to make culturally/economically related contributions just because of their status.

Some groups of minority students have not fared well in schools in this country (Schrag, 1997). Whereas a number of reasons have been offered for low achievement, contrary examples of great success of these same ethnic groups in local settings have been identified (Sizemore, 1985). Effective teacher evaluation distinguishes between significant teacher contributions and their lack. Two key tasks in teacher evaluation are to document the (1) needs of students and (2) specific teacher contributions that meet those needs.

Cummins (1986) reviewed research that identified four teacher contributions that benefit minority students:

1. Minority language and culture are incorporated into the school program
2. Community participation is an integral component of education
3. Pedagogy that uses language actively to generate knowledge is employed
4. Educators who are assessors are advocates for minority students

Cummins presented evidence that each of these teacher provisions is a valuable contribution to minority students' opportunity to learn.

Cazden and Leggett (1981) reported similar opportunities for teachers of minority students. They identified from research a number of cultural differences in cognitive style and interactive style that have been linked to higher achievement for some minorities. Equity means that teachers provide for these differences in their teaching. For example, cognitive style differences have been found that suggest that a multisensory curriculum is of value: "Certain mathematical concepts can be portrayed either by visual means such as graphs or Venn diagrams, or by equivalent works or numerical symbols" (Cazden & Leggett, 1981, p. 74).

A second area of teacher contribution to minority learners is to use appropriate interactive styles that maximize student engagement. Teachers can, for example, regulate the amount of cooperation and competition, teacher and student classroom domination, and verbal participation. Kagan and Madsen (1971) described a study in which Mexican and Mexican American children were much more successful in a game-task situation when only cooperative play was allowed. Anglo children were the most competitive in the study and performed relatively better in competitive settings. Jackson and Cosca (1974) presented evidence that teachers varied their levels of criticism when interaction related to student ethnicity. One disturbing finding of theirs was that minority children received critical teacher interactions detrimental to academic achievement. These teacher judgments can be mitigated by better understanding of student interaction preferences.

The third area of teacher contribution to minority students described by Cazden and Leggett (1981) is "bringing the community into the classroom." Similar to Cummins, the authors showed that the use of community events, artifacts, and procedures resulted in student learning. Community resources can be provided with parent participation, minority hiring, and inservice training.

Some writers have argued for even more subtle contributions of teachers to minority student learning and development. Castaneda and Gray (1974) detailed the importance of role modeling for field-sensitive students. Many minority children exhibit field dependency because of environmental differences between home and school. Erikson (1964) pointed out the need that developing children and adolescents have for adults who are able to recognize authentic student achievement (even when not up to adult standards). He described the function of the adult as the social entity responsible for responding to a young person's performance with recognition and verification. Erikson described how this external confirmation of value is a necessary basis for self-recognition, self-identification, and self-verification. Although these contributions of role model and value verifier are more subtle than test scores or classroom behaviors, they can be documented indirectly through teacher experiences and connections.

Although a case can be made for general links between teachers and contributions to minority students, evaluation requires that specific connections be made for individual teachers. Because each teacher has a degree of uniqueness in her teaching performance, each minority teacher may be expected to present a variable set of documentation.

Commonalties in Using Curriculum and Instruction Design, Action Research, School Improvement, and Unique Data Sources

Although the four data sources described in this chapter may seem to represent quite different activities, advocates, and payoffs, they share common needs and procedures to include them in a comprehensive teacher evaluation system. The burden of documentation as part of these data sources is great. The teacher is not only making a case that activity and results happened (as with other data sources), but also needs to establish: (a) a characterization of the activity and results, (b) that the activity and results are important, and (c) that the goals and data are credible. The teacher must make a case for need, logic of value, student learning (or a link thereto), results, side effects, and credentialling of importance. The good news is that teachers who are involved in these extraordinary curriculum design activities most often have done the preliminary documentation as a result of their involvement, and can meet these demands.

The process of credentialling is essential to the use of all four data sources. In this step, credible educators (e.g., peer teachers not politically connected, curriculum leaders in district, administrators) sign brief statements confirming the needs analysis, content, assessment measures, and gain outcomes as assembled by the teacher. It is not good enough to merely present raw data about activity to the summative evaluator(s); rather, the teacher is responsible to make the case for value of her efforts and results. Ultimately, the standards for evaluation of curriculum design activity are the same as the Pathway Model described in Chapter 3 (Table 3.1).

Data and decisions from these four activities are quite durable. Thus, evidence of teacher merit, value and impact can stand for a number of years, without an annual renewal. Results of these data sources may be used for three to five years, before updating is required.

The National Board for Professional Teaching Standards Licensing

The NBPTS was one result of an influential recommendation by the Carnegie Forum on Education and the Economy (1986). The purposes of the board are to provide leadership and standards for the teaching profession and to identify and certify accomplished practitioners. The board specifies five key areas of teacher performance: teachers (1) are committed to students and their learning, (2) know the subjects they teach and how to teach those subjects, (3) are responsible for managing and monitoring student learning, (4) think systematically about their practice and learn from experience, and (5) are members of learning communities.

The application process for teachers includes a school-site portfolio, which includes written descriptions of teaching in her own room, videotapes of teaching, and student work samples. In addition to the portfolio, a candidate teacher completes a one-day assessment center review in which they perform analyses of videotaped instruction and analyze student work samples. Local district teacher evaluation, as described in this book, provides pertinent data and experience for these national-level evaluation reviews. Successful NBPTS licensing is a positive use for the school district evaluation system.

NBPTS licensing is one data source to be combined with others in order to document the worth, merit, and value of a teacher's performance. This data source may be used in addition to one other from this chapter. NBPTS licensing is a unique data source in that its durability is career-long.

Recommended Procedures

Creating a unique data source involves one additional step to the actual data gathering and documentation of multiple data sources. Using a unique source requires the teacher to make a case (to the review audiences) for the value and pertinence of the data source itself, as well as the merit and worth of the performance. Thus the teacher should create a brief (one-page) description of the need for the data source. He also should include making a case for the validity and reliability of the data gathering.

INTERNET RESOURCES

Curriculum and Instruction Design

Thematic units

> http://www.atozteacherstuff.com//stuff/tusites.html

Teacher designed units

> http://www.design.iastate.edu/ART/NAB/strat.html

Teacher designed units

> http://edservices.aea7.k12.ia.us/edtech/teacherpages/index.html

Course

> http://spectrum.troyst.edu/~eddean/edu685/weeks/wk5files/ppwk5/

School Improvement

School improvement plan report

http://www.echhs.org/annualreport/report.htm

North Central Regional Educational Laboratory

http://www.ncrel.org/sdrs/pathwayg.htm

Florida State University, Office of School Improvement

http://osi.fsu.edu/

Action Research

Action Research Electronic Reader

http://www.beh.cchs.usyd.edu.au/~arow/Reader/welcome.htm

Action Research International

http://www.scu.edu.au/schools/sawd/ari/ari-home.html

Educational Action Research

http://www.triangle.co.uk/ear-o.htm

Links to Participatory Action Research Sites

http://www.goshen.edu/soan/soan96p.htm

MCREL: Action Research/Teacher as Researcher

www.mcrel.org/connect/action.html

National Writing Project

http://nwp.berkeley.edu

Networks

http://www.oise.utoronto.ca/~ctd/networks/

Participatory Action Research Network

http://www.parnet.org
http://www.imc.org.uk/imc/coursewa/doctoral/bobda.htm

Carnegie Foundation for the Advancement of Teaching, National Commission on Teaching & America's Future

http://www.tc.columbia.edu/~teachcomm/home.htm

National Board for Professional Teaching Standards

http://www.nbpts.org/nbpts/

15

Data Sources to Avoid

Previous chapters in Part II of this book present many ways to document the work of good teaching. Other methods show up in discussions about teacher evaluation, but these should be examined carefully with the criteria described for selection in Chapter 5. It is crucial that every method be subjected to tests of logic, practicality, reliability, validity, cost, and client acceptance. It is not enough to merely suggest a way of teacher evaluation because it has great intuitive, popular, or political appeal. Each recommended data source must be accompanied by a history of empirical test, parallel development by several sources, small-scale trials, real-world applications, and demonstrations of success. The results of this development should appear in refereed journals, as well as more popular professional magazines. This chapter describes nine attractive data sources that have shown problems in logic, implementation, or documentation about successful, real-world results.

Testimonials

Testimonials are statements from individuals about the quality, worth, or merit of the teacher. They most often are in the form of personal letters that state admiration for personal qualities, global approval, or glowing reports of single events or interactions. They may be solicited or written spontaneously.

Testimonials rarely have data about how accurately their views represent the total affected population. They often are exceptional cases, rather than representative reports. They may be provided by people who have little or no direct knowledge of the teacher's classroom performance. Testimonials rarely have corroborating evidence for their assertions. Conditions under which they are solicited or gathered most often are unspecified. Testimonial writers often have undisclosed motivations. People who submit testimonials may lack expertise for their judgments. Virtually any teacher will have some admirers and can be expected to produce testimonials if encouraged or required. Finally, testimonials usually are one dimensional in their topics; they do not speak to many important concerns.

Peer Classroom Visits

Peer teacher visits to classrooms usually have the same feature as conventional administrator reports. They are based on one or several visits, a report form checklist or open items, and a summary report. Sometimes peer visits are associated with the formative evaluations of "peer clinical supervision" (McFaul & Cooper, 1984) programs.

Peer classroom visits suffer from all the defects of traditional administrator observations: disruption caused by the visit, observer bias stemming from social or educational relationships with the teacher, domination of observer style preferences, inaccurate sampling of teacher performance, deficient recording forms (Wood & Pohland, 1979), bias of the role of the observer, and inadequate training and monitoring of observers (Scriven, 1981).

The special case of "expert" teachers who leave their classroom assignments for a year to become traveling observers is a bad practice. Once out of the classroom teacher role for several weeks, the teacher ceases being a peer because of sociological dynamics. A schedule of meetings with adults, lack of responsibilities with students, getting professional acknowledgment and reward, and lack of school community membership significantly change the teacher observer. Teachers taken from their classrooms face specific role changes that alter their perspectives, perceptions, and judgments. These include such experiences as having discretionary time, being taken seriously by adults, having authority and deference, and getting control over their own visits to the restroom. These differences make visiting teachers concentrate more on generalities of teaching and the conventional wisdom of nonteaching experts, and less on the specifics that make the difference for teachers in the front lines. Although expert teachers who leave the classroom for evaluation duties know their own classrooms well, they may not know others. They do not always respect the diversity of situations and specific successful teaching approaches that vary from their own.

Peer Consensus

Peer consensus most often is based on a survey questionnaire given to teachers within a school building that reports on teacher characteristics and quality (Hoogeveen & Gutkin, 1986). For example, a form may be circulated that asks colleagues to rate a teacher on classroom organization, learning, and cooperation. Peer consensus is quite different from peer review of materials in which disinterested peers base reports on examination of instruction materials submitted by the teacher.

A superficial survey of fellow teachers has serious conflict-of-interest problems. Consensus surveys may show high levels of agreement (reliability) but be quite inaccurate in agreement with objective evidence of outcomes (validity) (Hoogeveen & Gutkin, 1986). What is agreed on is the public perception of the teacher and her attributes. Some teachers have high needs for recognition among colleagues; others have low levels. What is measured in peer surveys is more likely to correspond to the teacher's need for recognition than performance quality. A serious drawback to peer surveys is the lack of direct knowledge that teachers have of each other's practice. Classroom visit exchanges are rare occurrences. As a result, peer consensus evaluations have little respect among colleagues. Cederblom and Lounsbury (1980) reported that peer consensus evaluation is more a report on popularity, friendship, or superficial impressions than on valid teacher quality.

Graduate Follow-Up

Graduate follow-up is documentation from former students some time after working with the teacher. This potential data source is appealing because the former students have had a chance to apply learnings, and they have the perspective of "real life" to more accurately assess the value of the teacher's work. In addition, former students have a more mature understanding of outcomes and presumably are able to use this wisdom to judge the quality of former teachers. Finally, graduates have had the most number of teachers and are able to compare the results of their teacher with other educational experiences.

The central technical problem with graduate follow-ups concerns adequate sampling. It is almost impossible to get a representative sample of students to question. Students disappear, even in populations that

appear stable from year to year. The wrong students are unusually motivated to participate—extreme cases of disaffection or support are over-
represented. Likewise, intervening variables color the viewpoints. Although more educational experience might be expected to inform
judgments, it is not uniform. Finally, it should be recognized that graduates are not completely expert in judging teachers. Scriven (1981) was critical of "alumni surveys" on the grounds that "they related to the ancestors
of present performance and . . . may exaggerate or underestimate the merit
of the only performance that should be used for current personnel decisions, namely current performance" (p. 254).

Competency-Based Teacher Evaluation

Competency-based teacher evaluation follows a general behaviorist
tradition of education in which the central tenet is a precise and encyclopedic description of ideal behavior (Heath & Nelson, 1974). Statements of
ideal behavior have the advantages of a public and thorough search for the
listing of competencies. These can be discussed and a consensus adoption
agreed to by teachers, the public, and evaluators alike. The argument for
competency-based evaluation is that once the performances are completely and accurately described, and valid and reliable observations and
other data-gathering devices are in place, evaluation becomes a technically
simple process of matching up the actual performance of competencies
with the ideal description (Provus, 1971; Stronge & Helm, 1991). The judgment process itself (the valuation part of evaluation) is direct, simple, obvious, and self-apparent. This discrepancy evaluation model has great appeal for its precision, specificity, clarity, comprehensiveness, and
objectivity. The behaviorist model has been expressed in a series of educational themes over the years, including behavioral structuring, mastery
learning, learning-by-objectives, management-by-objectives, and performance-based evaluation.

However, in practice these promises have been difficult to keep (Peterson & Kauchak, 1982; Watts, 1985). There is not agreement among interested persons on a system or set of components that describe the entirety of
the teaching performance. Also, generic teacher competencies are greatly
limited by the context dependency of actual teaching and learning (Coker
et al., 1980; Stodolsky, 1984). Next, actual teaching performance is not
merely a sum of distinct competencies. As described by Travers (1981),

The concept of teaching as an assembly of competencies lacks
substance at present. It has not led to the development of any defensible and usable set of criteria of teacher effectiveness. The approach has appeal, particularly to those who know little about

what has, and has not, been established about the nature of teaching. For the latter reason, it has had political attractiveness and has found some acceptance among some members of state legislatures, who have then brought pressure to bear on state departments of education to apply the concept to . . . teacher evaluation. (p. 21)

Teacher competencies are *not* provided by the process-product research findings on which some persons have claimed competency-based teacher evaluation is based (Scriven, 1987). Finally, teacher competency systems themselves have not been empirically verified; there is not a research basis for claims (or implications) that competency-based teacher evaluation produces superior teacher performances or more valid and reliable teacher evaluation decisions.

The most recent version of a behaviorist approach to teacher evaluation is outcome-based management (Brandt, 1993). Following this strategy, once the "outcomes" of teaching can be publicly identified, a technology of teacher evaluation can be designed to accommodate it. This latest expression of "precision planning," aligned with "precision teaching," followed by "precision assessment" has not been backed by empirical research that demonstrates superior results. The resurgence of a familiar but inadequate theme should sound a warning to designers of evaluation systems.

Standards-Based Teacher Evaluation (SBTE)

Standards-based education (SBE) is an attempt to present, in a systematic and organized way, the range of considerations to be taken into account in judging the quality of an educational system. Standards catalog the features, characteristics, or tasks important in designing or using the system. Standards may include levels of quality criteria as scoring guides or rubrics. Standards may provide benchmarks ("it has these dimensions") to compare a given application with the agreed-upon, explicit, organized descriptions of the ideal system. The SBE movement has produced standards for many educational components (e.g., what students should know and do in learning mathematics) (National Council of Teachers of Mathematics [NCTM], 1995).

Educational standards call for clarity and specificity to satisfy a variety of audiences:

Standards [for student learning] must be specific enough to enable everyone (students, parents, educators, policymakers, the public) to understand what students need to learn. They also must be precise enough to permit a fair and accurate appraisal of whether the standards have been met. . . . [S]tandards must make clear what is expected of students. (Linn & Herman, 1997, p. 9)

Standards must be written in clear, explicit language . . . detailed enough to provide significant guidance to teachers, curriculum and assessment developers, parents, students and others who will be using them. (American Federation of Teachers, 1996, p.19)

The standards-based education movement has produced catalogs for teacher performance. For example, Danielson (1996) described a

framework for teaching . . . [which] identifies those aspects of a teacher's responsibilities that have been documented through empirical studies and theoretical research as promoting improved student learning. Although not the only possible framework, these responsibilities seek to define what teachers should know and be able to do in the exercise of their profession. (p. 1)

The innovation of standards-based teacher evaluation (SBTE) is one of listing duties categories along with scoring guides for each category. Recent competitors have been "competencies" (Houston & Howsam, 1972), "performance analysis" (Heath & Nelson, 1974), and "teacher duties" (Scriven, 1987). Although SBE makes a contribution to educational systems, there are limitations to designing complete evaluation systems around the principles of the movement. SBTE offers the baits of "research basis" and "clarity, specificity, agreement" but then suffers from substantial switches in application. Table 15.1 presents a list of problems with SBTE, three of which will be discussed next.

Although the Danielson (1996) framework is based on documentation "through empirical studies" and "theoretical research" (p. 1), the author acknowledges that

factors combine to produce a research environment that is far from ideal. The ingredients required for clean research studies—educational goals, assessment measures, and control over extraneous variables—are compromised. Consequently, hard, empirical research in education is scanty—at least today, with our limited assessment measures and our evolving goals. (p. 22)

As described in Chapter 5, it is crucial to the development of teacher evaluation practice to empirically test the results. For example, if the intent

TABLE 15.1 Problems With Standards-Based Teacher Evaluation

Empirical studies of claims of acceptance and effectiveness are lacking

The logic of value is not made explicit

In practice, statements of standards rarely are "specific," "precise," "clear," and "detailed"

Need remains for informed, expert judgment

Teacher duties extend beyond any given system

There is more to teaching than just the topics in the standards

Can lead to practices at odds with professional tradition or empirical research

"Benchmarks" are not the same thing as the performance or task itself

May be irrelevant for the strongest performers (who easily exceed the standards) but fail to provide the resources for the weakest performers

Problems of conventional teacher evaluation remain (e.g., weak links with pupil achievement, portfolios call for work that many teachers do not want to do, principal may remain as single data source)

---

is improvement, it is important to have published instances (even small scale) of actual districts or groups of teachers who have been improved in performance, attitude, or pupil achievement. Other components of study should include comparisons, estimates of client satisfaction, and cost/benefit analysis. Research in teacher evaluation should provide empirical evidence that leads to, and supports, the claims made for the suppositions.

Three examples of teacher standards illustrate the practical difficulty of describing teacher performances in terms that are precise, clear, specific, detailed, and understandable to teachers, administrators, students, parents, and community alike:

> All the instructional goals are nominally assessed through the proposed plan, but the approach is more suitable to some goals than to others. (Danielson, 1996, p. 78)

> Students accept teacher insistence on work of high quality and demonstrate pride in that work. (Danielson, 1996, p.82)

> Teacher response to misbehavior is highly effective and sensitive to students' individual needs, or student behavior is entirely appropriate. (Danielson, 1996, p. 87)

The value of various performances is implied (e.g., expectations are clearly expressed for inclusive classroom participation). However, the logic of value or payoff is not discussed. Many components of teaching are cataloged with the implication for quality teaching that "the more of these components, the better the performance," rather than "do the components in play right now make the difference in this context?" Neither of these value positions is made explicit in the standards. Another question of value is the process of consensus weighting (Danielson, 1996, p. 53), which is left up to district groups without explicit statements of value.

Microteaching Performance

Microteaching is a teacher training process in which a teacher performs in a controlled setting (Allen & Ryan, 1969). The advantages of this approach to teacher education are that it (a) is "real" teaching, (b) creates a simplified context (size, time, content), (c) focuses on accomplishment of specific tasks, (d) increases control of teacher practice, and (e) offers greatly expanded feedback for teachers. These features allow focus on parts of teaching, as well as assessment of overall merit and worth.

The advantages of the focusing capacity of microteaching become the disadvantages of teacher evaluation. We are precisely interested in the capacity of the teacher to work in actual, complex settings, with nonspecified demands, uncontrolled settings, and little opportunity for teacher feedback. As stated by Brophy and Evertson (1976),

> Effective teaching is not simply a matter of implementing a small number of basic teaching skills. Instead, effective teaching requires the ability to implement a very large number of diagnostic, instructional, managerial, and therapeutic skills, tailoring behavior in specific contexts and situations to the specific needs of the moment. Effective teachers not only must be able to do a large number of things; they also must be able to recognize which of the many things they know how to do applies at a given moment and be able to follow through by performing the behavior effectively. (p. 139)

The latest versions of this approach are performance simulations advocated for licensing (Haertel, 1987, 1990). These assessments are context free; as a result, they measure teacher quality independent of the phenomenon of teaching itself. This information is just not very useful. In actuality, the context of actual students with a history and a future influences much of the consideration of value of instruction. In addition, many effective teaching practices (such as *clarity* and *supportiveness*) recognizable in a brief demonstration of teaching have a curvilinear rather than a linear effect of learning. Some demonstration of a teaching ability, at the proper time, en-hances learning, whereas too much of the same competency retards learn-ing (Soar, 1973). Thus teachers who score high on simulation situations may not be the best teachers with actual classes because they do not alter their behavior when the context calls for it.

Self-Evaluation

Self-evaluation is a frequently advocated data source for teacher eval-uation (e.g., Bodine, 1973; Carroll, 1981; McGreal, 1983). Self-assessment is an expected part of teachers' professional performance and can provide in-formation useful for planning and teacher improvement. Self-reports are valuable for several purposes. Because of their professional knowledge, teachers can suggest categories of performance and relations among teach-ing tasks, and in general give a perspective on teaching performance that is informative to data collectors (Centra, 1973, 1977). Teacher self-assessment is also of great value to administrators in helping to make good teaching as-signments.

Research has provided a good deal of information about teacher self-reports. Teachers do monitor their own behavior in relation to goals, expectations, and outcomes (Festinger, 1954) and are more likely to act on self-gained data than on information from other sources (Centra, 1972). In-structors have been shown to demonstrate significant improvement in sub-sequent student ratings when moderate discrepancies are identified be-tween initial student ratings and instructor self-reports (Carroll, 1981). Finally, teachers become more effective at self-assessment if training and opportunity to use self-reports are available (Weiner & Kukla, 1970).

The two major problems with use of self-report data in teacher evalua-tion are the teacher's perspective that produces inaccurate data and con-flicts with objective data, and a fatal conflict of interest (McNeil & Popham, 1973; Peterson & Kauchak, 1982).

Empirical studies generally have demonstrated that self-ratings show little agreement with students' ratings. (Student ratings are considered re-liable largely because they are an average of many reporters who balance each other's biases.) In a study involving 343 teachers from five colleges, Centra (1972) found a median correlation of 0.21 between self- and student ratings. In this study, Centra also found a tendency for teachers to give themselves better ratings than did their students. Blackburn and Clark (1975) found little agreement between faculty self-ratings of teaching effec-tiveness and ratings by students, colleagues, and administrators. The three external groups showed higher levels of agreement about teachers among themselves. Peterson and Yaakobi (1980) reported a study of high school classrooms in which student reports and teacher self-descriptions of classroom behaviors had a mean correlation of 0.30. They also found that teacher reports were inflated relative to student assessments. Hoogeveen and Gutkin (1986) found that teacher self-reports correlated at 0.02 with principal reports and 0.14 with peer reports. They concluded that "most ... overstate the quality of their own performance relative to others" (p. 379). Although these three studies were uniform in their findings, it may be the case that an optimistic view of oneself as a teacher, although unrealistic, is essential to performing the difficult role.

Self-interest precludes the use of self-reports in summative teacher evaluation. The task of data selection and gathering may come in to conflict with the best interests of the clients. The unfortunate choice is between the best data and decisions for the students or for the teacher. An evaluation design simply is bad if it structures this kind of conflict, and it should not be done. Persons should not be expected to objectively contribute to final decisions about their own salary, retention, or promotion.

Classroom Environment

Classroom environment evaluation focuses on judgments made about room arrangement, materials, appearance, attractiveness for visitors, and even cleanliness (Anthony, 1968). Specific instructional provisions may be looked for, such as learning centers, record keeping, and student products. The idea is to link teacher provisions with student learning with the environment as mediator.

The central problem with using classroom environment in teacher evaluation is the tenuous link with student learning. Another problem is that style preferences operate profoundly in judgments about classroom appearance. Legitimate environmental issues, such as pupil safety, can be addressed by administrator report. McNeil and Popham (1973) stated "too typically, classroom environment is viewed as an end—teacher's awareness of physical environment, care of property, management of pupils, teaching techniques and materials. The relation of the environment to more remote consequences is not questioned" (p. 133).

Some very good teachers work in spartan conditions; other good teachers *use* the classroom environment as a means of their quality performance. Some teachers are disadvantaged by scarce resources; other teachers manifest their impact by being remarkable resourceful. Some teachers overwhelm students with too busy environments. Some teacher preclude student structuring and control by imposing elaborate setups.

The best advice on classroom environmental concerns is to include them with peer review data. Knowledgeable peers are in the best position to describe the merit and value of these issues in the context of all of the teacher's materials.

INTERNET RESOURCES

Math (NCTM) and science (NSTA) standards

http://standards-e.nctm.org/1.0/89ces/Table_of_Contents.html.

Standards-Based Teacher Evaluation

http://www.enc.org/reform/index.htm

PART III

Tools for Improved
Teacher Evaluation

16

Authentic Assessment

Beyond Portfolios to Teacher Dossiers

One of the most important new directions in teacher evaluation is to collect a greater amount and variety of information about what teachers do and the people they affect. More comprehensive and accurate assessment of teachers means being more *authentic* in evaluation by basing judgments on a variety of evidence of the genuine teaching work and performance of the teacher, rather than on narrow indicators (such as a summary of 30 minutes of classroom behavior or postinstruction student achievement on paper-and-pencil tests) and hearsay general impressions.

The development of extensive and authentic teacher evaluation raises questions about how to organize and present the increased amount and variety of assessment materials (such as products, surveys, and peer reviews). This chapter describes two methods: the portfolio and the professional dossier. Dossiers will be recommended because of comprehensiveness and utility for review. The chapter concludes with recommendations for dossier assembly.

Authentic Educational Evaluation

Authentic evaluation is (a) realistic in content and performance and (b) comprehensive in scope and inclusion (Perrone, 1991). Authentic means that the full educative experience itself (materials, goals, people, knowledge, behaviors, attitudes, changes, and results) is captured and considered for its impact, merit, and worth. The focus is on lived experience, and not just the fate of planned events or goals.

Authentic also means that the processes of evaluation (purpose setting, data collecting, documenting, judging) are close to the actual and total performance under consideration. For example, a science curriculum should be judged by how it is presented by actual teachers and used by actual students in real classrooms. The focus in authentic evaluation is on natural whole performances in real-life contexts, rather than fragmented and abstracted parts in test situations.

Instead of focusing solely on discrepancies between inputs and outcomes, authentic evaluation includes (or "illuminates") the mechanisms of the phenomenon itself, or the "black box" between the planned treatment or materials and the results (Ginsberg, McLaughlin, Plisco, & Takai, 1992; Levitan, 1992). Authentic evaluation explicates changes, dynamics, relationships, adaptations, and problem solving. In another sense, authentic evaluation uses combinations of quantitative and qualitative assessment methods (Krueger, 1988) to capture complex dimensions of the phenomenon from varied perspectives.

An authentic evaluation is comprehensive. A complete evaluation includes descriptive characterization of the phenomena, demonstrated student learning gains, long- and short-term effects, costs, comparisons with competitors, reactions of multiple audiences, expert opinion about content, documentation of unintended side effects, and questioning of the goals themselves (Scriven, 1973a, 1973c).

By contrast, nonauthentic evaluation gathers data at a distance from the performance. Evaluation is less authentic when it relies on secondary indicators (e.g., completion rates of science activities), rather than primary indicators (e.g., representative samples of student questions and inventions as they do the activities). Evaluation is less authentic when narrowly based on a few components, rather than comprehensively on many dimensions. Evaluation is less authentic when it ignores the needs, purposes, and priorities of the primary participants for those of secondary clients (e.g., patrons).

Authentic Teacher Evaluation

The principles of authentic evaluation can be applied to teachers. Student and teacher artifact materials from the classroom are more authentic than simulated instructional sessions outside of the classroom. The educational experience reported by students over a 2-week period is more authentic than a checklist from a brief drop-in visit by a busy administrator. Analysis of the actual language of the classroom is more authentic than analysis of lesson plans. Teacher evaluation is more authentic when it comprehensively includes the extensive duties of the teacher, and not just narrow checklists of a handful of behaviors selected because they have been found in some teacher effectiveness studies to have low, but statistically significant, associations with generalized measures of student outcome.

Portfolios in Evaluation

One way to make educational evaluation more authentic is to gather representative artifacts and products into a portfolio. Originally meaning a portable case holding drawings, writing materials, and documents, evaluation portfolios are collections of materials that represent complex work. Portfolios are used by artists, architects, and others whose quality is best understood in examples of production. Currently, portfolio evaluation is actively under development in education (Herbert, 1992; Paulson, Paulson, & Meyer, 1991; Perrone, 1991, Wolf & Dietz, 1998). Portfolios are advocated as assessment that gets close to the activity of interest, can be shaped to specific settings ("ecological validity"), and provides rich data sources for value judgments (Ponzio, Peterson, Miller & Kinney, 1994). In spite of the intense current interest in portfolios for educational evaluation,

> surprisingly, a dearth of empirical research exists. . . . [O]f 89 entries on portfolio assessment topics . . . in the literature over the past 10 years, only seven articles either report technical data or employ accepted research methods. . . . [M]ost . . . explain the rationale for portfolio assessment; present ideas and models for how portfolios should be constituted and used; or share details of how portfolios have been implemented. . . . Relatively absent is attention to technical quality, to serious indicators of impact, or to rigorous testing of assumptions. (Herman & Winters, 1994, p. 48)

TEACHER PORTFOLIOS AND DOSSIERS

Teacher Portfolios

Portfolios have been suggested for teacher evaluation because they are well suited to capture the complexities of teaching (Sergiovanni, 1977; Wolf, 1991). Bird (1990) described portfolios as a way to see school teaching as "a form of expression, a humane project, an evolving state of affairs, and a situated accomplishment over time" (p. 249). Just as other kinds of portfolios are highly specialized, the unique possibilities of teacher portfolios need careful consideration before widespread adoption.

Selected Literature of Teacher Portfolios

Bird (1990) began a conceptual analysis of schoolteacher portfolios by discussing four central purposes. First, teacher selection and hiring can be enhanced by the detail and breadth of information presented in teacher portfolios. Second, professional development can be encouraged by documenting individual teacher activity in a form that invites "reflection, mutual assistance, or substantial support" (p. 245). Third, school reform can be furthered by the capacity of portfolio information to focus on teachers' needs for support, participation, and collegiality. Finally, professionalization of school teaching is encouraged as teachers use portfolio data to share wisdom, illustrate applications, acknowledge effectiveness, and break isolation.

Bird (1990) further advanced thinking about teacher portfolios in a matrix analysis in which he distinguished among (a) three sources of portfolio entries (teacher herself; others, such as colleagues and/or students; and teacher and others) and (b) three levels of guidance or mandate (informal norms, formal prescriptions, and mixed). The nine combinations of these two considerations (sources and mandates) provide different ways for thinking about and organizing the contents of a portfolio.

Another way in which Bird (1990) discussed the possible contents of a teacher portfolio was to list the array of documentation: photocopies, photographs, observation reports, videotapes, and others. The key for deciding what to include is for the teacher to consider the meaning and significance of possible entries that the teacher holds in common with the persons who use the portfolio. "The initial task is to organize . . . a penetrating and useful conversation about schoolteaching" (pp. 248-249). Further distinctions made by Bird in schoolteacher work were five task areas in a matrix with four areas of teacher concern for each of the task areas. Teacher tasks included teaching a class, planning and preparation, student evaluation, professional exchange, and community exchange. Each of these could be reflected in portfolio presentation. In each of these tasks, teachers are concerned about their responsibilities, subject matter, individual students, and class organizations. Clearly, there is much complexity about teacher work to document. It is important that teachers and their audiences be careful and explicit in their deliberations about how, why, and when to have teachers produce portfolios.

Wolf (1991) and colleagues reported on an exploratory study in which 20 elementary school teachers and 20 high school biology teachers developed portfolios in their respective subject areas. Wolf and his associates described portfolios more as an *attitude* of teacher behavior than as a *container* of information. They pointed out that portfolios are strong for capturing the complexity of teaching. Purposes of portfolios may include formative information, data for reward and recognition, or (even) avoidance of dismissal; additional purposes for portfolios need careful development. These researchers found that portfolios are best when they capture both classroom activity and teacher activity. Teacher activity should include integrated instruction, pupil assessment, and creating an environment. The biology teachers emphasized the four teacher areas of preparing and planning, teaching, evaluation and reflection, and exchanges with colleagues and the community.

Wolf (1991) and his associates advocated using portfolios to display both the artifacts of a teacher's work and her reflections on that work. They advised teachers to select 5 to 10 pieces of their classroom efforts for portfolio documentation and reflection. Sample lists of suggested contents included student work, teacher logs, journals, tests, lesson plans, text materials, notes from parents, video- and audiotapes, photographs, and diagrams. They found videotapes to be very helpful because they showed teacher responses to students, student participation, teacher management, and school context. However, some teachers reported that videotapes were difficult to make and disruptive to classrooms. The developers emphasized the need for substance over visual appeal in portfolio construction.

Problems with finding balances in definition, structure, and individual initiative and variety in portfolios were described by Wolf (1991) and his associates. They recognized that lack of specificity leads to a "paper chase" of large and unfocused collections (as experienced in some other field trials of portfolios for teacher evaluation in state-level systems). They argued for explicit directions for form and procedure, but permissiveness for content. They found that teachers want direction in portfolio assembly. Questions about how much to include are difficult to determine; these developers settled on a 1-year limit to contents. A dilemma about including representative or best work was resolved in the direction of best case presentations. Solo performances are preferred, but there is some room for joint production in a few settings.

Wolf (1991) and colleagues recommended holistic evaluation of portfolios that emphasize professional judgment. Their "middle course" assessment recommendations are for two stages of analysis. First, small specialist groups rate components on a 5-point scale, then larger groups (mixed with members from component groups) form consensus overall assessments on 5-point scales.

Wolf, Lichtenstein, Bartlett, and Hartman (1996) reported a study of portfolios for summative decisions in a pay-for-performance system in which volunteer teachers could elect evaluation for a 1-year, $1000 stipend and recognition as an *Outstanding Teacher*. Formative professional development was a secondary benefit of the program. The portfolio format was a notebook with seven components: resumé, philosophical statement, three brief commentaries on three scoring categories, six artifacts with rationale for selection, reflections on peer survey (four chosen by teacher) and client survey (20 students chosen by teacher and administrator), recent evaluation report, and a self-evaluation. The portfolio was judged by an administrator from the candidate's building who received 1 day of training. Three areas of review were (a) assessment and instruction, (b) content and pedagogy, and (c) collaboration and partnership. Three findings were possible: *Outstanding, Excellent* (with no reward), and *Not Meeting Criteria*. Judgment could include data or perspectives outside of the portfolio and was aided with suggested steps for review. Of the 829 eligible teachers in the district, 266 submitted portfolios and 236 (88.7%) were granted the reward. The middle category of excellent was not used by the administrators. The authors concluded that, in general, the program was well received (it remained in the negotiated contract). Specific benefits included clarification of goals for teachers, and for administrators, increased information about the good work going on in the building. Suggested changes for the future were to add a second administrator view, more emphasis on pupil achievement data and school improvement, and to minimize the negative effects on the teachers found not to meet criteria (those cases could be "devastating"). The authors were "enthusiastic" about the program and reported "important contributions to teaching and learning" (p. 286).

Wolf, Lichtenstein, and Stevenson (1997) summarized state of the art advice for teacher portfolios. They defined a teacher portfolio as "the structured documentary history of a carefully selected set of coached or mentored accomplishments, substantiated by samples of student work, and fully realized only through reflective writing, deliberation, and serious conversation" (p. 195). This documentation may include resumés, letters of recommendation, client surveys, lesson plans, and evidence of student learning tied to established standards. They warned against mere collections or scrapbooks of classroom life with "affectionate notes from students and parents." While they recognize that evaluation of portfolios is a "daunting task," they recommend as helpful remedies (a) identification of content and performance standards, (b) specifications for portfolio construction, and (c) design of an efficient evaluation system.

Disadvantages of Portfolios for Teacher Evaluation

Five serious problems with teacher portfolios preclude their use for summative evaluation. These problems mean that portfolios should be used as an optional data source for teachers, judged by peers who produce a one- to two-page summary (see Chapter 7), and included with other data sources in a summary professional dossier.

Although they are rich data sources, portfolios are notoriously difficult to use for judgment (Wolf, 1991). The open-ended nature of portfolios is an advantage for capturing the variety of teaching excellence and a disadvantage for deciding about quality. This structure allows individuals to custom present materials. It allows for individuality and documentation of specific examples. However, nonuniformity means difficulty in making comparisons or for judging overall adequacy. Unorganized collections of teacher and student artifacts provide few inherent standards for judgment.

The second set of problems with teacher portfolios concerns their physical qualities—they are bulky. Unless limited by ground rules, portfolios may grow to include artists' containers of poster-sized materials, boxes of papers, large collections of student work samples, and classroom realia (we received a student-made corn tortilla in one). Portfolios present difficulties with storage. If they are archived, they take up much room. Archived portfolios are rarely used, except for people who search them for ideas on how to put their own portfolios together, not to improve their teaching. A new set of problems begins if portfolios are not archived, but left with teachers. First, they are inaccessible for reference by others. Second, they are subject to raids by the teacher for materials and examples to use in the classroom, or to loan to others who are assembling their portfolios. It is rare for portfolios to stay intact if they are kept by the teacher who produces them.

A third problem of teacher portfolios for teacher evaluation is that they most often leave out a great number of needed perspectives. For example, portfolios show sample results, but not overall levels of pupil achievement. Portfolios rarely include systematic summaries of student and parent opinions about the impact of the materials on display. The reactions of peer colleagues are important guides to the value of portfolio contents. Also, the preparation and out-of-class duties of a teacher often are important concerns for summative evaluation. Of course, these perspectives can be included in a portfolio, but their inclusion often only complicates the organization.

A fourth problem with teacher portfolios is that they seriously underplay the strengths of teachers whose quality is *not* in materials or student products. Good teachers may be good because of personal interactions, pupil achievement in standardized dimensions, productive routines using few materials, a richly imaginative classroom, success in encouraging a divergence of student production, or educational payoffs with long-term visibility.

The final problem with teacher portfolios is that their mandated use in summative evaluation distorts both the evidence and process of judgment. Summative uses reward portfolio producers, not necessarily good teachers. Portfolios are a secondary or even a tertiary kind of evidence. An evaluation system that places a premium on portfolios soon creates an industry of portfolio assembly far beyond authentic samples of teacher work.

If teacher portfolios are used in teacher evaluation, they need to be compressed and commented on by educators in a position to tell the merit of the contents. It is extremely difficult to judge a portfolio—just what does all of the collection mean? One solution to this problem is the peer review of materials described in Chapter 7. The result of this review is a one- to two-page document that can be included in a teacher dossier of professional merit.

Teacher Dossiers

A dossier is a collection of documents related to a specific matter. A teacher professional dossier has the purpose of attesting to teacher quality (Scriven, 1973a, 1973c). Thorough and useful teacher dossiers can be limited to 12-15 pages in length while including many of the benefits of portfolio documentation (Peterson, 1984, 1988, 1990b). The distinction between portfolios and dossiers is nontrivial. Dossiers are much more compact, processed, and usable for judges of teacher quality. Central to the distinction between portfolios and dossiers are Scriven's original idea of *compression* in educational evaluation and related ideas of extraction and compaction. The voluminous data that can be gathered in authentic evaluations require treatment before judges can do their work. Compression is a process in which evaluation data are summarized, processed for key information, and subjected to prior subjudgments of specialized reviewers. One necessary preparation for teacher data is a credentialing of standards and claims in which expert views of the quality and importance of goals, methods, and results are documented. Compression greatly reduces size; for example, the peer review report from Chapter 7 (Figure 7.1) is a one-page summary of a box of materials that contained over 500 pages of plans, procedures,

TABLE 16.1 Contents of Three Teachers' Professional Dossiers

Teacher A

Documentation of professional activity: 2 pages

Peer review summary reports (1984, 1991): 2 pages

Student report data* (1984-1994): 2 pages

Administrator reports (copied, reduced 2/page): 4 pages

Parent survey data* (1984-1994): 2 pages

*1984-1987, 1989, 1991, 1993

Teacher B

Student achievement data (alternate years after 1985): 3 pages

Teacher test scores report: 1 page

Documentation of professional activity: 2 pages

Systematic observation report: 3 pages

Administrator reports: 1-page summary

Extended parent comment (reduced): 4 pages, with peer comments; Evaluation Unit description of
    comment selection

Teacher C

Administrator reports: 4 pages

Annual reports of Community Art Festival (reduced; 1980-present): 6 pages created by teacher C;
    student community learning projects

Student report data (1984-present): 3 pages

Parent report data (1992 focus groups; alternate years after 1988): 2 pages

and products! Lists of contents for three sample teacher dossiers are presented in Table 16.1. A visual comparison of portfolios and dossiers appears as Figure 16.1.

A central feature of evaluation is to examine collections of data and other information to make value judgments. Scriven (1967, 1973a, 1973c) described evaluation as a process to ascribe merit and worth to some product, preparation, performance, procedure, or outcome. There is quality in and of itself (merit), and the value in relation to some audience (worth). The judgment part of evaluation is to determine this merit and worth in relation to a specific audience, as near to their terms and values as possible. Teacher dossiers present the collection of data and other information to the groups or individuals who make the judgments about merit and worth.

Teacher dossiers can be reliably used for summative judgments about teacher merit and worth. Peterson (1988) reported defensible reliability with dossiers used to make decisions about teacher promotion in a career ladder system. In this study, 12 teacher dossiers were judged by 26 career ladder panelists, including teachers, administrators, university faculty,

Figure 16.1 Comparison of Teacher Professional Portfolios and Dossiers

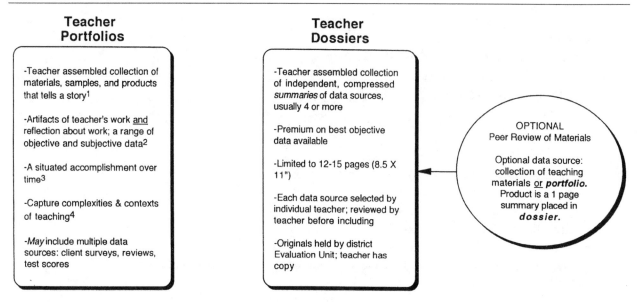

1. Ponzio, et al., 1994.
2. Wolf, 1991, 1996.
3. Bird, 1990.
4. Wolf et al., 1996.

and nursing educators. The dossiers in this study had a mean length of 12.7 pages and averaged 4.75 variable data sources. Panelists showed a 90.4% agreement level on the 312 promotion judgments. The mean rank order correlation coefficient among judges (Spearman's rho) was 0.729. Cohen's kappa for agreement on promotion was 0.808, an excellent reliability.

In another study (Peterson, 1990b), dossiers were reliably used to make simulated rankings of teacher performance by a computer expert program. The simulation was only for the purposes of better understanding human judgments about teacher data—no ranking purpose was suggested for actual teacher settings. Dossiers presented sufficient data in an organized fashion to be used to respond to a bank of 111 questions on teacher quality. The computer expert system was able to categorize (promote or no promote) and rank the dossiers as well as the top person in the middle third of the group of human judges. In this case, teacher dossiers were valuable for research purposes.

Authentic assessment, as represented in panel reviews of teacher professional dossiers, can be used for decision making, public relations, teacher education program designers, and other external audiences. Thus dossiers are a valuable asset for individual teachers, school districts, and others interested in teacher quality.

RECOMMENDATIONS FOR DOSSIER USE

Guidelines for Dossier Assembly

Each district should establish ground rules for dossier assembly and use (Peterson 1988, 1990b). Although teachers and dossiers should show individuality, personal strength, and authentic views, some guidelines and ground rules make them more usable and fair. Ground rules also give structure for teachers who need it. Ground rules may address size of dossier, information required for credibility, protection of due process, and guidelines on expectations for performance. Table 16.2 presents sample ground rules for dossier assembly. This section will discuss each of these considerations.

Dossiers that are too small do not given enough information for judgment. On the other hand, dossiers that are too large or rambling are difficult to interpret. Guidelines should be established for numbers of data sources, page size, and number of pages. Some oversized documents may need photoreduction to accommodate the limitations.

Credibility depends on confidence that dossiers contain honest information and that changes and alterations are not made to falsely enhance them. Ground rules can be agreed on to provide security to dossier storage. Storage should allow updates and protect confidentiality, but maintain accuracy of contents. It is necessary to have teachers keep a working copy and to deposit a safe copy with the district Evaluation Unit. The Evaluation Unit copy is used by the district Teacher Review Panel.

Due process in handling professional dossiers is important. Although safeguards are afforded by involving neutral participation of other people (district forms are used, independent clerks gather and score surveys, claims for professional activity are backed by letters, transcripts, testimonies in a teacher-held file), professional dossiers are voluntary and ultimately the property of the teacher herself. They are not be considered personnel files or employment files, which are the property of the school district. A teacher should have access to all dossier contents. The safeguards are to ensure confidence, not to restrict the rights of teachers to construct and maintain accurate records of their work.

Ground rules can assure technical adequacy. For example, some survey return rates on parent surveys can be inadequate. Particularly at the high school level, some good teachers may have less than 40% of mail surveys returned (Peterson, 1989b). This does not necessarily mean that the teacher practice is inadequate, only that the data-gathering technique is. Ground rules that establish lower limits for data in dossiers ensure technical accuracy. The overall ground rule is that each data source has guide-

TABLE 16.2 Sample District Guidelines for Dossier Assembly

1. Dossiers shall be no longer than 15 pages consisting of 8½ in. × 11 in. paper. They should be bound with heavy paper cover.
2. Dossiers should contain at least four data sources.
3. Each data source must follow the guidelines of that data source, as supplied by the Evaluation Unit.
4. District forms must be used. Alterations to the form (item deletion, editing, or additions) must be clearly indicated and explanations attached. This is not to discourage alterations, but to make them notable.
5. The following data sources must be collected and notarized by the Evaluation Unit: pupil survey, parent survey, peer review, systematic observation, and administrator report.
6. The Evaluation Unit must keep no records of data recalled by the teacher.
7. The following are guidelines for quality on certain data sources:
   Parent surveys, pupil surveys: 1 standard deviation below mean
   Teacher tests: above 40th percentile on national norms
   Peer reviews, administrator reports: "contributing, well functioning"
8. Back-up documents must be kept in accordion folders.

lines that must be respected (and documented). In the example of parent surveys, return rates must be clearly shown. District averages (obtained from the Evaluation Unit) indicate to the teacher and reviewers compliance with this guideline.

Finally, district ground rules can help to give perspectives on importance on reported values. For example, the absolute values of a global item on a student survey needs the perspective of district norms—what do averages (on a 5-point scale) of 4.9, 4.87, and 4.05 mean? Guidelines for value may be established, for example, good practice is indicated by averages at or above 1.5 standard deviations below the district mean. This guideline gives perspective on values as teachers gather data and panels review dossiers. This perspective may be difficult for individual teachers to assume, particularly when they are inexperienced with documentation. It is not pleasant for teachers to see themselves as below average, although half of them will be, and most of these in fact are showing good performance with these numbers.

Costs of Dossiers

Dollar and time costs of dossier preparation and maintenance are defensible; however, they need to be openly discussed and agreed on (Peterson, 1989c). Although dossiers are the initiative and property of teachers, school districts have distinct interests in encouraging and having high-quality teacher professional dossiers. To get good dossiers, districts have options about responsibilities for funding. The choices come from the amount of the costs borne by teachers, the district, or some combination.

Specific Dossier Costs

One area of dossier costs is in personnel time. Teachers need time to plan, talk with other teachers, research possibilities, and maintain their records. Evaluation Unit persons need time to file, review, and audit dossiers stored with the district. Another dossier cost is for production. This includes duplication of papers for the dossier itself. Also, the teacher's back-up file needs copies of transcripts, letters, test score reports, and testimonials. Organizing and presenting materials requires purchase of folders or dividers. Computer disks that contain teacher data may be an additional expense.

Although these costs may seem trivial, they should be openly presented and valued whether they are paid for by teachers or the district. Recognition and acknowledgement are key elements to the culture of the district and resulting respect for the evaluation system. The sociological value of district support far exceeds the monetary value (Johnson, 1990; Lortie, 1975; Peterson, 1989c).

Cost Options

Costs may be decided by the evaluation steering committee as policy. Some options are

District pays all assembly and maintenance costs
District pays all dossier costs for the first dossier; teacher maintains
District gives supplies; district gives supplies at a discount (bulk purchase)
Teacher pays all assembly and maintenance costs
District schedules time for dossier work versus teachers make time

Decisions about who takes responsibility for costs can be based on encouragement of teachers. If there is plenty of activity, the district can leave costs to teachers. If there is little activity, the district can encourage by increasingly providing supplies, money, and time.

17

Use of Computers in Teacher Evaluation

The new directions in teacher evaluation mean that teachers and school districts collect and use a great deal of information about teachers. The increase in quantity of information is matched by the increase in variety of information. Some teachers collect survey forms, peer review reports, and lists of professional activities. Other present student achievement data, classroom observation summaries, and administrator reports. District Evaluation Units prepare, process, and analyze many kinds of forms and surveys. Evaluation Review Panels consider the data and communicate their findings. Virtually all teachers need to communicate with others in preparation of dossiers or reactions to dossier review.

Computers help a great deal in teacher and district data gathering and use. "The computer can . . . keep records, sort and analyze data, prepare text and graphic displays, and enable teachers to contact each other in information networks" (Peterson & Edwards-Allen, 1992, p. 392). Table 17.1 presents specific uses of computers in teacher evaluation.

TABLE 17.1 Computer Uses in Teacher Evaluation

District evaluation forms and surveys
Directions for evaluation procedures (e.g., peer review)
Graphics for presenting data (charts, graphs, tables)
District form letters
Statistical analysis routines (e.g., means, standard deviations)
Bibliographies of evaluation techniques
District norms on surveys
Network data (e.g., teachers wishing to share information)
Records of evaluation costs and time
Student achievement data
Individual teacher records (e.g., resumés, course lists, scores)
Bibliographies in teacher evaluation
Legal reviews on teacher evaluation
Inservice instruction on teacher evaluation

Discussion of Uses

One of the simplest uses of computers in evaluation is for teachers to keep updated documentation of professional activity. Extended resumés contain lists of workshop attendance, university course work, consultations with experts, classroom visits, committee memberships, professional organization memberships, and consultations with other teachers. These can easily be updated several times a year using word processing or database software.

There are several important reasons for teachers to keep these records. Most teachers assume that their school district keeps track of the many outside-of-classroom activities that they are involved in. In practice, virtually no districts do. After 15 or more years in the teaching profession, it is difficult even for the teachers themselves to recall and document the various professional activities that make up this important consideration of teacher quality. A list of professional activities on computer disks enable easy updating for review in summative teacher evaluation.

Another reason for individual teachers to keep records of their professional activity is the ability for groups of teachers (or a district) to present aggregate records of teacher professional activities. For example, a district can report to newspapers the total number and range of teacher inservice hours, or range of student achievement activities. Publicity on what teachers are doing to update and support their profession are important political uses of teacher evaluation.

A second example of using computers in teacher evaluation is for districts to keep specific forms (e.g., parent or student surveys, peer review of materials report) in word processing format on disks. Often, good teacher evaluation calls for standardized forms. For example, pupil surveys should consist of items that have been conceptually and empirically tested (Peterson & Stevens, 1988). District-developed surveys, using the research literature and experts, are better than those constructed by one teacher or even by a committee of interested educators. Having an extensive set of forms enables teachers to choose appropriate ones and encourages their use. District forms include student and parent surveys, peer review of materials reports, teacher test results, administrator reports, and systematic observation summaries.

Another advantage of having evaluation forms on a computer word processing system is that it easily permits some level of customization for teachers. Specific items can be altered, deleted, or added to make a more useful and representative form for individual teachers. A teacher's central task in the more complex evaluation system presented in this book is to document and communicate the specific and individual contributions of their practice.

In addition to word processing, computers play an important role in data processing for teachers. Peterson et al. (1986) reported one career ladder system in which teachers used statistical analysis programs to examine and present data about their teaching. Statistical routines to compute averages, standard deviations, and distributions are useful in describing student achievement. Some teachers can use still more sophisticated programs, such as analysis of variance (t tests), for testing statistical significance of differences in class pre- and postinstruction examinations. Other procedures, such as correlations and distribution tests (chi-square), enable teachers to explore relationships among their data. Regression analyses enable educators to predict expected student gains, given pretest scores of actual classes and known pretest gain correlations for large populations.

Another kind of information that can be made available to teachers is normative data (averages) on district-level teacher results and activities. Examples of this information are survey results (e.g., item averages and return rates on parent surveys at different age levels; Peterson, 1989b) and test scores and item analysis on district standardized tests. Still another useful kind of data involves allocation of class and instruction time, which teachers can use to analyze their own practice. These normative data are helpful in formative evaluation as teachers reflect on their own work; they are helpful in summative evaluation as teachers make their own case for quality. Time and interaction analysis can be used in summative evaluation by some teachers who select systematic observation as a line of evidence. The indirect guidance to teachers offered by these data is rarely evident in the simple practices of current evaluation schemes.

Evaluation activity within a district can be significantly strengthened with computer-assisted networking. For example, teachers who voluntarily use parent surveys can enter their own names and schools in database programs for consultations with other teachers who are considering using the procedure. Resulting phone calls and visits among teachers enable better selection and use of evaluation procedures. Computer databases permit teachers to work together on complicated achievement data problems and presentations (Brauchle et al., 1989). An important function of these networks is sociological support afforded by mutual activity (Johnson, 1990; Lortie, 1975).

A final example of using computers is in staff development or inservice education. Computer materials and programs that simulate evaluation decisions and offer instruction in evaluation techniques help teachers to learn more about complex evaluation. In addition to helping teachers carry out improved evaluation, computers assist them in learning new ideas and procedures. Inservice education in evaluation can be assisted with examples, instructions, and support network information made available on computer disks.

Internet Resources

Many resources are available on the Internet for teacher evaluation. This development makes the sharing of ideas faster and more accessible. For example, some school district teacher evaluation systems have been placed on web sites. This allows educators in a school district charged with improving the teacher evaluation system to review sample specific documents such as parent surveys and listing of principles for district systems. Local district developers can contact other educators in similar positions in other districts or organizations. This section will present some examples from three kinds of web sites; specific sites for other topics are presented at the end of many chapters in this book.

School districts

No existing district system will be perfect, but many have interesting features for examination or adoption. A good strategy in Internet research is to look for strong components. Reviews of systems on the Internet should include a check for evidence (validity, reliability) that backs the claims of the system. School district contacts allow educators to get in touch with creators of systems and persons in similar positions or assignments. Two sample school district systems are

Davis School District, Utah
(http://www.davis.edu/staffdev/eas/index.htm)

Williamsburg-James City County Public Schools
(http://admin.sbo.wjcc.k12.va.us/public/teacheval.html)

Organizations

Groups have been formed to support development of teacher evaluation at a district level, or to engage educators in activities that directly support comprehensive teacher evaluation. Two examples are

Consortium for Research on Educational Accountability and Teacher Evaluation (CREATE)
(http://www.wmich.edu/evalctr/create/)

Teacher as Researcher, Special Interest Group of the American Educational Research Association
(http://www.ilstu.edu/depts/labschl/tar/)

Scholarly Journals

New academic journals pertaining to teacher evaluation have become available online. More than just adding convenience to research, this effort has gotten closer to the scholarly ideal of idea creation, critique, and dissemination. Gene Glass *(Education Policy Analysis Archives)* has been a creative visionary who saw beyond the details and traditions of academic inquiry to significantly lower barriers of time, cost, access, storage, elitism, and fragmentation of ideas with this single innovation. Two examples of journals are

Education Policy Analysis Archives (http://epaa.asu.edu/)

Educational Action Research
(http://www.triangle.co.uk/ear-o.htm/)

Although the information, perspectives, and contacts provided by Internet sites are valuable, there still remains the need for development of local expertise and discrimination. Whole teacher evaluation systems that can be imported do not yet exist. The difficult and long-term work of building a system still needs to go on.

Customized Uses and Programs

Using computers for evaluation goes beyond providing standard forms, procedures, and analysis. Teachers develop their own customized records and data presentation of their preparation for teaching, instructional performance, and student outcomes. For example, the ideas for database networks and district data banks for individual teacher use were suggested by participants in a career ladder program (Peterson et al., 1986). Improved evaluation challenges teachers to conceptualize and document their value and impact to the educational system. As with other uses of computers, we should expect to see many creative examples of how individual teachers can shape their own evaluation.

Research

Computers assist in research on teacher evaluation in straightforward ways, such as data analysis of pools of teachers, and in innovative ways, such as simulations of decision making. Early naturalistic investigations found actual classrooms quite different from ideal descriptions (Goodlad, 1970). Data on teacher performance found in evaluation reports give a better picture of actual practice as well as highlight exemplary practice. Computer records of teacher activity and pupil achievement are rich sources for researchers. For example, the variety of techniques that classroom teachers use to describe gain data shows the need to study how teachers assess pupil growth (Brauchle et al., 1989).

In another kind of research using computers, Peterson (1987c, 1990b) created a computer expert system that successfully simulated human panel decisions made on teacher dossiers created for a career ladder promotion system. This expert system was designed not to replace the necessary human professional judgments but rather to better understand how experts think about teacher quality.

CONCLUSIONS AND DISCUSSION

The purpose of computer-assisted teacher evaluation is to give teachers both information and increased control over their own data. This idea is very close to that of the computer itself; the value often is not so much in the *content* of computer use as it is in *empowerment of individuals* in their own work.

Not everyone agrees that teachers should increase their involvement in evaluation as described in this chapter. For example, not all educators agree that statistical analysis routines should be put in the hands of teachers. Some worry that inadequately trained practitioners will misuse statistical tests, for example, by substituting statistical significance for educational significance or by ignoring important mathematical assumptions. A counterargument is that dissemination of technical information will stimulate better training because demand for the statistical information will lead to the necessary inservice training. Also, researchers in the psychology of decision making consistently argue that increased knowledge of statistical concepts is central to improved decision making (Nisbett & Ross, 1980).

The activities described in this chapter call for higher levels of teacher contribution, reflection, and sharing than most districts now have in place. Certainly, the expectations for professional, technological, and sociological functioning are quite advanced and rare in practice. For instance, teacher proficiency and confidence in computer use is essential. However, policymakers should be encouraged to direct some of their energy toward giving autonomous professional teachers more tools and should direct less energy toward construction of rigid, uniform procedures for checklist teacher evaluation.

18

New School District Organizations,
Judging Teacher Dossiers, and New
District Payoff Structures

Teacher evaluation begins by having individual teachers select among possible data sources (such as students, peers, and observations) and then gather information about their practice. As described in Chapter 16, teachers collect summaries of their data in 10- to 15-page folders called professional dossiers. However, collecting information is only the first part of evaluation. The second part is to have knowledgeable people pass judgment about the merit, worth, and value of what is evidenced in the dossier. This chapter presents recommendations for organizing new groups in the school district to manage the data gathering and guide the judgment process, makes recommendations for judging the dossiers, and concludes with new payoff structures for quality performance such as teacher promotions and leadership positions.

Figure 18.1 District Decision-Making Organizations

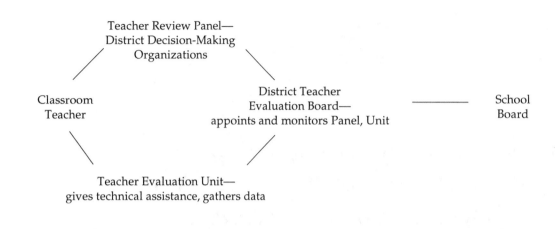

NEW SCHOOL DISTRICT ORGANIZATIONS

Several new district organizations are needed to guide and perform the increased teacher evaluation activities as recommended in this book. These district evaluation groups are depicted in Figure 18.1.

Teacher Evaluation Board

A school district Teacher Evaluation Board recommends policy, oversees, supports, and is responsible for overall district teacher evaluation activity, including the Teacher Review Panel. The board reports to the district administration; thus it is a new level of bureaucracy between teachers and administrators. The Teacher Evaluation Board is made up of administrators, elected teacher representatives, appointed parents, and older students. The size of the board should permit broad representation and input; its size can range from 8 to 18 members. Its responsibilities are to

- Appoint Teacher Review Panel members
- Support and monitor the Evaluation Unit
- Oversee development of teacher evaluation system
- Recommend and monitor district policies on teacher evaluation
- Assemble and distribute aggregate teacher data
- Hear appeals

Beyond these duties, the Teacher Evaluation Board should lead district development of teacher evaluation by establishing an agenda of study, testing new materials and procedures, resolving conflicts, advocating progress, commissioning research and development, and projecting the vision of improved and increased teacher evaluation. More than just one more district committee, the board is the new agency to initiate the new directions and practices.

Teacher Evaluation Unit

A school district teacher Evaluation Unit is a small group of data gatherers who work on teacher evaluation matters independently of administration and teachers' organizations. The unit reports to the Teacher Evaluation Board, and they to district administration. It consists of one or more clerks (depending on the size of the district) and a joint coordination team of one administrator and one teacher. Its size depends on need in the district, but may range from three to nine members. Small districts may decide to share interdistrict joint units. The Evaluation Unit responsibilities are to

- Give technical advice on teacher evaluation techniques
- Prepare and maintain forms and procedures and reviews
- Administer and score survey forms
- Schedule trained observers, standardized teacher tests, peer reviews, and other data gathering and preparation
- Archive teacher dossiers
- Maintain statistical records on district evaluation activity
- Give assistance in teacher inservice related to evaluation

Teacher Review Panel

The most important recommendation in this book to begin the new directions presented in Chapter 1 is for school districts to use a group called a Teacher Review Panel to make the summative judgments of teacher evaluation based on teacher-assembled and teacher-submitted dossiers.

A designated Teacher Review Panel should meet on a scheduled basis to consider the dossiers submitted by teachers in the district. The review panel should follow a review protocol with standardized procedures, guidelines, ground rules, participant training, and calendar. The panel reports results both for formative and summative evaluation purposes. An additional task for the review panel is to identify data to be used in district aggregate reports. This information subsequently is used by the Teacher Evaluation Board. Panel membership and functioning are overseen by a district Evaluation Board. The district Evaluation Unit assists teachers with technical support and adds credibility to the data collected.

Membership

Review panel members are appointed by the district Evaluation Board. In general, panel membership should represent the roles and perspectives present in the district. Specifically, this includes teachers, administrators, parents, and older students. Teacher members are dominant in number; they should represent a variety of grade levels. Peterson (1988) reported logistical and statistical success with panels having four teachers, two administrators, and two parents (or one parent and one student). Terms of service may be fixed at 2 to 3 years and staggered to maintain continuity. Large districts may require more than one panel. Small districts may share interdistrict panels.

Logistics

Evaluation decisions are made at meetings with all members present; decisions are made by majority vote. Teacher dossiers are delivered and monitored for security by the Evaluation Unit. Dossiers are kept at a central location for review by individual panel members. Dossiers also are discussed at work sessions with all members present. This permits deliberation of contents, procedures, and viewpoints. Teachers under review should not make personal appearances at the review panel for data presentation or clarification.

Appeals

Teacher appeals of review panel decisions and questions about district evaluation procedures should be addressed to the district Teacher Evaluation Board. The evaluation board makes recommendations to the district administration.

Organizations: Rational, Organic, and Irrational

Participants in a teacher evaluation system need to be critical of their own efforts. These new district organizations have been described as if the life of groups in a school district were rational: openly discussed, planned, negotiated, meritocratic, coordinated, informed, authorized, and supported. However, in real life organizations rarely function this cleanly. Instead, scholars have identified contrary and intermediary actual organizations (Corwin & Edelfelt, 1976). For example, an *irrational* system is one in which individuals pursue their own interests without regard for the organization, and in which the external supports (information, authority, resources) are absent. Still another organization is an *organic* system, which begins rationally, but then grows up as an accumulation of policy decisions that take on a life of their own until at last they define the organization. Status within the group becomes an issue itself. Subgroups form and negotiate; however, no one subgroup has the power to make changes they see as necessary. Open discussion diminishes. Perhaps the most telling change is a lack of merit as a basis for appointments and authority.

It is important for the participants in a teacher evaluation system to commit to rationality and merit. They should be aware of the hazards of mere organic growth, rather than the direction of good teacher evaluation: recognition of good teaching, prestige for the district, and high-quality education for students and the other clients of public schools.

JUDGING TEACHER DOSSIERS

Chapter 3 reviewed the principles of making judgments about teacher quality. The best judgments about quality and the best decisions about teacher evaluation are made by a panel of informed persons. Good judgments call for

- Explicit description of logic of value determination
- Best objective evidence available
- Control of bias inherent in human judgment
- Involvement of range of stakeholders

The best objective evidence available is the goal and intent of the multiple data sources from Part II of this book and the professional dossiers described in the last chapter. As future research and development improve the objective data-gathering procedures described in this book, new practices should supplement and supplant the recommendations presented here.

Bias is controlled by (a) having multiple judges (b) from several roles (c) interacting with each other as they make their judgments. Research (e.g., Peterson, 1988) suggests that panels made up of four teachers, two administrators, and two parents are able to produce defensible judgments about teacher quality. This arrangement will not eliminate all extraneous bias, but will control it sufficiently for reliable decisions and defensible costs.

Finally, the multiple roles represented on decision panels significantly involves stakeholders (Mark & Shotland, 1985). This provides some
assurance that needed points of view are involved.

Quotas

No quotas should be established for Teacher Review Panel decisions.
Although comparisons become an inevitable part of the culture of the decision-making process, essentially judgments of teachers can and should be
made independently of each other. Quotas imply that (a) there is some a
priori limited quantity or quality, (b) quality is defined as some fixed number of upper performers, or (c) there is some necessary limitation of recognition. None of these considerations is defensible for dossier review.

Guidelines for Decision Making

Districts may establish some guidelines for decision making. Table
18.1 is a sample set of guidelines from the panel reliability study by Peterson (1988). Guidelines are set after widespread discussions by the Evaluation Board and revised after each of the first several years of experience.
These guidelines help to reassure teachers and present some level of information prior to review. Having too many guidelines removes flexibility
and opportunities for professional clinical judgement from the panel.

Panel Instructions

Panel instructions are like those given to juries (see Chapter 3). They
should be clear, logical, and sequential. The following is a sample set of instructions:

> Examine the dossiers presented to you. You may make notes for
> your own use. Take some time for review by yourself, and some
> time to talk over your findings and reactions with other panel
> members. No ranking or weighting systems are expected of you
> or the panel—although these may be a part of how you form your
> own personal judgments (not all panel members make their
> judgments the same way). The entire panel should discuss each
> dossier, vote on a decision or statement, and record the statement
> on the report form.

TABLE 18.1 Sample Guidelines for Promotion Panel Decisions

---

1. Deciding for promotion means that a candidate has presented sufficient evidence of being a well-functioning, contributing, professional, quality teacher. The evidence should be compelling and sufficient so as not to raise doubts in the mind of the panelists.
2. Quality teaching means that the demonstrated needs of the clients have been met. The performance must be of a value in a specific context and to interested audiences. Quality may appear in a wide variety of teaching styles (e.g., systematic, open, outcome-based, humanistic, constructivist, task-oriented, disciplinary, interdisciplinary, or holistic). Good teaching meets ethical and fairness standards.
3. Evidence of teacher quality may be found in (a) preparation and potential, (b) process and performance, and/or (c) student outcome. Quality teaching is best understood in comparison with competitors in terms of effectiveness, durability, cost, and side effects.
4. There are no quotas for promotion. Numbers of successful or unsuccessful candidates from previous decisions should not be taken into account in deciding about current applicants.
5. Promotion requires submission of a minimum of four data sources, each judged as being of quality (e.g., pupil achievement or administrator report). Each data source must follow the district guidelines, ground rules, and restrictions of that source. Evidence is to be submitted in a bound dossier of no more than 15 8 ½ × 11 pages.
6. Lack of evidence in an areas (e.g., pupil report or parent report survey) should not be considered as negative. Only the evidence presented is to be taken into account in making decisions.
7. Promotion is to be recommended by the panel when four or more data sources are judged to represent quality performance.
8. Four of the data sources have levels of automatic quality rating. That is, certain ratings or scores have been determined to recommend for promotion without panel judgment. Numbers below these cut-in values *may* be considered as sufficient quality, but numbers above *must* be considered as recommending promotion for that data source.

Teacher tests:	60th percentile and above	
Student reports:	Grades K-6	> 4.51[a]
	Grades 7-12	> 3.88
Parent surveys:	Elementary	> 4.37
	Middle school	> 3.80
	High school	> 4.15
Administrator report:	Exemplary (4) or Well Functioning (3)	

---

a. These values are 1.5 *SD*s below district means.

Report Form

The report form for a panel review is a simple statement with signatures. Form 18.1 is a sample Teacher Review Panel report form.

FORM 18.1 Sample Teacher Review Panel Report

The King City School District
Teacher Evaluation Review Panel
finds:

Steven Simpson

to be qualified for tenure in the district. This judgment was based on materials submitted by
Mr. Simpson in accord with the panel review processes of the King City School District.

June 5, 2000

Panel members:

_____   _____

_____   _____

_____   _____

NEW DISTRICT PAYOFF STRUCTURES FOR TEACHER EVALUATION

A second key recommendation of this book is to expand the purposes of summative teacher evaluation to include teacher leadership based on panel review, tenure decisions, ranks achieved by promotion, and aggregated data for public release.

Leadership

Leadership appointments, such as to department chair positions, grade-level leaders, curriculum committee chairs, new teacher hiring committees, new teacher mentors, student teacher assignments, site councils, and team leaders, currently are most often made by administrators, or informally between administrators and teachers. They rarely involve merit, but more often represent seniority, influence of personality unrelated to professional merit, or political compromise. One important purpose of panel reviews is to enable districts to make these leadership appointments based on teacher evaluation data and thus take teacher merit into account. Eventually, membership on the Teacher Evaluation Board, Teacher

Review Panel, and Evaluation Unit should be based on dossier review excellence.

Tenure

Purposes for the review panel vary according to the situation of the teacher. One kind of review can be at the end of 3 years of practice, or when tenure normally is granted (Strike & Bull, 1981). Tenure is defined differently in various states and essentially follows a 1- to 3-year probationary period. Tenure represents a long-term commitment on the part of a district to its teachers. The review panel can be charged with examining the dossiers of teachers in their third year and making a recommendation for or against tenure.

Teacher Promotion and Ranks

Promotion and rank systems are virtually nonexistent in the public schools, although they are successful in postsecondary education (Murphy, Peterson, & Kauchak, 1985; Peterson, Wilson, Ulmer, Franklin, Mitchell, & Winget, 1984). A promotion system has ranks (or titles) for teachers, with a review eligibility each 5 to 7 years. Sample ranks are Professional Teacher at 3 years, Associate Teacher at 5 years, and Senior Teacher at 10 years. The promotion is based on a successful Teacher Review Panel decision. Quotas for promotion are not appropriate. These ranks may or may not have additional pay; additional pay can be token or substantial. Some leadership positions may be reserved for ranked teachers, for example, all department chairpersons must be Associate or Senior Teachers. An unfavorable review should not influence subsequent reviews.

Optional Review

Another function of the review panel process is to give voluntary reviews to teachers. This process, although limited in numbers of teachers who are interested, gives teachers an opportunity for individual acknowledgement. Reasons for this include job security, option for professional feedback, desire for recognition, or preparation for hiring at another school district.

DISCUSSION AND CONCLUSIONS

Decision Making

The recommendations of this chapter assume a decision-making process in which several knowledgeable human judgments are aggregated to produce a value decision. The decision is not made with a simple addition of subjudgments that then produces an objective final decision. The method of judging teacher dossiers described here is one of recognizing emergent values in a specific case in a specific setting. This is an independent determination of quality rather than a dependent judgment of acceptable level of discrepancy from an ideal.

District-Level Organizational Support

Adoption of the decision-making structures presented in this chapter have significant technical, sociological, and political implications. Although teacher dossier assembly and construction are a relatively gentle addition to teacher evaluation practice, use of an Evaluation Unit, Teacher Review Panel, and Teacher Evaluation Board represents a landmark departure from current practice. A key element of this change is the commitment of all participants to rational organizational change. The role of the district leadership (teacher and administrative) in making these organizational changes is complex (Corwin & Edelfelt, 1976). The keys are the following:

- Novel, creative, unconventional ideas about teacher evaluation are introduced
- Creative, competent, flexible socialization persons work with the participants in these ideas
- A relatively complex and decentralized organizational structure is created in which participants make key decisions
- District-level organization has enough slack to permit changes and give needed resources
- Teachers are given security and protections from status-risk changes
- External support coalitions (e.g., other districts, community organizations such as the League of Women Voters) are formed

PART IV

Evaluation of Other Educators

19

Hiring, Caring for, and Evaluating New Teachers

The hiring, care, and assessment of new teachers are special cases of teacher evaluation with a great deal at stake. They are interrelated topics because their activities support or hinder each other, and they occur in sequence.

Judging inexperienced teacher applicants is difficult because they lack a track record and their practice is not yet fully developed. Yet hiring new teachers must be done well because selecting bad ones damages the educational system, strains the evaluation program for good teachers, and results in either difficult and expensive dismissal procedures or toleration of bad teachers for the length of their careers. This chapter reviews the current haphazard practices and makes recommendations for more successful efforts. Assessment techniques already presented in the book are mobilized to improve the quality of the most important input for districts: new teachers. Improvement in hiring decisions has the single greatest potential for cost-effective improvement in public education.

Once hired, new teachers require special care. They have predictably characteristic needs for reassurance, professional development, and sociological induction into the profession. Caring for new teachers includes evaluating them well (particularly reassuring them), removing barriers to good teaching, meeting needs in order to enable the best teaching as soon as possible, and creating good attitudes and participation toward career-long evaluation. Giving special treatment to beginning teachers is virtually nonexistent in current practice. This lack produces greater difficulties later in evaluation, more disruptive dismissals, and greater problems in establishing the new directions presented in this book. Good care for beginning teachers means changing current practices in the vast majority of school districts.

The two reasons for evaluating new teachers are to give them reassurance that they are beginning well and to create good attitudes for the extensive evaluation program that is to be with them throughout their careers. If the selection process is rigorous, then the needs for detailed evaluation of teachers in their first several years are limited to encouragement and minimal monitoring. It is a serious mistake to use high-stakes evaluation on beginning teachers that weeds out, criticizes less-than-perfect performance, and shows domination of administrators. Current practice in beginning teacher evaluation results in professionals who are nonidealistic, timid, conservative, alienated, and (ultimately) of lower quality.

SELECTED LITERATURE

Hiring New Teachers

Hiring decisions are difficult to make because so much is at stake. Employing a public school teacher has been called the "million dollar decision" because of the financial commitment of the school district to the teacher's career. In addition, the talents and spirit that a beginning teacher brings to a district affect the morale and effectiveness of those around her. Selection is the first stage of teacher evaluation and begins the career-long process. Good hiring mitigates problems of evaluation later on—well-screened teachers require less diagnosis and remediation; they produce less uncertainty and conflict.

Bolton (1973) advocated that school districts use a systems analysis type teacher selection process. He included eight components: position analysis, established standards, recruitment, applicant description from multiple data sources, behavior predictions, comparison of predicted behavior with standards, choice, and analysis of error sources in process. This detailed process "may be performed by a single person or independently by several people" (p. 49). Bolton's faith in information and process ("management by objectives"; p. 51) downplays the roles of judgment, multiple views, and variation in decision making by individual. Bolton's strongest contributions are his ideas for recruitment to get a large pool for selection, attention to many possible decision concerns, and collection of multiple data sources. Other ideas, such as behavior specification and prediction, have not been demonstrated in practice.

Scriven (1990) analyzed four key topics associated with teacher selection: what to look for, how data should be gathered, how decisions are made, and who should do the selection. For the first topic, he suggested that the qualities or achievements sought in the candidates be derived from (a) a district mission statement, (b) a duties statement for teachers in the district, (c) a job description of the specific position, and (d) a school-based needs assessment. Included in selection considerations should be candidate merit in terms of knowledge of subject matter, competence with student testing, teaching ability, intellectual and personal qualities, and worth to the district in terms of specific needs. Scriven identified topics that must not be taken into account in hiring decisions, including (a) family and personal life; (b) particular personality type or appearance; (c) sex, race, religion, or age (except for district worth considerations); (d) unverifiable statements (e.g., reasons for wanting to teach); and (e) particular teaching style or methodology.

Data for teacher selection, according to Scriven (1990), should be taken from an application form, further information solicited from the candidate, references from persons knowing the work of the person, interviews, and test or trials. Information should be independently verified, including phone calls to others than those named by the applicant as references. Important data may include the classroom teaching track record (including possibility of student surveys); subject matter expertise, skills, and knowledge in testing and evaluation; out-of-class professional activity; and an interview for verification of competence or excellence. All of these data sources need to be used thoughtfully with attention given to their limitations. For example, Scriven warned against selection solely by interview. He cited hazards of learning more about the interviewers than candidates, premium on the peak performer rather than the constant achiever, undue influence of show qualities unrelated to classroom teaching, and general unreliability of interview data gathering. He also cautioned about the method of trial teaching: "because the teacher is going in cold, is not there for long enough for observers to pick up a sense of . . . conscientiousness and perseverance and is under atypical stress" (p. 91). However, data with known limitations are better than no data at all.

Data analysis in the teacher selection process points toward identification of a short list of highest quality candidates for more extensive data gathering and review. To get to this group, a selection committee should eliminate the least promising candidates, identify stars, and gradually prioritize (rank) the remaining candidates. Scriven (1990) distinguished between global and analytical decision making. The former is holistic and comparative. Analytical choice is based on agreed-on criteria and weightings. Each emphasis, global or analytical, is important at different stages of selection. Individual judges may prefer one approach over the other, and make their personal decisions in a manner different from others in the selection group. Scriven recommended that selections be made by a range of players in a school district: principals, assistants, district office specialists, consultants, school board members, and teachers.

Bridges (1992) gave valuable perspectives on hiring new teachers, evaluating them, and making the crucial decision to award tenure. He began his advice on teacher hiring by recommending that school districts be aggressive in letting colleges know what information is helpful and what is meaningless in their written recommendations for teacher candidates. He continued by advocating a district selection committee that includes three of the best teachers and three of the best evaluators to be active in teacher hiring. He encouraged the use of 30- to 45-minute videotapes of candidate teachers presenting a lesson. Bridges recommended that finalist candidates be observed by members of a selection committee while they taught a lesson based on an objective written by the selection team.

The features of Bridges's (1992) evaluation system for beginning teachers include commitment from the top administration, defensible criteria, multiple sources of evidence, staff development, personal assistance, sufficient resources, principal accountability, a tenure committee, and a faculty staffing plan. This ambitious activity means less attention to the evaluation of veterans because so many of the scarce resources are diverted to the beginners. It also means more time spent on recruitment and selection, some errors in denying tenure, more strain on probationary teachers, and more money than conventional practice. The payoff, however, is a lessening of strain on the entire educational system because of the bad teacher, which represents a much bigger problem.

Bridges (1992) also had specific advice for making tenure decisions. He gave highest priority in the limited evaluation system to the tenure-granting process. His position was one of "hard on the standards but soft on the people" (p. 151). By "hard on the standards," he meant that there should be absolute reliance on (a) some clear criteria (e.g., maintain discipline, impart material) and (b) a "flair" factor in which the person is outstanding in some dimension (e.g., talent in art, multilingual). In terms of "soft on the people," he advocated that resources be used for attention to beginners, inservice education, intensive care for problem teachers, and finally, substantial career assistance to those few denied tenure.

Support of New Teachers

A number of authors, including Peterson (1979), Johnston and Ryan (1983), Veenman (1984), and Huling-Austin (1987), have studied the needs of beginning teachers. Emerging from this research is a clear picture of how districts can support new teachers, and the extraordinarily positive impact this has on educational systems. Peterson (1990a) summarized the needs into three particular areas of support for beginning teachers: professional growth, sociological development, and personal. These needs are to be expected, and districts should plan to address them as a matter of normal operation. Meeting these needs brings long-term benefits to both teachers and the district. For example, early orientation for new teachers to specific programs and students produces a career-long teacher sensitivity to finding out about student needs.

Professional support involves inservice targeted to new teachers. The first need for the beginner is familiarity with current district students and programs. These differ from the student teaching assignment and are an initial source of uncertainty and confusion. Next, staff development should address gaps in teacher training programs; no program completely addresses all that a teacher needs to know. An early inventory of skills in planning, evaluating students, and working with parents is sure to identify some specific needs in these crucial performance areas. Classroom discipline is a chronic problem for virtually all new teachers.

Sociological support is a relatively unheard of area of beginning teacher needs. Indeed, most people think of technical inservice needs rather the environmental system of expectations, rewards, sanctions, roles, and responsibilities of teachers. However, without sociological support, beginning teachers soon lose their idealism and turn to the most conservative educational practices because their "personal social norms and sentiments profoundly and predictably change to conform to a schoolteacher's perspective" (Peterson, 1990a, p. 106). Alternatives to these normal conservative forces are authoritative reassurance, countermeasures to isolation, rewards and acknowledgement, resources (such as stable classroom assignments), and feedback about effectiveness. This last support is well provided by good beginning teacher evaluation.

The third area of beginning teacher need is personal. New teachers often have moved their residences from another city or location. They can be expected to be low on money. Early, advance paychecks keep them eating and able to settle their housing arrangements. Their human support systems and personal relationships are changing. District-arranged support networks help them to interact with others in the same situation and to exchange mutual assistance.

Driscoll, Peterson, and Kauchak (1985) described how mentors are an important part of beginning teacher development. Mentors fulfill all three areas of professional, sociological, and personal needs of beginning teachers. These authors reported a study in which new teachers (who were mentored) were asked about what activities were most helpful to them. The beginning teacher rankings of mentor tasks are presented in Table 19.1.

Evaluation of New Teachers

Three problem areas of evaluation for beginning teachers are shared by veterans: Current evaluation practices provide little information, the principal is in a conflicting role of supporter and summative judge, and formative and summative evaluation are mixed at the same time—by the same person (Crow & Peterson, 1983). A fourth problem that is unique to new teachers is the change from extensive university supervisor/cooperating teacher feedback to virtually none for the beginning teacher.

Peterson (1990a) advocated aggressive and extensive new programs for the evaluation of beginning teachers, basing these recommendations on three arguments. First, the sociology of the school workplace means that new teachers need authoritative reassurance provided by a formal evaluation system. Also, the principal role of summative judge is mitigated by having a complex evaluation system in place that frees her up to be more supportive. Second, beginners need the technical feedback provided by good teacher evaluation to refine their practice. Haphazard information, from informal evaluation systems, is not adequate to the technical demands. Third, good teacher evaluation meets the political need in the society for information about teacher performance. For example, resources for new teachers are in competition with resources for new prisons.

Peterson (1984, 1990a) reported five innovations in teacher evaluation that have applications for beginning teachers: multiple data sources, variable data sources, increased teacher control, panel judgments of teacher dossiers, and uses of evaluation for reassurance and recognition.

SELECTION PROCEDURES TO BE DONE WITH GREAT CARE OR AVOIDED

Five teacher hiring practices found (or advocated) in current practice have great limitations, but too often are used at face value where the *results* directly determine the hiring decision, rather than *deliberation* about the re-

TABLE 19.1 Beginning Teacher Rankings of Importance of Mentor Tasks

---

Observes and comments on your classroom performance (5.06)[a]

Gets involved in solving specific problems (5.00)

Assists you to know how well you are doing as a teacher (4.60)

Helps you to cope with practical details of being a teacher (4.57)

Addresses your feelings about being a teacher (4.51)

Becomes a friend (4.45)

Helps with your understanding and coping with school authorities (4.40)

Listens to day-to-day concerns, progress, and questions (4.27)

Sets up a visit of her or his classroom (3.96)

Introduces you to people in the district (3.63)

SOURCE: Driscoll, Peterson, and Kauchak (1985). Used with permisson.
a. Rating scale: 1 = *not needed*; 4 = *important*; 7 = *crucial*.

sults. All create significant problems if they are used without great care and recognition of their limits.

Interviews

In current practice, interviews are relied on entirely too much. They are used too early in the selection process, treated as evidence for all kinds of teacher quality, and misemphasize personal qualities that have nothing to do with the classroom. However, at this final stage of selection interviews can be used to clarify data from other sources, give one more chance for new information from personal expression, and eliminate candidates whose public performance with adults in a nonclassroom, high-stakes pressure setting is not acceptable (e.g., a poor listener with parent questions, unable to clarify a professional choice to colleagues).

Psychological Profile Test Batteries

One selection technique uses a standardized battery of questions in interviews or on a survey that are scored to yield a categorical diagnosis of applicants. These commercial interviews and surveys disclose profiles of preference and personality types. There is no empirical evidence to suggest that any set of personal preferences or styles differentially affects student learning, but adults in educational organizations often prefer to work with people who think or act like they do. Standardized profiles may determine and facilitate agreement with current personnel. This may be the opposite of what is needed for healthy educational organization growth. Such personal characteristics are a wash in classrooms where the variety of student

styles and preferences mixes and clashes with a wide variety of adult characteristics with equanimity. There simply is no most effective personality
for education or organizations. Controlled studies would be required to
link the results of these tests to student learning or organizational effectiveness, but these research strategies are impractical. The value of standardized testing batteries depends on one's belief in the value of pigeonholing
by psychological testing.

Videotapes

Videotapes that show teacher candidates in former classrooms are becoming more common. These are attractive to people who think that they
can tell the quality of teaching by looking for brief episodes, but videotapes
(just like classroom visits) should be used with great caution. Videotapes
are best at providing evidence of acceptable studied appearance: students
under control, compliant with work requests, and showing respect (or,
best of all, affection) for the teacher (Lortie, 1975). However, they present
no guarantees for endurance of these appearances. Videotapes communicate little about the appropriateness of the teacher behavior. They do not, of
course, provide an opportunity to ask students what they think is going on.
Of crucial importance is that videotapes do not document student learning,
merely manifest behavior. They rarely show the teacher dealing with unexpected events or problems, something quite normal in most classroom settings. They most often represent the idealized instruction time of the day
(and week), infrequently showing the beginning or ending of the day,
Mondays and Fridays, and just before or after breaks. Brief episodes do not
present the context of what has happened before, and what is to follow, in
classroom events. Videotape appearances of students appeal to the greatest effect of stereotyping on the part of the observer. The quality of videotaped instruction depends a great deal on selection of particular episodes,
editing, camera position, sound quality, and cooperation of pupils. Sin-
gle-camera techniques at times show the teacher when student action is
key, and at other times show the students when teacher behavior is of most
interest. Finally, it should not be forgotten that videotaping is sure to distort the actual routines of a classroom and its occupants.

Teaching Tryouts

Teaching tryouts are brief teaching sessions with actual students.
Sometimes they are done with objectives provided by the district, sometimes chosen by the candidate. These trials do show spontaneous teacher
abilities. However, some teachers are disadvantaged by tryouts because
their strength is in their long-term program. Crucial relationships have not

been established with the pupils. The applicant is at the mercy of the students and cannot use a substantial (even majority) of her classroom discipline and motivational techniques. The candidate is under a great deal of stress that is not a part of the teaching job. The observers distort the situation, and unless there are at least several of them in the room, minority points of view will prevail in judgments about the performance. Glass (1974) discussed the unreliability of judgments of any pupil gains that come from such short periods of instruction.

Selection at Tenure

One possible rigorous teacher selection procedure is to have a genuine probationary period in which teachers are tried out. At the end of 2 or 3 years, only the highest quality teachers are retained and tenured. This solution is used in some higher education institutions in which assistant professors are hired with the knowledge that perhaps 1 in 15 (or more) will be retained; the appointment essentially is to a postdoctoral position. This solution to the problematic nature of teacher hiring is not going to happen in public schools. Selection at tenure would result in teacher candidates avoiding those districts that began the practice, and many avoiding the uncertainty altogether if it became widespread by not entering the profession.

RECOMMENDED PRACTICES FOR HIRING TEACHERS

Allocate Resources

Both the payoffs for districts in having the highest quality teachers and the costs of dismissing bad teachers mean that districts must allocate sufficient specific resources to the teacher hiring process. Allocation of personnel and money in most districts is the responsibility of the superintendent. Allocation of time is the responsibility of the principal.

Personnel

Personnel assignments to the task are key for good hiring. People are needed from various roles to be representative of different points of view. This will both counter unproductive prejudices and biases, and expand the considerations about what criteria are taken into account. For example, administrators see the orderly functioning of interrelationships in the district, teachers concentrate more on individual classroom and program operation, and parents are concerned about actions in individualized situations.

Numbers of people are needed to share the numerous tasks of reviewing, checking, verifying, comparing, and judging. Also, review and improvement of the hiring system itself is needed. The tasks are too time consuming and onerous for only several people to do; spreading the labor makes it more possible. In addition, having more persons involved leads to greater feelings of participation and ownership.

Finally, persons involved in new teacher selection need to be rewarded (in their terms) for their efforts. Recognition, acknowledgment of time costs, and compensation (even if token) are essential to complete the process.

Money

Searches for new teachers cost money. Budgets should be developed for communication (phone calls), travel expenses, duplication of documents, refreshments, and gratuities for public volunteers. Getting a large applicant pool (Bolton, 1973) requires publicity, solicitations, personal contacts through phone calls, and advertisements. Refreshments for selection committee and visiting candidates make the process more comfortable and communicate the appreciation of the district for players in the process. Several actual hirings can be used to develop a generic budget for future efforts. Specific dollar figures from tentative budget should be used to discuss choices for allocation of money resources for teacher selection.

Time

Time is the most valuable commodity for individual educators. Yet hiring decisions are the most important activity for the entire system. Thus it is justified to request teacher time. The actual amount of time spent by individuals can be shortened by including sufficient personnel in the process. Teachers can be compensated with recognition, discretionary time, or released time.

Specific time needs to be allocated for data gathering about the candidates. They will supply much of their own information, but some requires solicitation; all data need to be organized. Next, time is required for deliberation; clarification and discussion are essential to decision making. Finally, time must be set aside for annual review of practices and outcomes. The temptation is to fold up operations as soon as the new person is signed on. What is needed instead is a thorough review of the process, analysis of strengths and weaknesses, and final brainstorming and creativity about new practices in teacher selection. In fact, hiring practices are not likely to improve in a district unless something is learned and changed by each round of hiring. Focus groups debriefings are an efficient tool for this process (Krueger, 1988; Morgan, 1988).

Form a District Selection Panel

The final recommendation for teacher hiring should be made to the superintendent and school board by a diverse panel. The teacher selection panel should include veteran teachers, parents, older students, administrators, and several of the most recently hired teachers in the district. The balance of numbers should favor teachers. Volunteers may be used, but effort needs to be made to use teachers who have demonstrated outstanding classroom performance. Veteran teacher dossier review is a very appropriate source of membership. This adds recognition and a premium to teacher evaluation. The current practice of taking only volunteers or outspoken teachers for tasks such as new hiring needs to be revised to get the best performing teachers in the district into these visible decision-making roles.

Some panel members may be appointed in small numbers. For example, one or two older students serve the purpose of introducing student views, moderating adult behavior in meetings, and keeping a focus on youth as the center of quality work. Large numbers of student members are not needed to serve these functions.

Solicit Applications

Once resources have been allocated, solicitation of applicants can begin with the goal to get a large pool of candidates. Placement offices in colleges and universities in the region around the district should be notified of openings. Advertisements in local newspapers may attract qualified persons not using placement services. District representatives should seek career fairs scheduled in many regions of the country. Timely announcements and a somewhat lengthy window of opportunity help to increase the number of applicants. Beyond these specific suggestions, it is important to use local creativity to enlarge the applicant pool. The selection committee should brainstorm ways of getting the maximum number of candidates in their setting.

Gather Data

Data gathering and screening are the most time-consuming part of the hiring process. Data gathering should be extensive, but divided into stages that bring increasing information for a decreasing number of the highest quality candidates. Equal treatment of candidates is across all applicants at each stage, not for all applicants regardless of their fate at the sequence of stages. Each of the stages of data concludes with decision making that reduces the number of candidates. This section describes the data gathered at each of four stages and the decision-making process itself.

Stage 1: Initial Screening

A sample application form, presented as Form 19.1, is a beginning source of information about candidates. This form asks for demographic information, indicates several minimal qualifications, and begins the description of each candidate.

In addition to an application form, candidates should furnish a number of other materials. Of primary importance is a college placement service file. Included in the file, or supplied by candidates, must be letters from student teaching supervisors and cooperating teachers. Additional recommendations are helpful to establish credibility and reputation. Former teaching positions should be represented by letters from the principal and lead teachers. A brief statement of interest shows fit of applicant and position and is a limited test of written communication. Other information should include descriptions of teaching licenses, academic degrees, work experience, and other significant activities. Candidates should be made aware that the next selection stages will include positive verification (e.g., phone calls) of application and supporting data claims.

Once the deadline has passed, a small team from the selection panel (e.g., an administrator, two teachers, a parent, and a clerk) makes a consensus reduction of initial applicants to those with complete files and appropriate licenses. The team is larger than absolutely necessary for this task because it familiarizes more people with the applicant pool and helps to spot the rare outstanding applicant who barely qualifies the screening of appropriate license and position fit, test of communication, and complete file. Decision making at the first stage should consist of global, holistic judgments. Candidates are put into one of three categories by majority vote: not qualified, well qualified, or outstanding. Those found not qualified are eliminated. The remaining applicants that meet the general needs of the position are retained in the pool.

Stage 2: Document Review Reduction

At the second stage of selection, applicants are given direction for submission of an additional application portfolio. The portfolio was not requested at the first stage to limit the paper flow. Form 19.2 presents a sample district solicitation for assembly of these data. Key additional information is requested in this portfolio. One component is a two-page,

FORM 19.1 Application for Teaching Position

Name _____   Phone numbers _____

Address _____

_____

Email address _____

Teaching licenses held (includes titles, endorsements, states, lengths of authorization or expiration):

Academic experience (list all colleges or universities attended and dates, majors and minors, degrees, and certificates):

Teaching experience (indicate public school experience, student teaching, private tutoring or educational program, volunteer work; dates, locations, contact persons):

Student teaching (dates, location, cooperating teacher[s], university supervisor, administrator; grades or subjects):

Work experience; other significant preparation (descriptions, dates, locations, duties, contact persons):

Statement of interests and preparation: In no more than one page, describe (a) the positions (grades, subjects, areas) you are professionally prepared to teach and (b) the positions of your greatest strengths and interests.

Other information: Please send your placement file. It is important that letters of recommendation be received from cooperating teacher(s) and university supervisor. Additional letters of recommendation from persons who have observed you teaching are very helpful.

Verification: As part of its deliberations, the Selection Panel will contact some of the persons and institutions you have listed. It is helpful for you to include phone numbers of contact persons and those recommending you.

word processed (for ease of reading) statement with a general topic, such as "What is most important in student achievement?" A second component is a highly selected, brief (limit 10 pages) sample of instructional materials. The third component consists of expanded assessments of cooperating teacher at student teaching, administrator during student teaching, and university supervisor. Analysis should include (a) the assessments themselves, (b) candidate self-report of the value of the assessment, and (c) selection committee assessment of the value of the recommendations. Most public school hirings do not sufficiently use the important information about student teaching performance. Other information should be college and university transcripts and more letters of recommendation. Additional contents are at the option of the applicant, but in no case more than 10 additional pages.

This stage includes data review by the entire selection committee. This stage should include phone calls to references for additional information and spot-check verifications. The entire committee reduces the pool to five to seven, depending on how close the bottom two of this group are to the top five.

Stage 3: Telephone Interviews

Stage 3 consists of phone calls to the candidates conducted by subgroups (including three or more of the teachers) of the committee. These interviews are a chance for peers to ask about preferences, successes, and interests. They should be restricted to questions agreed on by the committee, and a standardized report form. The entire committee uses these interviews to reduce to a final three top candidates for the next stage of selection. This is a ranking decision, based on global judgments.

Stage 4: Final Selection

The work of the committee on final selection begins with selective confirmation of data submitted by the three remaining candidates. Committee members divide up the task of spot-checking references and activity lists with phone calls to school districts, job sites, and universities.

This last stage also includes solicitation about additional information. Candidates can be asked to submit work samples that contain not only their plans and materials but also evidence of student learning associated with this teaching. Follow-up phone calls, made by persons other than those who made the prior calls, should be made to student teaching supervisors and cooperating teachers.

The final selection can include the selection tools that show limitations. These include videotape viewing and teaching tryouts. Although

---

FORM 19.2 Sample Letter for Second Stage of Teacher Selection

---

Dear Applicant,

The Teacher Selection Panel of the King City School District has included your application in the group of candidates found to be well qualified and having appropriate background, preparation, and interest in the position for which you applied.

More information about you is required at this point in the selection process. Please send to us, by May 15th, the following information:

1. A two-page, word-processed statement by you on what is most important about student achievement in the subject areas for which you are applying.

2. No more than 10 pages (8½ in. × 11 in.) of *highly selected* instructional materials that represent an important theme in your teaching. These may be designed or selected by you. One idea or many may be represented. Activities, assessments, work samples are appropriate.

3. Student survey data summaries from previous teaching (if available). This information should be no more than 5 pages.

4. A letter of recommendation, speaking to this specific position, from your student learning cooperating teacher. This letter is in addition to the one you supplied with your original application.

5. Additional letters of recommendation.

6. Transcripts of all college and university courses.

7. Additional information that supports your application. In no case should this be more than an additional 10 pages.

You may phone Ms. Cynthia Jenkins at (503) 555-1423 if you have questions about this information.

Thank you for your continued interest in our school district.

---

they do not disregard the limitations of the short-term, artificial nature of tapes and performance trials, these situations can provide additional information about spontaneous moves, short-term planning, communication with new students, and availability of limited subject matter. It is best if these situations are negotiated with the candidates so that they are not placed in a situation where they have little chance to be successful. The severe limitations of judgment by observation must be taken into account. Care must be taken to ensure equal opportunity; for example, each candidate may be asked to choose one additional form of evidence.

Each member should rank the candidates on a personal global or analytical system. Either way, this is a subjective decision, but one having informed subjectivity: based on the best objective data available, controlled for bias, and involving interested audiences. The best decision is a consensus agreement. If this cannot be achieved, then a mean rank of ranks can be computed and the choice given to the highest-averaged rank applicant.

Review and Learn From the Selection Process

Selection of the new teacher is not the final act of the selection panel. Their last task is to review the hiring process and learn from it. These findings should be made part of the next panel. One member of the hiring panel should be put in charge of this review activity and be a member of the next selection panel.

Six major questions or areas should be addressed at the selection panel review. These topics are presented in Table 19.2. Information about the round of hiring should be analyzed and discussed. For example, the videotape viewing should be thoroughly reviewed. How adequate were the tapes? Who got to see them, what guidelines should be changed, and were they fair? This review should be extended to all of the components listed in Table 19.2.

RECOMMENDATION FOR SUPPORT OF NEW TEACHERS

Hiring teachers well contributes to the strength and dynamism of a school district. It signals to the new teacher that evaluation is taken seriously in the district, with multiple data sources and points of view in judgment. Also, the new teacher begins her work with a concrete collection of professional data—the beginnings of a professional dossier. The next step is to support the newly hired teacher. Beginning teacher support is *not* an option or a frill; it is the way to get the best out of the selection and to set the stage for continued teacher quality and a good evaluation system. Table 19.3 presents the kinds of support required.

Orientation to tasks and district should be staged throughout the year to avoid overwhelming new teachers. *Appropriate job assignment* means that beginners teach within their academic preparation and student teaching strengths. *Supportive working conditions* include a desirable room (not shared), sufficient and available materials, protected planning time, limited extracurricular duties, fewer preparations than assigned veterans, private workspace, released time for discretionary visits or preparation, and small classes of school-successful students. The current teacher culture that thrives on putting newcomers through the worst conditions must change if more positive attitudes about evaluation and collaborative practice are to be created (Peterson, 1990a).

Inservice education should be targeted to specific, local programs that the new teacher uses. It also should include individualized diagnostic

TABLE 19.2 Topics and Questions for Review of Teacher Selection Process

1. What information had the most predictive value? Which specific data sources most influenced this hiring decision? Which sources did not work well?
2. How adequate were the recommendations? What distinguished certain ones?
3. What logistical problems happened? Where were the bottlenecks and frustrations? What did not work, on time?
4. How adequate were the resources? Were enough time, money, and personnel available?
5. How did those who were selected view the process? What are their suggestions for the next round? How did those who were not selected view the process?
6. How did selection panelists view the process? What improvements should be made?

inservice for gaps and a gradual blend into the long-term district inservice system. *Mentor systems* provide guides, consultants, and advocates (Driscoll, Peterson, & Kauchak, 1985). Mentors should not be evaluators. They should be given released time, with good substitutes, to carry out their service. *Visitation programs* cut teacher isolation, give immediately useful ideas, provide models for mundane teacher tasks, and provide reassurance. Good substitutes (the best in the district) are important to encourage beginner participation and enable teachers to leave their classrooms with confidence. *Support groups* permit beginners to share stories, gain perspectives, feel good about their work, cut isolation, and reward each other. Involving some new teachers from neighboring districts gives a perspective above local conditions.

Finally, an extensive *evaluation system* for beginners is an essential kind of support with many payoffs. It provides technical feedback for self-regulation. Early activity familiarizes teachers with evaluation procedures, such as focus groups and systematic surveys, that are new practices. Finally, nothing creates good attitudes toward evaluation like positive early experiences. Lortie (1975) presented evidence that beginning teachers both want and expect good teacher evaluation systems.

RECOMMENDED PRACTICES FOR EVALUATING NEW TEACHERS

Following closely in time to processes for hiring new teachers is the task of evaluating teachers during their first several years of teaching. There will be a difference in experienced teachers newly hired in the district and

TABLE 19.3 Ways to Support Beginning Teachers

Orientation to tasks and district
Appropriate job assignment
Supportive working conditions
Inservice education
Mentor systems
Visitation programs
Support groups
Evaluation system

SOURCE: Peterson (1990).

teachers beginning their careers. This section focuses on the evaluation of persons new to the profession.

The evaluation of new teachers has two major functions. The first is to reassure teachers that they are doing a good, expected, and valuable job. The second function is to introduce them well to the long-term district evaluation system. A gentle and positive introduction to data collection in the first several years orients beginners to the complex system. New teachers can add to the materials they gathered for the position application by experimenting with new surveys, collecting instructional materials, and trying out documentation of pupil achievement. Accumulations of inservice training will reassure many that they are on the path to good professional development.

The sociology of teaching is such that teachers need authoritative reassurance (Lortie, 1975). Teaching is an occupation that does not provide much credible feedback to practitioners. Other occupations provide reassurance in terms of repeat customers and staged entry. Beginning teachers expect the feedback provided by college supervisors and cooperating teachers. They expect that there are norms for practice such as those provided by teacher education programs; however, they are not to be found. Instead, they encounter isolation, alienation, and a generally negative environment for collaboration (Cusick, 1973; Johnson, 1990; Lortie, 1975). Rather than staged entry (such as for law clerks or architect or surgical interns), new teachers face the same conditions and problems as 15-year veterans.

Because of this lack of institutional support, it is important to provide simple, reassuring data and other indications that teachers are doing a good and respected job (Peterson, Yaakobi, & Hines, 1981). This reassurance can be provided in a number of ways. Panels of senior teachers giving favorable reviews are well received. Some districts give a celebration at tenure time. These supportive responses do not simply create more dependency; rather, they take the place of returning customers, concrete products, and stagewise success to show the beginning teachers the worth of their contributions, effort, and caring.

Giving room to grow is good policy for the evaluation of new teachers, as well as for their support. There is not a pressing need to hover over them; rather, some degree of moratorium is appropriate. Most often, beginning teachers are better than average on any objective measure—but not all because of the best reasons. Beginners are driven by idealism, care, hard work, oversensitivity, optimism, and fear. This last source of motivation is not the best, but does help with their quality of performance until the time when experience and wisdom replace it.

COSTS AND BENEFITS OF BEGINNING TEACHER SUPPORT AND EVALUATION

Costs for teacher induction and evaluation systems are substantial, but defensible. Personnel, materials, and time are required for beginning teacher mentoring, data gathering, and visitation programs. However, resources for support and evaluation offset replacement costs for teachers who otherwise leave the system (Johnston, 1985). Cynical attitudes and arrested professional development caused by haphazard induction have long-term (although hidden) costs. Teachers made reticent and conservative by early career bad experiences are not as likely to respond effectively to challenges as those given initiative and confidence through inservice, data, and sense of efficacy.

The support and evaluation ideas in this chapter are recommended to improve public schools. This assistance and assessment is not merely for a more pleasant or effective first year, but to promote positive career-long attitudes and development. The emphasis is not on personal, idiosyncratic development or individuals, but rather on the thoughtful shaping of groups of teachers who control social forces that otherwise detract from good teaching.

The ideas of this chapter are good for teachers of any experience level. Proactive support, multiple and variable data sources, feedback tied to inservice education, and teacher control make sense at any career stage. However, the key for beginners is to develop sound data and attitudes. Without a successful foundation, such as described in this chapter, teachers become remarkably poor consumers of evaluation, permitting disastrous practices and failing to demand good ones.

Lack of advocates for better support and evaluation of new teachers means a low priority for such activities. The persons with the primary interest, beginning teachers, lack power and perspective. It is the responsibility of veteran teachers and administrators to install effective beginner support and evaluation. The need for farsighted action on behalf of new teachers is crucial. Veteran teachers in particular must be challenged to support this strategy—through short-term sacrifices of time, assignments, and resources—to get better and more professionally aggressive colleagues (Peterson, 1990a; Peterson & Chenoweth, 1992).

20

Evaluating Administrators, Support Personnel, and Other Teacher Groups

T he main focus of this book is the evaluation of classroom teachers. However, an adequate district personnel evaluation system needs to assess a variety of educators other than teachers, and some teachers in contexts other than classroom settings (e.g., as project team members). Both of these categories have some unique assessment considerations, although the evaluation of all educators should be coordinated into the district program.

Evaluation of educators other than classroom teachers is important to round out the responsibilities of a school district. The first group for consideration is administrators. The literature suggests that much work needs to be done to create adequate evaluation for this key group of educators. A second group includes support personnel such as counselors, media center specialists, health workers, staff development specialists, and social workers. This chapter cites evaluation developments in the literature, but continues to break new ground by extending strategies described for classroom teachers to these special groups. Evaluation of teachers for reward and leadership is a new focus for public education and constitutes a third, special group for consideration. Teacher-of-the-year programs should be replaced with more systematic, far-reaching, and effective techniques for teacher recognition. A final special group for evaluation is teachers in specific projects. This evaluation leads not only to benefits for individual teachers but also to stronger arguments for the programs themselves.

ADMINISTRATORS

The evaluation of administrators is a very important component of district systems. Their work is important to the overall efforts of the district. Good administrators make a difference not only in the operation of the school but in how teacher functioning in classrooms is affected. The central purpose for principal evaluation presented in this book is to set the stage for teacher evaluation. Fairness to teachers, understanding of teacher impact, and leadership by example all call for evaluation of administrators. The other benefits of improved administrator evaluation are for the practitioners themselves.

Selected Literature on Administrator Evaluation

Weller, Buttery, and Bland (1994) surveyed the literature of school principal evaluation as a part of their development of the Teacher Evaluation of Principals Survey study. They concluded that

> principal evaluations (if conducted at all) are frequently done by the immediate supervisor, who rarely if ever visits the principal's school. Most evaluation processes are often superficial and based on informal feedback. These procedures do little to assist principals in strengthening their job performance in order to make their schools instructionally effective. (p. 112)

Ginsberg and Berry (1990) provided a comprehensive review of the literature concerning evaluation of public school principals. They cited the Natriello, Deal, Dornbusch, and Hong (1977) view that principal evaluation is in the Stone Age. Ginsberg and Berry characterized "the process of principal evaluation as being minimally studied and minimally changed over the years" (p. 207).

Ginsberg and Berry (1990) described the literature concerning administrator evaluation in five categories: home recipes, literature reviews, guidelines and textbooks, surveys of practice, and research and evaluation studies. They concluded that particularly the first three of these sources offered very few defensible practices for good evaluation. For example, they stated that "textbooks and guidelines . . . offer no conclusive evidence as to which is the best approach to utilize" (p. 215) and "[literature] reviews offer policymakers little in the way of specific information for framing evaluation programs" (p. 213). These authors reported that the research and evaluation literature has begun to disclose directions for improved practice.

Ginsberg and Berry (1990) took this fragmentary advice and findings to piece together state-of-the-art advice for principal evaluation. First, they advised that any strategy be examined in terms of its reliability, validity, and utility. These are key benchmarks for defending the quality of any particular system.

Second, the purpose of the administrator evaluation needs to be carefully considered. The most common purpose is improvement of performance, but other reasons may be included or may be even more important for some settings. Certainly, formative and/or summative purposes need to be specified. The value of a particular approach or set of materials is in relation to the district purpose for evaluation.

Third, criteria (what is to be measured) should be examined carefully. Three possibilities are (a) traits or attributes, for example, dependability; (b) behaviors, for example, planning; and (c) tasks, for example, school climate improvement. Although most districts use mixtures of these criteria types, task-oriented systems are gaining favor.

Fourth, Ginsberg and Berry (1990) recommended that standards for meeting the criteria be carefully selected and explained. In particular, it is important that participants understand what performance or accomplishment levels are expected of them. For example, it makes a difference if complete attainment is expected or merely that minimal achievement is required.

Fifth, instruments and evidence to be used in principal assessment require thoughtful development and presentation. Kinds of instruments include rating sheets, observation procedures, interviews, surveys, portfolios, and self-reports. Some data sources are designed to be quantitative, whereas others allow for narrative reports. Numerical-based decision making is featured in some approaches; others emphasize professional judgment.

Finally, the authors focus on processes of judgment. Quality rests on validity, reliability, utility, and clear standards of defensible criteria, Also adequate training of evaluators is key.

Assessment centers present a possible option for nonbiased principal data. An assessment center is a designated location at which an administrator is required to "perform a number of simulations while being observed by trained assessors to obtain a score that can be used to determine the present or predicted level of administrative skills expertise" (Bryant, 1990, p. 353). One example of administrator assessment centers are those of the National Association of Secondary School Principals (NASSP). NASSP Assessment Centers focus on 12 administrative behaviors: problem analysis, judgment, organizational ability, decisiveness, leadership, sensitivity, stress tolerance, oral communication, written communication, range of interest, personal motivation, and educational values.

Although the strategy of assessment center data gathering appears promising, the problems in practice are lack of predictive validity and the context-free simulation quality of the experience. For example, Schmitt, Noe, Meritt, Fitzgerald, and Jorgensen (1979) reported a 3-year validation study in which assessment center scores were correlated with ratings of self, supervisors, teachers, and support staff from the administrator's own practice. Bryant (1990) described these findings:

> For the self-evaluation, 86 percent . . . of the items were correlated at .15 or less. Eighty-two percent . . . of the items correlated between support staff ratings and Assessment Center ratings were at or below .15. The percentage of stronger correlations (.16 to .45) increased when superior ratings and teacher ratings were correlated. . . . Still, the bulk of the correlations were .15 or less (59 percent for supervisors and 66 percent for teachers). What may be observed here is a Rashomon effect where one's version of reality differs depending upon how one was involved in the crime. (p. 359)

In another study of administrator assessment centers, Bryant (1990) examined the records of 80 participants at one site and found that the NASSP Assessment Center does not capture the assumed expertise (experience) possessed by participants on many dimensions. He reported that "the Assessment Center process does appear to distinguish between experience and inexperience on one, probably two, dimensions: problem analysis and organizational ability" (p. 359).

Weller et al. (1994) surveyed Georgia teachers, principals, and superintendents for their views concerning use of teacher evaluations of principals in the evaluation of administrators by their superiors. "The teacher responses were in the strongly agree category while both principals and superintendents only slightly favored the use of teacher evaluation by superiors" (p. 114). Weller et al. recommended surveys by teachers that focus on "effective-school leadership dimensions" type variables such as quality of school curriculum and instructional climate. The results of these surveys then should be used by the evaluators of administrators.

Recommended Practices for Administrator Evaluation

Recommendations for administrator evaluation follow strategies suggested for teachers, with several modifications. In some respects, the work of an administrator is more circumscribed than that of a classroom teacher. For example, administrators work simultaneously with multiple audiences, each of which views and limits the work of the administrator. The following recommendations for administrator evaluation procedures reflect this difference from the classroom teacher context.

Purposes

The multiple purposes for administration evaluation are similar to those of classroom teachers. Perhaps the most important purpose of administrator evaluation is to reassure the practitioner herself of valuable, meritorious, and even just plain competent work. Just as with teachers, in current practice there is little or no systematic feedback to let principals know that they are doing a good job. Good administrators should enjoy laurels to show off and, at times, to rest on. A good administrator evaluation system can provide this information.

Related to reassurance of individual administrators is reassurance of the audiences that good work is going on. These audiences include parents, the lay public, teachers, fellow administrators, and legislators. Irresponsible policy positions such as "public school administrators are a bloated, unneeded part of the schools" need to be countered with empirical data about function, impact, merit, and value (Berliner & Biddle, 1995).

A third purpose for administrator evaluation is to support the classroom teacher evaluation system. It is difficult to expect teachers to participate fully, take risks, and do the difficult work of evaluation if they do not see the building leadership likewise participating. Also, estimates of teacher impact on pupil learning require estimates of contributions by administrators, parents, and community.

A fourth purpose for administrator evaluation is acknowledgment and dissemination of good administrative practice. It is important to educators everywhere to be made aware of good performances, procedures that satisfy or make a difference, and highlights from a variety of locations. Good administrator evaluation can help disseminate the best practices from the front lines. Administrator training programs benefit from direct examples of good strategies and techniques documented in district evaluation records.

A somewhat distant fifth reason to evaluate administrators is to provide an opportunity for improvement. This reason receives much of the lip service for doing personnel evaluation, but there is very little evidence that anyone in fact takes it seriously. Especially because administrator evaluation is mostly described as nonexistent, this purpose cannot be of much value at present. However, collecting data for *summative* evaluation purposes, as described in this chapter, presents some good materials and perspectives for administrators to do helpful *formative* evaluation on their own.

Multiple Data Sources

Administrator evaluation should be based on a number of lines of evidence that correspond to dimensions of administrator quality. Just as with teachers, overall administrator quality requires information from a number of perspectives. These include principal knowledge (determined by test or expert interview), client survey, objective district evidence, professional activity, and unique data concerning administrator initiative.

Variable Data Sources.

Compared with teachers, administrator tasks are more narrowly defined and less stylistic. There is more responsibility for uniform performance and expectation. Therefore, administrator evaluation is somewhat more uniform than teacher evaluation. Although more mandatory data sources are to be expected, there certainly is variability by individual. The principal should have the opportunity to create *some* of her case for quality. This means that some data are optional or customized for the individual practitioner.

Specific Data Sources

Table 20.1 presents seven kinds of data to be used in administrator evaluation; these data sources are discussed below. The first four are expected of each person; the last three are optional additions that serve to complete information about the value and merit of performance. Optional materials should be collected by the district Evaluation Unit and inspected by the administrator before she decides to include the information in her review.

Required Administrator Data Sources

Administrator knowledge. A number of specific areas of knowledge are important for school administrators. These include promising educational practices, teacher evaluation, legal concerns, emergency procedures, management (business, human resources, conflict resolution), and information about specific audiences such as parents.

Data sources for administrator knowledge may be standardized tests, assessment centers, university course passing grades, or face-to-face interviews with superintendents. Accumulating more than one assessment

TABLE 20.1 Types of Data Sources for Administrator Evaluation

Required
      Administrator knowledge
      Systematic client opinion
      Objective district data
      Professional activity

Optional
      Peer review of personal data
      Assessment center results
      Other data, individually selected

strategy, for example, paper-and-pencil test and performance center, is preferable. This is not an annual activity for each principal, but it should be done frequently enough to ensure continuing up-to-date-knowledge. Administrators who do well in knowledge assessment may want to present evidence from all four techniques. One way to extend these opportunities for administrators is to form a pool of area superintendents who perform this service for each other's districts several days each year. This is a significant time investment, but an important one because it puts into practice the value for administrative knowledge.

Systematic client opinion. An important source of information about administrator quality comes directly from the people with whom he works. Systematic surveys of important audiences document the necessary and important work of the administrator. These audiences include teachers, students, parents, staff, and district contacts. Central purposes of surveys are to build up a record of levels of satisfaction over a period of years and to indicate areas of strength and accomplishment. Survey items should be tied to tasks, simple and direct, and few in number. An overall, global item is quite helpful (Peterson, Gunn, et al., 1984). Survey design and population sampling are technically difficult tasks. Expertise in these topics should be sought by districts developing instruments for administrator evaluation. The surveys should be studied by factor and correlational analysis and improved using the empirical data from trial applications of volunteers.

Despite the recommendations of some advocates, there is little evidence to suggest that one certain style of management is the sine qua non of successful school administration. Duty-based or task-oriented items are the most defensible strategy at present.

Sample interviews or focus groups of audiences, such as students or clerical staff, may be helpful for expanding information found in surveys

(Krueger, 1988; Morgan, 1988). Surveys present standardized responses to major categories of expectations; focus groups highlight the administrator mechanisms, provide concrete examples, and elicit unexpected responses. Group interviews should be conducted and summarized by outsiders. Such additional data gathering can be at the option of the principal.

Objective district data. An important component of administrator evaluation is evidence concerning important duties and tasks. One example is routine paperwork; it is the responsibility of the administrator to keep the information flow in his school, and between school and district, efficient and on time. Another example is requests for transfer by faculty; there is an optimum level where good teachers are encouraged, but bad teachers are pressured to seek greater comfort elsewhere. Other district data might be initiatives for instructional improvement, progress on district goals, and context-indexed effectiveness of student discipline management. Clearly, much local development is required for this data source. Administrators themselves are in a good position to generate and test possibilities. The task is less to weigh principals down with exhaustive, detailed job descriptions but more to give them credit for the good routine work that they do.

Professional activity. Part of educational leadership is consistent participation in activities that develop and encourage up-to-date practice and personnel support. This professional activity includes dissemination of information about educational practice, such as is found in curriculum organizations. Interactions with the business community and employers are important. Youth service agencies and community support groups permit administrators to coordinate efforts. Documentation of professional activity should include logs of contacts, meetings, topics, persons, and dates. Patterns or strategies of participation should be provided by the individual administrator. Her goal statements are important, not for examining achievement or discrepancies but for communicating her insight and intention.

Optional Administrator Data Sources

Peer review of personal data. Individual administrators should have the opportunity to collect evidence of their work in work samples, a portfolio, or a less organized collection of materials in a box. These are reviewed by peer administrators who are not socially, professionally, or personally connected with the person under review. The peer review report consists of a one-page description of the process and a one-page summary of peer findings. The important contents are a summative statement of "contributing, well functioning" or "contributing, well functioning with the following exemplary practices: . . ." or "deficient in these respects . . ." A useful form for reporting the administrator peer review can be made by modifying Form 7.1, The Teacher Peer Review form.

Assessment center results. Although the studies of assessment center strategies (Bryant, 1990) are discouraging as sole indicators of administrator quality, they add to the multiple perspectives that are needed for administrator evaluation. Some individual administrators should use the option to present high assessment center scores as corroborating evidence of their merit.

Other data, individually selected. Finally, individual administrators should have the opportunity to design and assemble evidence of quality performance in a data source that is unique to their situation or practice. This optional evidence can address special circumstances, vision, practical developments, themes, or outcomes. A principal who is responsible for an inordinate amount of success with, for example, school-to-work transitions, local parent involvement and support, complex involvement of child care programs in his building, or high graduation rates should have the opportunity to bring this story to considerations of his merit and worth.

Administrator Review Panels

Summative judgments for administrator retention and remediation should be made by superintendents. These judgments should be informed by administrator professional dossiers and recommendations from administrator review panels, similar to those outlined in this book for teachers. Summative judgments for recognition should be made by panels that have a majority in number of principals, but include teachers and parents as well as associate superintendents.

Needed Research in Administrator Evaluation

These recommendations for evaluation of administrators are, at this point, near the level of "home recipes" in Ginsberg and Berry's (1990) terms, because they are the borrowed ideas of teacher evaluation practices detailed earlier in this book. For example, the student surveys of teacher performance recommended in Chapter 6 were studies with field tests of over 20,000 surveys, factor analysis, and standardized procedures (Peterson & Stevens, 1988). The recommended client surveys in this section on principal evaluation have not been subject to field tests and research. Thus there is considerable research needed to forward these ideas.

Needed research for the evaluation of administrators can follow the same direction as outlined by Peterson (1984) in his call for research on teacher evaluation. He specified research in three dimensions: sociological, political, and technical. For the technical development of evaluation, Peterson recommended studies of the audiences for evaluation, models for designing and doing evaluations, lines of evidence (or data sources), and formats (metrics) for reporting results. Thus research for improved administrator evaluation needs to include not only development of instruments and procedures but also studies of policies and the all-important sociology of administrator evaluation.

Although there are great needs for research in this area, the best advice for local school districts is to begin assisting administrators to collect multiple and variable data sources. Volunteer participation is a good place to start.

EVALUATION OF SUPPORT PERSONNEL

Classroom teachers present specific assessment problems. This book has described processes for tailoring evaluation to the audiences, needs, and performance of teachers. However, not all educators who work for school districts are classroom teachers. These other educators include librarians, special education teachers, counselors, health educator-nurses, physical and arts education specialists, social workers, and home educators. Like teachers, these educators have their own special requirements for effective evaluation.

Stronge and Helm (1991) presented a thorough discussion of evaluation issues concerning educational support personnel. They reported that "the literature on the evaluation of non teaching, non administrative professional personnel in education . . . remains skimpy and difficult to locate" (p. xi). These authors advocated a systems analysis approach that includes six steps: identify system needs, relate expectations to job responsibilities, select performance indicators, set job performance standards, document performance, and evaluate performance. This is a discrepancy evaluation model following the guidelines of Provus (1971).

Recommended Practices for the Evaluation of Support Personnel

In general, strategies for the evaluation of nonclassroom educational specialties should follow the techniques outlined for classroom teachers. This advice is a significant departure from the current practice of administrator-based and discrepancy model personnel evaluation. As with administrator evaluation, the lack of basic research on evaluation of support personnel means that much of this advice relies on empirical work done with classroom teachers.

Multiple Purposes Emphasizing Reassurance of Practitioners and Audiences

It is important that support personnel, evaluators, collaborators, and clients be clear about the purposes for evaluation. Although much rhetoric exists for evaluation to improve performance, it is recommended that the purposes of reassurance, acknowledgment, and dissemination of good practice take great precedence over improvement.

Multiple and Variable Data Sources

Various data sources for support personnel include demonstrations of knowledge (e.g., in standardized test scores), client surveys (e.g., teachers, students, administrators, parents), client change or achievement data, peer reviews of materials and work samples, documentation of professional preparation and activity, administrator reports, and other data unique to individual support personnel. Circumstances may mean that some of these data sources are required, whereas others are optional.

Evaluation of support personnel calls for survey instruments developed especially for the roles. For example, nurses may call for surveys of classroom teachers to document their perceptions of merit and worth of services. Items that call for frequency of use are important parts of specialist surveys. Use of focus groups of client teachers works well for school specialists, where individual teachers vary a great deal in their knowledge of specialist performance.

Assembly of Professional Dossiers

Support personnel should be responsible for guiding the assembly of personal professional dossiers of compressed evidence supporting their case for valuable and meritorious performance. The dossiers are maintained by a district Evaluation Unit, but directed by the individual educators. Selection of materials for the dossier and value of results can be credentialed by socially and professionally neutral consultant experts.

Panel Review of Dossiers

Ultimate value and merit of dossier contents should be determined by a district review panel. The panel should be dominated in number by support personnel, but include teachers, administrators, and parents. Retention remediation decisions can be made, as presently, by administrators.

TEACHER ACKNOWLEDGMENT AND LEADERSHIP

As was described in Chapter 1, teacher evaluation has as a main function the recognition and acknowledgment of good practice. Some additional provisions are available for supporting leadership and acknowledging exemplary practice.

Teacher leadership positions in a district include department chairs in high schools, cluster leadership in middle schools, and grade-level leaders in elementary schools. Other leadership positions are committee memberships and chairs on curriculum decisions, textbook adoption, advisory bodies, and parent relations. Some districts have developed site councils for local control. Mentors for newly hired teachers are a kind of leadership position. Finally, having student teachers assigned provides still another kind of leadership. Typically, teachers are selected for the above kinds of service based on volunteering, an unsystematic tradition of leadership, or personal influence unrelated to merit. It is recommended that teacher leadership placement decisions be based on successful dossier review. A selection process that recognizes quality, merit, and value gives prestige to the teacher, selection process, and ultimately to the evaluation system itself.

Teacher acknowledgment currently consists of teacher-of-the-year programs. These programs are not respected by practitioners who see recipients as making an end run around the scarce reward possibilities in the district (Lortie, 1975). One desirable replacement is leadership and service assignments based on dossier review. Another possibility is a "high-quality practice" fair at which well-documented teacher accomplishments are highlighted for their exemplary practice. The goal for these staff development opportunities is more for emulation than for setting aside some teachers.

TEACHERS IN SPECIFIC PROJECTS

Teachers may collaborate in special projects or subgroups. For example, a group of teachers forms a school-within-a-school, language immersion program, writing project, or other specialized grouping. When this happens, teachers have a vested interest in the prestige and survival of their program. Teacher evaluation, as advocated in this book, can support these groups by coordinating and highlighting performance of the teachers within the specific project. For example, teachers in a foreign language immersion program can use this focus to bring in external reviews and concrete data that highlight their emphasis. This strategy helps to document individual teacher merit and value, but it also can be turned to bring attention to the program itself.

Teacher evaluation is a tool of teacher groups to build and maintain their identity and to compete for scarce resources. The contribution of concrete information to the system results in increased power in recognition and decision making for these teachers. Gathering support and data for one's program is an essential political component of any school district.

21

Evaluating Deficient Teachers

Bridges (1992) defined the deficient teacher as one who persistently fails one or more of the expectations for teachers to maintain discipline, properly treat students, impart subject matter, accept teaching advice from superiors, demonstrate subject matter knowledge, and produce student learning or other objectives. *American Law Reports* stated that

> the incompetent teacher is rarely deficient in one respect alone; rather, incompetence seems to manifest itself in a pervasive pattern encompassing a multitude of sins and bringing in its wake disorganization, disharmony, and an atmosphere unproductive for the acquisition of knowledge or any other ancillary benefit. (4 A.L.R. 3d 1090 at 1102)

The evaluation of the deficient teacher has received more attention and description than most other topics of teacher evaluation.

Evaluation itself addresses only one part of the problem of the deficient teacher. The situation of the bad teacher calls for a decision about remediation or dismissal, generates considerable expense, and causes severe sociological disruption. This chapter looks at how the problem of the deficient teacher fits into teacher evaluation practice. It will give advice for strengthening the teacher evaluation component of dealing with the bad teacher.

Thus far in the book, it has been recommended that data sources be voluntarily selected by teachers. However, this chapter recommends that the deficient teacher be *required* to gather evidence to determine competence and retention. Increased and targeted evaluation leads to more precise data for personnel actions to remediate or terminate the bad teacher.

THE BAD TEACHER DRAWS ATTENTION TO TEACHER EVALUATION

Educators pay little attention to teacher evaluation unless there are severe problems. This makes sense; the central activity of education is working with students and most attention is directed to that end. Also, Lortie (1975) described the sociological "presentism" of schools that pressures teachers to create short-term impressions of control, work compliance, and respect and affection, not longer term information about performance quality coming from systematic evaluation data and decisions. The sociological force of presentism directs attention away from evaluation, which is treated as a relatively unimportant long-term activity. Additionally, evaluation is stressful for both teachers and administrators; unpleasant experiences tend to be ignored in favor of pleasant ones. Finally, evaluation rarely drives improvement or practice, so attention is not generated by hopes for future effect.

What does draw attention to teacher evaluation is the infrequent problem of the bad teacher. The actual number of deficient teachers is small; an estimate has been made by Bridges (1992), Johnson (1984), Neill and Custis (1978), and Tucker (1997) of 5% of the total teaching corps. However, this small number attracts the greatest share of teacher evaluation attention. This small group is a morale killer among teachers. The public relations problem is significant. Fear of the bad teacher situation creates much upsetting professional lore. The presence of the deficient teacher is one of the few times when educators want a thorough, comprehensive, objective, and respected teacher evaluation system.

The existence of the bad teacher in a school generates a cycle of problems. Allegations of bad teaching generate much conflict among educators and clients. Disagreements about events and remedies for the conflict abound. Action calls for a basis in fact and data, which most often have not been gathered. Lack of reliable and valid information causes educator inaction. Teachers, who are in a position to support decisive remediation or removal of bad teachers, withdraw their involvement and demand that the administrators take sole responsibility. Teachers' organizations must first protect individual members; long-term protection of the entire membership by controlling quality is a secondary responsibility. Hesitation in personnel actions causes doubt in the public and greater conflict for the teacher at risk, administrators, and the majority of teachers who are not directly involved. Much attention and discussion is generated in all audiences by the topic of evaluating and acting on the deficient teacher. Few in the organization can be mobilized to deal with the problem.

SELECTED LITERATURE

Lawrence et al. (1993) distinguished between the self-assured teacher and the marginal teacher. They described the self-assured teacher as "predisposed to success in the classroom largely due to a firm belief that he or she has the power to nurture higher order thinking and social learning skills in even the most recalcitrant student" (p. 3). The marginal teacher is "unlikely to experience a great deal of success in the classroom" (p. 3). The hallmark of the marginal teacher is low pupil performance. Work of the marginal teacher is characterized by "boring, uninspiring, and ineffective instruction" (p. 5). Indicators of poor teaching include an inordinate number of disciplinary referrals, complaints from parents and colleagues, and requests for transfer from parents.

Lawrence et al. (1993) suggest that in current practice administrators can contribute only somewhat to the assurance of teachers. They listed such minor acknowledgments as providing business cards, work areas, keys to classrooms, and public recognition of excellence. However, they recognized that qualities for self-assurance are largely internal (knowledge, confidence, energy, vitality, flexibility, nonbias, accommodation, sensitivity) and not subject to change by external forces. Thus the future of the marginal teacher is grim. These authors provided 34 sample letters and forms, regularly scheduled throughout a school year, to set the stage for fair identification and dismissal of the marginal teacher. For example, one document recommended by Lawrence et al. is an informal observation form for administrators. It contains information about "criteria established by the school district" (p. 18) and columns to check scale values of "outstanding", "above average," "average," "fair," "unsatisfactory," and "not applicable." A second formal observation form uses the same checklist scale in seven categories: planning/instructional strategies, understanding the curriculum, assessment of instructional plan, classroom management, classroom environment, schoolwide involvement, and professional development. In each category, a listing of specific district criteria is called for. The authors also developed a self-report Teacher Expectancy Analysis Instrument and a Professional Development Needs Assessment Instrument.

Bridges (1992) provided a thorough analysis of the problems of dealing with the incompetent teacher. His perspective is an empirical report of practices, rather than a collection of home recipes; he tells it like it is practiced. Bridges began by reviewing the statistics of bad teachers. He continued with a discussion of the lack of action against them on the part of most educators. The central reasons for inaction are to avoid unpleasant situations and the great cost of action (dismissal procedures may cost $50,000-$100,000). Districts are not likely to dismiss bad tenured teachers unless the district places an unusually high value on action, the district is small, parent complaints are up or enrollment is down, or financial problems are severe.

Bridges (1992) described the first response of school districts to bad teachers as a salvage attempt. Although this rarely leads to improvement, salvage generally passes through seven stages. The first is a change from the usual tepid praise to unmitigated criticism. This leads, second, to a defensive reaction on the part of the teacher. The third stage is a behavioral description of problems—which may or may not be entirely accurate. Next is limited assistance because effective techniques are not actually available. A fifth common response is restrained support of the teacher. This comes from the complexity of improvement, which is not likely to happen soon, and the legal problems of positive evaluations at this point when termination is a possibility. Sixth, extensive documentation is characteristic as the administrator seeks to buttress the case and establish a number of positions, including "I'm thorough, nonbiased, reasonable, and trying to help the teacher improve; the teacher is incompetent (and other people agree), and not misassigned." Finally, remediation attempts result, predictably, in little improvement.

Bridges (1992) reviewed the induced exits employed by school district, including pressure (indirect such as transfer to undesirable assignment or direct such as persuasion, threat, or probation), notice of incompetence, negotiations, involvement of teacher unions, or inducements to leave (such as early retirement). Finally, formal termination proceedings begin.

Tucker (1997) reported a survey study of 112 Virginia principals on their responses to teacher incompetence. In addition to estimates of rates of deficiency, one study hypothesis stated that the presence of certain components in a district system might be associated with increased administrator action on incompetence. Tucker identified 35 components of a district evaluation system including five from each of the following seven categories: presence and use of criteria, established procedures, remedial procedures, priority of evaluation activity in the district, collaboration among those involved in evaluation and supervision, training, and integration of evaluation with other district components (such as staff development).

The principals in the Tucker study reported a mean rate of incompetence among their teachers of 5% (range 0%-15%). However, the sample formally identified incompetence for action at the mean rate of 2.65% of teachers. Thus, Tucker concluded that "principals and school systems are avoiding a serious problem that undermines the education of millions of children, staff morale, and the public's perception of education" (p. 103). In addition, she concluded that:

> The most disturbing finding of the study was the lack of any relationship between evaluation system components and the incidence of administrative response to incompetence. Based on these findings, a comprehensive evaluation [system] does not ensure that a principal will address incompetence. (p. 116)

Tucker hypothesized that factors other than the formal teacher evaluation components play into the administrators' reluctance to act on incompetence. She listed

1. Personality characteristics, such as discomfort with confrontation
2. Lack of requisite skills for identification, assistance, and assessment of satisfactory progress
3. Role conflict when required to offer both assistance and final judgment on performance
4. Inadequate time to work with teachers experiencing difficulty
5. Lack of support from superintendent and school board
6. Lack of financial resources for all phases of evaluation (including possible litigation in cases of dismissal)

Scriven (1997) provided a thorough, explicit, logical analysis of due process in dismissal actions. Although he argued for the need for expert local legal advice (an attorney), he devised a checklist of practical, ethical, legal, and social issues for consideration. His timeline framework suggested informal notice and formal specification (with seven essential components, such as bill of particulars, logical connections with contract, specifics of improvement, and time specifications). In addition to the formal specifications, there are specific requirements for district actions, namely (a) sticking to time specifications, (b) adding no related increase in load, (c) attention to teacher-initiated decrease in load, and (d) the nature of help offered to teacher. A district must be thorough in its response to the teacher's rebuttal. The reevaluation period is crucial; it must include pertinent review, documentation, standards, and careful consideration of time.

RECOMMENDED PRACTICES

Once the deficient teacher has been identified, two main courses of action may be taken by administrators. If the problem is immediate, irremediable, unacceptable, and intolerable, the administrators should move for immediate suspension and dismissal. As specified in local state statutes (or administrative rules), grounds for dismissal might include physical abuse, immorality, insubordination, physical incapacity, unprofessional conduct, or gross incompetence (Gee & Sperry, 1978; Strike & Bull, 1981; Valente, 1987). Documentation concerning the specific act(s) or problem, and lack of remediation as a remedy, is required. Also important are witnesses and evidence of damages, where appropriate. Provision for procedural due process should be in place in the district (Annunziata, 1998, 1999; Fischer & Schimmel, 1973: Rebell, 1990; Scriven, 1997), as described in Chapter 25.

A second kind of response to deficient teaching is for less acute and egregious problems. This action is for deficient or marginal teaching that can be improved and presents less an immediate (and more a long-term) threat to students. The following recommended evaluation practices are for this second kind of bad teaching. These strategies begin with a declaration by the administrators of probationary status for the teacher. The period of probation also should be accompanied by strict procedural and substantive due process. The following sections address evaluation concerns (for example, data gathering) and not other managerial requirements (for example, appointment of mentors to probationary teachers and inservice education).

Mandatory Multiple Data Sources

Mandatory multiple data sources are put in place at declaration of probation. This is a significant departure from the option data gathering recommended for the vast majority of teachers as part of their routine evaluation. Teachers on probation should be assisted in gathering the evidence. Administrators should assemble this evidence for remediation and improvement. Failing a correction of deficiencies, the data become evidence for dismissal.

Data Source Selection

The data sources should be selected by administrators in relation to the problem. The problem of *ineffective teaching* calls for pupil achievement data, peer review of materials, systematic observation, and pupil reports. *Human relations problems* call for student reports, parent surveys, and the less systematic evidence of spontaneous complaints. *Lack of knowledge* will be evident in teacher testing, peer review of materials, and professional activity. The teacher may call for additional data, but should not be allowed to exclude the lines of evidence decided on by the administrators.

The teacher is notified that collection of these data is mandatory and arrangements have been made to proceed. The teacher should get copies of the results at the same time the administrator does.

Data Collection

Data for probationary teachers should not be collected by the Teacher Evaluation Unit. The purpose of this agency is reassurance and recognition. Rather, data should be collected under the direction of administrators. Data collectors can be agreed on by teacher and administrator, although some situations will preclude this negotiation. It is best to have ad hoc personnel external to the district for data gathering, for example, on loan from another district under a reciprocal agreement. Data should be collected using the general district guidelines, for example, concerning sample size and assurance of credibility. Most often, the usual district procedures and instruments are appropriate. Additional instrument items may need to be added by either party.

Decision Making

Decisions about bad teaching should be made by administrators. Due process provides such features as hearings, details of the evidence, and chance for rebuttal (Annunziata, 1998, 1999; Fischer & Schimmel, 1973; Rebell, 1990; Scriven, 1997; Strike & Bull, 1981). Remediation and termination proceedings must not be handled by the district Teacher Review Panel. This body has a distinct function of reassurance and acknowledgment of excellence that is threatened by involvement in retention and dismissal cases.

RESPONSES TO BAD TEACHING

There is general agreement that remediation is preferably to dismissal. First, thoughts should turn to specific information, evaluation data, and supported opportunities to improve. Simply too much time and money are invested in teachers, and too many hazards in quick dismissal exist, to not take the opportunity for remediation seriously. The idealism of the best efforts at remediation and salvage is important.

District Teamwork With Deficient Teacher

Figure 21.1 depicts a possible complex organization for school district teamwork with a deficient teacher. The goals for this system are (1) sufficient resources and safeguards, (2) flexibility for the range of responses needed, and (3) support for the individual building principal. The intent is for the district to take more frequent and better responses to poor practice.

Key features of the district support system include:

Principal who initiates most remediation and dismissal actions based on her monitoring and review of teacher-provided data.

Administrator Review Team (ART) who meets with the principal soon after he flags the bad practice; their function is to review the nature and process of the action. The ART consists of experienced upper-level district administrators whose purpose is to give the principal perspective and advice. It is important that the ART not merely look for ways to back the principal, but to thoughtfully review the wisdom and adequacy of the responses; in fact, they may advise to rescind initial actions. The views of the ART are not formally used in the job action, but are intended to give helpful support and counsel to the principal.

Rating System where a rating of "N" (needs improvement) on the annual administrator report calls for remediation on the part of the teacher. The teacher may be told anytime during the year that (at this time) this is the rating to be given at the end of the year. The teacher then can informally work with the principal during the year to have the rating moved to a "W" (well functioning). This feature gives the principal leverage in her work with a deficient teacher without involving formal district notice.

Performance Assistance Phase where an experienced veteran teacher is appointed to work with the teacher for a specified period. This mentor does not gather evidence nor write a report that is to be used in the job action. The mentor is a joint appointment of the district administration and the teachers' organization.

Remediation Team Phase where a four-person team works for remediation. In this group the principal is joined by three veteran teachers—one each appointed by the teacher, teachers' organization, and district administration. In addition to providing coaching, referrals, materials, inservice education, observations, and conferences, they gather evidence that may be used to document remediation or as evidence for a dismissal action.

Figure 21.1 Teamwork With the Marginal Teacher

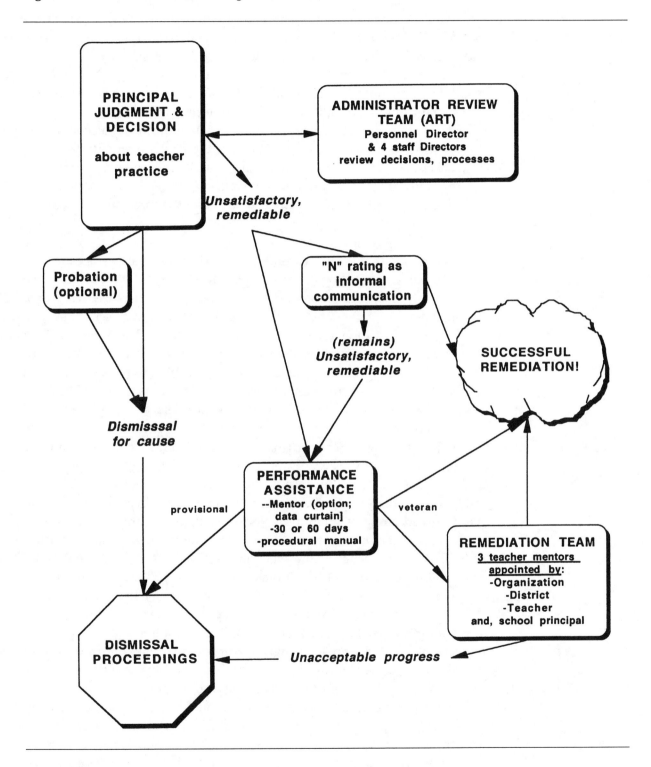

Dismissal of the Deficient Teacher

Public education has the reputation of not dealing with poor performance. Consider, for example, this editorial calling for educators to "Toss bad apples from class" (*Salt Lake Tribune,* April 9, 1997):

Many school principals—and their superiors—obviously are reluctant to go through the complex due-process procedures required to terminate teachers. Strict rules on monitoring teachers, alerting them to problems and helping them improve, divert supervisors from other tasks. The process can disrupt entire communities if targeted teachers have allies who use union power, the courts and social pressure to overpower their principals. (editorial page)

The reason that it takes careful effort to dismiss a teacher is called the United States Constitution (Cooper, 1997). The careful effort that administrators put into teacher personnel actions strengthens the society for all of its members. The safety and well functioning of the entire school system and larger society depends on the care of many people. The time and effort spent by school districts considering the rights and due-process concerns are valuable and necessary, and ultimately contribute to the safety of each citizen. Although it should be expensive to badly dismiss a teacher or to try to dismiss a good teacher, it certainly is possible to dismiss a bad teacher.

The conventional wisdom that it is virtually impossible to dismiss the bad teacher is a myth. School districts can and do effectively deal with the marginal teacher (Andrews, 1995; Annunziata, 1998, 1999; Cooper, 1997; Scriven, 1997; Tucker, 1997). The problem of bad teacher practice is routinely dealt with by (1) successful remediation of certain problems, (2) mutually agreed upon resignations (Fossey, 1998), (3) negotiated early retirements, and (4) dismissals for serious, irremediable problems. Tucker (1997) estimated the incidence of these actions at 45% for remediation, 24% for resignation/retirement, 17% for reassignment, and 7% for termination.

Four requirements for successful dismissal are listed in Table 21.1. First, the actions and documentation in a specific case must be reasonable. The district establishes that there is a specific problem with clear consequences: Students are not learning. It should be clear that there are patterns of problems—not just isolated mistakes. Reason means that there is documentation that establishes the facts of the charges.

Second, the evaluation system itself should indicate the problem (i.e., the system has not merely been used to get the teacher after the problem is known). Far too often, districts are aware of the deficiencies, then mobilize the evaluation system to document the prior decision. These cases are easy

TABLE 21.1 What Is Required to Dismiss a Poor Teacher

Reasonableness in this specific case—this person, situation, action
The teacher evaluation system indicates the problem
The teacher evaluation system and policy are strictly followed and applied
Fairness

to recognize by teacher attorneys and courts, and clearly are not appropriate. Third, the teacher evaluation system must be followed. If features are in the system, either as written or traditionally practiced, they must be done as specified; this means that mistakes such as overly complicated systems, specious jargon, and vague language built into a district system must be applied. Finally, in order to dismiss deficient teachers, fairness is an absolute. People cannot be treated differently, arbitrarily, or capriciously.

What is not necessary in a teacher evaluation system that responds well to incompetence is extensive documentation, an expensive "research-based" system, and overly complex policies. However, these approaches are commonly used in the mistaken hope that they are effective remedies for incompetent practice.

In addition to the above requirements, the new directions and practices of teacher evaluation add considerable support to dismissals of deficient teachers. First, objective evidence such as parent views and pupil achievement data can be systematically documented independently of the principal. Second, additional mandatory data can be made available as a part of dismissal action. Third, broad-based support for the principal actions, as shown in Figure 21.1, encourages principals to respond to teacher incompetence.

Further Thoughts on Dismissal

Bridges (1992) pointed out that remediation assumes that the problem is mere lack of information or modeling of good practice. However, it is virtually unthinkable that a teacher can survive a minimum of several years in public education without having been shown or exhorted to display good practice. Schools of education abound with good examples, assignments, and even requirements for good practice. Also, the idealism of new teacher colleagues is infectious and should have affected every beginner. Few schools do not have *some* senior colleagues who spontaneously render opinions and aid to newcomers. Even the busiest of administrators have a self-interest in the good practice of new teachers and act at times to help aid or correct new teachers. All of this means that a bad practitioner is that way because of some fairly profound and specific problems. These deficiencies are not likely to be amenable to the simplistic, routinized, and logical-linear solutions of remediation. Also, it should be recognized that the intellectual, technical, and monetary resources to address these problems simply do not exist. Thus Bridges is quite justified in his pessimism about remediation of the bad teacher, and he is supported by his empirical studies of actual school district experience.

Teacher dismissal should be accepted as a needed part of professional teacher life. Given extensive safeguards, opportunities for professional growth, and remediation programs, all educators must support inevitable dismissals. Of course, teacher unions will always experience ambiguity in this process. Their function is to protect their members, directly in dismissal cases and indirectly in support of teacher quality checks. The educational system needs the less ambiguous influence of teachers in the problems of deficient practice. Three systematic features can help the greater acceptance and support of teachers in dismissal cases. First, rigorous teacher selection is key to reducing the need for dismissal, but highlighting its importance. Second, the tenure-granting process and decision need to be strengthened—tough actions are needed at this point in professional careers. Third, supportive development of teachers is important. Inservice education needs to be deeply conceived, patient, broadly involved, and teacher directed. All three of these features can help to dispel reasons to tolerate bad teaching.

Finally, one nonsystematic feature needs strengthening: the professional regulation behavior of teachers. Making the administrator the sole player in teacher dismissals is tempting for teachers who are not directly involved, but ultimately creates more difficulties for teachers. Public confidence in teacher quality is lessened, individual teachers experience greater uncertainty, administrators are distanced from teachers, and the dismissal process itself is made more personally damaging. Instead, teachers' representatives and organizations need to make their support visible in addressing the problem of the deficient teacher by participating in teacher evaluation (as described in this book), voicing clear standards and expectations, and monitoring the dismissal process for positive (as well as negative) actions.

INTERNET RESOURCES

ERIC clearinghouse on teacher dismissal

http://www.ericae.net/db/edo/ED259448.htm

ASCD on supervision of poor teacher

http://westy.jtwn.k12.pa.us/users/sja/Supervision-3.html

Principal on teacher evaluation

http://llanes.panam.edu/ed63000/Ethnomethodology.html

Miami-Dade County Public Schools

http://paces.dade.k12.fl.us/

PART V

School District Responsibilities and Activities

22

School District Concerns

This book has focused on a significantly more central role in evaluation for the individual teacher. However, support at a school district level is essential to make and maintain this transformation of responsibility. This chapter presents four topics toward this end. First, district responsibilities for increased and improved teacher evaluation are listed and described. These include administrator evaluation, improved forms and procedures, technical assistance and advice, and enhanced community relations. The second topic is costs of teacher evaluation. This chapter presents specific cost estimates (taken from field trials and research reports) on data sources such as student surveys, peer review of materials, teacher tests, and systematic observation. A specific teacher evaluation budget is highlighted and strategies for districts to manage evaluation costs are presented. Third, a section on improving the culture and politics for teacher evaluation details steps for districts to work on a positive climate for teacher participation and community support for teacher evaluation, which leads to increased public support for the entire school program. The technical improvements of Parts II and III *require* these collateral sociological and political changes. Finally, stagewise transition to increase evaluation activity is important for districts to take the necessary time, engage volunteer teachers, conduct local research and development, train personnel, and build the infrastructure for improved teacher evaluation.

SCHOOL DISTRICT RESPONSIBILITIES

Good teacher evaluation is a partnership among teachers, administrators, staff and community. Specific contributions of policies and resources at the school district level are needed to encourage the teacher initiative required for fully effective and credible teacher evaluation. Table 12.1 lists seven district-level provisions; they are discussed individually in this section. It is more important to make good progress in all of these areas than to fully complete only one or two of them.

Administrator Evaluation

Literally, the first step in improved and expanded *teacher* evaluation is to begin a visible and complex *administrator* evaluation system. Before mobilizing the teachers and beginning the development of complex teacher assessment procedures, all of the educators in the district need the example, leadership, and common risks of administrators under equal scrutiny and burden for data gathering. As described by Scriven (1981), "A system for the evaluation of administrators must be *in place* in order to avoid the entirely justifiable resistance of the serfs to being evaluated by those in the castle, who are above such things themselves" (p. 245). It is necessary to have the administrator evaluation system working for at least a short period of time before initiating similar developments with teachers.

District Principles for Educator Evaluation

Each school district should prepare a list of principles of educator evaluation, which will serve as a guide and standard to the many activities of building a system. This list of principles should be discussed and revised regularly as district personnel become more competent and experienced in teacher evaluation. Table 22.2 presents a sample set of principles.

Improved Forms and Procedures

Virtually all school districts currently have a set of teacher evaluation forms and procedures. These usually include principal report forms and policy descriptions in district employee handbooks. Some districts may have separate evaluation handbooks, with position and policy statements, forms, and research study citations.

It is important to the development of new directions in teacher evaluation for district personnel to see systematic and widespread activity to im-

TABLE 22.1 School District Responsibilities for Increased Teacher Evaluation

Program of administrator evaluation
District principles for education evaluation
Improved evaluation forms and procedures
Technical assistance and advice for individual teachers
Inservice on teacher evaluation
Teacher mentor and visitation programs
Substitute pool for teacher evaluation released time
Community relations on teacher evaluation issues

prove current forms and procedures. This should include a visible literature research effort, where best practices and principles are sought out. Development of forms should include prototype models and publicized pilot volunteer studies and data gathering, so that an empirical and rational basis and tradition are established. Teachers need to see that routine public debate is held over new forms and procedures, that discussion is based on data, and that changes are made as a result of debate (Lortie, 1967).

Reliance on a specific set of forms and procedures is much less important than having a systematic and ongoing process of local research and development. The assessments and judgments are best understood as estimates, which can be improved in time. The developmental strategy should be one of successive, improving approximations of estimating the merit and worth of individual teachers. Although the forms and procedures presented in this book are defensible starting points, the empirical experience of each school district over a period of at least 5 years is essential to building a good local system.

Technical Assistance and Advice

New directions in teacher evaluation mean that teachers take on much increased individual professional responsibility for their own evaluation. To do this successfully, teachers need access to technical assistance and advice in evaluation practice. For example, technical consultations help them to decide to try one data source, but not use another. The advice can lead them to make choices, for which they then become responsible. The consultants are not the authority, but are guides for individual steps that a teacher takes to create her evaluation program.

Consultants and advisers need to be politically and sociologically neutral. They should not be members of the administrative staff who have

TABLE 22.2 Guiding Principles of Educator Evaluation

The Teacher Evaluation System Should:

1. Conform to state statutes concerning educator evaluation.
2. Be understood, credible, valued, and used by district personnel, board, and community.
3. Recognize and acknowledge good teaching, reassure practitioners and audiences, give security to good educators, highlight exemplary practices for emulation, inform hiring practices, and foster improvement.
4. Supply information about educator quality for accountability, educator planning, retention decisions, and public and professional dissemination.
5. Include distinct formative, summative, and monitoring functions.
6. Be based on the best objective evidence available, show a logical analysis for procedures and decisions, control bias, and involve the interested audiences. Value the use of multiple and variable data sources.
7. Promote equality of opportunity for student learning.
8. Include the central involvement of individual educators and their responsibility for their own professional evaluation. Promote equality of opportunity for professional practice and documentation of merit, value, and impact.
9. Be based on role expectations derived from national professional standards.[a]
10. Meet professional standards for sound personnel evaluation, including *propriety, utility, feasibility,* and *accuracy.*[b]
11. Support fairness and the rights of both educators and the institution.[c]
12. Include all categories of personnel, and be supported by assessment of other educational components that influence student achievement. The district should show balance in assessing students, staff, and programs, and reciprocity and parallelism in rigor and frequency of assessment.
13. Show special emphasis on assessment and assistance for beginners.
14. In cases of poor practice, supply specific information for effective remediation, or make a case for dismissal.
15. Be subject itself to evaluation, validation, refinement, and updating.

NOTES: a. National Board for Professional Teaching Standards (1996); Danielson, C. (1996).
b. Joint Committee on Standards for Educational Evaluation (1988).
c. Strike, K. & Bull, B. (1981).

summative or monitoring responsibilities. Their central role is to provide information and options. They can be critical and demanding in a technical sense, but not in terms of the teacher's classroom practice.

Consultants should be available to work one-to-one with teachers (Berman & McLaughlin, 1978). They need to give advice about specific populations, data, and situations, for example, how to show learning gains in a multiage primary classroom. Assistance is required to plan overall data gathering and corroboration, and to look at specific data, for example, parent surveys about a middle school, team-taught, block-scheduled class on community health problems. Advice is needed on data presentation, as well as gathering and interpretation; for example, statistical and graphical analysis and presentation are important topics for advisers.

Without this technical support, teachers lack confidence to control their own evaluation. They are expert in what goes on in classrooms and how to assess student activity, but much less expert in professional personnel evaluation. Their familiarity with many of the tools and vocabulary of educational evaluation makes the job easier, but teacher evaluation is a new task for teachers.

Inservice Education on
Teacher Evaluation

Related to the teacher's need for advice and consultation is a regular program of inservice education on teacher evaluation issues. Without inservice training, for example, on topics of sampling and statistical analysis, teachers lack the tools and confidence to take initiative. They are less able to make decisions for which they take responsibility. The knowledge of teachers needed to design and complete good teacher evaluation is considerable and should be built over a period of years. This not only strengthens teacher work on their own evaluation but it becomes a resource for the district as the collective teacher wisdom and experience accumulate. The advice for allowing years of development for teacher evaluation development recognizes this need for building teacher knowledge.

One justification for inservice work in teacher evaluation topics is the transfer to classroom teaching practice. Ideas about teacher performance assessment and authentic evaluation directly apply to student learning and assessment. For example, the dossiers of teachers have a parallel in student portfolios. The ideas of data gathering and presentation are important in student work. Principles of sampling, evidence, and documentation serve teachers well as they plan student curriculum.

The advice of Berman and McLaughlin (1978) about effective dissemination of educational innovations is important in designing effective teacher inservice on evaluation. Their findings are for districts to include (a) concrete, teacher-specific, ongoing advice; (b) assistance on individual teacher evaluations; (c) visits and observations of successful evaluation programs in other locations; (d) regular meetings on teacher evaluation progress; (e) teacher participation in evaluation program decisions; (f) local development of evaluation materials; and (g) inclusion of administrators in training. They found that successful advice avoids outside consultants, packaged management approaches, one-shot presentations, payment for participation, formal evaluation of the evaluation process, and large-scale programs for too many people and locations at once.

Mentor and Visitation Programs

Mentor and teacher visitation programs are loosely structured opportunities for practitioners to informally assist each other. Mentor programs are generally designed for beginning teachers and are arranged for a fixed period of time (Driscoll, Peterson, & Kauchak, 1985). Teacher visitation programs are less formal and shorter in duration. They provide brief opportunities for teachers to watch each other in practice. Such visits are appropriate for both beginning and veteran teachers. They work best when focused on specific topics identified by the teacher visited and the visitor, for example, how to begin the day, or the logistics of complex sets of hands-on materials. It is not always the case that the teacher who is visited has the best practice. When the visitor turns out to have the better practice, she benefits from confirmation in her own teaching. The professional exchange and reassurance provided by these visits is essential to professional growth and perspective on one's own work.

The link between teacher evaluation and mentor or visitation programs is the sharing of professional wisdom and perspective of individual experience, and the idea that teachers pass ideas on and encourage each other. Specific examples and generalizations in a given context of practice are essential to the development of the individual teachers who are competent to direct their own evaluation and to participate in the evaluation of colleagues. Thus mentors and visits set the stage for increased teacher participation in teacher evaluation.

Without mentoring and visitation programs, teachers are reluctant to form opinions about each other's practice. Without a positive and profitable history of looking at each other's classrooms and materials, the more critical requirements of teacher evaluation (e.g., in a peer review of materials) are too novel and threatening for many teachers to carry out successfully. The foundational development of teachers in these programs is essential to more complex teacher evaluation schemes.

Substitute Pool

Teacher evaluation activities take time from teachers. Efficient evaluation systems mean little lost classroom practice time. However, a complex and developing teacher evaluation system will require, on occasion, time for some teachers during classroom instruction schedules. One example of this is visitation programs, which must take place while students are in session. Another example is the meeting of Teacher Review Panels that may occur during school time.

An important barrier to teacher participation in teacher evaluation activities is the disruption to their own classrooms. Field tests consistently find a somewhat unexpected barrier in the form of an inadequate number of good classroom substitute teachers. Although this problem does not seem like a huge one in terms of all of the activities and logistics needed for a complex teacher evaluation system, it turns out to be a critical barrier. The remedy is to find several very good substitutes and to include them in a pool for teacher evaluation/visitation times. The priority in scheduling these substitutes goes to those doing teacher evaluation activities. This removes one important distraction. It means giving up some secret and favored persons, but also means a more stable pool for evaluation activities.

Two strategies are important in building the substitute teacher pool. First, individual teachers should nominate good candidates. This will operate *against* the individual teacher interest in that the substitute will then be less available to that individual teacher than before it was known how good that person is. Second, the district should begin an aggressive search and recruitment of new substitutes for the purpose of teacher evaluation support. These would be persons in the community who want part-time work. This cadre should be specially trained and recognized.

Without this provision, many good and key teachers will eventually be burned out on their participation and leadership because their own classrooms are not supported well enough. This is a subtle but significant barrier to development of the entire teacher evaluation system. It is too often overlooked because the problems do not surface for several years.

Community Relations

A further responsibility of school districts that are setting up complex teacher evaluation systems is to work on community relations surrounding teacher performance and teacher evaluation. It is one thing to expect teachers to take initiative to tell the story of their practice and to document successes and unfilled needs. However, teacher evaluation is not done in the absence of a context; it needs an environment of community understanding and support. A central reason for teacher evaluation is to reassure audiences, and certainly the community is a central audience. The school district is in the position to best develop relations within this context.

Good community relations begin with a working knowledge of the community. Neighborhoods, sections of large cities, and small towns vary considerably. Community study may follow the example of Narode, Rennie-Hill, and Peterson (1994). Although this study was done with preservice teachers, similar activities are productive with veteran teachers. These authors reported on how teachers spent time with community recreation centers, teen health programs, churches, and youth gang task forces. At each location, teacher candidates asked about community expectations for schools. They found two largely different populations. For one segment of the community, schools work well. For the other, schools do not work well. In both cases, teachers learned a great deal about community expectations. They gained confidence that their efforts were pointed in the right direction. They tapped into the strong support for schools felt even by community members who did not feel well served by schools. Gestwicki (1987) presented still other ideas for community study. His more simple approaches include (a) study of local newspaper stories and (b) "walk arounds" of neighborhoods.

All of these community study activities take time. But without them, teachers lack specific knowledge, perspective, and the certainty of community support. Polls (e.g., Gallup, 1985) consistently show that persons approve of their own schools, whereas they are critical of education in general. Community study gains this support for teachers. Once school districts better understand communities, they are in position to make the moves for better relations. For example, one idea from Narode et al. (1994) is to create parent welcome rooms at local high schools. This is a relatively low-cost provision with payoffs of increased support.

Improved community relations continue with information about teachers and efforts to increase documentation of teacher work. Parent surveys create a direct line of feedback information from community to school. Information sessions for the community on results of surveys and achievement data should be scheduled. The climate where the community cares about teacher performance data is created by the district providing meeting times and places about the efforts. More such ideas about building good community relations are presented in Chapter 26.

COSTS OF TEACHER EVALUATION

Two facts of life are that love hurts and evaluation costs. Too often in current practice, teacher evaluation is treated as an activity with zero expense. A critical deficiency of many discussions of teacher evaluation systems is the failure to include debate about costs (e.g., Lewis, 1982; McGreal, 1983; Millman, 1981). In fact, teacher evaluation procedures and practices have time and dollar costs. Scriven (1973a, 1973c) pointed out that there are many costs associated with educational evaluation: money, time, materials, morale, and lost opportunities from competitor activities. All of these need to be figured in teacher evaluation program design and openly considered and deliberated.

Ideas about cost-benefit analysis are important features of educational evaluation (Levin, Glass, & Meister, 1987; Scriven, 1973a, 1973c; Thompson, 1980). Evaluation designers should estimate and monitor costs as a fundamental activity. These costs need to be analyzed in terms of the payoffs. Some good evaluation ideas should be supported because of their cost-benefit justification; other ideas should be discarded because of indefensible costs. It should be kept in mind that every dollar spent in teacher evaluation ultimately is taken from more immediate support of students in materials, class size, or teacher salary.

Hoenack and Monk (1990) provided a background of the economics of teacher evaluation. They began with a discussion of production theory and efficiency, in which information is analyzed in terms of its relation to production. From this perspective, justification of costs of evaluation should be based on its effect on production; in this case, student learning. A second area of consideration is the economics of information in which although "better decisions often can be made with more complete information, the costs of added information should be justified by the resulting incremental value of desired outcomes" (p. 392). The authors pointed out that any evaluation activity creates (intentionally or not) incentives for participants. Thus the costs of a teacher evaluation system should be examined in terms of incentives created. Hoenack and Monk continued with a description of how evaluation systems create differential distribution of effects. Any evaluation activity will benefit some audiences more than others, for example, parents more than teachers, some teachers more than others, or some kinds of students more than others. These differential effects are costs, and they should be weighted in program design and maintenance.

Hoenack and Monk (1990) showed that different types of teacher evaluation data sources have their own cost-benefit dynamics. The four types they analyzed were (a) teacher records, (b) teacher tests, (c) teacher observations, and (d) student learning. Each approach requires a separate economic analysis from its own point of view.

Finally, Hoenack and Monk raised three additional issues about teacher evaluation cost analysis. First, the tradeoffs between taxpayer benefits and teacher benefits need to be carefully considered. Better results for teachers that do not result in better learning require careful justification. Second, teacher evaluation systems that focus on the teacher as the cause of student learning (production) are in error. Student learning is produced by much else in the system (e.g., prior achievement, materials, environment) that needs good cost analysis. Third, close economic analysis of teacher performance discloses that individual teachers are most productive in certain specific settings of subjects, age levels, and student characteristics. The goodness of the match between the teacher and the setting is important for understanding that particular teacher, and needs to be made explicit.

Cost Estimates

Peterson (1989c) analyzed the costs incurred in complex teacher evaluation systems. Table 22.3 shows the evaluation costs by data source. Indi-

TABLE 22.3 Costs of Teacher Data Sources

	$ Per Student	$ Per Class (N = 25)	$ Per Teacher	Teacher Time [a]	Staff Time	Administration Time
Student survey	.17	4.25	8.50[b]	10	30	0
Parent survey	.65	16.25	32.50[b]	10	30	0
Principal report	—	—	—	10	0	2 hrs
Teacher tests	—	—	41.00	3 hrs	5 hrs[c]	0
Professional activity	—	—	2.00	1 hr	0	0
Peer review	—	—	29.00	12 hrs	8 hrs[c]	0
Systematic observation	—	—	85.00	2 hrs	16 hrs	1 hr
Pupil gain	.50	12.50	25.00	3 hrs	10	15

SOURCE: Peterson (1989c). Used with permission.
a. Time is in minutes, unless indicated as hours.
b. Assumes 50% elementary (one class) and 50% secondary (three classes).
c. One time per year cost for all district teachers.

vidual costs of procedures are more completely described in the previous chapters on each data source.

District Budget for Teacher Evaluation

The costs to the district of each data source are not only the direct expenses but the effect of the rates of use for that data source (Peterson, 1989c). For example, 75% of the sample of teachers chose to gather parent surveys, whereas only 33% chose to have peer reviews of their teaching materials. Second, actual costs depend on how often each data source is used. For example, once a teacher has established her patterns, student surveys are recommended on alternate years, whereas teacher tests are recommended only once each 7-year period. The final cost to the district for the data source (AC) is the cost of source per teacher (CT) multiplied by the percentage of teachers in the district electing to use the source (N) multiplied by the percentage frequency of use of data source by each teacher (F). For example, teacher tests cost $41.00, were selected by 40% of the teachers, and are taken once every 7 years, or AC = $41.00 × .40 × .143 = $2.35. Table 22.4 presents a budget cost per teacher per year. This table shows the annual dollar cost of providing eight data sources for teacher was $44.71 per teacher (in 1985 dollars). Computations for this table assumed a class size of 25. Costs per student for three data sources affected by class size (student survey, parent survey, pupil gain) were 89 cents.

TABLE 22.4 Dollar Costs to District for Teacher Evaluation Data Sources

	$ Cost Per Teacher	*Usage in District*	*Frequency by Teachers*	*Source Cost Per Teacher*
Pupil survey	8.50	0.85	0.600	4.34
Parent survey	32.50	0.75	0.600	14.63
Teacher test	41.00	0.40	0.143	2.35
Professional activity	2.00	0.90	1.000	1.80
Peer review	29.00	0.33	0.143	1.37
Systematic observation	85.00	0.80	0.143	9.72
Pupil gain	25.00	0.70	0.600	10.50
		Total dollar cost per teacher in district = $44.71		

SOURCE: Peterson (1989c). Used with permission.

Cost Sharing

Although the Peterson (1989c) study estimated costs of approximately $45.00 per teacher per year (in 1985 dollars), school districts have many options in controlling evaluation costs. These estimates were made on systems with no dollar costs to teachers; however, such systems are not always needed. Teachers can share costs if they see the activities and data to be in their interest. Thus the district can pay for 0% to 100% of the costs, depending on the attraction to teachers. Installation of user fees can add significant resources to the district, with a minimal effect on data gathering.

One way to decide about putting the cost burden on teacher or district is the timing of the data gathering. For example, a school district may decide to pay costs for the first year (or 5) years of a teacher's career. Then, cost sharing begins. Or the district may pay all system costs until the system is well established. Then, cost sharing begins for all teachers in the district. Another version is to subsidize costs of certain data sources. For example, in a district with low rates of teacher testing, subsidization will increase the numbers of participating teachers.

The question for school districts in considering support is the current level of participation. If participation is satisfactory, there is room for cost sharing. If participation is too low, then subsidization is called for. Local school districts can be expected to vary considerably in the need for financial support for teacher evaluation.

IMPROVING THE CULTURE AND POLITICS FOR TEACHER EVALUATION

As described in Chapter 4, an essential element for change in the directions and procedures for teacher evaluation is for school districts to specifically act to change the current culture and politics for evaluation activity. At present, teacher evaluation is not highly thought of, and distinctions created by evaluation are minimized by teachers. Participation or cooperation in evaluation is not seen as desirable, and sanctions of distancing are taken by colleagues of teachers who are involved. Teachers who earn attention by documentation of good or outstanding work are shunned by others.

School district leaders (both administrative and teacher) need to create a sociological and political environment that supports teacher evaluation. Without this change, the technically best teacher evaluation designs will not survive. There simply is no option to a district beginning the activities outlined in this following section.

Begin With Beginners

The most significant, extensive, and long-lasting changes in teacher culture come from treating the beginners differently. Thus the best ways to improve the culture and politics of educators concerning teacher evaluation is to begin with the beginners.

Peterson (1990a) outlined a program of assistance and assessment of beginning teachers that emphasized sociological development along with changes in evaluation. These procedures have the aim of creating good initiation experiences for teachers and a strong support system in order to produce well-functioning professionals. Peterson's specific district provisions are presented in Table 19.3. Beyond the activities uniquely targeted at beginning teachers, for example, mentors and beginner orientations, his advice is to create better than average working conditions for at least the first year. For example, (whenever possible) beginning teachers should have small classes with a preponderance of school-successful students. This advantage, paid for by the other veteran teachers having slightly larger classes (and a few more difficult students), creates lifelong, positive, professional attitudes in newcomers. For a second example, abundant, positive, and reassuring feedback data for first-year teachers changes their long-term attitudes about evaluation.

Organizational Climate and Leadership

Berman and McLaughlin (1978) found in their studies of successful educational innovations that "the local institutional setting had the major influence on project outcomes and continuation" (p. 30). Their findings have great relevance for making changes in teacher evaluation. Three elements of the organizational climate having the greatest effect are (a) quality of teacher's relationships, (b) involvement and support of administrators, and (c) quality of program staff. Additionally, these authors found that change is more difficult at the secondary level, teachers with more experience were *less* likely to innovate, and that "teachers' attitudes about their own professional competence . . . may be a major determinant of what happens to projects" (p. 32). A circular dynamic of teacher evaluation activity by teachers is that it both requires and engenders a positive attitude about professional competence.

McLaughlin (1990) recognized the key element of a positive school culture for successful teacher evaluation:

> Teacher evaluation will be no more effective than the extent to which teachers support it. An effective teacher-evaluation system assumes candor on the part of teachers and requires opening classroom doors . . . rather than the dog-and-pony show teachers say most evaluators witness. An effective evaluation system demands teachers willingness and ability to act on the outcomes of an evaluation. An effective evaluation system insists on trust between teachers and administrators. (p. 404)

She described five elements for building a supportive district culture for teacher evaluation: (a) evaluation embedded in an overall movement for improvement, (b) involvement of stakeholders (teachers, administrators, parents, board members, and citizen groups), (c) active commitment of the superintendent, (d) joint training for administrators and teachers, and (e) resources to support needs of individual teachers.

Focus Groups on Barriers

A spirit of patient problem solving is important in establishing a comprehensive teacher evaluation system. If difficulties are experienced with any constituency, it is important to find out why. This can be done with the data-finding technique of focus groups (Krueger, 1988; Morgan, 1988). The essential questions for groups of teachers, administrators, parents, and public audiences are, What is happening with teacher evaluation? What is not working? What should be done next?

Open and Rational Public Talk

A new cultural norm needs to be recognized and supported in the district for rationality and open talk in the school district about teacher evaluation direction and practice. As described by Lortie (1967), talk in school districts about teacher evaluation should point toward certain political decision-making values that favor rationality. These include active debate followed by decisiveness on questions of value. It means delineation and certainty about responsibilities. Rational discussion should focus on creating specific terminology, rather than general and hazy language. Decisions on goals, rather than compromises, encourage rationality. Finally, restraint by all participants in use of pressure tactics is important.

Corwin and Edelfelt (1976) discussed rationality in organizations in terms of clear goals, well-planned and coordinated activities, available information, enough power and authority for decisive action, and authority generated by demonstrated expertise and achievement. They contrasted rational organizations with organic ones in which individual units set their own goals above the organization, status is more important than contribution, survival is the most important goal, decisions are made as compromises and bargains, power and authority are diffused, and authority is not derived from expertise and achievement. From this perspective, districts interested in rational development of teacher evaluation programs must be explicit from the beginning that initial consensus discussions must result in decisions that will be carried out, and that those in leadership positions demonstrate their competence and experience in teacher evaluation practice.

Another alternative to rational systems is described as *realistic* in which clarity, order, decisiveness, restraint, higher vision, and recognition of competence are not commonly found. Rather, realism means that people act according to their needs and not their ideals. From this point of view, it is naive to think that a teacher evaluation system can avoid petty dissension, self-serving participation, focus on survival, incompetence, instances of subversion, and genuine divisiveness. In fact, these "minor" forces can be expected to accumulate until the best thought out and best led system collapses into a situation of every person for himself. Perhaps the best stance in relation to the pessimism of realism is for teacher evaluation advocates to include tolerance and acceptance in their perspectives and to work on the elements that best support innovation.

Lightfoot (1983) described characteristics of one kind of educational organization that supports quality. She characterized the "good high school" in which certain norms are realized. These include "enduring qualities of nurturance, kindness, stimulation, and stability" (p. 311). But perfection in these qualities, and in school organizations, is not to be found; rather, she recommended "removing the absolutist standard and admitting human frailty and vulnerability as integral to worthiness" (p. 311). Acceptance of disappointment occurs in the context of "a consciousness about imperfections, and the willingness to admit them and search for their origins and solutions [that] is one of the important ingredients of goodness in schools" (p. 309). The value is for "tough self-criticism, clear recognition of unevenness and weakness," and delight in facing problems openly. Participants in the good school see "goodness, frustration, and criticism as compatible responses" (p. 310).

Cusick (1973) described quite a different school in which the organization did not recognize imperfections in idealism and consequently generated little progress toward achieving goodness. In his school, he found many constraints placed on teachers, with no apparent opportunity to "forgive and forget" deviance. Second, the school placed very narrow boundaries on teacher behavior, in terms of time, instruction, activity, and even furniture arrangement. Finally, the whole school suffered under the responsibility to run a trouble-free operation in the eyes of the community. All of these precluded the consciousness about imperfections and the open discussion and problem solving they require.

Opening up direct lines of questioning is helpful to changing a culture because it emphasizes open information and opinion, rather than covert and rigid positions. Behind-the-scenes subversion needs the competition of open directness and honesty, followed by genuine response from decision makers. In rigid cultures without invitation to talk, the premium is on colleagues who are most secretive, biting, sarcastic, and subversive. With more open communication, the premium changes to the most articulate, creative with alternatives, and willing to speak out. Focus groups are an example of a technique to encourage greater openness; they invite discussion on the unspeakable. By doing so, they open up lines of organization. This is a significant change in the culture of problem solving.

The goal for districts is to create discussions about teacher evaluation that, although patient, move toward specific decisions for trial. Conflict of values—for example, over what is quality teaching—should be openly expressed, but pushed for specificity, operational understanding, and open trials for deliberation. All of this discussion should take place with interest groups and individuals holding back on quid pro quo arrangements, historical conflicts, single-issue partisanship, and pressure tactics. Consensus must give way to decisiveness, followed by refinement.

Table 22.5 presents the complexities of balancing acceptance and determined action in a school district teacher evaluation program. This perspective involves what Elbow (1986) and McLaughlin (1990) called "embracing contraries" as a necessity in complex educational affairs. That is, the effective change of cultures requires participants to move flexibly to both incorporate and then implement a unitary action.

Co-Sponsorship

Essential to cultural and sociological health in an organization is visible participation of all constituencies. A way to destroy or seriously limit a

TABLE 22.5 Embracing Contraries in District Teacher Evaluation Systems

At first:	*But then:*
Accept human imperfection; be realistic about organizations	Be idealistic about teacher evaluation procedures and results
Support participants; give security	Recognize and stand up to bad practice
Give nurturance, kindness, stimulation, and stability	Confront subversion, self-serving behavior, incompetence, divisiveness
Seek and give voice to divergent views and individuality	Seek and set group goals
Accept ambiguity, express tolerance	Seek clarity, focus, and definition
Seek consensus	Expect decisive, unitary action
Show restraint	Commit to quality

complex program like a comprehensive teacher evaluation system is to make it the function of one single stakeholder—the "teachers' program" or the "administrators' program," or "student outcome-based program." Instead, ownership has to be openly that of all participants. Virtually all activities, publications, and monitoring need to be co-sponsored by administrators and teachers. Key players from parents, community, employers, and students need to be frequently visible. One particularly effective strategy is to have the teachers' organization(s) and the administration co-sponsor early pilot teacher evaluation activities, for example, the test trails of parent surveys for volunteer teachers and administrators. Later co-sponsorships might include the League of Women Voters, Urban League, and PTA.

Reward Structure

Lortie (1975) described public school teaching as having a scarce reward structure. Essentially, little recognition, acknowledgment, payoff, prestige, and reassurance are available to public school teachers. For instance, they work in isolation. Teachers are in an environment where adult contact and interaction are discouraged. They work in a setting that is dominated by presentism rather than long-term accomplishment. Current reward systems favor the appearance of control, getting students to work, and displays of respect and affection. There are no rewards for creativity, scholarship, initiative, innovation, hard work, or dedication. The economies of public education preclude private offices, conference areas, telephones, faxes, classroom keys, assistants, and even business cards.

When rewards in an institution are scarce, people adjust to the inadequate recognition. For example, currently it is not considered good form for teachers to go public with exemplary practice when there are not enough rewards to go around. They see colleagues who get attention as making an end run around the current system; for example, teacher-of-the-year programs are negative experiences for most recipients.

One example of scarce rewards in education is the conventional wisdom that high-quality teaching is reserved for a small number. Some observers maintain that the number of truly great teachers is in the 5% to 20% range. Terms like *excellent* and *outstanding* suggest that the practice of teaching has a small number whose practice is head and shoulders above the merely average teacher. There are no empirical data to suggest that very good teaching is reserved for a small elite of teachers. To the contrary, our data suggest that the amount of what can be defended as very good teaching is far greater than many critics estimate (Driscoll, Peterson, Crow, & Larson, 1985; Peterson, 1987a, 1987b, 1989b; Peterson et al., 1990; Peterson & Stevens, 1988). In our school district samples, we found that upward of 70% of the teachers were able to assemble very impressive data about their practice. Indeed, our numbers matched those of pollsters, who find that large a number of the public are satisfied with the *local* schools, as opposed to education in general in this country (Gallup, 1985).

The estimates of limited levels of good teacher performance are most likely based on style preferences. Each observer has preferred styles that limit the number of performances he or she would call outstanding. Some like task-oriented producers; others prefer more relaxed and supportive processors as teachers. There is no empirical evidence that one of these styles is consistently, across the board, more effective for stimulating student learning. More objective, style-free evidence shows far more teachers are doing a good job than conventional wisdom suggests.

Changes in Reward Systems

Changes in the reward system are important. The most significant improvement is to drastically increase the number and kinds of rewards available to teachers. This needs to be done in two ways, formal and informal. Formal rewards include tenure and promotions based on dossier/panel reviews and teacher leadership positions based on superior reviews. Still another kind of formal reward is a certificate of accomplishment from a prestigious institution. Titles that acknowledge seniority and quality performance should be established.

Informal rewards are more difficult to pin down, but include a number of specific strategies to be commonly and frequently bestowed. One example is spoken appreciation for results evidenced in dossiers. It means acceptance of diversity of what quality means—whether in student activity, teacher test, professional involvement, materials development, student achievement, or client response. Informal reward means setting aside time and resources to acknowledge accomplishment. Recognition at hurdle times, for example, tenure, are important informal rewards. Finally, there is a sense of negative action in informal reward systems. For example, teachers who have not demonstrated their achievements in the evaluation system should not participate in some of the public acknowledgments.

STAGEWISE TRANSITIONS TO IMPROVED TEACHER EVALUATION

Time Requirements

The most important transition strategy for improved teacher evaluation is to take sufficient time (Harris, 1986; McLaughlin, 1990). It is a mistake to immediately impose all of the changes in expectation, procedure, and decision making. Certainly, more comfortable time frames are needed. The practices outlined in this book should be installed gradually over a 5-year period. This gives sufficient time for groundwork to be laid and experience to be gathered.

Early participants should be volunteers. These self-selected persons are quite likely to have good practices and to have good experiences with the change in documentation and recognition. Care must be taken to gradually install mandates, and teachers should be involved in this decision. The fall-back position is to have intermediate areas of teacher choice.

An extensive transition period provides the time to accumulate an experience base for the district. Problem solving becomes cumulative. For example, difficulties with survey sample sizes at the high school level can be addressed as experience is gained with sufficient and insufficient returns.

Participant training needs to be complex and ongoing. The knowledge and skills of teacher evaluation require time and experience for assimilation and practice by teachers. Few teachers currently are able to sample audience opinions or prepare student achievement data for use outside of their classrooms. Professional decision making and accountability are scarcely developed in most settings.

Research, development, and validation studies need to be ongoing and extensive. These gradually build confidence and good evaluation practices. Gradual improvement of surveys and procedures should be expected. Levels of confidence should be established; this means that some good ideas need to be tempered by studies of actual practice. Some confidence levels need to be lowered, as well as others gained. A systematic schedule for R&D (e.g., parent surveys this year, student surveys next year, a review of parent surveys in the fourth year) communicates the scope of needed work and attention to problems. The tentative nature of early work should be emphasized. The district Teacher Evaluation Board must assume a great deal of new responsibility for this effort.

An infrastructure of teacher evaluation takes time to build. Committees must be formed, units developed, and descriptions and materials adopted and developed. New procedures require schedules, assignments, protocols, and resources. For example, the Evaluation Unit needs to develop its procedures for initiation.

Finally, it takes time for the sociology of the teacher workplace to change. A new openness to documentation, novel procedures, and effective use of results all are needed before the goals of greater confidence and reassurance can be felt. Former relationships and fears need replacement by newer ones. This takes a great deal of time, patience, and stagewise changes in thinking.

Specific Stages

Peterson and Chenoweth (1992) identified three stages for change in teacher evaluation in the district. The first stage is traditional, in which the developmental perspective is one of survival. The second stage is transitional, in which teachers participate in exploratory and innovative activities. The third stage is emergent, in which teacher initiative, responsibility, and involvement are heightened. It is important for districts to go through these stages, rather than to fully impose the highest expectations on all participants. Thus districts should plan for a rather lengthy (5-year) introduction to new evaluation directions and practices to allow for distinctly different stages of teacher thinking and doing.

INTERNET RESOURCES

Guidance for mentors

http://teachermentors.com/MCenter%20Site/GuideMentors.html

Classroom visits

http://www.wisc.edu/MOO/recipform.html

Public relations

http://www.heavypen.com/promote/index5.htm

http://www.people.virginia.edu/~dbb5n/EAF/
communication.html

National School Public Relations Association

http://www.nspra.org/

Pennsylvania School Public Relations Association

http://www.pcpe.org/

Texas School Public Relations Association

http://www.tspra.org/

Missouri School Public Relations Association

http://info.csd.org/mosprahome.html

23

New Roles in Teacher Evaluation for Principals

Principals and other administrators who evaluate teachers have high hopes for their roles (Drake & Roe, 1986; Greenfield, 1987). They want to exert leadership that supports successful instruction and curriculum, enables quality teacher performance, creates a school that functions as a learning community, and (ultimately) fosters pupil growth and achievement in knowledge, skills, and attitudes. It is clear to practitioners and scholars alike that the principal can make these differences in school quality (National Association of State Boards of Education, 1984; Wiles & Bondi, 2000). A key role for principal leadership is that of teacher evaluation. Although it is only one administrator duty and only one part of the whole picture of school operation, teacher evaluation is a central educational function. In this important school role, no other player has such a range of involvement as does the principal. No other single participant can tip the balance between perfunctory, noneffective teacher evaluation and practices that foster the best in teacher performance, student learning, and school well-being.

It is important to emphasize the potential good of the principal's role in teacher evaluation. However, it also is necessary to recognize that in the real world, few tasks diminish principal leadership opportunities like teacher evaluation. Administrators face conflicting roles, instances of overwhelming demands on time, behind-the-scenes power struggles, crippling limits to their own behavior, and feelings of frustration. Scarce administrator time and influence can be squandered by ritualistic, required classroom visits and conferences that neither administrators nor teachers respect (Johnson, 1990; Kauchak, Peterson, & Driscoll, 1985; Lortie, 1975). Teacher data restricted to narrow checklists or brief narratives fail to use principal insights about actual teacher practice. Intimidation of teachers by the role of the principal as sole summative judge constricts teacher initiative, behavior, and thought around the principal (Lortie, 1975). Opportunities to lead by developing beginning teachers are hindered by the lack of time (Peterson, 1990a). Finally, the onerous responsibility to deal with the problem of the bad teacher discourages and further isolates the principal from her faculty and from chances to provide leadership in curriculum and instruction (Blumberg & Greenfield, 1980).

The good that has resulted from current conventional teacher evaluation practice is more the result of the individuals doing the activity than of the designs, tools, and district evaluation systems being used. At present, administrators produce better results than educators have any right to expect given traditional teacher evaluation practices and directions. Yet practitioners and scholars agree on the need for administrators who continue to strive for the best. It is time for school districts to do a better structural job of teacher evaluation; the need is clear for systems that are worthy of the people who take on the tasks.

This chapter will make recommendations for new roles of the administrator in teacher evaluation consistent with the data-based, dossier-based new directions of this book. The principal's opportunity for leadership can be enhanced by rethinking teacher evaluation in four ways. First, valuable time can be saved by eliminating much of the principal's current ineffective role in veteran teacher evaluation. At the same time, several new monitoring activities can be added that permit more open, effective, and satisfying technical and sociological interactions. Second, principals can share the process of data gathering with teachers, which strengthens the data and shares the power. This not only opens up valuable time for administrators, it positively affects the sociological work relationships with teachers. Third, additional administrator roles and contact with beginning teachers and marginal teachers helps shape their development and extends principal leadership where it clearly makes a difference. Fourth, a reduction in the isolation and burden on individual principals with the problem of the marginal performer can be made by bringing more persons and data into the process.

These necessary changes in practices and directions are important for two reasons. First, the technical role differences of time, data use, and specific tasks enable the administrator to do more of what he does best. Second, the role changes allow the administrator to put into effect the strategies of the previous chapter on sociological changes for districts. These sociological improvements benefit administrators, teachers, and the entire organization. Although the principal cannot make the sociological transformations all by herself, she is a key player who interacts with the most participants, and her ability to focus on improved teacher evaluation is essential for the efficient functioning of the entire school system.

PERSPECTIVES ON TECHNICAL AND SOCIOLOGICAL PROBLEMS OF TRADITIONAL TEACHER EVALUATION PRACTICE FOR ADMINISTRATORS

Before presenting new directions and practices for administrators, it is important to have perspectives of problems in current teacher evaluation. The central technical problem is administrator time for the evaluation role. For some teacher evaluations, particularly at the secondary level, there is the added technical problem of a lack of specialized subject matter expertise by the administrator. Sociological problems are more complicated but also need to be addressed by new practices.

Roles for School Administrators and the Problem of Time

The roles of the public school administrator are many and complicated (Black & English, 1986; Drake & Roe, 1986; Greenfield, 1987) as depicted in Table 23.1. The great number and complexity of administrator roles means significant time demands on administrators. Her time and focus on any single role is limited by the nature, number, and priorities of required duties. In addition to the demands of roles and preferences, the pressure of administrative details are a constant force for determining what a principal actually does. For example, Krajewski (1978) found that instructional supervision and leadership was the single most desired role for principals, but it ended up in time and effort priority behind tasks such as administration of materials and facilities, discipline, teacher evaluation, and pupil services coordination. Figure 23.1 shows the differences between desirable and actual time usage reported by principals as described by Drake and Roe (1986).

Current practice means that principals face time restrictions to do their teacher evaluation. The lack of time may produce feelings of guilt for conscientious administrators who do not have room for the task. Many administrators describe the time of year when they just shut out all other re-

TABLE 23.1 Public School Administrator Roles

Organizational head, stabilizer
Instructional leader
Decision maker, adjudicator
Disciplinarian
Resource economist
Personnel manager
District, community, parent liaison
Local legal authority
Team player
Physical plant manager

sponsibilities and "get out of the way" the dreaded end-of-the-year evaluation report process. It is clear that any new directions for teacher evaluation practice must take into account the priorities and time demands placed on administrators in the system.

Sociological Problems for Administrators

Just as with time demands in actual practice, sociological environment factors are another set of limitations on administrators (Wilson, 1991). As described in Chapter 4, the sociology of the school workplace is largely invisible and unspoken. However, the influences on a principal of such sociological realities as power, resistance, leadership, and morale can do more to enhance or limit good teacher evaluation than even the problem of inadequate time allocation. For example, the formal evaluation roles of supervisor/worker make it difficult for the teacher to speak openly of doubts, pride, and ideas for change. As a second example, scarce rewards for teachers prevent principals from singling out exemplary practitioners. The goal of new directions in teacher evaluation set out in this book is to make a more satisfactory social environment for administrators. Improved teacher evaluation should result not only in better data, decisions, and teacher enhancement but also in increased administrator satisfaction.

NEW DIRECTIONS AND PRACTICES FOR ADMINISTRATORS

New directions and practices for administrators mean a number of role changes. Three essential changes, described next, are evaluation activities for veteran teachers, methods of data gathering for all teachers, evaluation

Figure 23.1 Principals' Desired and Actual Use of Time
Drake and Roe (1986). Used with permission.

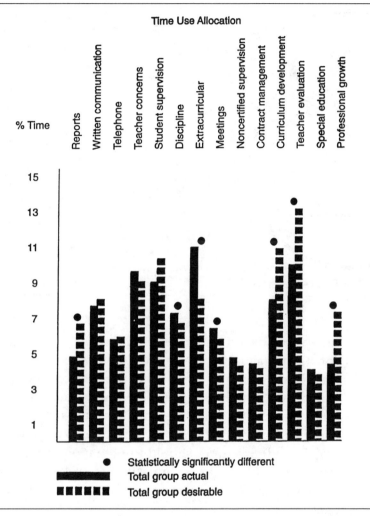

work with beginning and marginal teachers, and responsibilities for decisions about inadequately performing teachers. Figure 23.2 depicts these changes.

Veteran Teacher Evaluation

The role of the principal in teacher evaluation can be changed to one of monitor, with a brief annual report, rather than a clinical supervisor (except in the few cases where that role is desired or needed). The "dog and pony show" is given up in favor of a dossier of the best objective data available and the knowledge gained from frequent monitoring. The time-consuming responsibility for interviews and detailed observations should

Figure 23.2 Change in Amount and Allocation of Principal Evaluation Time

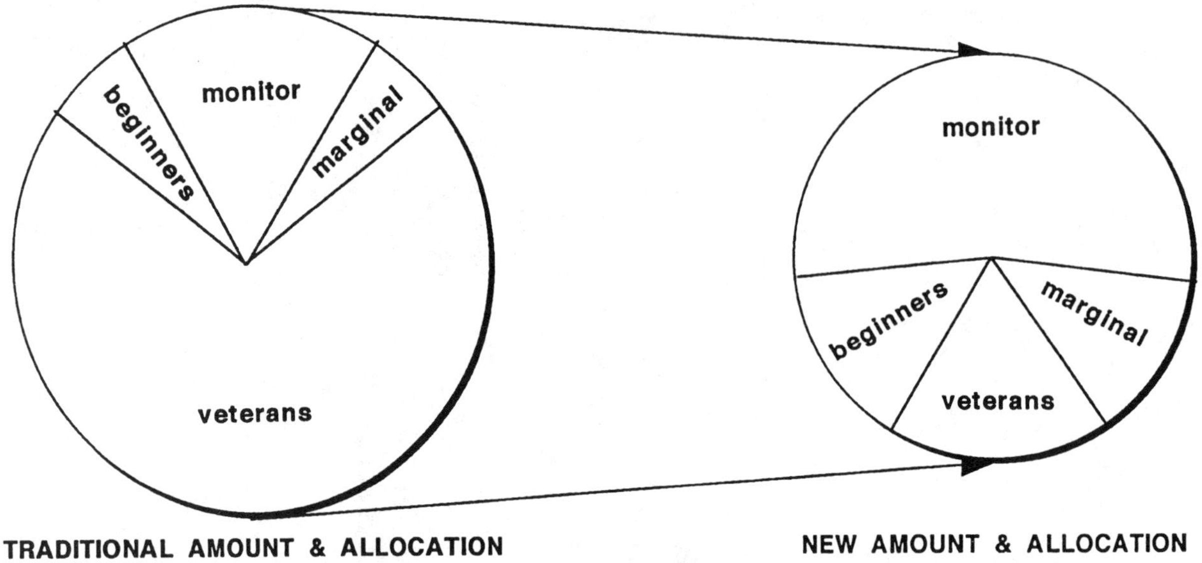

TRADITIONAL AMOUNT & ALLOCATION   **NEW AMOUNT & ALLOCATION**

be replaced by a complicated but more realistic and manageable expectation for principals to be broadly aware of what is happening in their schools, especially in terms of teacher performance. Eight dimensions of monitoring include things such as walk-throughs, sampling the goods, and sharing. Although these activities may sound like mere slogans, experience and sophistication are required to do them well.

The administrator should use the monitoring contacts to communicate with teachers, to be himself, and to be frank about what is seen. These very important sociological dynamics will be discussed later in this chapter.

Share Evaluation Data Gathering With Teachers

Additional administrative time is saved as teachers become involved in providing some of the data on which crucial personnel decisions are made. These changes free up time for principals to be more of the instructional leaders they want to be. Teachers select from a menu of data sources: pupil achievement, parent or teacher surveys, teacher tests, documentation of professional activity, and information unique to individual teachers. They are assisted in gathering and presenting these by a sociologically/politically neutral district evaluation unit.

TABLE 23.2 Principal Monitoring

Frequently walk-through classrooms and other areas of learning
Put ear to the ground
Sample the goods
Ask the customers
Interact with individual teachers on more than two topics
Share what you see
Share what you know about good practice
Listen, listen, listen

Principal Leadership With Beginning and Marginal Teachers

Although the time and expectations for principal evaluation of veteran teachers have been decreased overall, the expectations for administrators to work with beginning and marginal teachers has been *increased*. A list of duties with beginning teachers is presented in Table 23.3 and for marginal teachers in Table 23.4. The purpose of this increased attention is to focus principal leadership on the relatively small number of teachers at these two quite different places and situations in teacher careers. Good principal leadership for these two groups can have inordinate impact and value for the entire system. Opportunities for principals to do what they care most about are very important to the entire system and the satisfaction of administrators with the new directions in teacher evaluation.

SOCIOLOGICAL CHANGES AND OPPORTUNITIES AFFORDED BY NEW DIRECTIONS AND PRACTICES

The greatly enhanced monitoring role in the new directions and practices for teacher evaluation gives the school administrator a strong opportunity to affect many sociological dynamics that limit teacher effectiveness. Educational researchers and sociologists such as Cusick (1973), Lightfoot (1983), and Blumberg and Greenfield (1980) have provided sound advice for specific topics and strategies for administrators to employ during their monitoring work. Nine of these themes are presented in Table 23.5.

The administrator can give teachers many positive comments during the monitoring walk-throughs and casual (relative to formal observations and conferences) discussions. When the administrator authentically sees

TABLE 23.3 Principal Leadership With Beginning Teachers

Two or more conferences per year, *not just one*

Stagewise orientations to teacher tasks and district expectations, *not just one at the beginning of the year*

Appropriate, supportive assignments, *not just the leavings of the senior faculty*

Continuing, targeted professional education, *not just the "off-the-shelf" inservice for all teachers in the school*

Mentors and networks found, *not just happenstance introductions*

Visitations of other classrooms, *not just an occasional vague recommendation*

Support groups of fellow beginning teachers, *not just casting beginners out on their own*

Career-long evaluation program begun, *not just ignoring needs for reassurance, feedback, and documentation of success*

TABLE 23.4 Principal Leadership With Marginal Teachers

Mandate data gathering according to perceived problem—for example, parent surveys for communication or relationship problems

Cooperate with district performance assistance teams (mentor teachers for remediation support)

Contact educators to give support to marginal teacher (otherwise abandoned while in difficulty)

Arrange for remediation in form of professional education and visits

Heighten monitoring

good practice, effort, persistence, or competence, she can articulate what she sees, state her pleasure, and express appreciation. Direct efforts must counter the current teacher culture, which makes it bad form to go public with one's own exemplary practice. Teachers need encouragement to express justifiable pride in their work. When the administrator sees doubt, upset, or uncertainty, he can reassure, express confidence in future success, and remind the teacher of educator solidarity.

The administrator can single out teachers who make clear and compelling statements about good practice and echo these statements to other educators and audiences. The administrator can look for unusual, resourceful, clever, and adaptive teaching; she can state her appreciation and bring the attention of others to the teacher and his practice. The administrator can identify with teachers who are courageously willing to state publicly the views that forward quality, value, equity, and accomplishment in the district.

TABLE 23.5 Opportunities for Effective Sociological Intervention by Administrators While Performing Evaluation Monitoring and Work With Beginning and Marginal Teachers

1. Communicate nurturance, kindness, stimulation, and stability.
2. Acknowledge, praise, and otherwise support those educators who are articulate, creative, and willing to speak out.
3. Soften unnecessary boundaries on teacher and administrator practice, behavior, speech, and initiative.
4. Be conscious of imperfections in programs and personnel; remove the standard for absolute perfection; admit human frailty and vulnerability as integral to worthiness.
5. Show tough self-criticism, clear recognition of unevenness and weakness. Search for origins and solutions to problems. Delight in facing problems openly.
6. Complete instances of forgiving and forgetting.
7. Communicate goodness, frustration, and criticism as compatible experiences in schools.
8. Reconcile inevitable school problems and pressures to appear trouble free to the community and district administration.
9. Confront subversives, backbiters, and sarcastic practitioners.

SOURCE: Based on Blumberg and Greenfield (1980), Cusick (1973), and Lightfoot (1983).

The principal can do a great deal to encourage teachers to be more their individual selves rather than to always emphasize the stereotypic role of teacher. The administrator can recognize the pressures to conform to narrow views of teachers rather than to represent the true variety of selves that make up the teacher corps. The administrator can put these same practices in his own behavior: Principals should use more of their own personal strengths and styles in their work—to do the things that are successful rather than just the narrow expectations of the role, to say thoughts genuinely held but "outside the lines" that bound a school principal, to begin actions that are potentially of value but not clearly the "way" of a school administrator.

Good relationships can be built with flexible but rational and caring behavior on the part of the administrator. Rather than insistence on "clear, universal standards" and the hazard of enforcing debilitating absolutist criteria, she can encourage diversity toward solutions. The relationship between administrator and teacher is one of two individuals, as well as of two professional role players.

The administrator can deal with mistakes and errors with less perfectionism and more a sense that although teachers should be correct a high percentage of the time, the human territory means accepting a certain level of mistakes. In addition, the administrator can reinforce the reality that valuable, competent humans can be damaged, hurt, sad, angry, and upset. Interactions around mistakes are especially important; administrators can author situations in which teachers truly experience the capacities to for-give and forget errors rather than to store them up for future conflict.

The administrator can speak to the reality that there are unspoken pressures for schools to look perfect and errorless—whereas the reality is that all fall short. Principals can encourage more witnesses of competence to counter the fear of talking openly about problems.

The principal can call for more teachers to come forward and partici-pate in their evaluations rather than sit on the sidelines and complain. The administrator can confront and speak out (with care and mainly in private) with teachers who tear down programs and people behind the scenes. The whiners, complainers, and groaners can be confronted and told of their rec-ognition and disapproval.

The Special Problem of the Bad Teacher

Bad teachers are few in number, but they are real morale killers. The vast majority of teachers are embarrassed by bad practice, the public media feature suspicious stories along with a few spectacular successes, and prin-cipals are under great pressure to find the bad teachers. Effective teacher evaluation systems use a complicated structure of sharing the burden. One central purpose is to avoid isolating the principal as the "bad guy" so that his leadership with not only the marginal teacher, but with all other educa-tors, is limited. Experiences with terminating the bad performer affect principal effectiveness for careers (Blumberg & Greenfield, 1980).

Good teacher evaluation, as described in this book, gives support for terminating the bad performer (Chapter 21). Remediation teams, group re-views, and additional data gathering all reduce the isolation of the princi-pal and the sense of leaving her out on a limb during this most difficult ad-ministrator task. An additional support is strong coaching about legal matters, especially courtroom testimony strategies, at times *when no specific litigation is at hand.* Lawyers are limited in their pretrial preparation of ad-ministrators for ongoing litigation because specific coaching (as opposed to witness "preparation") is ethically limited. The sociologically restricting experience of terminating a bad performer must be supported by the dis-trict teacher evaluation system.

The powerlessness an administrator can feel in the face of clear knowl-edge of inadequate practice needs to be addressed; the evaluation system must clearly identify and address marginal practice. Administrators need the sociological reassurance of bad practice being remedied or rejected by teachers and administrators alike.

Principal job description

> http://jobprofiles.com/edu912principal.htm

K-8 principals

> http://www.naesp.org/prinpro.htm

Principal evaluation form

> http://www.charterproject.org/res-ev1.html

School accountability report card

> http://www.nusd.k12.ca.us/Nusd/newarkhssarc.html

Evaluation procedures

> http://www.centralvalleyea.org/the_contractf.htm

24

Making the Transition From Traditional Teacher Evaluation to New Directions and Practices

The ideas and techniques presented in this book require complicated and challenging changes for any individual educator or school district. Part I of this book presented key ideas and background information for thinking about teacher evaluation. Parts II through IV gave tools and techniques for gathering data and making decisions. This chapter presents realistic strategies for change toward these new directions and practices.

Realistic change in a district teacher evaluation system must take into account a great number of considerations. For one, the time frame for a successful transition from traditional to improved practice is on the order of 5 years. Another reality is that for the many steps and problems encountered along the way, districts will find many possible options and a wide variety of solutions to problems rather than encountering a well-defined catalog of behaviors, standards, or outcomes. In fact, a history of successful problem solving by a district is one necessary building block of increased competence of the entire system. For example, as small districts face the necessity to share evaluation resources with neighboring districts, and large districts deal with problems of regional differences, techniques of collaboration and governance will be created for subsequent operation and development of the teacher evaluation system. This chapter will give advice about how to initiate participation, begin a tradition of teacher data gathering, change the locus of decision making, create a district infrastructure, shape sociological change, and finally alter the purpose and intent of teacher evaluation itself.

STAGES OF INCREASED EDUCATOR PARTICIPATION

Participation in enhanced teacher evaluation should begin on a small scale and build on success rather than be imposed on a whole district all at once. Participation can begin with volunteer pioneers—educators who, for a variety of reasons, step forward to be included. It is important that these people have a good experience, their vision of quality teaching be confirmed, and they take pride in their accomplishments as evidenced in the new process of evaluation. (Of course, all of these payoffs should not protect volunteers from the consequences of evidence of mediocre and bad practice.) The second phase of participation will recruit additional volunteers who base some of their motivation on observed success of the initial pioneers. Third in participation will be teachers who choose new practices as options that work better for them. The fourth stage should include all teachers in the district, except those who actively opt out (the mirror image of the early pioneers). Participation should be increased gradually and be based on the success, ideas, and advocacy of those who go first. Districts have the option to run dual programs and to allow practitioner choice during this time of transition.

TRANSITIONS TOWARD TEACHER DATA GATHERING IN DOSSIERS

Teachers can begin collecting evidence with the perspective that it takes on the order of a minimum of 2 years to complete the first adequate dossiers. For some teachers with complex performances or outcomes, documentation may take 4 years. Beginning teachers can be expected to be heavily involved in data gathering, because most current teacher education programs already use portfolios and work samples (Schalock, 1998; Wolf, Whinery, & Hagerty, 1995). The minority of veteran teachers who refuse the new directions for data gathering may be given options such as clinical supervision or traditional principal judgment, and can be maintained with traditional evaluation until retirement. Overall, changing teacher culture in terms of teacher initiative for data gathering is more than a decade-long process.

TRANSITIONS OF DATA-BASED DECISION MAKING

Perhaps the most significant and difficult transition to new directions in teacher evaluation is that of changing the responsibilities for data gathering and decision making. Table 24.1 depicts four recommended phases of development that gradually increase the authority and involvement of teachers in their own evaluation. These four phases are discussed in this section.

Traditional Principal Hegemony

Most districts begin with the principal as the data gatherer and summative decision maker for routine annual teacher evaluation (Loup, Garland, Ellett, & Rugutt, 1996; Wiles & Bondi, 2000). In this practice, the building administrator collects data through observation, some form of clinical supervision, and anecdotal records. She then makes the decision for retention, remediation, or dismissal. This is a time-honored practice that produces the least effort and conflict for participants. It is a technique with strong legal precedents.

Districts have several options in using this traditional practice. It may be retained for teachers who request no change in their evaluation. This choice requires little consensus among other educators in the district. Also, it may be retained by individual principals who assert that clinical supervision is a necessary part of their practice. This second option requires consensus agreement and teacher organization approval to be used. Little is lost with retention of traditional practices for some teachers, as this is what has been done for years. Diverting some resources in this direction can do little harm, and much good if it satisfies a few practitioners who otherwise might sabotage the new system.

Teacher-Controlled Data, Principal Decision Making

The first transition to new directions and practices is to allow teachers to make their case for positive annual evaluation by submitting (via the Evaluation Unit) a dossier of credible evidence about their merit, value, and impact for that year, and for their career. This second phase of teacher evaluation does not alter the decision-reporting role of the principal, but does change the overall evaluation process significantly: The power is

TABLE 24.1 Transition Phases of Data-Based Decision Making

1. Traditional practice: principal gathers data, writes summative report
2. Teacher controls data gathering; principal writes summative report; principal retains monitoring role
3. Teacher-dominated panels make "auxiliary" decisions: leadership, mentors, permanent status, promotion, student teacher supervision, recommendation for national board licensing; principal monitors
4. Panels make summative teacher retention decisions, reports; principal retains monitor role

shared, and the principal must justify her decision making in terms of the data presented. This phase is a necessary transition to fully innovative practices; districts must have successful experience with teacher-directed data gathering before moving on to other changed roles in teacher evaluation.

One district option for teacher evaluation is to stay at this level of change. This choice permits the advantage of multiple and variable data sources, and increased teacher autonomy, but stops short of the logistics of panels and further sharing of principal authority.

Panels for "Auxiliary" Decisions Other Than Routine Summative

When a district becomes experienced with complex data gathering and has the necessary infrastructure in place (e.g., forms and scoring procedures, the Evaluation Unit), there is the opportunity to move to teacher-dominated panel decision making. However, the innovation away from current principal hegemony requires experience with decisions that are technically and sociologically easier to make than are those involved in summative retention. These *auxiliary* decisions do not involve retention, remediation, or dismissal, but do affect appointments, assignments, status, and responsibilities, which should be based on meritorious performance. Examples of these decisions are grade-level or department chairs, permanent (tenure) job status, rank promotions, eligibility for student teachers or mentor assignments (paid or unpaid), and a district recommendation for national board licensing. Some of these judgments are new to the system and thus do not have the baggage of tradition and precedent. Some judgments involve low stakes and are noncontroversial themselves; the real changes are in the authority to make the decision and the nature of evidence to be used.

As with earlier phases of change in decision making, districts have the option of staying at this level of innovation (i.e., change in data gathering, but not in decision making), or making this level available for individual teachers who do not want to participate at the final level, which involves judgments of other teachers. Little is lost with these individuals having their way; much can be lost in the system if they become subversive.

Panels for Routine, Dossier-Based Summative Teacher Evaluation

The most sophisticated and advanced phase for district development of decision making is for most teachers to rely on a teacher-dominated panel, including administrators and parents, for routine teacher evaluation decision making. That is, most teachers are evaluated by successfully passing panel reviews on a biennial basis. Included in this process is active and up-to-date data gathering directed by individual teachers. (Problems of substandard performance should be retained by administrators for action, although individuals can be flagged for attention by district review panels.)

TRANSITIONS IN DISTRICT INFRASTRUCTURE

Developing an infrastructure for successful teacher evaluation requires creating a number of new institutions and resources in a school district. This combination of support people, procedures, and documents has been previously described in this book. Table 24.2 summarizes the kinds of infrastructure needed for a successful transition from traditional to new directions and practices.

Development of infrastructure takes time to accumulate experience, create alternatives, and put a stamp of local application and versions on the materials and products of teacher evaluation. Initial formation of organizations and materials requires a period of moratorium on extreme pressure for results and compromise. Both people and materials require a chance to mature to the demands that will be placed upon them by serious teacher evaluation. Developed capacity is the process of creating local expertise, experience, and professional wisdom. As described by the North Central Regional Educational Laboratory (NCREL, 2000), this local development requires schools to define their problems using their own goals, initiate changes in accordance with local conditions, and evaluate to decide what more needs to be done. NCREL further advises locals to use research-based knowledge, get expert advice, look for demonstrations of successful practice, and use self-study tools.

TABLE 24.2 Infrastructure Development

Organizations, e.g., Evaluation Board, Evaluation Unit
Responsibilities, e.g., data gathering, scoring and reporting of surveys
Time structures, e.g., opportunities to meet with Evaluation Unit, gather data
Forms and procedures, e.g., parent surveys, focus groups for students
Teacher ranks, e.g., "Professional" and "Senior"

SOCIOLOGICAL DEVELOPMENT

Transition to a sophisticated teacher evaluation requires changes in sociology. Although Chapters 4 and 23 presented many details, it is important to highlight the topics that require special attention. This movement should be championed by several key district agencies. The Evaluation Board described in Chapter 18 is the formal advocate for good teacher evaluation. The cosponsors of the superintendent and teachers' organization must remain vocal supporters of the system. Strong substantive support for sociological development must come from staff development inservices, which increase capacity one workshop at a time. The Evaluation Unit should be expected to change the sociological relationships with every consultation and provision of materials. Finally, the school board must remain resolute in taking the new directions.

A conscious effort must be made to increase rational and scholarly decision making relative to organic growth as the infrastructure is built. Examples of irrational decision making should be illustrated and its influence greatly restricted. Several years of explicit attention to sociological realities and the vocabulary of sociology will make a difference in the technical and political actions. Inservice education should not only address the techniques of teacher evaluation, but also the sociology of change. Rational development can be fostered by acknowledging those who practice good decision making.

The sociological structures of the district will be changed as collaboration in teacher evaluation increases, which will, in turn, foster new relationships. For example, teachers who participate in peer review acknowledge the permanent change in interactions that result from that experience (McCarthey & Peterson, 1987). Teachers must be given the necessary time and recognition to work with each other. Educators who spend time on district evaluation activity, for the benefit of colleagues, should be acknowledged.

Shifts in educator sociology require open discussions about power and authority. As decision making becomes more shared, debates about consequences, benefits, and new discomforts should be encouraged. The increased participation by parents and students, which is a part of the new directions, should be highlighted and discussed.

Finally, changes in the sociology of the district can be fostered by pay-offs and recognition; rewards are increased by a conscious and deliberate plan. Exemplars of documentation and practice should be publicized. The goal is for recognition of the good work already going on, not to maintain the never silent drumbeat of change. The shift to appointments and teacher leadership based on demonstrated merit is a major revolution in the profession. The great need to increase the types and number of rewards for public school teachers (Lortie, 1975) is a major component in improved teacher evaluation.

PURPOSE FOR TEACHER EVALUATION

The traditional purpose of evaluation is a vague mix of a never-ending push for change, accountability, fulfilling past expectations, and some need to get bad practice. As better evaluation develops in a district, purpose evolves into a more complex set of functions, which interlock, sharing resources and techniques. The purpose begins to recognize the needs of teachers themselves, as well as those of external audiences. Purposes of improvement diminish in relation to other payoffs, such as recognition of excellence in practice. The sense of purpose begins to include more individual visions of teachers as they make actual strong performance contributions. More profound performances should be documented along with the collection of mundane, repetitive tasks of traditional teacher evaluation. The concept of the nature of good teaching must show its overwhelming contextual basis. Good teaching must show its preparation and process, as well as its outcomes. Teacher evaluation should document actual instances of increased ordered intellectual power in students, developed imaginations, service to others, and exercise of a will to happiness, as fostered by teachers.

25

Justifying a School District Teacher Evaluation System

A school district teacher evaluation system needs to be sufficiently justified by those creating and using it. Sufficient does not mean because this is what

> We have always done
> The evaluation committee has decided
> The policies of the superintendent are
> We are required to do
> Neighboring districts do
> Our consultant gave us

Instead, sufficient justification means that the system, its practices, and results are defended from four perspectives. First, the validity (including reliability) is established. Second, issues of fairness and equity are considered in the design and implementation. Third, the system is consistent with state, federal, and case law. Finally, the district teacher evaluation system is analyzed using the Personnel Evaluation Standards. This chapter examines these interrelated issues of justification.

VALIDATING A TEACHER EVALUATION SYSTEM

Validating a teacher evaluation system means completing a number of steps in building a case that is "sound; well grounded on principles or evidence; able to withstand criticism or objection, as an argument" (Friend & Guralnik, 1960, p. 1608). Validation consists of creating a public, reviewable description that shows that the system addresses what it ought to address in teacher performance, and then actually assesses what it claims that it assesses. A valid teacher evaluation system functions dependably, accurately, and with known limits. Validity means that it operates with the best techniques and materials available. The system and its results are believable. Table 25.1 lists these and other attributes of validity in a teacher evaluation system. No single one of these attributes confers validity; rather, a sufficient number of them combine to increase the validity of the teacher evaluation system to a sufficient level.

Because the concept of validity is complicated to define, some more statements about it may be helpful:

1. The exercise of judgment is necessary in creating valid procedures. No wholly empirical or quantitative processes of validation exist.
2. The validity of teacher evaluation is a matter of degree, not an all-or-none quality. Procedures are not valid or invalid; they are more or less valid.
3. The validity of teacher evaluation is not determined solely by the procedure itself. It depends on the purpose, group, and way in which it is used.
4. Validity is the extent to which the procedure is useful for a given purpose.
5. Not all operational definitions of teaching are equally rational or useful.
6. The more fully and confidently a procedure can be specified and described, the greater its validity.
7. Many validation problems arise from lack of clear and generally accepted definitions of what is to be measured.
8. Teacher evaluation procedures may not, in fact, measure what they claim to measure.
9. Validity may be determined directly by critical analysis of the procedures, specifications, and contents—or indirectly by analysis of its correlation with a criterion or with other intrinsically valid measures.
10. To be valid, a procedure must be both relevant and reliable.
11. Validity is the degree to which a procedure is absolutely correct in measuring what it purports to measure.
12. Different types of validity exist.

TABLE 25.1 Attributes of a Valid Teacher Evaluation System

Has good reasons behind it
Has reasons that are good in the specific setting it is used in
Does not have good reasons against it
Does not leave out important considerations about teaching
Fits into the larger scheme of education
Is associated with other things that are valued in education
Predicts other things that are valued in education
Does a good job of sampling
Usually means that other valuable things will occur as a result
Is agreed on by experts in the field
Is agreed on by local practitioners
Documents what it appears to document
Documents what we say it documents
Documents accurately, consistently, predictably, and dependably

Table 25.2 presents types of validity described by educational and psychological evaluators (Cohen, 1981; House, 1980; Joint Committee on Standards for Educational Evaluation, 1988; Scriven, 1987; Stanley, 1971).

Components of Validation

Specification. Validation begins by describing what the system addresses (assesses, measures, considers, documents, analyzes). It explains its domain, analysis, ground rules of operation, and system of evidence. It justifies that it addresses what it ought to address. Specification is a process of logic and description. It should rule out some concerns, for example, organizations that the teacher belongs to in his or her personal life.

Link of specifications to practice. Validation should demonstrate that a system addresses what it claims to address in its public statements of concern. This means, for example, that data are presented to show that student surveys show what students think of their teachers and that peer reviews give pertinent information about how fellow teachers judge teacher materials. This sense of validity is that the proclaimed topics and issues are followed through in actual practice.

Specification of limitations. Valid teacher evaluation means recognition of the limitations of the data. For example, pupil achievement data are a logical concern for teacher evaluation. However, because there are technical limits to gathering student achievement data on all teachers (e.g., lack of good tests for some subject areas, overly expensive test administrations for others), validity statements for pupil achievement as a data source require

TABLE 25.2 Types of Validity

Has good reasons behind it [CONSTRUCT]
Has reasons that are good in the specific setting it is used in [ECOLOGICAL]
Does not have good reasons against it {CONSTRUCT]
Does not leave out important considerations about teaching [CONTENT]
Fits into the larger scheme of education [CONSTRUCT]
Is associated with other things that are valued in education [CONCURRENT; FACTORAL]
Predicts other things that are valued in education [PREDICTIVE]
Does a good job of sampling {CONTENT; RELIABILITY]
Usually means that other valuable things will occur as a result [PREDICTIVE]
Is agreed on by experts in the field [EXPERT]
Is agreed on by local practitioners [CONSENSUS]
Documents what it appears to document [FACE]
Documents what we say it documents [FACE]
Documents accurately, consistently, predictably, and dependably [RELIABILITY]

declarations of limits. Thus the *optional* use of pupil achievement data increases the validity of their use in teacher evaluation.

Use of best practices. Validation continues with evidence that the system uses the best practices that are available. Every system will be imperfect in actual practice; it simply is not possible to meet every logical demand and test of data gathering and analysis in an actual school setting. Time, expense, and technical limits prevent perfection. However, the burden for good evaluation is not for perfection but that the effort be the best that currently is attainable. Surveys, reports, and reviews should be the best available. There should not be systems that are better; if other districts or research groups have better procedures, then the district has the burden to adopt new practices.

Reliability. A valid teacher evaluation system needs to be dependable and consistent. When there is variation, as with any system in actual practice, users need some estimate of the magnitude of the inaccuracy or undependability. Validation requires that measurements are made to see how accurate and variable the practices are. For example, when a class is surveyed, how accurate and reproducible are the reported averages? Should audiences judge whole numbers or tenths? Will the result of one administration be the same as another made several days later? Data are dependable at some level; a valid teacher evaluation system estimates at what level dependable judgments can be made. For example, when judges see an average response of parents of 4.65 (on a 5-point scale) on the survey item "overall satisfaction" for the past 3 years, they also need to know that if the survey were given again it may range as much as plus or minus .13 points.

Comprehensiveness. If data represent all of the experience under consideration, then validity is high. For example, if all of a teacher's students or parents are surveyed, then we can be sure of the summaries. However, very often in teacher evaluation only samples are assessed or judged. For example, teacher materials are not all that a teacher actually uses. For high school teachers with many students, not all students will be surveyed. Not all parents will respond to surveys. In these cases, samples are used. Some samples are adequate and others are not. A valid system will attend to the adequacy of samples. It will, for example, announce acceptable return rates for parent surveys, for example, 80% with no known selection bias.

Multiple perspectives. Validity is enhanced by using multiple judges to temper the inevitable biases of human judgment. Also, validity is strengthened by multiple data sources; each line of evidence answers some questions and confirms answers to others. Replications of data gathering done on a systematic basis help with confidence.

Credibility. Finally, validity means that the procedures, data, and judgments are believable. The assumption is that they are true, and not inaccurate, dishonest, or misrepresented. For example, validity means that peer reviews are not conducted by friends of teachers, surveys are scored by neutral parties, report forms are managed by persons other than the teacher herself, and reports and dossiers are maintained so that they cannot be altered. Credibility means that teachers are not put in the impossible situation of conflict of interest between their clients (students and parents) and their own self-interest, for example, as occurs in self-evaluation.

How Is Validation Accomplished?

Table 25.3 presents components of district validation. Each of these activities contributes to the argument, or case, that a district teacher evaluation system is valid: It does what it says it does and it does what it should be doing. These activities may seem formidable and intimidating. However, they can be done with a sufficient time frame. Not all of these have to be done at once, but they do need to be completed and to be ongoing. A reasonable amount of time is up to 5 years. During this time, a district may be operating with volunteers and a no-harm policy. Not all of these have to be done with perfection; the standard is what the competition is doing, and what state-of-the-art professional behavior is. Each component contributes to the overall validity.

TABLE 25.3 Validating a District Teacher Evaluation System

Establish purpose statements
Document data-gathering procedures
Analyze empirical data: norms, comparisons
Estimate empirical reliability of data
Establish multiple measures: data, judges
Establish safeguards: units, safe storage, oversight
Collect examples from other districts, literature
Conduct studies on current and proposed procedures
Archive data

Establish Purpose Statements

Validation begins by publishing, discussing, reviewing, and revising purpose statements. Purpose statements should include protection of clients, monitoring for minimal professional performance, and compliance with district expectations and requirements. Purpose statements should encourage and recognize good professional behavior and excellence in performance. They should provide information for ongoing professional development. It is best to promise to improve practice directly by evaluation feedback.

Document Data-Gathering Procedures

Data-gathering procedures, such as surveys and peer review protocols, should be collected and bound for public review. These collections should include examples, ground rules, materials, and descriptions of the procedures themselves. It is important to include examples of *inadequate* applications, for example, surveys that were collected by the teacher, or testimonial letters unsystematically gathered. Districts should show ranges of acceptable applications; for example, well-done lists of professionalism or minimally adequate test score reporting.

Once the data-gathering procedures, materials, and sample results are collected, copies should be made and distributed. This gives participants and stakeholders a chance to be familiar with expectations, to suggest changes, to spot problems, and finally to lend agreement to the entire system. Another component is to get expert reviews of the data gathering. This is what Scriven (1973a, 1973c) called "credentialing."

Analyze Empirical Data and Estimate Empirical Reliability

Once the teacher evaluation system is under way, it produces much specific information. The analysis of these data begins by computing population norms. This enables a district to uncover realistic expectations and comparisons. It allows individual teachers to locate their own data with that of colleagues. A district Evaluation Unit should calculate ranges, averages (mean, median, mode), and distributions (variances, standard deviations, standard errors of measurement). This information should be prepared in descriptive, tabular, and graphic forms. For example, parent surveys should show the averages of return rates, rating on specific items, and samples of comments. Next, comparisons, such as correlations with other measures and performance assessments, should be made.

One particularly important area of data analysis is to estimate empirical reliability. Surveys, reports, and even panel judgments will not be perfectly replicable or representative. It is important to know the practical limits of measures used in the teacher evaluation system. It also is important to build confidence in the dependability of these measures. For example, student surveys are more stable than thought of by most teachers who are not familiar with them (Kauchak et al., 1985). Reliability can be determined by such procedures as administration-readministration, split-half, internal, and multimethod comparison (e.g., survey and interview) (Peterson, 1988, 1990b; Stanley, 1971).

A final area for documentation is that of costs. These costs include dollar, time, personnel, materials for individual procedures, per teacher expenses, and procedures for sharing costs between district and individual teacher. Comprehensive cost data include installation, maintenance, and displacement costs as well as the direct expenses for the evaluation itself (Scriven, 1973a, 1973c).

Establish Multiple Measures and Judges

Multiple data sources are necessary for difficult-to-measure phenomena such as those assessed in teacher evaluation. Triangulation or multiple indicators are a more valid look at complex teacher performances (Mehrens, 1990; Peterson, 1984). Multiple judges are needed to incorporate different points of view (Epstein, 1985).

Establish Safeguards

Safeguards should include independent Evaluation Units. These limit the use of teacher evaluation as a control mechanism for administrators and concentrate the data on the issue of performance. Another necessary safeguard is safe storage; it is important that information collected not be subject to change, alteration, or tampering. Finally, safeguards should include oversight: some credible agency and specific persons accountable for watching the procedure, giving arbitration for disputes, and seeing that provisions are carried out.

Collect Examples From Other Districts, Literature

Specific teacher evaluation examples from other districts show that a district is doing what it should do, from the perspective of what competitors are doing. Descriptions and materials can be exchanged every several years. Likewise, an examination of the current literature on teacher evaluation will show examples of the state of the art. The argument should be made that the current practice is up to date and that there are not major alternative strategies that have not been considered. The standard is not perfection, but that a defensive, ongoing effort is made.

Conduct Studies on Current and Proposed Procedures

Not all of the teacher evaluation procedures used in a district system will be equally tried and true. Preliminary usage is defensible, if current studies are a part of development. Such studies follow the expectations for any teacher evaluation data: What are population norms? What are comparisons with other measures? What levels of user satisfaction are there? What are the benefits and costs of the procedures? How can the procedures be improved?

Archive Data

A final validation activity is to create archives for review, checking, and as a resource for future development. Some individual record may be identified for destruction in 5 years. When this is the practice, a small number of random samples should be archived indefinitely. For individual teachers, summary records should be kept indefinitely, whereas most other data and materials can be destroyed after a 5-year period. Some representative examples should be archived by individuals. Long-term data need to be protected from fire, invasions of privacy, alteration, and disturbance.

Validation Calls for Increased Professional Activity

As pointed out by Rebell (1990), the courts have not required [a school] board to show that assessment devices used to justify a finding of incompetence [in a tenured teacher dismissal action] were professionally validated. As the court explained in *Board of Fort Madison v. Youel* (1979), the preponderance of the evidence standard means that the board must list specific findings of fact on each of the major points to support its conclusions reached in routine evidence procedures, and the courts are not likely to probe beyond the conclusions to consider the adequacy of the assessment criteria used. (p. 344)

Because the courts are not likely to require the additional validation work recommended in this chapter, the only reason for this effort is to achieve professional quality. Thus the term *professional* has a distinct meaning in this context. Technical knowledge and responsibility go beyond legal requirement and mandate from noneducators, as educators take control of evaluation and practitioner quality.

FAIRNESS AND ETHICAL ISSUES

A school district teacher evaluation system not only should be justified in terms of its technical validity, it also should meet standards for its treatment of people in terms of fairness and ethics. Values about quality in human learning and teaching are inextricably bound with values about how people treat each other. These ideas about how a society and a profession should work present additional guidelines and restrictions to those who design and use teacher evaluation systems.

Rawls (1971) described three theories of ethics and justice to consider in teacher evaluation. The first is utilitarian in which the evaluation system is designed to get the greatest total of satisfaction for everyone concerned. This theory assumes a common measure or index of teacher quality that provides satisfaction to students, administrators, parents, colleagues, community, scholars, and society. A second kind of ethical system is plural/intuitive in which the system is designed to accommodate different notions of quality, which are individual and context dependent. The third kind of system is based on justice as fairness, which combines elements of the first two theories. It begins with agreement on the ends of the activity, or "what is right." Then, participants are free to create their own descriptions of how they get there. This system is consistent with Rawl's ideas "that to respect another as a moral person is to try to understand his aims and interests from his standpoint" (p. 338). Thus one part of a moral teacher evaluation system is that it have mechanisms to document the aims and interests of each teacher from his or her own standards. The limits to this are the agreed-on sense of right of the entire system: the demonstrated needs of the clients and the corresponding work needs of the educators.

Rawls (1971) described two principles for justice. The first was that "each person is to have an equal right to the most extensive system of equal basic liberties compatible with a similar system of liberty for all" (p. 302). The second included that "social and economic . . . benefits[s] [are] . . . open to all under conditions of fair equality of opportunity" (p. 303). The evaluation system should present a chance for each teacher to have an equal and fair opportunity to document his or her own contributions and thus to make a case for merit, worth, and value.

House (1980) maintained that it is necessary for participants in an evaluation system to arrive at a "fair evaluation agreement." This understanding may include written and unwritten elements. A public school system will have much less latitude in its concerns than the entire society. A fair agreement is one that has "noncoercion, rationality, acceptance of terms, joint agreement, disinterestedness, universality, community self-interestedness, equal and full information, nonriskiness, possibility, counting all votes, and participation" (p. 173). An evaluation system requires four values: moral equality, moral autonomy, impartiality, and reciprocity.

Strike and Bull (1981) described fairness in terms of two components: equal respect and reasonableness. Equal respect for all teachers derives from both their intrinsic value and equal worth. Teacher evaluation should not harass, belittle, or use some informative methods (e.g., covert surveillance). Equal respect does not mean identical treatment; rather, the purposes and results of evaluation shape differential treatment. It does mean that only relevant criteria may be used. Reasonableness requires that evaluation practices and results not be arbitrary or capricious. Rather, they should be based on the best possible evidence and not consist of haphazard, single-person focus or irregular, covert, or untimely procedures. Strike and Bull included effectiveness as a central value of teacher evaluation systems than can be simultaneously considered with fairness.

Strike (1990) continued this analysis of ethics in teacher evaluation by combining the ideas of equal respect and maximizing benefits of evaluation activity for all participants, clients, and audiences. He expressed the ethics of teacher evaluation in eight principles: due process, privacy, equality, openness of procedures to public, humaneness, client benefit, academic freedom, and respect for autonomy. He applied these ideas to a Bill of Rights for Teacher Evaluation, which is reproduced as Table 25.4.

Scriven (1981) described as a key ethical consideration that teacher evaluation systems not be based on certain teaching styles. Too often in education, singular approaches to teaching (e.g., structured, stepwise lessons) are advocated as a singular description of good teaching. Although some of these styles have been demonstrably (usually through statistical correlation analysis) successful at enabling learning with some populations at some times (at low to moderate levels), these relationships simply

TABLE 25.4 Bill of Rights for Teacher Evaluation

Rights of educational institutions

1. Educational institutions have the right to exercise supervision and to make personnel decisions intended to improve the quality of the education they provide.
2. Educational institutions have the right to collect information relevant to their supervisory and evaluative roles.
3. Educational institutions have the right to act on such relevant information in the best interest of the student whom they seek to educate.
4. Educational institutions have the right to the cooperation of the teaching staff in implementing and executing a fair and effective system of evaluation.

Rights of teachers

1. Professional rights
   a. Teachers have a right to reasonable job security.
   b. Teachers have a right to a reasonable degree of professional discretion in the performance of their jobs.
   c. Teachers have a right to reasonable participation in decisions concerning both professional and employment-related aspects of their jobs.
2. Evidential rights
   a. Teachers have the right to have decisions made on the basis of evidence.
   b. Teachers have a right to be evaluated on relevant criteria.
   c. Teachers have the right not to be evaluated on the basis of hearsay, rumor, or unchecked complaints.
3. Procedural rights
   a. Teacher have the right to be evaluated according to general, public, and comprehensible standards.
   b. Teachers have the right to notice concerning when they will be evaluated.
   c. Teachers have the right to know the results of their evaluation.
   d. Teachers have the right to express a reaction to the results of their evaluation in a meaningful way.
4. Other humanitarian and civil rights
   a. Teachers have a right to humane evaluation procedures.
   b. Teachers have the right to have their evaluation kept private and confidential.
   c. Teachers have the right to evaluation procedures that are not needlessly intrusive into their professional activities.
   d. Teachers have the right to have their private lives considered irrelevant to their evaluation.
   e. Teachers have the right that evaluations not be used coercively to obtain aims external to the legitimate purposes of evaluation.
   f. Teachers have the right to nondiscriminatory criteria and procedures.
   g. Teachers have the right not to have evaluation used to inhibit the expressions of unpopular views.
   h. Teachers have the right to an overall assessment of their performance that is frank, honest, and consistent.

Principles of conflict resolution

1. Remediation is to be preferred, where possible, to disciplinary action or termination.
2. Mediation is to be preferred, where possible, to more litigious forms of conflicts.
3. Informal attempts to settle disputes should precede formal ones.

(continued)

TABLE 25.4 Continued

Rights of the public

1. Parents and the members of the community have a right to expect that the educational welfare of children will be the paramount concern in any system of teacher evaluation.
2. Parents and the members of the community have the right to expect that their children will be taught by competent people.
3. Parents and the members of the community have the right to expect that the competence of teachers will be assessed on a regular basis and in a fair and functional way.
4. Parents and the members of the community have the right to expect that evaluation will be acted on in a way that improves the education of their children and protects their children against maliciousness or incompetence.
5. Parents and members of the community have the right to have their concerns and complaints fairly considered.
6. Parents and the members of the community have the right to have teachers evaluated according to publicly known standards and by publicly known practices.

SOURCE: Strike (1990). Used with permission.

must not be extended to making assumptions about the effectiveness of other teachers at other times. Much better evidence than these "predictions" comes from the actual track record of the teachers. Only as a last resort for poor teachers should formulistic prescriptions for teaching be applied as guides for quality performance. Beyond being "scientifically indefensible" (p. 268), Scriven (1981) described the use of style-related questions and observations in teacher evaluation as unethical.

LEGAL CONCERNS ABOUT TEACHER EVALUATION

Suggestions in this book about measures that a school district should take to ensure legal justification of a teacher evaluation system should not replace the advice of competent legal counsel. However, a number of ideas and concrete steps can help to construct systems that are fair, equitable, and in compliance with statutes and court precedents concerning teacher evaluation.

There are many existing good sources of advice about legal issues in teacher evaluation (Bridges, 1992; Fischer & Schimmel, 1973; Gee & Sperry, 1978; Rebell, 1990; Rossow & Parkinson, 1992; Strike & Bull, 1981; Sullivan & Zirkel, 1998; Valente, 1987; Zirkel, 1979). Thus the information presented in this section is brief. The discussion begins with eight legal principles related to teacher evaluation. Next follows a set of specific steps recommended for districts as part of justifying the evaluation system. Third is discussion of new issues likely to be raised by the new directions and procedures recommended in this book. Increased involvement and responsibility for teachers will bring new legal relationships. Many of these issues have not been subject to litigation or completely analyzed for legal implications.

Legal Principles and Precedents

Teacher evaluation necessarily means concern with legal procedures and precedents. Teachers, parents, and legislatures use the courts and the law to settle educational controversies. Teachers use the courts and law as "a form of protection against termination or other negative employment decisions" (Rossow & Parkinson, 1992, p. 1). The state has a legitimate interest in the instructional competence of its teachers (*Shelton v. Tucker*, 1960; Strike & Bull, 1981); thus legislative bodies make laws about teacher licensing, competence, evaluation, and termination. Designing and using teacher evaluation systems call for awareness and study of legal concerns.

Legal concerns with teacher evaluation are matters of the U.S. Constitution and constitutions of the states, federal and state laws (statutes, administrative rules), and of precedents from court cases. As stated by Zirkel (1979), "although there are a federal overlay and local interplay, the law of teacher evaluation—like that of public education in general—is largely a matter of state control" (p. 17). The U.S. Constitution has no provisions for education and the Tenth Amendment reserves educational issues to the states (Rebell, 1990); however, property and liberty rights play a part in teacher evaluation. Legislatures have passed laws on teacher tenure, licensing, and collective bargaining. More than half of the states have laws concerning teacher evaluation; these laws vary considerably. For example, Connecticut's laws are permissive for local school board discretion, whereas Nevada is quite specific in terms of procedures and expectations. Finally, case law precedents provide much of the detail for teacher evaluation practices and limits. For example, a teacher cannot be negatively evaluated for exercise of protected speech as a result of a series of court case precedents, including *Pickering v. Board of Education* (1968), *Mt. Healthy City School District v. Doyle* (1977), and *Connick v. Meyers* (1983).

Lawful due process is a central concern in teacher evaluation. The Fourteenth Amendment to the U.S. Constitution declares that "a person should not be deprived of property without due process." This protects *procedural* due process, which includes the right of notice of dismissal, a hearing, and in some instances a written statement of the reason for dismissal. Fischer and Schimmel (1973) provided a complete list based on the Supreme Court decision of *Goldberg v. Kelly* (1970):

A hearing scheduled at a reasonable time and place

Timely and adequate notice giving details of the reasons for the proposed suspension or dismissal

An opportunity to defend oneself, including oral presentation of evidence, data, and arguments

An opportunity to cross-examine witnesses and challenge evidence

Right to representation and legal counsel (including an attorney)

A decision following established rules, and based on evidence and data presented in writing and at the hearing

A written statement of the decision and reasons for the determination and the evidence used to reach the decision

Unbiased and nonpartial decision makers

In general, the courts have strictly applied the procedural requirements of teacher evaluation laws. Dismissal charges against teachers in Pennsylvania were not sustained in cases where the rating systems were not strictly followed, where the evaluation form did not contain unsatisfactory ratings, and where the required anecdotal records were not provided. In addition, courts in various jurisdictions have overturned dismissal decisions based on unsatisfactory evaluations due to failure to provide written warnings about remediable teaching deficiencies (Zirkel, 1979).

Substantive due process means that the topics and reasons are defensible. For example, in noneducational cases, courts did not support inappropriate use of performance evaluations in instances where (a) ratings were based on subjective or vague factors, (b) observational ratings did not indicate an adequate sampling of behavior or there was evidence to indicate rater bias, and (c) standard conditions were not employed for the collection and scoring of ratings (*Griggs et al. v. Duke Power Company*, 1971).

Courts traditionally have been very deferential to school districts in matters of teacher evaluation (Scheelhaase v. Woodbury Central Community School District, 1973). In particular, "state courts tend not to probe the substance of the evaluative criteria or methods used. [The] courts tend to defer to administrator expert judgment and to accept the results of their evaluations without undertaking any independent analysis" (Rebell, 1990, p. 345). When local administrators and school boards comply with state statutes and negotiated agreements, the courts generally support school authorities. Rossow and Parkinson (1992) state that "if the stipulated [teacher evaluation] procedures are followed, the courts will be unwilling to substitute their judgment for the judgment of educators when teachers challenge an evaluation rating" (p. 4). They cited as an example *Rogers v. Department of Defense Dependents School, Germany Region* (1987).

The courts generally have deferred to the discretion of school authorities concerning the validity of teacher evaluation systems. In reaching this conclusion, Zirkel (1979) cautioned that the specifics of a case such as whether the teacher was tenured and the specific state statutes involved could influence court decisions. Within broad general limits, the courts do not appear to be interested in determining the particular methods of evaluation or the criteria that are applied. One accepted rule is for generally accepted practice. The courts do, however, expect the evidence obtained to be job related and nondiscriminatory.

Districts have an interest in and legal rights to keep teacher evaluation records. Part of a school district's employee supervisory function is to keep personnel records. These contain information necessary for the school board to make decisions about assignment and retention. Such records document professional licenses and certificates, educational records, and hiring documents. Also included are records of administrative actions such as assignments and performance remediation. They also contain performance evaluations.

The courts have long recognized the sensitive nature of personnel records:

> The personnel records of the district are maintained as confidential files; . . . such matters are among the most confidential and sensitive records kept by a private or public employer, and their use remains effective only so long as the confidence of the records, and the confidences of those who contribute to those records, are maintained. It does not matter that here the employees themselves sought disclosure of the records; the records are the property of and are in the custody and control of the district, not the employees. (*Board of Trustees of Calaveras Unified School District v. Leach*, 1968)

Thus the public and teachers (and even grand juries) are restricted from access to files. Personnel files can be kept confidential with limits to teacher access. Teachers can inspect performance evaluations before they are placed into the file; usually district forms require a signature of acknowledgment. Individual administrators can keep personal notes separate from the personnel files.

Many states differentiate between evaluation of beginning teachers and that of veterans. Probationary periods have been established to "provide teachers an opportunity to learn their craft, and school districts . . . to assess teachers' competence, before a permanent hiring commitment is made" (Rebell, 1990 p. 342). After generally what is a 2- to 3-year period, teachers are entitled to tenure. Dismissal for a probationary teacher in most states can be for reasons that can be offered by a school district after the fact, whereas dismissal from a tenured position may be based only on specified grounds and good cause that are enumerated in legislation.

Tenured teachers may be dismissed for a number of specific reasons. Grounds for dismissal of tenured teachers include incompetence (student control or poor instruction), incapacity, insubordination, unprofessional conduct, immorality (dishonesty or sexual misconduct), or good cause (declining enrollment, district consolidation) (Rossow & Parkinson, 1992; Valente, 1987). The standard for these decisions is stricter than for probationary teachers. The burden of proof must be competent and substantial evidence or a preponderance of the evidence (e.g., *Meredith v. Board of Education of Rockwood*, 1974; Rebell, 1990). Incompetence is the most time-consuming and evidence-requiring grounds for evaluation leading to dismissal (Rossow & Parkinson, 1992).

Legal restrictions contribute to the complexity of dismissing bad teachers. For example, Zirkel (1979) stated,

> In Pennsylvania which has probably the most lengthy and well-developed legal history concerning teacher evaluation, only about 100 teachers have been charged with incompetence by local boards since 1940, averaging 2.7 per year, and the charges have been upheld against only slightly above 50 percent of the teachers. (p. 21)

One response to the perceived difficulty of following procedural due process is to develop more detailed and specific teacher evaluation procedures. But this action can be counterproductive. The more detailed the procedures, the greater the possibility that some procedural shortcoming will occur. According to Cohen (1981), "Paradoxically, if an institution's personnel practices are vague or unspecified, it is more difficult for faculty members to challenge decisions on specific procedural grounds" (pp. 281-310). When district-level procedural policies exist, they must be closely followed and administered in a nonbiased fashion (Rossow & Parkinson, 1992; Zirkel, 1979). Nonbiased means that all persons are treated the same way, that no special provisions are made, and that there is equal opportunity for all to be informed and participate in the same way. Nonbiased means that personnel who apply the district policies do not discriminate against or exclude individuals but rather treat groups with uniformity.

Recommended Safeguards for Practice

Form 25.1 presents measures that school districts can take to strengthen the validity, ethics, and legal safeguards for their teacher evaluation program. Taking these steps increases the justification for the system and its results.

FORM 25.1 Steps to Strengthen Justification of Teacher Evaluation System

---

A.   Steps before evaluation begins
1.   Establish evaluation criteria: what is acceptable or notable and what is not. Relate criteria to critical work behaviors. Describe connections of criteria to district educational goals.
2.   Analyze evaluation criteria to eliminate discrimination in terms of race, sex, national origin, religion, and physical handicap.
3.   Describe the relationship of indirect teacher assessments (such as test data, peer reviews, parent surveys) to the educational goals or the district.
4.   Gather precedents (descriptions and findings from prior use) for each evaluation procedure.[a]
5.   Prepare clear definitions, descriptions, and examples of criteria, procedures, and precedents. Give these to data gatherers and teachers.
6.   Prepare criteria and examples of evaluations that will result in negative results, such as nonpromotion, nonaward of tenure, and dismissal.
7.   Communicate evaluation criteria, procedures, and precedents clearly and explicitly to all teachers and administrators. Communicate in writing (district employment handbook and special evaluation handbook) and in interactive workshops.
8.   Train evaluation personnel. Provide readings, examples, case studies, discussions, and information and performance tests.

B.   Steps during evaluation
1.   Follow and complete procedures exactly as stated.
2.   Monitor potential bias and conflict of interest of personnel involved in evaluation.
3.   Monitor evaluation personnel to ensure that they are equitable in their work and do not apply procedures to some teachers but not to others.
4.   Gather evidence as described in procedures. Follow rules and ground rules for data gathering.
5.   Keep data gathering confidential.
6.   Follow rules and ground rules of decision making. Base decisions on documented facts.
7.   Complete required written records, including decision.

C.   Steps after evaluations are completed
1.   Keep evaluation record confidential.
2.   For teachers with remedial defects, give written specifications and opportunities to correct deficiencies.
3.   Use due process for teachers facing dismissal: written charges, use of counsel, opportunities for rebuttal, hearings.
4.   Make all participants aware that specific evaluation procedures and decisions are precedents for the future.

---

a. If procedures are new in a district, for example, peer reviews, establish precedents with "no harm," voluntary pilot tests.

Legal Issues Concerning New Directions in Teacher Evaluation

New directions in teacher evaluation mean both innovative procedures (e.g., variable data sources, panel decisions) and outcomes (e.g., teacher promotions, distinctions). These developments raise questions about current legal precedents and principles. In some dimensions, conflict between teachers and districts may decrease because teachers are given much more choice and participation in their own evaluations. For example, a teacher who selects and inspects pupil survey data can hardly claim inappropriate use of these data. In other dimensions, conflict may increase. For example, more different kinds of people (e.g., parents, students, and peer teachers) will be involved in teacher evaluation—most have *less* specific training in personnel evaluation than do present administrators. This section presents eight topics where legal understandings and precedents face challenge and change.

Participation

These new directions greatly expand the kinds of people who may participate in teacher evaluation. Decision-making panels may include teachers, parents, and even students. In the past, courts generally have not directly analyzed the training or qualifications of teacher evaluators. (*Kudasik v. Board of Directors, Port Allegany School District*, 1983; *Rosso v. Board of School Directors*, 1977). However, in *Trask v. Board of Education of the City of St. Louis* (1981), the judge held that professional educators were expected to have exclusive control of teacher evaluation matters. Some teacher challenges based on inadequately trained Teacher Review Panel members may be expected.

Standing of New Evaluation Outcomes

At present, tenured teachers are considered to have a property interest in retention of their jobs and a liberty interest in their professional reputations that are protected by the Fourteenth Amendment (*Board of Regents v. Roth*, 1972; Rebell, 1990). New evaluation outcomes for public school teachers may include promotions, titles, leadership positions, and other distinctions based on dossiers and panel reviews. The standing of these outcomes has not been tested. Presumably, precedents from postsecondary education promotion systems will apply.

Due Process

In the past, procedural due process generally has meant that all teachers are evaluated with exactly the same procedures, forms, and data. These new directions include the opportunity for teachers to vary their evaluation. A newer understanding of fairness in this situation is an *equal opportunity to document quality*. Another sense of due process is that it means equal treatment of classes of teachers in a school district, for example, all teachers under consideration for retention should be treated the same way. However, if new classes are created (e.g., teacher leaders or Senior Teachers), it may be permissible to vary treatment among classes.

Procedural due process for termination or suspension of a tenured teacher has meant a complex set of expectations (Fischer & Schimmel, 1973; *Goldberg v. Kelly*, 1970). It is not clear if all of these provisions will be required for new evaluation procedures such as Teacher Review Panel decisions. New requirements may be expected for actions of teacher promotion and distinction. At a minimum, expectations to follow written procedures and to avoid arbitrary and capricious acts are likely for new evaluation outcomes.

Standards of Evidence

The presumption that teachers are competent because of their licensing is an important one for the traditional purposes of teacher evaluation: tenure and retention. The focus of evaluation for these purposes is compliance or evidence of incompetence or interference with the normal educational process. However, for newer distinctions such as teacher leadership, acknowledgment, and reward, it will be necessary to focus evaluation activity to show distinction. It is not clear what new burdens of documentation, opportunity, and comparison will be required for this new focus of teacher evaluation. Certainly, the voluntary nature of these reward distinctions will affect legal actions and decisions.

For probationary teachers, there is a standard that evaluation procedures merely are not arbitrary or capricious. For tenured teachers the standard becomes higher: "Competent and substantial evidence" or "a preponderance of the evidence" (e.g., *Meredith v. Board*, 1974; Rebell, 1990) is required for evaluation activities. The standard for newer procedures and outcomes is unclear.

Validity of Teacher Evaluation Systems

Rebell (1990) stated that the courts have not required a school board "to show that assessment devices used to justify a finding of incompetence [in a tenured teacher dismissal action] were professionally validated" (p. 344). The courts traditionally have been very deferential to school districts in matters of teacher evaluation. However, they may become interested in more objective components of teacher evaluation (e.g., surveys, tests, peer reviews). For example, courts have been willing to be involved in questions about teacher testing (e.g., Rebell, 1988; *St. Louis Teachers' Union, Local 420 v. Board of Education of the City of St. Louis*, 1987).

The validity of the new practices discussed earlier is to be established *professionally* beyond basic legal expectations and requirements. Active and ongoing validation work by school districts (e.g., record keeping, reliability estimates, studies of results) may be respected by courts.

Initiative in Teacher Education

Courts recognize the rights of the institution to supervise its employees, including personnel evaluation (e.g., *Shelton v. Tucker*, 1960). Teacher initiative in evaluation in the new directions can go considerably beyond district activity. Because it is a voluntary action, much of the adversarial setting will be changed. The new ground rules for this activity are unclear. Conflicts can be expected between administrators and teachers in the new evaluation setting. For example, teacher leaders may conflict with the responsibilities of administrators in education direction. Such conflicts could be defined as interference with the normal educational process or insubordination.

Record Keeping

In current practice, teacher personnel records generally are the property of the school district. They are private and not open to public inspection. Access to teacher files by individual teachers can be greatly restricted, for example, to inspect performance records (*Board v. Leach*, 1968; Gee & Sperry, 1978). Under the new directions, some teacher record keeping is more open; it combines personal dossiers with dossiers on record with the district teacher Evaluation Unit. Because this documentation is voluntary and monitored by teachers, more leeway in access may be permitted. Dossiers are on file with the district to increase their credibility. The teacher can add to or delete from his or her professional dossier. However, they should not be open to public inspection. Questions about who owns and controls teacher evaluation documents will arise.

Increased Use of Professional Judgment

Finally, one characteristic of new directions in teacher evaluation is increased use of professional judgment (Popham, 1987). Teacher peer review teams and district Teacher Review Panels will be given complex objective data on which to make their judgments. Part of the nature of these decisions is that they are not based on clearly written guidelines but rather depend on the expert perspective of the decision maker.

In the past, courts have held that personnel decisions not be subjective but be based on objective measures and careful written descriptions of procedures (*Albermarle Paper Company v. Moody*, 1974; Rebell, 1990; Rossow & Parkinson, 1992; *Rowe v. General Motors Corporation*, 1972). Courts have recognized that some level of subjectivity is inevitable and valid in teacher evaluation judgments, for example, *Tyler v. Hotsprings School Dist. No. 6* (1987) and Rossow and Parkinson (1992). Some litigation may be expected in terms of standards for objectivity and clarity of decision-making guidelines.

USING *THE PERSONNEL EVALUATION STANDARDS*

The last step of teacher evaluation program justification is a systematic analysis with the best standards in mind. For educational personnel evaluation, these are *The Personnel Evaluation Standards*, developed and maintained by the Joint Committee on Standards for Educational Evaluation (1988), chaired by Daniel Stufflebeam. The final section of this chapter will present advice for using these national standards for teacher evaluation.

Although the components of teacher evaluation system justification described in this chapter are complex, lengthy in performance, and technical, the more that can be accomplished locally, the better the design and functioning of the system. As described by Piaget, "to invent is to understand." Justifying or thinking about the teacher evaluation system takes time and experience but is a crucial activity for system development and use. Smaller districts should share this process with others in a network, or link with a large district. All should be careful about an early adoption of an intact program from another location and be keen about pushing for understanding and innovation of their own.

DEVELOPING THE STANDARDS

The 16-member Joint Committee (1988) includes members from organizations such as

American Association of School Administrators
American Educational Research Association
American Federation of Teachers
American Psychological Association
National Education Association
National School Boards Association

Representatives of these organizations, and seven others, used nationally distributed hearings, existing literature, drafts with revisions, and expert panels to list a total of 21 standards that "present criteria for judging evaluation plans, procedures, and reports" (p. 9). The standards are "elaborated general principles" that are commonly agreed upon by "people engaged in the professional practice of evaluation" (p. 8).

Each standard is presented with an explanation, rationale, guidelines, common errors, illustrative cases, and a listing of supporting documentation. The 21 standards are organized into four general categories: Propriety, Utility, Feasibility, and Accuracy. The standards are not a definition of good teaching or other educational performance. The standards do not present criteria differentiation, such as levels or rubrics for scoring. Table 25.5 presents the Standards as described by the Joint Committee (1988).

TABLE 25.5 The Personnel Evaluation Standards

PROPRIETY STANDARDS

The propriety standards require that evaluations be conducted legally, ethically, and with due regard for the welfare of evaluatees and clients of the evaluations.

P1 Service Orientation—Evaluations of educators should promote sound education principles, fulfillment of institutional missions, and effective performance of job responsibilities, so that the educational needs of students, community, and society are met.

P2 Formal Evaluation Guidelines—Guidelines for personnel evaluations should be recorded in statements of policy, negotiated agreements, and/or personnel evaluation manuals, so that evaluations are consistent, equitable, and in accordance with pertinent laws and ethical codes.

P3 Conflict of Interest—Conflicts of interest should be identified and dealt with openly and honestly, so that they do not compromise the evaluation process and results.

P4 Access to Personnel Evaluation Reports—Access to reports of personnel evaluation should be limited to those individuals with a legitimate need to review and use the reports, so that appropriate use of the information is assured.

P5 Interactions with Evaluatees—The evaluation should address evaluatees in a professional, considerate, and courteous manner, so that their self-esteem, motivation, professional reputations, performance, and attitude toward personnel evaluation are enhanced or, at least, not needlessly damaged.

UTILITY STANDARDS

The utility standards are intended to guide evaluations so that they will be informative, timely, and influential.

U1 Constructive Orientation—Evaluations should be constructive, so that they help institutions to develop human resources and encourage and assist those evaluated to provide excellent service.

U2 Defined Uses—The users and the intended uses of a personnel evaluation should be identified, so that the evaluation can address appropriate questions.

U3 Evaluator Credibility—The evaluation system should be managed and executed by persons with the necessary qualifications, skills, and authority, and evaluators should conduct themselves professionally, so that evaluation reports are respected and used.

TABLE 25.5 Continued

U4 Functional Reporting—Reports should be clear, timely, accurate, and germane, so that they are of practical value to the evaluatee and other appropriate audiences.

U5 Follow-Up and Impact—Evaluations should be followed up, so that users and evaluatees are aided to understand the results and take appropriate actions.

FEASIBILITY STANDARDS

The feasibility standards call for evaluation systems that are as easy to implement as possible, efficient in their use of time and resources, adequately funded, and viable from a number of other standpoints.

F1 Practical Procedures—Personnel evaluation procedures should be planned and conducted so that they produce needed information while minimizing disruption and cost.

F2 Political Viability—The personnel evaluation system should be developed and monitored collaboratively, so that all concerned parties are constructively involved in making the system work.

F3 Fiscal Viability—Adequate time and resources should be provided for personnel evaluation activities, so that evaluation plans can be effectively and efficiently implemented.

ACCURACY STANDARDS

The accuracy standards require that the obtained information be technically accurate and that conclusions be linked logically to the data.

A1 Defined Role—The role, responsibilities, performance objectives, and needed qualifications of the evaluatee should be clearly defined, so that the evaluator can determine valid assessment data.

A2 Work Environment—The context in which the evaluatee works should be identified, described, and recorded, so that environmental influences and constraints on performance can be considered in the evaluation.

A3 Documentation of Procedures—The evaluations procedures actually followed should be documented, so that the evaluatees and other users can assess the actual, in relation to intended, procedures.

A4 Valid Measurement—The measurement procedures should be chosen or developed and implemented on the basis of the described role and the intended use, so that the inferences concerning the evaluatee are valid and accurate.

A5 Reliable Measurement—Measurement procedures should be chosen or developed to assure reliability, so that the information obtained will provide consistent indications of the performance of the evaluatee.

A6 Systematic Data Control—The information used in the evaluation should be kept secure, and should be carefully processed and maintained, so as to ensure that the data maintained and analyzed are the same as the data collected.

A7 Bias Control—The evaluation process should provide safeguards against bias, so that the evaluatee's qualifications or performance are assessed fairly.

A8 Monitoring Evaluation Systems—The personnel evaluation system should be reviewed periodically and systematically, so that appropriate revisions can be made.

Source: Joint Committee on Standards for Educational Evaluation (1988).

INTERNET RESOURCES

Joint Committee on Standards for Educational Evaluation

http://www.wmich.edu/evalctr/jc/

The Standards (summary)

http://www.theriver.com/aea/EvaluationDocuments/
perseval.html

State (Hawaii) level application

http://arch.k12.hi.us/staff/standards/overview.htm

26

Using Teacher Evaluation Data

This chapter presents new payoffs of a sophisticated and ambitious teacher evaluation system. The ideas begin with a link between teacher data and the district inservice education program. Next, aggregated teacher evaluation data (e.g., student achievement examples or district averages on parent survey items) can be used by school districts to demonstrate the impact and value of educational programs. Suggestions are presented about publicity for aggregated teacher evaluation data, for example, in press releases and community meetings and focus groups. A third use for evaluation data is to make teacher leadership appointments, for example, grade-level chairs, based on Teacher Review Panel findings of teacher dossiers. Next, institutional review boards from teacher training colleges and universities can provide recognition of successful track records of teachers in their first several years of teaching. Fifth, an important extension of high-quality evaluation data is organization and extension into the National Board for Professional Teaching Standards Licensing. Finally, reasons are given to seek these and additional uses for new directions and practices in teacher evaluation. The examples of using teacher evaluation data may inspire still other benefits created by individual school districts involved in serious teacher evaluation.

LINKS BETWEEN TEACHER EVALUATION
DATA AND INSERVICE EDUCATION

Teachers readily find links and interests in using the evaluation results they get and in working on their practice. District inservice programs can begin with the opportunity for teachers to explore how to get better evaluation results. Then, inservice education becomes more sophisticated as teachers get behind the results, to the reasons for the data and practices of effective teaching. For example, teachers begin with an interest in more consistent and higher parent ratings and then move to topics of communication with parents and specific parent concerns (e.g., home support of learning). They consider teacher tests and then begin to do more reading on professional topics assessed by the tests, such as school law or the status of schools in the society. These topics can be addressed at a more profound level than that of the first coverage in college teacher training courses.

Good inservice education requires strategizing and planning by personnel other than the teachers themselves. Staff developers should analyze recent dossier reviews and distribute needs analysis surveys to teachers to find topics of interest. Next, staff developers can assemble readings, literature reviews, and sample materials to address these areas. For example, curriculum writing techniques are appropriate for persons interested in strengthening their peer review of materials (before or after actual reviews). Texts for this inservice are teachers' own dossiers, new materials pertinent to dossier themes supplied by inservice educators, and finally a teacher-controlled viewing of each other's dossiers. This inservice is a combination of time for reflection, input of new content, and teachers helping each other. Teachers should be encouraged to assist others from positions of knowledge and accomplishment ("Well, this is how I handled and documented that situation with parents . . .").

Another kind of inservice education is to disseminate the practices of teachers who get the most spectacular data reports and reviews. Teachers can be invited to present the programs behind their results. Assistance with theoretical backing, and collateral literature, helps to conceptualize the practice and to make transfer to other situations more likely. Although in most years the inservice is internal to an individual school (or district), a variation is to have exchanges with other school districts every several years. For example, an idea fair based on teacher evaluation results and the programs behind them forms a good basis for such an exchange.

AGGREGATING AND PUBLICIZING TEACHER DATA

School districts increasingly need credible evidence that they are doing a good job. Research experience suggests that most school districts already *are* doing a job that needs to be seen to be believed. The responsibility for district aggregation should be delegated to a strong individual leader and advocate; generalized interest is not sufficient to get the work done. Oversight for this activity should be done by the Teacher Evaluation Board. Such oversight should include identification of highlights, priority setting, protecting individuals, and maintaining credibility of findings.

Data for Aggregation

Individual teacher evaluation results are aggregated for the information of audiences interested in the school district. Three kinds of organizations are made: averages of normative data, exemplars of specific data sources, and outstanding performances of individual teachers in their combinations of data sources.

Averages

District averages on student and parent surveys present key information about important audiences. For example, the average response on the parent survey item "overall satisfaction," along with distributions (ranges, standard deviations), will challenge many critics of public education. For example, the Peterson (1988) field study with parent surveys found an average of 4.49 (SD = .39) on a 5-point scale of this global item. This represented over 12,000 parent surveys and a very positive point of view about teacher performance quality.

Parent comments can be aggregated independently of individual teachers. Content analysis will raise issues of parent concern, priority, and attention. What topics do they raise, what are their issues of praise? Our studies found, for example, that parents of all students cared about self-esteem development and ability of students to concentrate in their studies. (Focus groups could have been helpful to understand these issues but were not performed.)

Teacher test score results give a picture of teacher knowledge in a school district. Group analysis of these results is helpful: How many teachers have taken tests? How representative are the teachers? What are comparisons with national norms? What do these scores mean in absolute terms of knowledge? Are there differences by experience, grade level taught, or subject area? What are the trends in recent hires?

Another kind of average is the categorical finding of peer review of materials. Here, the majority will be "well functioning"; many will be "well functioning, with . . . exemplary practices." Numbers of teachers in these categories and specific examples of outstanding performances are helpful. For example, if 20% of the teachers are found to be exemplary on curriculum writing, some further investigation and explanation about how these skills and products were acquired is well worth publicizing.

These aggregate averages are anonymous and should not be threatening to individual teachers. They create a sense of accomplishment, but also standards and expectation. The results will look high to external audiences, but low to individual teachers who have unrealistic expectations of perfection. Only more experience with aggregate data can help these teachers.

Highlight Individual Teachers

Individual teacher results can be highlighted in two ways. The first is to show specific examples of individual teachers on single data sources. One kind of aggregation is to collect typical, but strong, examples of teacher evaluation data. These generally are anonymous, but outstanding. They show how teachers accomplish quality in different dimensions: pupil achievement, parent relations, development of materials, and continuous updating of professional knowledge. These exemplars are helpful to show public audiences how teachers work on quality and they cue individual teachers about what good performance looks like.

In a very different way, outstanding overall performances function to communicate what all teachers are doing. This publicity shows the values, ideals, and directions of practice. The purpose is to communicate a value for excellence to audiences other than teachers themselves. To not do this is to say that teachers really do not care much for quality, or that educators do not know the differences in quality that exist. Either way, audiences are not reassured by this lack of recognition.

The second strategy is to select a number of teacher dossiers that paint a picture of what excellent teachers do in the district. These selections should be recommended by Teacher Review Panels and made by the Teacher Evaluation Board. These data show teachers who are strong for several reasons. These should be done with the agreement of the individual teachers. The culture being changed is currently negative in terms of recognizing outstanding data.

Disseminating the Data

Once data are aggregated, they should be distributed in regular channels of communication. Dissemination of teacher evaluation data should be done by someone designated by the Teacher Evaluation Board. One gradually gets better at this task with experience; for example, it soon becomes apparent that it is better to hold meetings with the PTA before sessions with chambers of commerce, an audience less familiar with schools. Teacher participation in presentations should be on a rotating basis. This is an additional teacher duty, but one with big payoffs. Good teacher collaboration keeps these duties from becoming distracting and onerous. Ultimately, most teachers will be energized and restored by participating in them. In a consumer-oriented society, there simply is no choice for the public schools but to do these activities (Gooler, 1973). Promotion of school success and public relations concerning teacher data are important and effective activities. Many resources exist for district planning for public relations, for example, Lober (1993), Warner (1994), Warner and Curry (1997), and West (1995). Four avenues for publicizing teacher evaluation data are described next.

Regular News Releases

Regular district news releases that aggregate data, give examples, and describe problem solving are helpful to bring educational issues to the public. In some instances, these reports balance other negative stories. In other situations, they serve to broaden the public debate about teachers and schools. One vital function is to build the pride of teachers in their results. Figure 26.1 shows the results of one such press release.

Community-District Interaction Nights
With Aggregated Teacher Evaluation

Interaction nights are programs regularly scheduled (e.g., twice a year) by the school district to present aggregated data of teacher evaluation. They should begin with handouts and graphics, and follow with presentation of priorities and evidence. Later in the session, it is a good idea to open the floor for community comments and directions. These meetings are a chance for presentation, reactions, self-expression, and learning. Debate can be developed about various priorities, for example, the place of self-concept development in an overall educational program. Another

Figure 26.1 Sample Newspaper Article on Teacher Evaluation Data
SOURCE: "297 Utah Teachers" (1986). Reprinted with permission.

The Salt Lake Tribune, Sunday, April 13, 1986

297 Utah Teachers Strut their Stuff, Score in Top 18% on National Test

Nearly 300 teachers from Granite, Nebo and Park City school districts have received high scores on the National Teachers' Examinations as an optional part of career-ladder evaluations.

Kenneth D. Peterson, associate professor of educational studies at the University of Utah, said the average score of the 297 Utahns was in the top 18 percent nationwide.

He said 27 scores were in the top 1 percent for their subject areas and 44 percent were in the top 10 percent.

Dr. Peterson is director of the Utah Teacher Evaluation Project, which has a grant from the U.S. Education Department to study teacher evaluation and career ladders in Utah.

The career ladder is a teacher pay reform adopted in Utah school districts for the 1984-85 school year in which teachers judged superior receive extra pay for extra work.

"The teachers opted to take the tests as part of the career-ladder programs which allow test scores as part of the evaluation process," said Dr. Peterson. He said there are no plans to require the tests of all teachers.

"While Utah citizens and legislators should be pleased with these scores, I'm not surprised by them," he said. "I've seen many academically well-prepared teachers in these districts. In addition, Utah teachers tend to do well on these tests."

The tests, produced by Educational Testing Service, are the most commonly used teacher examinations. They are designed to measure teach-

ers' knowledge of their subjects and their professional knowledge about classroom work.

Dr. Peterson said using teacher tests is controversial.

"High test scores alone do not guarantee good teaching. We need teachers to communicate with young people, create active classrooms and do the hundreds of other jobs expected of them," he said.

"Because educators are concerned that teachers know their stuff, I think we should look for ways to increase the use of teacher tests," he said.

However, Dr. Peterson warned against mandating tests for veteran teachers, as recently done in Arkansas and Texas.

"Not all of our best teachers score well on these tests. It's just one form of excellence. Also, teacher tests are estimates that may become less accurate with people who have been away from test practicing for several years," he said.

While the tests are "quite good," he said it is difficult to write tests that match what all teachers actually teach in their classrooms.

"All of us in Utah need to create school working conditions that keep academically talented teachers in the classroom," said Dr. Peterson.

issue is the thorny problem of comparing data of one community with that from another location. Socioeconomic analysis and perspectives should be a part of any of these community meetings. These meetings have great value, even if attendance is low, or if the audience changes the subject. The district is doing its job—educators are not responsible for expressions of community interest.

Aggregated data and examples of the best practices and achievement should be used for *interactive presentations* with community organizations. Examples of such organizations are PTA (as a good starter), League of Women Voters, Urban League, chambers of commerce, service clubs (Lions, Kiwanis, Rotary), state legislative study committees, and war veteran groups. These sessions should present information, but also systematically gather responses and ideas from these audiences. Topics, priorities, and problems are appropriate subjects for these sessions. Rotations of teacher participants mean that a good number of practitioners will gain experience with these audiences. Slick presentations are not as valuable as specific examples, interchanges of values, and openness to a variety of points of view.

Focus Group Reviews of Data

Focus groups (Krueger, 1988; Morgan, 1988) can be held by school districts to review teacher evaluation data. A sample of parents, in groups of 8 to 10, are invited in for 2-hour sessions in which they review aggregated teacher evaluation data and respond to a series of questions. The questions elicit reactions, values, questions, and creative ideas that the district can use to better understand and communicate with its audiences. The ideas also can be used to structure the educational program and teacher evaluation system.

As with other focus groups described in this book, several key organizational strategies hold. It is best if the parents do not know each other ahead of time. The meeting should be in a pleasant and quiet location, with food and comfortable furniture. The purposes, needs, and limits of the activity should be made clear to participants ahead of time.

Focus groups provide greater depth of reaction than the interaction nights. They create an opportunity to study the teacher payoffs and goals in the terms of a key audience. Focus groups are the most controlled sessions of dissemination and study. They give the district a chance to develop ideas and concepts about teacher performance. For example, development of student self-esteem is controversial, but it consistently arises in parent comments that are appreciative of teachers who provide it. What is the proper priority for this educational outcome? How should districts best describe it to their patrons?

Teacher-Parent Discussion Groups

Teacher-parent discussion groups are series meetings. They usually are scheduled in evenings, over a 3- to 5-week period. The groups should have several teachers, but more parents than teachers. Conversation begins with teacher data. Teachers can choose to use some district aggregate data and some of their own. The discussions move from teacher performance to more general ideas of education, to still more personal positions about being a teacher and being a parent.

Discussion groups are a longer term usage of teacher evaluation data than the one-shot community interactions. This is a chance for teachers to process their own ideas and presentations. Discussion groups are a significant dialogue between teacher and a key client. These exchanges lead to clarity and mutual valuing. Discussion groups grasp an important link of teaching, appreciation, and reflection in a way that very few teachers enjoy and that the present culture of teaching entirely lacks.

ASSIGN DISTRICT TEACHER LEADERSHIP TASKS BASED ON DATA REVIEW EXCELLENCE

An important new use for teacher evaluation data is to have teacher leadership positions filled based on dossier reviews by Teacher Review Panels. Teacher leadership positions include department chairs, grade-level leaders, curriculum development committee chairs, textbook selection chairs, site council memberships, and ad hoc problem-solving task force committees. Other leadership activities include service on teacher hiring panels, mentorships for beginning teachers, and student teacher placements. In current practice, appointment to such leadership positions is made by seniority, elections, or appointment. These are based on years of experience, personal prestige, or desire for recognition of individual teachers. A significant new direction and practice for school districts is to base these appointments on merit ranking of dossier reviews. This policy opens up new areas of teacher reward, professional status, and controlled competition for superior teaching.

INSTITUTIONAL REVIEW BOARDS

Peterson (1989a) described Institutional Review Boards as

> a source of information for program evaluation, as well as a bene-fit to candidates. Three to four years after [teacher training] pro-gram completion, graduates may elect to assemble dossiers of evaluation data from a variety of sources (e.g., pupil achieve-ment, student and parent surveys, teacher tests, peer reviews, and professional activity). These data present the performance track record of the recent graduates. Dossiers are reviewed by a panel of teachers, administrators, and lay persons given institu-tional guidelines and a framework of goals. Upon successful re-view a Certificate of Merit is awarded. Board Reviews provide data to answer questions about teacher preparation program quality and acknowledge meritorious performance in the field. (p. 14)

Such boards give beginning teachers the recognition of quality early track records. They have the advantage of coming from outside of the district and conferring the prestige of the granting institution. Such prestige ranges from slight to important, but many more methods of rewarding teachers need to be tried and developed. Institutional Review Board show promise for this purpose. They may do a lower cost job of what is sought with national certification programs.

NATIONAL BOARD FOR PROFESSIONAL TEACHING STANDARDS LICENSING

An important extension of teacher evaluation data is organization and ex-pansion of materials to be submitted to the National Board for Professional Teaching Standards (NBPTS). The NBPTS was one result of an influential recommendation by the Carnegie Forum on Education and the Economy (1986). The purpose of the board is to provide leadership and standards for the teaching profession and to identify and certify accomplished practitio-ners. The board specifies five key areas of teacher performance: Teachers are (1) committed to students and their learning, (2) knowledgable about the subjects they teach and how to teach those subjects, (3) responsible for managing and monitoring student learning, (4) thinking systematically about their practice and learn from experience, and (5) members of learning communities (NBPTS, 1996).

The application process for teachers is based on a school-site portfolio, which includes written descriptions of the teacher's classroom teaching, videotapes of the teaching, and student work samples. In addition to the portfolio, a candidate teacher completes a 1-day assessment center review in which he performs analyses of videotaped instruction and student work samples. Local district teacher evaluation, as described in this book, provides pertinent data and experience for these national-level evaluation reviews. Successful NBPTS licensing is a positive use for the school district teacher evaluation system.

THE NEED TO DO MORE TEACHER EVALUATION

Peterson and Chenoweth (1992) described the needs for increased teacher involvement in evaluation that

> benefits teachers, the educational system, audiences for teacher performance, and students. The positive effects of teacher evaluation are *technical* as assessment is made more accurate and comprehensive; *sociological* as relationships, roles, and rewards are altered; *psychological* as career satisfaction is enhanced; and *political* as public decision making is improved. (p. 184)

There is no more important work in the society than the educational care of the young. Teachers have dedicated their working lives to this service; it is necessary that they bask in the acknowledgment of their role, value, and impact in the community. Teacher-parent interaction groups make this real in a way that other teacher duties, activities, and responsibilities do not. The value of teaching must be *felt* by teachers to be fulfilled.

In addition, the political uses of teacher evaluation data by public schools must not be ignored. Current political forces are to limit resources for public education and to support ideas for private education. The link between a breakaway economic elite and diverted resources from public education should be clear to all. Although it is naive to think that these developments will be fully informed by data, public school advocates should operate from the strong position of the already impressive results of public school teachers.

These ideas for new dissemination practices take time to develop, implement, and show benefits. The payoffs are long term rather than immediate. The ideas themselves are not perfect in theory or practice. However, the goal in evaluation is not perfection, but incremental improvement over the most recent efforts of close competitors. To fail even to make an effort to improve is to fail to evaluate well. Educators have three choices: Do the activities in this book, do better ones, or do nothing whatsoever to improve teacher evaluation amid clear signals and substantial needs for new directions and practices.

INTERNET RESOURCES

Public Relations

http://www.heavypen.com/promote/index5.htm

http://www.people.virginia.edu/~dbb5n/EAF/communication.html

National School Public Relations Association

http://www.nspra.org/

Pennsylvania School Public Relations Association

http://www.pcpe.org/

Texas School Public Relations Association

http://www.tspra.org/

Missouri School Public Relations Association

http://info.csd.org/mosprahome.html

References

Acheson, K., & Gall, M. (1980). *Techniques in the clinical supervision of teachers.* New York: Longman.

Aleamoni, L. M. (1981). Student ratings of instruction. In J. Millman (Ed.), *Handbook of teacher evaluation* (pp. 110-145). Beverly Hills, CA: Sage.

Aleamoni, L. M. (1987). Student rating myths versus research facts. *Journal of Personnel Evaluation in Education, 1,* 111-119.

Alfonso, R. J. (1977). Will peer supervision work? *Educational Leadership, 34,* 594-601.

Allen, D., & Ryan K. (1969). *Microteaching.* Reading, MA: Addison-Wesley.

Amatora, M. (1954). Teacher rating by younger pupils. *Journal of Teacher Education, 5*(2), 149-152.

American Education Research Association. (1953). Second report of the Committee on the Criteria of Teacher Effectiveness. *Journal of Educational Research, 46,* 641-658.

American Federation of Teachers. (1996). *Making standards work.* Washington, DC: Author.

American Law Reports (4 A.L.R. 3d 1090 at 1102). (1992). In L. F. Rossow & J. Parkinson (Eds.), *The law of teacher evaluation* (p. 15). Topeka, KS: National Organization on Legal Problems of Education.

Anderson, H. M. (1954). A study of certain criteria of teaching effectiveness. *Journal of Experimental Education, 23,* 41-71.

Annunziata, J. (1998). Understanding and ensuring due process. *CREATE Newsletter, 1*(1), 3.

Annunziata, J. (1999). Richard Fossey: If a practitioner cleans the windows, will you look in? *Journal of Personnel Evaluation in Education, 13*(1), 83-92.

Anthony, B. M. (1968). A new approach to merit rating of teachers. *Administrators Notebook, 17*(1), 1-4.

Applebome, P. (1995, December 13). Have schools failed? *New York Times,* p. B16.

Barr, A. S., & Burton, W. H. (1926). *The supervision of instruction.* New York: Appleton.

Batista, E. (1976). The place of colleague evaluation in the appraisal of college teaching. *Research in Higher Education, 4,* 257-271.

Bergman, J. (1980). Peer evaluation of university faculty. *College Student Journal, 14* (3, Pt. 2), 1-21.

Berk, R. A. (1988). Fifty reasons why student achievement gain does not mean teacher effectiveness. *Journal of Personnel Evaluation in Education, 1,* 345-363.

Berliner, D. C., & Biddle, B. J. (1995). *The manufactured crisis: Myths, fraud, and the attack on America's schools.* New York: Addison-Wesley.

Berman, P., & McLaughlin, M. W. (1978). *Federal programs supporting educational change: Vol. 8. Implementing and sustaining innovations* (R-1589/8-HEW). Santa Monica, CA: RAND.

Bingham, R.D., Heywood, J.S., & White, S.B. (1991). Evaluating schools and teachers based on student performance. *Evaluation Review, 15,* 191-218.

Bird, T. (1990). The schoolteachers' portfolio: An essay on possibilities. In J. Millman & L. Darling-Hammond (Eds.), *The new handbook of teacher evaluation: Assessing elementary and secondary school teachers* (pp. 241-256). Newbury Park, CA: Sage.

Black, J.A., & English, F.W. (1986). *What they don't tell you in schools of education about school administration.* Lancaster, PA: Technomic Publishing.

Blackburn, R., & Clark, M. (1975). An assessment of faculty performance: Some correlates between administrators, colleagues, students, and self ratings. *Sociology of Education, 48,* 242-256.

Bloom, B. S. (Ed.), Engelhart, M., Furst, E., Hill, W., & Krathwohl, D. (1956). *Taxonomy of educational objectives. Handbook I: Cognitive domain.* New York: McKay.

Blumberg, A., & Greenfield, W. (1980). *The effective principal: Perspectives on school leadership.* Boston: Allyn & Bacon.

Bodine, R. (1973). Teachers' self-assessment. In E. House (Ed.), *School evaluation: The politics and process* (pp. 169-173). Berkeley, CA. McCutchan.

Bolton, D. L. (1973). *Selection and evaluation of teachers.* Berkeley, CA: McCutchan.

Borich, G. D. (1977). *The appraisal of teaching concepts and process.* Reading, MA: Addison-Wesley.

Borich, G. D. (1990). *Observation skills for effective teaching.* Columbus, OH: Merrill.

Borich, G. D., & Madden, S. K. (1977). *Evaluating classroom instruction: A source book of instruments.* Reading, MA: Addison-Wesley.

Boyce, A. C. (1915). Methods of measuring teacher's efficiency. *Fourteenth yearbook of the National Society for the Study of Education, Part II.* Bloomington, IL: Public School Publishing.

Brandt, R. (1993). On outcome-based education: A conversation with Bill Spady. *Educational Leadership, 50*(4), 66-70.

Braskamp, L. A. (1980). What research says about the components of teaching. In W. R. Duckett (Ed.), *Observation and the evaluation of teaching* (pp. 62-86). Bloomington, IN: Phi Delta Kappa.

Brauchle, P., McLarty, J., & Parker, J. (1989). A portfolio approach to using student performance data to measure teacher effectiveness. *Journal of Personnel Evaluation in Education, 3,* 17-30.

Braunstein, D., Klein, B., & Pachio, M. (1973). Feedback expectancy and shifts in student rating: Reliability, validity, and usefulness. *Journal of Applied Psychology, 58,* 254-258.

Bridges, E. M. (1992). *The incompetent teacher* (2nd ed.). Phildelphia: Falmer.

Bridges, E.M., & Groves, B. R. (2000). The macro- and micropolitics of personnel evaluation: A framework. *Journal of Personnel Evaluation in Education, 13,* 321-337.

Brookover, W. (1940). Person-person interaction between teachers and pupils and teaching effectiveness. *Journal of Educational Research, 34,* 272-287.

Brophy, J. & Evertson, C. (1976). *Learning from teaching: A developmental perspective.* Boston: Allyn & Bacon.

Bryan, R. (1966). Teacher's image is stubbornly stable. *Clearing House, 40,* 459-461.

Bryant, M. T. (1990). A study of administrative expertise in participant performance on the NASSP Assessment Center. *Journal of Personnel Evaluation in Education, 3,* 353-364.

Carnegie Forum on Education and the Economy. (1986). *A nation prepared: Teachers for the 21st Century.* Washington, DC: Author.

Carroll, J. (1981). Faculty self evaluation. In J. Millman (Ed.), *Handbook of teacher evaluation* (pp. 180-200). Beverly Hills, CA: Sage.

Carson, C. C., Huelskamp, R. M., & Woodall, T. D. (1993). Perspectives on education in America. *Journal of Educational Research, 86*, 259-311.

Castaneda, A., & Gray, T. (1974). Bicognitive processes in multicultural education. *Educational Leadership, 32*(2), 203-207.

Cazden, C. B., & Leggett, E. L. (1981). Culturally responsive education: Recommendations for achieving Lau remedies II. In H. T. Trueba et al. (Eds.), *Culture and the bilingual classroom.* Rowley, MA: Newbury House.

Cederblom, D., & Lounsbury, J. (1980). An investigation of user-acceptance of peer evaluations. *Personnel Psychology, 33*, 567.

Centra, J. A. (1972). *Strategies for improving college teaching.* Washington, DC: American Association for Higher Education.

Centra, J. A. (1973). Self-ratings of college teachers: A comparison with student ratings. *Journal of Educational Measurement, 10*, 287-295.

Centra, J. A. (1975). Colleagues as raters of classroom instruction. *Journal of Higher Education, 46*, 327-337.

Centra, J. A. (1977). The how and why of evaluating teaching. *New Directions for Higher Education, 17*, 93-106.

Centra, J. A. (1980). *Determining faculty effectiveness.* San Francisco: Jossey-Bass.

Christensen, C. (1960). Relationships between pupil achievement, pupil affect need, teacher warmth and teacher permissiveness. *Journal of Educational Psychology, 51*, 169-173.

Cizek, G. J. (1993). Rethinking psychometrician's beliefs about learning. *Educational Researcher, 22*(4), 4-9.

Cohen, D. K. (1973). Politics and research. *Review of Educational Research, 40*, 213-238.

Cohen, P. A. (1981). Student ratings of instruction and student achievement: A meta analysis of multisection validity studies. *Review of Educational Research, 51*, 281-310.

Cohen, P. A., & McKeachie, W. J. (1980). The role of colleagues in the evaluation of college teaching. *Improving College and University Teaching, 28*, 147-154.

Coker, H., Medley, D. M., & Soar, R. S. (1980). How valid are expert opinions about effective teaching? *Phi Delta Kappan, 62*(2), 131-134, 149.

Combs, A. W. (1965). *The professional education of teachers.* Boston: Allyn & Bacon.

Cook, M. A. & Richards, H. C. (1972). Dimensions of principal and supervisor ratings of teacher behavior. *Journal of Experimental Education, 41*(2), 11-14.

Cooper, C. (1997). Presentation to Educator Assessment Development Committee of the Davis County School District, Farmington, Utah.

Corwin, R. G., & Edelfelt, R. A. (1976). *Perspectives on organizations: Viewpoints for teachers.* Washington, DC: American Association of Colleges for Teacher Education.

Crow, N., & Peterson, K. (1983). *The common sociology between teacher evaluation and teacher development.* Salt Lake City: University of Utah. (ERIC Document Reproduction Service No. ED 244960)

Cummins, J. (1986). Empowering minority students: A framework for intervention. *Harvard Educational Review, 56*(1), 18-36.

Cusick, P. A. (1973). *Inside high school: The students' world.* New York: Holt, Rinehart & Winston.

Danielson, C. (1996). *Enhancing professional practice: A framework for teaching.* Alexandria, VA: Association for Supervision and Curriculum Development.

Darling-Hammond, L., Wise, A. E., & Pease, S. R. (1983). Teacher evaluation in the organizational context: A review of the literature. *Review of Educational Research, 53*, 285-328.

DeCharms, R. (1968). *Personal causation.* New York: Academic Press.

Delandshere, G., & Petrosky, A. R. (1994). Capturing teachers' knowledge: Performance assessment. *Educational Researcher, 23*(5), 11-18.

Dishaw, M. (1977). *Description of allocated time to content areas for the A-B Period* (Beginning Teacher Evaluation Study). San Francisco: Far West Laboratory or Educational Research and Development.

Drake, T. L., & Roe, W. H. (1986). *The principalship.* New York: Macmillan.

Driscoll, A., Peterson, K., Browning, M., & Stevens, D. (1990). Teacher evaluation in early childhood education: What information can young children provide? *Child Study Journal, 20*, 67-79.

Driscoll, A., Peterson, K., Crow, N., & Larson, B. (1985). Student reports for primary teacher evaluation. *Educational Research Quarterly, 9*(3), 43-50.

Driscoll, A., Peterson, K., & Kauchak, D. (1985). Designing a mentor system for beginning teachers. *Journal of Staff Development, 6*, 108-117.

Elbow, P. (1986). *Embracing contraries: Explorations in learning and teaching.* New York: Oxford University Press.

Epstein, J. L. (1985). A question of merit: Principals' and parents' evaluations of teachers. *Educational Researcher, 14*(7), 3-8.

Erffmeyer, E. S., & Martray, C. R. (1990). A quantified approach to the evaluation of teacher professional growth and development and professional leadership through a goal-setting process. *Journal of Personnel Evaluation in Education, 3*, 275-300.

Erikson, E. H. (1964). A memorandum on identity and Negro youth. *Journal of Social Issues, 20*(4), 29-42.

Erlandson, D. A. (1973). Evaluation and an administrators' autonomy. In E. House (Ed.), *School evaluation: The politics and process* (pp. 20-26). Berkeley, CA: McCutchan.

Etzioni, A. (1969). *The semi-professions and their organization.* New York: Free Press.

Evertson, C. M., & Burry, J. A. (1989). Capturing classroom context: The observation system as lens for assessment. *Journal of Personnel Evaluation in Education, 2*, 297-320.

Evertson, C. M., & Holley, F. M. (1981). Classroom observation. In J. Millman (Ed.), *Handbook of teacher evaluation* (pp. 90-109). Beverly Hills, CA: Sage.

Festinger, L. A. (1954). A theory of social comparison process. *Human Relations, 7*, 117-140.

Fischer, L. & Schimmel, D. (1973). *The civil rights of teachers.* New York: Harper & Row.

Fisher, C., Filby, N., Marliave, R., Cahen, L., Dishaw, M., Moore, J., & Berliner, D. (1978). *Teaching behaviors, academic learning time, and student achievement* (Final Report of Phase III-B, Beginning Teacher Evaluation Study). San Francisco: Far West Laboratory for Educational Research and Development.

Flanders, N. A. (1970). *Analyzing teaching behavior.* Reading, MA: Addison-Wesley.

Fortune, J. C. (1985). *Understanding testing in occupational licensing.* San Francisco: Jossey-Bass.

Fossey, R. (1998). Legal notes: Secret settlement agreements between school districts and problem employees. *Journal of Personnel Evaluation in Education, 12*, 61-68.

French, R. L. (1984). Dispelling the myths about Tennessee's career ladder program. *Educational Leadership, 42*(4), 9-13.

French-Lazovik, G. (1981). Peer review: Documenting evidence in the evaluation of teaching. In J. Millman (Ed.), *Handbook of teacher evaluation* (pp. 73- 89). Beverly Hills, CA: Sage.

Friend, J. H. & Guralnik, D. B. (Eds.). (1960). *Webster's new world dictionary.* New York: World Publishing.

Gallup, G. (1985). The 16th annual Gallup poll of the public's attitude toward the public schools. *Phi Delta Kappan, 66*, 23-28.

Gathercole, C. E. (1968). *Assessment in clinical psychology.* Baltimore: Penguin.

Gee, E. G., & Sperry, D. J. (1978). *Education law and the public schools.* Boston: Allyn & Bacon.

Gestwicki, C. (1987). *Home, school, and community relations. A guide to working with parents.* Albany, NY: Delmar.

Ginsberg, A., McLaughlin, M., Plisco, V., & Takai, R. (1992). Reinvigorating program evaluation at the U.S. Department of Education. *Educational Researcher, 21*(3), 24-27.

Ginsberg, R., & Berry, B. (1990). The folklore of principal evaluation. *Journal of Personnel Evaluation in Education, 3*, 205-230.

Glasman, N. S., & Biniaminov, I. (1981). Input-ouput analysis of schools. *Review of Educational Research, 51*, 509-539.

Glass, G. V. (1974). A review of three methods of determining teacher effectiveness. In H. J. Walberg (Ed.), *Evaluating educational performance* (pp. 11-32). Berkeley, CA: McCutchan.

Glass, G. V. (1990). Using student test scores to evaluate teachers. In J. Millman & L. Darling-Hammond (Eds.), *The new handbook of teacher evaluation: Assessing elementary and secondary school teachers* (pp. 229-240). Newbury Park, CA: Sage.

Goebel, B. L., & Cashen, V. M. (1979). Age, sex and attractiveness as a factor in student rating of teachers. *Journal of Educational Psychology, 71*, 646-653.

Good, T. L. (1980). Classroom observations: Potential and problems. In W. R. Duckett (Ed.), *Observation and the evaluation of teaching* (pp. 2-44). Bloomington, IN: Phi Delta Kappa.

Good, T., & Brophy, J. (1980). *Educational psychology: A realistic approach* (2nd ed.). New York: Holt, Rinehart & Winston.

Good, T., & Brophy, J. (1987). *Looking in classrooms* (4th ed.). New York: Harper & Row.

Good, T. L. & Mulryan, C. (1990). Teacher ratings: A call for teacher control and self-evaluation. In J. Millman & L. Darling-Hammond (Eds.), *The new handbook of teacher evaluation: Assessing elementary and secondary school teachers.* (pp. 191-215). Newbury Park, CA: Sage.

Good, T. L., Sikes, J. N., & Brophy, J. E. (1973). Effects of teacher sex and student sex on classroom interaction. *Journal of Educational Psychology, 65*, 74-87.

Goodlad, J. (1970). *Behind the classroom door.* Worthington, OH: Jones.

Goodman, N. (1992). *Introduction to sociology.* New York: HarperCollins.

Gooler, D. D. (1973). Evaluation and the public. In E. House (Ed.), *School evaluation: The politics and process* (pp. 306-318). Berkeley, CA: McCutchan.

Grayson, D. A., & Martin, M. D. (1990). *GESA: Gender/ethnic expectations and student achievement.* Earlham, IA: GrayMill.

Greenfield, W. (Ed.) (1987). *Instructional leadership: Concepts, issues, and controversies.* Boston: Allyn & Bacon.

Gunne, C., & Peterson, K. D. (1990). Use of an academic aptitude test for teacher preservice admissions. *Teacher Education Quarterly, 17*(2), 85-92.

Guthrie, J. (1970). Survey of school effectiveness studies. In A. Mood (Ed.), *Do teachers make a difference?* (pp. 25- 54). Washington, DC: U.S. Government Printing Office.

Haak, R. A., Kleiber, D. A., & Peck, R. F. (1972). *Student evaluations of teacher instrument II, manual.* Austin: University of Texas, R&D Center for Teacher Education.

Haertel, E. H. (1987). Toward a national board of teaching standards: The Stanford Teacher Assessment Project. *Educational Measurement: Issues and Practices, 6*(1), 23-24.

Haertel, E. H. (1990). Performance tests, simulations, and other methods. In J. Millman & L. Darling-Hammond (Eds.), *The new handbook of teacher evaluation: Assessing elementary and secondary school teachers* (pp. 278-294).Newbury Park, CA: Sage.

Harris, B. M. (1986). *Developmental teacher evaluation.* Boston: Allyn & Bacon.

Harris, W. (1981). Teacher command of subject matter. In J. Millman (Ed.), *Handbook of teacher evaluation* (pp. 58-72). Beverly Hills, CA: Sage.

Hass, G. (1978). *Curriculum planning: A new approach.* (2nd ed.). Boston: Allyn & Bacon.

Hastie, R., Penrod, S., & Pennington, N. (1983). *Inside the jury.* Cambridge, MA: Harvard University Press.

Heath, R., & Nelson, M. (1974). The research basis for performance-based teacher education. *Review of Educational Research, 44*, 463-484.

Help! Teacher can't teach! (1980, June 16). *Time,* pp. 54-73.

Herbert, E. A. (1992). Portfolios invite reflection—from students and staff. *Educational Leadership, 49*(8), 58-61.

Herman, J. L., & Winters, L. (1994). Portfolio research: A slim collection. *Educational Leadership, 52*(2), 48-55.

Hill, C. W. (1921). The efficiency ratings of teachers. *Elementary School Journal, 21*, 438-443.

Hoenack, S. A., & Monk, D. H. (1990). Economic aspects of teacher evaluation. In J. Millman & L. Darling-Hammond (Eds.), *The new handbook of teacher evaluation: Assessing elementary and secondary school teachers* (pp. 390-402). Newbury Park, CA: Sage.

Holly, P., & Southworth, G. (1989). *The developing school.* New York: Falmer.

Homans, G.C. (1950). *The human group.* New York: Harcourt & Brace.

Homans, G.C. (1961). *Social behavior: Its elementary forms.* New York: Harcourt, Brace & World.

Hoogeveen, K., & Gutkin, T. B. (1986). Collegial ratings among school personnel: An empirical examination of the merit pay concept. *American Educational Research Journal, 23,* 375-381.

House, E. R. (Ed.). (1973). *School evaluation: The politics and process.* Berkeley, CA: McCutchan.

House, E. R. (1980). *Evaluating with validity.* Beverly Hills, CA: Sage.

Houston, W. R., & Howsam, R. B. (Eds.). (1972). *Competency-based teacher education.* Chicago: Science Research Associates.

Huling-Austin, L. (1987). Teacher induction. In D. Brooks (Ed.), *Teacher induction: A new beginning.* Reston, VA: Association of Teacher Educators.

Hunter, M. (1976). *Rx improved instruction.* El Segundo, CA: TIP.

Hyman, R. T. (1884). Testing for teacher competence: The logic, the law, and the implications. *Journal of Teacher Education, 35*(2), 14-18.

Jackson, G., & Cosca, C. (1974). The inequality of educational opportunity in the Southwest: An observational study of ethnically mixed classrooms. *American Educational Research Journal, 11,* 219-229.

Jackson, P. W. (1968). *Life in classrooms.* New York: Holt, Rinehart & Winston.

Johnson, S. (1984). *Teacher unions in the schools.* Philadelphia: Temple University Press.

Johnson, S. M. (1990). *Teachers at work: Achieving success in our schools.* New York: Basic Books.

Johnston, J. M. (1985). Teacher induction: Problems, roles, and guidelines. In P. Burke and R. Heideman (Eds.), *Career-long teacher education* (pp. 194-222). Springfield, IL: Thomas.

Johnston, J. M., & Ryan, K. (1983). Research on the beginning teacher: Implications for teacher education. In K. Howey & W. Gardner (Eds.), *The education of teachers: A look ahead* (pp. 136-162). New York: Longman.

Joint Committee on Standards for Educational Evaluation. (1988). *The personnel evaluation standards.* Newbury Park, CA: Corwin.

Kagan, S., & Madsen, M. C. (1971). Cooperation and competition of Mexican, Mexican American, and Anglo American children of two ages under four instructional sets. *Developmental Psychology, 5,* 32-39.

Kalven, H., & Zeisel, H. (1966). *The American jury.* Boston: Little, Brown.

Kauchak, D., & Peterson, K. (1982). Student evaluations: An additional source of information. *Colleague, 4*(3), 1-5.

Kauchak, D., Peterson, K., & Driscoll, A. (1985). An interview study of teachers' attitudes toward teacher evaluation practices. *Journal of Research and Development in Education, 19*(1), 32-37.

Kearney, C. P., & Huyser, R. J. (1973). The politics of reporting results. In E. House (Ed), *School evaluation: The politics and process* (pp. 47-59). Berkeley, CA: McCutchan.

Kerlinger, F. (1971). Student evaluations of university professors. *School and Society, 99,* 353-356.

Kimbrough, R. B. (1964). *Political power and educational decision-making.* Chicago: Rand McNally.

Kliebard, H. M. (1993). What is a knowledge base, and who would use it if we had one? *Review of Educational Research, 63,* 295-303.

Knezevich, S. J. (1977). Designing performance appraisal systems. In G. Borich (Ed.), *The appraisal of teaching: Concepts and process* (pp. 206-215). Reading, MA: Addison-Wesley.

Krajewski, R. J. (1978, September). Secondary principals want to be instructional leaders. *Phi Delta Kappan,* p. 65.

Krathwohl, D. R., Bloom, B. S., & Masia, B. B. (1964). *Taxonomy of educational objectives: Handbook II. Affective domain.* New York: David McKay.

Krueger, R. A. (2000). *Focus groups: A practical guide for applied research (3rd ed.).* Thousand Oaks, CA: Sage.

Landis, L. M., & Pirro, E. B. (1977). Required, elective student differences in course evaluations. *Teaching Political Science, 4,* 405-422.

Larsen, O. N., & Catton, W. R. (1962). *Conceptual sociology.* New York: Harper & Row.

Lawrence, C. E., Vachon, M. K., Leake, D. O., & Leake, B. H. (1993). *The marginal teacher.* Newbury Park, CA: Corwin.

Levin, H. M., Glass, G. V., & Meister, G. R. (1987). Cost-effectiveness of computer-assisted instruction. *Evaluation Review, 6*(1), 50-72.

Levitan, S. A. (1992). *Evaluation of federal social programs: An uncertain impact.* Washington, DC: George Washington University, Center for Social Policy Studies.

Lewis, A. C. (1982). *Evaluating educational personnel.* Arlington, VA: American Association of School Administrators.

Lewis, L. S. (1975). *Scaling the ivory tower: Merit and its limits in academic careers.* Baltimore: Johns Hopkins University Press.

Lieberman, M. (1972). Should teachers evaluate other teachers? *School Management, 16*(6), 4.

Lightfoot, S. L. (1983). *The good high school.* New York: Basic Books.

Lind, M. (1997). *Up from conservatism.* New York: Free Press Paperbacks.

Linn, R. L., & Herman, J. L. (1997). *A policymaker's guide to standards-led assessment.* Denver, CO: Education Commission of the States. (ERIC Document ED 408 680)

Lloyd-Bostock, S. (1989). *Law in practice: Applications of psychology to legal decision making and legal skills.* Chicago: Lyceum.

Lober, I. M. (1993). *Promoting your school: A public relations handbook.* Lancaster, PA: Technomic Press.

Lortie, D. C. (1967). Rational decision making: Is it possible today? *EPIE Forum, 1*(3), 6-9.

Lortie, D. C. (1975). *Schoolteacher: A sociological study.* Chicago: University of Chicago Press.

Loup, K., Garland, J., Ellett, C., & Rugutt, J. (1996). Ten years later: Findings from a replication of a study of teacher evaluation practices in our 100 largest school districts. *Journal of Personnel Evaluation in Education, 10,* 203-226.

Lyons, G. (1979). Why teachers can't teach. *Phi Delta Kappan, 62,* 108-112.

MacDonald, B. (1973). Briefing decision makers. In E. House (Ed.), *School evaluation: The politics and process* (pp. 174-188). Berkeley, CA: McCutchan.

Madaus, G. F. (1988). The influence of testing on the curriculum. In L. N. Tanner (Ed.), *Critical issues in curriculum. Eighty-seventh yearbook of the National Society for the Study of Education* (pp. 83-121). Chicago: University of Chicago Press.

Madaus, G., & Mehrens, W. A. (1990). Conventional tests for licensure. In J. Millman & L. Darling-Hammond (Eds.), *The new handbook of teacher evaluation: Assessing elementary and secondary school teachers* (pp. 257-277). Newbury Park, CA: Sage.

Manatt, R. P., & Daniels, B. (1990). Relationships between principals' ratings of teacher performance and student achievement. *Journal of Personnel Evaluation in Education, 4,* 189-202.

Manatt, R. P., & Manatt, S. B. (1984). *Clinical manual for teacher performance evaluation.* Ames: Iowa State University Research Foundation.

Mark, M. M., & Shotland, R. L. (1985). Stake-holder based evaluation and value judgments. *Evaluation Review, 9,* 605-626.

Marsh, H. W. (1980). Research on student evaluations of teaching effectiveness: A reply to Vecchio. *Instructional Evaluation, 4*(2), 5-12.

McCall, W., & Krause, G. (1959). Measurement of teacher merit for salary purposes. *Journal of Educational Research, 53,* 73-75.

McCarthey, S. J., & Peterson, K. D. (1987). Peer review of materials in public school teacher evaluation. *Journal of Personnel Evaluations in Education, 1,* 259-267.

McFaul, S. A., & Cooper, J. M. (1984). Peer clinical supervisor: Theory vs. reality. *Educational Leadership, 41*(7), 4-9.

McGreal, T. L. (1983). *Successful teacher evaluation*. Alexandria, VA: Association for Supervision and Curriculum Development.

McKeachie, W. (1979). Student ratings of faculty. *Academe, 65,* 384-397.

McLaughlin, M. W. (1990). Embracing contraries: Implementing and sustaining teacher evaluation. In J. Millman & L. Darling-Hammond (Eds.), *The new handbook of teacher evaluation: Assessing elementary and secondary school teachers* (pp. 403-415). Newbury Park, CA: Sage.

McNeil, J., & Popham, W. (1973). The assessment of teacher competence. In R. M. Travers (Ed.), *Secondary handbook of research on teaching* (pp. 131-147). Chicago: Rand McNally.

Medley, D. M., & Coker, H. (1987). The accuracy of principals' judgments of teacher performance. *Journal of Educational Research, 80,* 242-247.

Medley, D. M., Coker, H., & Soar, R. S. (1984). *Measurement-based evaluation of teacher performance: An empirical approach*. New York: Longman.

Meehl, P. E. (1954). *Clinical versus statistical prediction*. Minneapolis-St. Paul: University of Minnesota Press.

Meehl, P. E., & Dahlstrom, W. G. (1960). Objective configural rules for discriminating psychotic from neurotic M.M.P.I. Profiles. *Journal of Consulting Psychology, 24,* 375-387.

Mehrens, W. A. (1990). Combining evaluation data from several sources. In J. Millman & L. Darling-Hammond (Eds.), *The new handbook of teacher evaluation: Assessment of elementary and secondary school teachers* (pp. 322-336). Newbury Park, CA: Sage.

Millman, J. (1981). Student achievement as a measure of teacher competence. In J. Millman (Ed.), *Handbook of teacher evaluation* (pp. 146-166). Beverly Hills, CA: Sage.

Mills, G. E. (2000). *Action research: A guide for the teacher researcher*. Upper Saddle, NJ: Merrill.

Morgan, D. L. (1988). *Focus groups as qualitative research*. Newbury Park, CA: Sage.

Morine-Dershimer, G. (1976). *Teacher judgments and pupil observations: Beauty is in the eye of the beholder*. Paper presented at the American Educational Research Association annual meeting. San Francisco.

Murphy, J. (1987). Teacher evaluation: A comprehensive framework for supervisors. *Journal of Personnel Evaluation in Education, 1,* 157-180.

Murphy, M., Peterson, K., & Kauchak, D. (1985). *Analysis of Utah career ladder plans*. Salt Lake City: University of Utah. (ERIC Document Reproduction Service No. ED 256 031).

Murray, S. L. (1986). *Considering policy options for testing teachers*. Portland, OR: Northwest Regional Educational Laboratory.

Nagel, N. (1995). *Real world problem solving*. Thousand Oaks, CA: Corwin Press.

Narode, R., Rennie-Hill, L., & Peterson, K. D. (1994). Urban community study by preservice teachers. *Urban Education, 29,* 5-21.

National Association of State Boards of Education. (1984). *A policymakers guide to improving conditions for principals' effectiveness*. Alexandria, VA: Author.

National Board for Professional Teaching Standards. (1996). *What teachers should know and be able to do*. Detroit, MI: Author.

National Commission on Excellence in Education. (1983). *A nation at risk: The imperatives for educational reform*. Washington, DC: Department of Education.

National Council of Teachers of Mathematics. (1995). *Standards for school mathematics*. Reston, VA: Author.

Natriello, G., Deal, T., Dornbusch, S., & Hong, M. (1977). *A summary of the recent literature on the evaluation of principals, teachers and students* (Occasional Paper No. 18). Stanford, CA: Stanford University, Stanford Center for Research and Development in Teaching.

Neill, S. B., & Custis, J. (1978). *Staff dismissal: Problems and solutions*. Arlington, VA: American Association of School Administrators.

Nisbett, R. E., & Ross, L. (1980). *Human inference: Strategies and shortcomings of social judgment*. Englewood Cliffs, NJ: Prentice Hall.

North Central Regional Educational Laboratory (2000). *Pathways to school improvement*. (Website: http://www.ncrel.org/sdrs/pathwaysg.htm/). Oak Brook, IL: Author.

O'Barr, W. M. (1982). *Linguistic evidence: Language, power and strategy in the courtroom.* New York: Academic Press.

Ober, R. L., Bentley, E. L., & Miller, E. (1971). *Systematic observation of teaching.* Englewood Cliffs, NJ: Prentice Hall.

Osmond, P. (1978). *Teacher assessment of supervisory evaluations.* Detroit, MI: Wayne State University. (ERIC Document Reproduction Service No. ED 200 514).

Ostrander, L. P. (1995). *Multiple judges of teacher effectiveness: Comparing teacher self-assessments with the perceptions of principals, students, and parents.* Doctoral dissertation, University of Virginia.

Owens, R. G. (1991). *Organizational behavior in education.* Englewood Cliffs, NJ: Prentice Hall.

Parsons, T. (1937). *The structure of social action.* New York: McGraw-Hill.

Parsons, T. (1964). Levels of organization and the mediation of social interaction. *Sociological Inquiry, 34,* 207-220.

Paulson, F., Paulson, P., & Meyer, C. (1991). What makes a portfolio a portfolio? *Educational leadership, 48*(5), 60-63.

Perrone, V. (Ed.). (1991). *Expanding student assessment.* Alexandria, VA: Association for Supervision and Curriculum Development.

Perry, R., Abrami, P., & Leventhal, L. (1979). Educational seduction: The effect of instructor expressiveness and lecture content on student ratings and achievement. *Journal of Educational Psychology, 71,* 107-116.

Perry-Sheldon, B., & Allain, V. A. (1987). *Using educational research in the classroom.* Fastback #260. Bloomington, IN: Phi Delta Kappan.

Peterson, K. (1979). Teacher performance and development: A structural model. *The Teacher Educator, 15,* 22-30.

Peterson, K. (1984). Methodological problems in teacher evaluation. *Journal of Research and Development in Education, 17*(4), 62-70.

Peterson, K. (1985, February). *Politics of the use of teachers academic tests.* Paper presented at the annual meeting of the Association of Teacher Educators, Las Vegas.

Peterson, K., Gunne, M., Miller, P. & Rivera, O. (1984). Multiple audience rating form strategies for student evaluation of college teaching. *Research in Higher Education, 20,* 309-321.

Peterson, K., & Kauchak, D. (1982). *Teacher evaluation: Perspectives, practices and promises.* Salt Lake City: University of Utah. (ERIC Document Reproduction Service No. ED 233 996)

Peterson, K., & Kauchak, D. (1983). *Progress in development of lines of evidence for teacher evaluation.* Salt Lake City: University of Utah. (ERIC Document Reproduction Service No. ED 228 228)

Peterson, K., Kauchak, D., Mitchell, A., McCarthey, S., & Stevens, D. (1986). *Utah Teacher Evaluation Project: The Park City career ladder design.* Salt Lake City: University of Utah. (ERIC Document Reproduction Service No. ED 265 143)

Peterson, K., & Mitchell, A. (1985). Teacher controlled evaluation in a career ladder program. *Educational Leadership, 43*(3), 44-49.

Peterson, K., Wilson, J., Ulmer, D., Franklin, N., Mitchell, T., & Winget, L. (1984). *Teacher career ladders in Utah: Perspectives on early development.* Salt Lake City: University of Utah. (ERIC Document Reproduction Service No. ED 246 051)

Peterson, K., & Yaakobi, D. (1980). Israeli science student and teacher perceptions of classroom role performance: Concepts, reports, and adequacy. *Science Education, 64,* 661-669.

Peterson, K., Yaakobi, D., & Hines, S. (1981). Self-concept and behavior perception changes of student teachers. *Educational Research Quarterly, 5*(4), 41-50.

Peterson, K. D. (1987a). Teacher evaluation with multiple and variable lines of evidence. *American Educational Research Journal, 24,* 311-317.

Peterson, K. D. (1987b). Use of standardized tests in teacher evaluation for career ladder systems. *Educational Measurement, 6*(1), 19-22.

Peterson, K. D. (1987c). *Expert system knowledge base for a computer simulation of judgments on dossiers of school teacher performance.* Portland, OR: Portland State University. (ERIC Document Reproduction Service No. ED 291 339)

Peterson, K. D. (1988). Reliability of panel judgments for promotion is a school teacher career ladder system. *Journal of Research and Development in Education, 21*(4), 95-99.

Peterson, K. D. (1989a). Teacher education program evaluation through an institutional board review of graduates. *Journal of Research and Development in Education, 22*(4), 14-20.

Peterson, K. D. (1989b). Parent surveys for school teacher evaluation. *Journal of Personnel Evaluation in Education, 2,* 239-249.

Peterson, K. D. (1989c). Costs of school teacher evaluation in a career ladder system. *Journal of Research and Development in Education, 22* (2), 30-36.

Peterson, K. D. (1990a). Assistance and assessment for beginning teachers. In J. Millman & L. Darling-Hammond (Eds.), *The new handbook of teacher evaluation: Assessing elementary and secondary school teachers* (pp. 104-115). Newbury Park, CA: Sage.

Peterson, K. D. (1990b). DOSSIER: A computer expert system simulation of professional judgments on schoolteacher promotion. *Journal of Educational Research, 83,* 134-139.

Peterson, K. D., Bennet, B., & Sherman, D. F. (1991). Themes of uncommonly successful teachers of at-risk students. *Urban Education, 26,* 176-194.

Peterson, K. D., & Chenoweth, T. (1992). School teachers' control and involvement in their own evaluation. *Journal of Personnel Evaluation in Education, 6,* 177-189.

Peterson, K. D., Deyhle, D. & Watkins, W. (1988). Evaluation that accommodates minority teacher contributions. *Urban Education, 23,* 133-149.

Peterson, K. D. & Edwards-Allen, J. (1992). Uses of microcomputers in school teacher evaluation. *Journal of Research on Computing in Education, 24,* 392-398.

Peterson, K. D. & Stevens, D. (1988). Student reports for schoolteacher evaluation. *Journal of Personnel Evaluation in Education, 1,* 259-267.

Peterson, K. D., Stevens, D., & Driscoll, A. (1990). Primary grade student reports for teacher evaluation. *Journal of Personnel Evaluation in Education, 4,* 165-173.

Peterson, K. D., Stevens, D., & Ponzio, R. C. (1998). Variable data sources in teacher evaluation. *Journal of Research and Development in Education, 31*(3), 123-132.

Ponzio, R. C., Peterson, K. D., Miller, J. P., & Kinney, M. B. (1994). A program portfolio/panel review evaluation of 4-H sponsored community-based, social action projects for at-risk youth. *Journal of Research and Development in Education, 28,*(1) 55-65.

Popham, W. (1971). Performance tests of teaching proficiency: Rationale, development, and validation. *American Educational Research Journal, 8,* 105-117.

Popham, W. J. (1984). Teacher competency testing: The devil's dilemma. *Teacher Education and Practice, 1,* 5-9.

Popham, W. J. (1985). *The evaluation of teachers: A mission ahead of its measures.* Invited address at the annual meeting of the American Educational Research Association, Chicago.

Popham, W. J. (1987). The shortcomings of champagne teacher evaluations. *Journals of Personnel Evaluation in Education, 1,* 25-28.

Popham, W. J. (1988). The dysfunctional marriage of formative and summative teacher evaluation. *Journal of Personnel Evaluation in Education, 1,* 269-273.

Popham, W. J., Cruse, K. L., Rankin, S. C., Sandifer, P. D., & Williams, P. L. (1985). Measurement-driven instruction: It's on the road. *Phi Delta Kappan, 66,* 628-634.

Provus, M. (1971). *Discrepancy evaluation.* Berkeley, CA: McCutchan.

Rakow, E. A., & McLarty, J. R. (1990). Equating a multiple-data source evaluation system. *Journal of Personnel Evaluation in Education, 3,* 261-274.

Rawls, J. (1971). *A theory of justice.* Cambride, MA: Harvard University Press.

Read, L. F. (1973). An assessment of the Michigan assessment. In E. House (Ed.), *School evaluation: The politics and process.* Berkeley, CA: McCutchan.

Rebell, M. (1988). Legal issues concerning bias in testing. In R. Allan, P. Nassif, & M. Elliot (Eds.), *Bias issues in teacher certification issues.* Hillsdale, NJ: Lawrence Erlbaum.

Rebell, M. A. (1990). Legal issues concerning teacher evaluation. In J. Millman & L. Darling-Hammond (Eds.), *The new handbook of teacher evaluation: Assessing elementary and secondary school teachers* (pp. 337-355). Newbury Park, CA: Sage.

Rodger, T. F., & Mowbray, R. M. (1961). Clinical method in psychological medicine. *Journal of Medical Education, 36,* 167-172.

Rosenbloom, P. (1966). *Characteristics of mathematics teachers that affect students learning.* Minneapolis: University of Minnesota. (ERIC Document Reproduction Service No. ED 021 707)

Rosenshine, B. (1970). The stability of teacher effects upon student achievement. *Review of Educational Research, 40,* 647-662.

Rosenshine, B. (1980). How time is spent in elementary classrooms. In C. Denham & A. Lieberman (Eds.), *Time to learn.* Washington DC: U.S. Government Printing Office.

Rosenshine, B., & McGaw, B. (1972). Assessing teachers in public education. *Phi Delta Kappan, 44*(10), 640-643.

Rosenshine, B., & Stevens, R. (1984). Classroom instruction in reading. In P. D. Pearson (Ed.), *Handbook of reading research* (pp. 745-798). New York: Longman.

Rossow, L. F., & Parkinson, J. (1992). *The law of teacher evaluation.* Topeka, KS: National Organization on Legal Problems of Education.

Rothberg, R., & Buchanan, L. (1981). Teacher perceptions of teacher assessment. *Phi Delta Kappan, 62, 527.*

Sagor, R. (1992). *How to conduct collaborative action research.* Alexandria, VA: ASCD.

Sanders, W. L., & Horn, S. P. (1995a). Educational assessment reassessed: The usefulness of standardized and alternative measures of student achievement as indicators for the assessment of educational outcomes. *Educational Policy Analysis Archives, 3*(6).

Sanders, W. L., & Horn, S. P. (1995b). The Tennessee Value Added Assessment System (TVAAS): Mixed model methodology in educational assessment. In A. J. Shinkfield & D. Stufflebeam (Eds), *Teacher evaluation: Guide to effective practice* (pp. 337-350). Boston: Kluwer.

Sanders, W. L., & Horn, S. P. (1998). Research findings from the Tennessee Value-Added Assessment System (TVAAS) database: Implications for educational evaluation and research. *Journal of Personnel Evaluation in Education, 12,* 247-256.

Sanders, W. L., Saxton, A. M., Schneider, J. F., Dearden, B. L., Wright, S. Paul, & Horn, S. P. (1994). Effects of building change on indicators of student academic growth. *Evaluation Perspectives, 4*(1), pp. 3, 7.

Schalock, M. D. (1998). Accountability, student learning, and the preparation and licensure of teachers: Oregon's teacher work sample methodology. *Journal of Personnel Evaluation in Education, 12,* 269-285.

Schalock, H. D., Schalock, M. D., Cowart, B., & Myton, D. (1993). Extending teacher assessment beyond knowledge and skills: An emerging focus on teacher accomplishments. *Journal of Personnel Evaluation in Education, 7,* 105-133.

Schlechty, P. C., & Vance, V. S. (1981). Do academically able teachers leave education? The North Carolina case. *Phi Delta Kappan, 63,* 106-112.

Schmitt, N., & Cohen, S. A. (1990). Criterion-related validity of the assessment center for selection of school administrators. *Journal of Personnel Evaluation in Education, 4,* 203-212.

Schmitt, N., Noe, R., Meritt, R., Fitzgerald, M., & Jorgensen, C. (1979). *Criterion-related and content validity of the NASSP Assessment Center* (Tech Rep.). East Lansing: Michigan State University.

Schrag, P. (1997, October). The near-myth of our failing schools. *The Atlantic Monthly,* pp. 72-80.

Schubert, W. H. (1986). *Curriculum: Perspective, paradigm, and possibility.* New York: Macmillan.

Scriven, M. (1967). The methodology of evaluation. In R. Tyler, R. Gagne, & M. Scriven (Eds.), *AERA monograph review on curriculum evaluation: No. 1* (pp. 39-83). Chicago: Rand McNally.

Scriven, M. (1972). Prose and cons about goal-free evaluation. *Journal of Educational Evaluation, 3*(4), 1-4.

Scriven, M. (1973a). *Handbook for model training program in qualitative educational evaluation.* Berkeley: University of California Press.

Scriven, M. (1973b). Goal free evaluation. In E. House (Ed.), *School evaluation: The politics and process* (pp. 319-328). Berkeley, CA: McCutchan.

Scriven, M. (1973c). *The evaluation of educational goals, instructional procedures and outcomes.* Berkeley: University of California. (ERIC Document Reproduction Service No. ED 079 394)

Scriven, M. (1976). Evaluation in science teaching. *Journal of Research in Science Teaching, 13,* 363-368.

Scriven, M. (1977). The evaluation of teachers and teaching. In G. Borich (Ed.), *The appraisal of teaching: Concepts and process* (pp. 186-193). Reading, MA: Addison-Wesley.

Scriven, M. (1981). Summative teacher evaluation. In J. Millman (Ed.), *Handbook of teacher evaluation* (pp. 244-271). Beverly Hills, CA: Sage.

Scriven, M. (1987). Validity in personnel evaluation. *Journal of Personnel Evaluation in Education, 1,* 9-24.

Scriven, M. (1988). Duty-based teacher evaluation. *Journal of Personnel Evaluation in Education, 1,* 319-334.

Scriven, M. (1994). Using student ratings in teacher evaluation. *Evaluation Perspectives, 4*(1), 1-2, 4-6.

Scriven, M. (1997). Due process in adverse personnel action. *Journal of Personnel Evaluation in Education, 11,* 127-137.

Sergiovanni, T. (1977). Reforming teacher evaluation: Naturalistic alternatives. *Educational Leadership, 34,* 602-607.

Shimberg, B. (1985). Overview of professional and occupational licensing. In J. C. Fortune (Ed.), *Understanding testing in occupational licensing* (pp. 1-14). San Francisco: Jossey-Bass.

Shulman, L. S. (1987). Knowledge and teaching: Foundations of the new reform. *Harvard Educational Review, 57*(1), 1-22.

Sizemore, B. A. (1985). Pitfalls and promises of effective schools research. *Journal of Negro Education, 54*(3), 269-288.

Smith, G. P. (1984). The critical issue of excellence and equity in competency testing. *Journal of Teacher Education, 35*(2), 6-9.

Soar, R. S. (1973). Teacher assessment problems and possibilities. *Journal of Teacher Education, 24,* 205-212.

Soar, R. S., Medley, D. M., & Coker, H. (1983). Teacher evaluation: A critique of currently used methods. *Phi Delta Kappan, 65,* 239-246.

Spring, J. (1997). *Political agendas for education.* Mahwah, NJ: Lawrence Erlbaum.

Stake, R. E. (1973). Measuring what learners learn. In E. House (Ed.), *School evaluation: The politics and process* (pp. 193-223). Berkeley, CA: McCutchan.

Stanley, J. C. (1971). Reliability. In R. L. Thorndike (Ed.), *Educational measurement* (2nd ed.) (pp. 356-442). Washington, DC: American Council on Education.

Stedman, C. H. (1984). Testing for competency: A Pyrrhic victory? *Journal of Personnel Evaluation in Education, 3,* 7-15.

Stiggins, R. J. (1989). A commentary on the role of student achievement data in the evaluation of teachers. *Journal of Personnel Evaluation in Education, 3,* 7-15.

Stodolsky, S. S. (1984). Teacher evaluation: The limits of looking. *Educational Researcher, 13*(9), 11-18.

Strike, K. A. (1990). The ethics of educational evaluation. In J. Millman & L. Darling-Hammond (Eds.), *The new handbook of teacher evaluation: Assessing elementary and secondary school teachers* (pp. 356-373). Newbury Park, CA: Sage.

Strike, K., & Bull, B. (1981). Fairness and the legal context of teacher evaluation. In J. Millman (Ed.), *Handbook of teacher evaluation* (pp. 301-343). Beverly Hills, CA: Sage.

Stronge, J. H., & Helm, V. M. (1991). *Evaluating professional support personnel in education.* Newbury Park, CA: Sage.

Stronge, J., & Ostrander, L. (1997). Client surveys in teacher evaluation. In J. H. Stronge (Ed.), *Evaluating teaching: A guide to current thinking and best practice* (pp. 129-161). Thousand Oaks, CA: Corwin.

Sullivan, K. A., & Zirkel, P. A. (1998). The law of teacher evaluation: Case law update. *Journal of Personnel Evaluation in Education, 11,* 367-380.

Tanner, D., & Tanner, L. N. (1980). *Curriculum development: Theory into practice.* New York: Macmillan.

Thompson, M. S. (1980). *Benefit-cost analysis for program evaluation.* Beverly Hills, CA: Sage.

Toss bad apples from class. (1997, April 7). [Editorial] *Salt Lake Tribune,* p. B2.

Trask, A. (1964). Principals, teachers and supervision: Dilemmas and solutions. *Administrators Notebook, 13*(4), 1-4.

Travers, R.M.W. (1981). Criteria of good teaching. In J. Millman (Ed.), *Handbook of teacher evaluation* (pp. 14-22). Beverly Hills, CA: Sage.

Tucker, P. D. (1997). Lake Wobegon: Where all teachers are competent (or, have we come to terms with the problem of incompetent teachers?). *Journal of Personnel Evaluation in Education, 11,* 103-126.

Tuckman, B. W., & Oliver, W. F. (1968). Effectiveness of feedback to teachers as a function of source. *Journal of Educational Psychology, 59,* 297-301.

297 Utah teachers strut their stuff, score in top 18% on national test. (1986, April 13). *Salt Lake Tribune,* p. B3.

Valente, W. (1987). *Law in the schools* (2nd ed.). Columbus, OH: Merrill.

Veenman, S. (1984). Perceived problems of beginning teachers. *Review of Educational Research, 54,* 143-178.

Wang, M. C., Haertel, G. D., & Walberg, H. J. (1993). Toward a knowledge base for school learning. *Review of Educational Research, 63,* 249-294.

Warner, C. (1994). *Promoting your school: Going beyond PR.* Thousand Oaks, CA: Corwin.

Warner, C., & Curry, M. (1997). *Everybody's house—the schoolhouse: Best techniques for connecting home, school, and community.* Thousand Oaks, CA: Corwin.

Watts, D. (1985). Teacher competency testing: Causes and consequences. *The Teacher Educator, 20,* 15-21.

Webster, W., & Mendro, R. (1995). An accountability system featuring both "value-added" and product measures of schooling. In A.J. Shinkfield & D. Stufflebeam (Eds.), *Teacher evaluation: Guide to effective practice* (pp. 350-376). Boston: Kluwer.

Weiner, B., & Kukla, A. (1970). An attributional analysis of achievement motivation. *Journal of Personality and Social Psychology, 15,* 1-20.

Weller, L. D., Buttery, T. J., & Bland, R. W. (1994). Teacher evaluation of principals: As viewed by teachers, principals, and superintendents. *Journal of Research and Development in Education, 27*(2), 112-117.

West, P. T. (1985). *Educational public relations.* Beverly Hills, CA: Sage.

Wiles, J., & Bondi, J. (2000). *Supervision: A guide to practice* (5th ed.). Upper Saddle, NJ: Merrill.

Wilson, B. L. (1991). Influence in schools and the factors that affect it. In S. C. Conley & B. S. Cooper (Eds.), *The school as a work environment* (pp. 92-106). Boston: Allyn & Bacon.

Wise, A. E., Darling-Hammond, L., McLaughlin, M. W., & Berstein, H. T. (1984). *Teacher evaluation: A study of effective practices.* Santa Monica, CA: RAND.

Wise, A. E., & Gendler, T. (1990). Governance issues in the evaluation of elementary and secondary schoolteachers. In J. Millman & L. Darling-Hammond (Eds.), *The new handbook of teacher evaluation: Assessment of elementary and secondary schoolteachers* (pp. 374-389). Newbury Park, CA: Sage.

Wolf, K. (1991). The schoolteacher's portfolio: Issues in design, implementation and evaluation. *Phi Delta Kappan, 73,* 129-136.

Wolf, K. (1996). Developing an effective teaching portfolio. *Educational Leadership, 53*(6), 34-37.

Wolf, K., & Dietz, M. (1998). Teaching portfolios: Purposes and possibilities. *Teacher Education Quarterly, 25,* 9-22.

Wolf, K., Lichtenstein, G., & Stevenson, C. (1997). Portfolios in teacher evaluation. In J. H. Stronge (Ed.), *Evaluating teaching: A guide to current thinking and best practice* (pp. 193-214). Thousand Oaks, CA: Corwin Press.

Wolf, K., Lichtenstein, G., Bartlett, E., & Hartman, D. (1996). Teacher portfolios and professional development: The Douglas County outstanding teacher program. *Journal of Personnel Evaluation in Education, 10,* 279-286.

Wolf, K., Whinery, B., & Hagerty, P. (1995). Teaching portfolios and portfolio conversations for teacher educators and teachers. *Action in Teacher Education, 17,* 30-39.

Wolf, R. (1973). How teachers feel toward evaluation. In E. House (Ed.), *School evaluation: The politics and process* (pp. 156-168). Berkeley, CA: McCutchan.

Wood, C. J., & Pohland, P. A. (1979). Teacher evaluation: The myth and realities. In W. R. Duckett (Ed.), *Planning for the evaluation of teaching* (pp. 73-82). Bloomington, IN: Phi Delta Kappa.

Woolfolk, A. E. (1993). *Educational Psychology* (5th ed.). Needham Heights, MA: Allyn & Bacon.

Wright, B., & Sherman, B. (1965). Love and mastery in the child's image of the teacher. *The School Review, 73*(2), 89-101.

Wright, S. P., Horn, S. P., & Sanders, W. L. (1997). Teacher and classroom context effects on student achievement: Implications for teacher evaluation. *Journal of Personnel Evaluation in Education, 11,* 57-67.

Zahorik, J. A. (1980). Research on teaching as a basis for the evaluation of teaching. In W. R. Duckett (Ed.), *Observation and the evaluation of teaching* (pp. 46-50). Bloomington, IN: Phi Delta Kappa.

Zirkel, P. (1979). Teacher evaluation: A legal overview. *Action in Teacher Education, 2,* 17-25.

Legal Cases Cited

Albemarle Paper Company v. Moody, 422 U.S. 405 (1974)

Board of Education of Fort Madison Community School District v. Youel, 282 N. W. 2d 677 (Iowa 1979).

Board of Trustees of Calaveras Unified School District v. Leach, 258 Cal. App. 2d 281, 65 Cal. Rptr. 588, 539 (1968)

Board of Regents v. Roth, 408 U.S. 564 (1972).

Connick v. Meyers, 461 U.S. 138 (1983).

Goldberg v. Kelly, 38 U.S. L. Week 4223, 24 March (1970).

Griggs et al. v. Duke Power Company, 401 U.S. 424 (1971).

Kudasik v. Board of Directors, Port Allegany School District, 455 A.2d 261 (Pa. Cmwlth. 1983).

Meredith v. Board of Education of Rockwood, 513 S.W. 2d 740 (Mo. App. 1974).

Mt. Healthy City School District v. Doyle, 429 U.S. 274 (1977).

Pickering v. Board of Education, 391 U.S. 563 (1968).

Rogers v. Department of Defense Dependents Schools, Germany Region, 814 F.2d 1549, 1551 (Fed. Cir. 1987).

Rosso v. Board of School Directors, 388 A.2d 1238 (Pa. Cmwlth. 1977).

Rowe v. General Motors Corporation, 457 F.2d 348 (5th Cir. 1972).

Scheelhaase v. Woodbury Central Community School District, 488 F.2d 237 (8th Cir. 1973), *cert. denied*, 417 U.S. 969.

Shelton v. Tucker, 364 U.S. 479 (1960).

St. Louis Teachers' Union, Local 420 v. Board of Education of the City of St. Louis, 652 F.Supp. 425 (E.D.Mo. 1987).

Tyler v. Hotsprings School Dist. No. 6., 827 F.2d 1227, 1229 (8th Circ. 1987).

Index